The
Complete
Works
Of
Thomas
Boston

Volume 11

The
Complete
Works
Of
Thomas
Boston

Volume 11
of
12 Volume Set

Sovereign Grace Publishers, Inc.
P.O. Box 4998
Lafayette, IN 47903

Printed In the United States of America
By Lightning Source, Inc.

CONTENTS OF VOL. XI.

PART II.—OF THE BREACH OF THE COVENANT OF WORKS.

PART III.—OF THE IMPUTATION OF ADAM'S FIRST SIN TO HIS POSTERITY.

PART IV.—SECT. I. THE STATE OF MAN UNDER THE BROKEN COVENANT OF WORKS.

DISCOURSES ON PRAYER.

OF THE NATURE OF PRAYER IN GENERAL; WITH THE IMPORT OF PRAYING WITHOUT CEASING. *

1 Thess. v. 17,

Pray without ceasing.

These words are an exhortation briefly delivered, as laws use to be; and therein we have, 1. A duty proposed, "Pray." 2. The manner of it, "without ceasing."

I. We have the duty itself, "Pray." It may be asked, What is prayer? I answer, It is "an offering up of our desires to God, for things agreeable to his will, in the name of Christ, with confession of our sins, and thankful acknowledgement of his mercies." Here I shall consider,

1. The object of prayer, or whom we are to pray to.
2. The parts of prayer.
3. The matter of it.
4. In whose name we are to pray.
5. The several kinds of prayer.

First, I am to consider the object of this duty, or whom we are to pray to; that is, God: not to saints and angels, as the Papists do; for prayer is a part of religious worship, and therefore due to God only, Matth. iv. 10; and he only knows all things, and is present everywhere to hear us, Isa. lxiii. 16. To all the three persons in the Trinity prayer is due. That it is so to the Father, nobody doubts. That it is due to Christ, the Son, appears from Stephen's calling upon him in his last moments, and saying, "Lord Jesus, receive my spirit," Acts vii. 59. Even Christ the Mediator is to be worshipped, though his divine nature is the reason why he is worshipped, Heb. i. 6, "And let all the angels of God worship him." The Holy Ghost also is to be worshipped, as appears from the apos-

---

*The substance of two Sermons preached at Etterick, in the year 1727.

tolical benediction, 2 Cor. xiii. 14, " The communion of the Holy
Ghost be with you all."

In respect of the object of worship, people would do well to satisfy
themselves, in their addresses to God, with the belief of the Trinity
of persons in the Godhead, who are but one object of worship, and
not think to comprehend God, but to make use of the names and
titles he has taken to himself in the word. Beware of imaginations
of God or the three persons, and of dividing the object of worship, as
if praying to the Father, you did not also pray to the Son and the
Holy Ghost.

It is most necessary our prayers begin with such a description of
God, as may both strike fear and dread in our hearts, and confidence of being heard; as, " Our Father which art in heaven ;" " O,
Lord, the great and dreadful God, keeping the covenant, and mercy,"
&c., Dan. ix. 4. And this will readily be the case, if we have due
thoughts of his glorious majesty and infinite excellency.

Secondly, The parts of prayer are three, (1.) Confession, (2.)
Thanksgiving, and (3.) Petition.

1. Confession, Dan. ix. 4, 5, " I prayed unto the Lord my God,
and made my confession, and said, O Lord the great and dreadful God, keeping the covenant, and mercy to them that love
him, and to them that keep his commandments : we have sinned,
and have committed iniquity, and have done wickedly, and have re-
belled," &c. It well becomes sinful dust and ashes, in addresses to
God, to come with a blush in the countenance, and tears in the eye,
and confession in the mouth. It is necessary to humble us in the
sight of God, and it is the humble only that are heard, Psalm x. 17.
Confession is the vomiting up of the sweet morsel, and God has
joined pardon and confession together, 1 John i. 9, " If we confess
our sins, he is faithful and just to forgive us our sins, and to cleanse
us from all unrighteousness." God's ears are shut to those whose
mouths are bound up from this. Some say they cannot pray : O can
ye not confess what you are, have done, and daily are doing ? How
can ye want matter of prayer, while ye have so many sins to
confess ?

2. Thanksgiving, Phil. iv. 6, " In every thing by prayer and
supplication with thanksgiving, let your requests be made known
unto God." Every man is God's debtor for mercies, as well as
sins ; the least return ye can make, is to acknowledge debt. He that
is unthankful for what he has got, cannot think to come speed in
addresses for more.

3. Petition, wherein prayer properly consists. It is an offering
up of our desires to God. Wherein we may note the act of prayer,

" offering up our desires." The prayer that God makes account of is first in the heart, 1 Cor. xiv. 15, " I will pray with the spirit, and I will pray with the understanding also." It is a pouring out of the heart to God, Psalm lxii. 8. The Spirit of God moves on the waters of our affections, and then they are poured out before the Lord, as the water of the well of Bethlehem was by David. Many times our prayers come as mud out of a vessel; but as water they should flow freely. Then

In prayer there are real desires of what we seek of God, which desires are offered to the Lord. The mouth must not speak out anything but what is the desire of the heart. It is dangerous to mock God, who knows the heart; to confess sin, and not have the heart affected with it; to seek supply of wants from him, and not have the heart impressed with a due sense of the want of them. There are two sorts of desires.

(1.) There are *natural* desires, which are the mere product of our own spirits, offered unto God, but not regarded as prayer (Hos. vii. 14.) by the Lord. These may be not only for temporal things but for spiritual also, as those who said to Christ, " Lord evermore give us this bread." A natural man, from a gift of prayer, may seek grace and glory, as a bridge to lead him over the waters of wrath; but coming only from their own spirits, such a prayer is not acceptable.

(2.) There are *spiritual* desires, Zech. xii. 10; which the saints breathe out unto God, having them first breathed into them by the Spirit, Rom. viii. 26. And these may be for temporal things, as well as spiritual, accepted, seeing they are put up in a spiritual manner. These are always sincere and fervent, so as the soul earnestly craves the things sought.

Thirdly, The matter of prayer, or what we are to petition and seek for. These are, the things that are agreeable to God's will. To pray for the fulfilling of unlawful desires, is horrid, Jam. iv. 3. But the will of God is the rule of our prayers, 1 John v. 14, " This is the confidence that we have in him, that if we ask anything according to his will, he heareth us." We find the will of God in his commands and promises. Whatever God has commanded us to seek, whatever he has promised, that we may and ought to pray for. These are, (1.) Spiritual mercies, grace, glory, the increase of grace, comforts, &c. (2.) Temporal mercies, health, strength, &c., mercies relating to our bodies and temporal estate in the world.

Some have no freedom to bring their temporal concerns to their prayers. ANS. That we may and ought to do it, is plain.

1. In that God has given them a place in his covenant; they are

promised as well as spiritual mercies, 1 Tim. iv. 8, " Godliness is profitable unto all things, having promise of the life that now is, and of that which is to come." Isa. xxxiii. 16, " Bread shall be given him, his water shall be sure." Psalm i. 3, " Whatsoever he doth shall prosper."

2. It has been the practice of the saints in all ages. Memorable is Agur's prayer, Prov. xxx. 8, " Give me neither poverty, nor riches, feed me with food convenient for me."

3. Christ teaches us so to do in that pattern of prayer, Matth. vi. 9, &c., " Give us this day our daily bread," where we may observe, that they ought to have a place in our prayers daily.

4. God has commanded it, Phil. iv. 6, " Be careful for nothing : but in every thing by prayer and supplication with thanksgiving, let your requests be made known unto God. Ezek. xxxvi. 37, " Thus saith the Lord God, I will yet for this be inquired of by the house of Israel, to do it for them." Compare vers. 30, 33, &c., " I will multiply the fruit of the tree," &c. It is a general command, " In all thy ways acknowledge him," Prov. iii. 6.

5. Sin and duty are very large. Men are under a law as to their management of temporal concerns, and light and wisdom should be sought for the same from the Lord, Psalm cxii. 5, " A good man will guide his affairs with discretion." No doubt many things go the worse with us, that God is so little owned in them. If that be true, that " God doth instruct the plowman to discretion, and doth teach him," Isa. xxviii. 26, there is a good reason we pray, that " God may establish the work of our hands upon us," Psalm xc. ult. Surely those Christians that neglect it, deprive themselves of many experiences of the Lord's kindness. For the temporal mercies they meet with, were they answers of prayer, would be so many experiences of the Lord's love, Isa. xli. 11. Nay, I think it were a piece of Christian prudence, for the child of God, when he finds his heart not so affected as he would have it for spiritual mercies, to make an errand to God of a temporal mercy, whereby his heart may be the more fitted for asking spiritual blessings ; as we have instances often in the Psalms, and also in the famous wrestling of Jacob. Only,

(1.) Pray for temporal mercies for the sake of spiritual, not contrariwise, Matth. vi. 33, " Seek ye first the kingdom of God, and his righteousnesss, and all these things shall be added unto you. Prov. xxx. 8. 9, " Give me neither poverty, nor riches, feed me with food convenient for me : lest I be full, and deny thee, and say, Who is the Lord ? or lest I be poor, and steal, and take the name of my God in vain."

(2.) Keep within the bounds of the promise. Now, all promises of temporal things have this condition, if they be for God's glory and his children's good. Pray so as you may be content to want them, if God see it meet. But as for grace, the favour of God, and communion with him here and hereafter, it can never be our duty to be content to want them, 1 Thess. iv. 3, " For this is the will of God, even your sanctification.

Fourthly, In whose name are we to pray ? In the name of Christ, John xiv. 13, 14, " Whatsoever ye shall ask in my name, that will I do, that the Father may be glorified in the Son. If ye shall ask any thing in my name, I will do it." This is to plead the merits of Jesus Christ. We must come to God in the name of Christ, laying all the stress upon his merits. All things go by favour in the court of heaven ; the Father hears us for the Son's sake. This implies that we must be in Christ, before we can pray acceptably. But I shall consider this particular more fully, when I come, in course, to speak of praying in the name of Christ.

Fifthly, There are several kinds of prayer. I shall speak a word to these three, ejaculatory, secret, and family.

1. Ejaculatory prayer, which is a sudden dispatch of the desires of the soul to heaven, upon any emergent occasion ; sometimes with the voice, and sometimes without it. I will say of it,

(1.) It has been the practice of the saints. Thus Jacob, when making his testament, says, Gen. xlix. 18, " I have waited for thy salvation, O Lord." And when giving charge to his sons concerning Benjamin, chap. xliii. 14, " God Almighty give you mercy before the man," &c. Moses, when brought into a great strait at the approach of the Egyptians, Exod. xiv. 15, " The Lord said unto Moses, Wherefore criest thou unto me ? Speak unto the children of Israel, that they go forward." David, when told of Ahithophel's being among the conspirators with Absalom, says, 2 Sam. xv. 31, " O Lord, I pray thee, turn the counsel of Ahithophel into foolishness." And Nehemiah, when in the king's presence, and asked by him his request, says, chap. ii. 4, " I pray to the God of heaven."

(2.) Such prayers are very necessary. Light and strength for duty, against temptation, &c., are often needed, when we cannot get to our knees.

(3.) They are very useful for present help, and are notable means to keep the soul habitually heavenly and in a proper frame, when we make more solemn approaches to God.

(4.) It is no small mercy, that God's door stands always open, and that our prayers may be at heaven, before we can be at a secret place.

2. Secret prayer, wherein the man or woman goes alone to a secret place, and they pour out their souls before the Lord.

(1.) It is commanded expressly by our Lord, Matth. vi. 6, " When thou prayest, enter into thy closet, and when thou hast shut thy door, pray to thy Father which is in secret," &c.

(2.) They will have much ado to evidence their sincerity, whose prayers are all before men, Matth. vi. 5, 6, " When thou prayest, thou shalt not be as the hypocrites are : for they love to pray, standing in the synagogues, and in the corners of the streets, that they may be seen of men," &c. A hypocrite may pray in secret ; but a sincere soul will be loath to neglect it.

(3.) As no man knows our case so well as ourselves, so it is a sign of little acquaintance with our own hearts, if we have not something to tell Christ, which we cannot tell before others, Cant. vii. 11, 12, " Come, my Beloved, let us go forth into the field : let us lodge in the villages. Let us get up early to the vineyards, let us see if the vine flourish, whether the tender grape appear, and the pomegranates bud forth : there will I give thee my loves."

(4) The greatest enjoyments of the people of God have been in secret prayer ; as in the case of Jacob, Daniel, &c.

3. Family prayer. God must be worshipped in our families, as well as in our closets.

(1.) God commands it, in so far as he requires every kind of prayer, Eph. vi. 18, " Praying always with all prayer." The scripture speaks of a church in Aquila's house, Rom. xvi. 5. Surely the family was not such a one that shut God out of doors. The family sacrifice was God's ordinance, Exod. xii. 21, " Draw out, and take you a lamb, according to your families, and kill the passover."

(2.) It was the practice of Christ, Matth. xxvi. 30, John xvii. and of the saints, as Job, chap. i. 5, Joshua, chap. xxiv. 15, and Cornelius, Acts x. 2. Elisha prayed with his servant, 2 Kings iv. 33.

(3.) The master of the family has the charge of the souls under his roof ; and surely the case of a family requires family prayer. Are there not family wants, sins, and mercies, that require such an exercise ?

O what a heavy vengeance abides families that are without the worship of God ! Jer. x. 25, " Pour out thy fury upon the heathen that know thee not, and upon the families that call not on thy name." That house that is not sanctified by prayer, is like to be the house of the wicked, where God's curse is. How will ye answer for the souls committed to your charge, who do not pray in your families ? No wonder godly persons should scare at your family ; though indeed it is to be lamented, that many professors like Jonah will flee from the presence of the Lord, out of a praying family to a prayerless one ; whom a storm sometimes pursues.

Before proceeding to the other head, the manner of praying, permit me to make a very brief improvement of what has been said.

1. Let me address myself to those that live in the total neglect of this duty of prayer. O repent and amend, and set about this necessary duty. Consider,

(1.) A prayerless person is a graceless person, in a state of wrath, in the gall of bitterness and the bond of iniquity. No sooner is Paul converted, but, "behold, he prayeth." Still-born children cannot be heirs. The Spirit of grace is the Spirit of supplication. The Spirit makes us to cry, " Abba, Father."

(2.) A prayerless person is a thief and a robber of what he possesses in the world. How darest thou use God's creatures, and not ask his leave? 1 Tim. iv. 4, 5, " For every creature of God is good, and nothing to be refused, if it be received with thanksgiving: for it is sanctified by the word of God and prayer." Surely, thou prayerless one, a curse is on thy house, thy basket, and thy store. But, alas! many live like swine; they never look up to heaven, nor cry till the knife of death be at their throat.

(3.) It is a privilege that God will allow us to come so near him, and to pour out our hearts before him, a privilege bought by the blood of Christ. The prayless person undervalues this rich privilege, trampling on that blood that bought it, which will be a worm in his conscience in hell that will gnaw it for ever.

(4.) Thy soul lies at stake. That dumb devil that possesses thee, must be cast out of thee, or thou art undone for ever. Thou art lost by nature; wilt thou not cry for the life of thy poor soul? God says to thee, as Pilate to Christ, John xix. 10, " Speakest thou not unto me? knowest thou not, that I have power to *damn* thee, and have power to save thee?" Thou canst not be saved, without calling on the Lord by prayer.

But perhaps one may say, I will pray on a deathbed. ANSW. What if God cut thee off in a moment? what if thou die in the rage of a fever? how knowest thou that God will then hear thee? Ponder and seriously consider what the Lord says, Prov. i. 24—31, "Because I have called, and ye refused, I have stretched out my hand, and no man regarded; but ye have set at nought all my counsel, and would none of my reproof: I also will laugh at your calamity, I will mock when your fear cometh; when your fear cometh as desolation, and your destruction cometh as a whirlwind; when distress and anguish cometh upon you. Then shall they call upon me, but I will not answer; they shall seek me early, but they shall not find me: for that they hated knowledge, and did not choose the fear of the Lord. They would none of my counsel: they despised all my

reproof. Therefore shall they eat of the fruit of their own way, and
be filled with their own devices." And remember that such a conduct will bring you to that miserable pass described, Isa. viii. 21,
22, "And they shall pass through it, hardly bestead and hungry:
and it shall come to pass, that when they shall be hungry, they shall
fret themselves, and curse their king, and their God, and look upward. And they shall look unto the earth: and behold trouble and
darkness, dimness of anguish; and they shall be driven to darkness."

Another may say, I cannot pray. ANSW. Will ye try, for God
calls thee; thou mayst expect assistance, Exod. iv. 11, "Who hath
made man's mouth? or who maketh the dumb, or deaf, or the seeing,
or the blind? have not I the Lord?" Seriously consider thy state
and sins, and thou shalt have matter for confession; consider thy
mercies, and thou shalt have matter for thanksgiving; consider thy
wants, and thou shalt have matter for petition. Though thou canst
not express thyself as some others, yet be sincere. Parents love to
hear their babes that are learning to speak; and God will never
refuse to hear the sincere language of a heart, though it is not expressed in the most proper words.

2. To praying persons I would say, Continue constantly in this
duty of prayer, and never give it over as long as you live. Consider,

(1.) Your need, wants, temptations, snares, &c. never cease, nor
will cease while ye are here; and why should ye cease to pray?
God will have his people live from hand to mouth, because he loves
to have them always about his hand.

(2) Praying is a soul-enriching trade. It is a trade with heaven,
and brings down temporal and spiritual mercies. He that drives
this trade most diligently, will be found the most thriving Christian.
Surely the leanness among professors is owing to this neglect in a
great measure.

(3.) If ever a time called for prayer, this time does, while the ark
of God is in hazard, and damnable errors are spreading. O then
pray, and pray frequently, and ere long your prayers shall be turned
to praises.

II. I proceed to consider the manner of praying, or to shew, in
what respects we are to "pray without ceasing." This is not to be
understood as if we should spend our whole time in the exercise of
prayer: for there are many other duties, both of our station in life
and as Christians, that we are bound to perform; and these must
have their time; and God does not bind us to inconsistencies. But
we must,

1. Pray frequently, as David did, Psalm cxix. 164, "Seven times
a-day do I praise thee: because of thy righteous judgments."

The Christian should be no stranger to, but often at that work. It is a piece of walking with God, wherein the soul seeks communion with Heaven, and wherein he should abound, Col. ii. 6, 7. We find Daniel frequently at it, when it was death to pray, Dan. vi. 10. See Psalm lv. 17, "Evening and morning, and at noon will I pray, and cry aloud: and he shall hear my voice." Hereby may be known what case the soul is in; the more diligent one is in this duty, he will be the more thriving.

2. Pray statedly, without ceasing from the set times of prayer. These are evening and morning. The morning and evening sacrifice were called "the continual burnt-offering," Exod. xxix. 39, 41, 42., as being offered continually at these times. And these times were the times of prayer, Acts iii. 1. The light of nature itself teaches us to begin and end the day with the worship of God. And they should be reckoned lost days that are not so begun and ended.

3. Pray occasionally, without ceasing from embracing occasions of praying which the Lord puts in your hand. Do as David did, Psalm xxvii. 8, "When thou saidst, Seek ye my face; my heart said unto thee, Thy face, Lord, will I seek." An observing Christian will sometimes find himself called to pray between hands; and it is dangerous to sit the motion of an occasional tryst that God sometimes sets a person. To such a tryst there concurs, (1.) An inward moving of the soul to converse with God by prayer, Psalm xxvii. 8, just cited; the Spirit of the Lord exciting to duty, by representing a particular need, or fit occasion of converse with God, and so pressing a man forward to the throne to supplicate. (2.) A fair opportunity for it, Gal. vi. 10. And forasmuch as there may be motions to prayer, that are not from the Spirit of God, they may thus be discerned by the unseasonableness of them; for the Spirit of God puts people to duty seasonably, Psalm i. 3.

4. Pray constantly, Eph. vi. 18, "Praying always with all prayer and supplication in the Spirit, and watching thereunto with all perseverance." There must be a persevering in this duty, in the several kinds thereof, as the Lord gives opportunity. And this imports a continuing the course of praying, never giving up with it while breath remains, nor giving it over for a time, Psalm cxix. 112. The latter makes way for the former, as swooning does for dying for good and all.

5. Pray "importunately," not fainting nor giving over your tabled petitions as long as your needs remain, but resolutely pursuing them before the throne; Luke xviii. 1, "And he spake a parable unto them, to this end, that men ought always to pray, and not to faint." Pray till you get the answer of your prayers, if it should

be never so long delayed. God loves to have such petitioners about him as are resolute, and will not take a nay-say, as in the woman of Canaan's case; Matth. xv. 22—28.

6. Be *habitual* in the use of ejaculatory prayer; for this is a kind of prayer that can be mixed with whatever other good thing ye are about. There is an occasion for lifting up the heart to the Lord in an ejaculatory petition, in every business that is lawful, and in every company; and there is always an opportunity for it too. All our actions should be seasoned with it.

7. *Lastly*, Keep your hearts always in a praying frame; that whenever God calls you, you may be ready as the soldier at the sound of the trumpet; Eph. vi. 18. Hereto two things are necessary. (1.) That ye keep a clean conscience, watching against sin, having habitually recourse to the blood of sprinkling; Heb. ix. 14. (2.) That ye use moderation in all things, Phil. iv. 5. That joy or sorrow, eating or drinking, working or diversion, that unfits a man for prayer, is too much; for glorifying God is our chief end, to which all other ends must be subordinated; 1 Cor. x. 31, "Whether ye eat or drink, or whatsoever ye do, do all to the glory of God."

Use I. Of reproof to those that, being come to years of discretion,

1. Have not yet begun to pray; but live like beasts, eating, working, or playing, and sleeping, but have not begun to pray to the God that made them. Ah! know ye not that ye must die, and live eternally in another world? that ye are criminals, and have forfeited your life by your sin? that ye must be pardoned, or perish? And ye that have not set up God's worship in your families, will ye not give God house-room with you? Know your danger, and flee from the fury which the Lord will pour out on those who call not on his name.

2. Those that have left off praying. Sometimes they have prayed, but have given it over now; some in secret, and some in their families. Remember that this makes you apostates, and that apostasy is very dangerous. Consider the two following scripture-passages; 2 Pet. ii. 21, "It had been better for them not to have known the way of righteousness, than after they have known it, to turn from the holy commandment delivered unto them." Heb. x. 38, "If any man draw back, my soul shall have no pleasure in him."

3. Those that pray now and then only, as it suits with their conveniency. Some will pray on the Sabbath-day, when they have no other thing to do. Sometimes they are in a good mood, and take a start of praying; at other times they will rise from bed, and go to it, without ever bowing a knee to God. They will pray at even, but not at morn. Some cannot be got to set up the worship of God in

their families in the morning, others for several days in a week
have no family worship, sometimes in the year in the throng of
business. Let conscience say, if that be "praying without ceasing."
Is it not a contempt of God in his worship, and like the hypocrite;
Job xxvii. 10, of whom it is said, " Will he always call upon God ?"

USE II. Pray without ceasing. For, (1.) Satan never ceases to
seek your destruction, 1 Pet. v. 8. (2.) Your need of the Lord's
help never ceaseth; ye need direction, protection, life, strength,
mercies of all kinds, spiritual and temporal. (3.) *Lastly*, Time
never ceases to run, and ye know not when it may run out. There
is good reason we pray always, since we know no time wherein
death may not overtake us.

OF THE SPIRIT'S HELP IN PRAYER.*

ROMANS viii. 26,

*Likewise the Spirit also helpeth our infirmities ; for we know not what
we should pray for as we ought ; but the Spirit itself maketh intercession for us with groanings which cannot be uttered.*

SOMEWHAT of the nature of prayer in general, with the import of
praying without ceasing, has been explained to you; but it is not
every kind of prayer that is acceptable to God. Among praying
people there is a twofold cry that goes to heaven, (1.) The cry of
strangers, not known and approved there. That is prayer wrought
out by ourselves, in virtue of a natural sense of want, by a gift of
knowledge and utterance. (2.) The cry of children; that is prayer
wrought in us by the help of the Holy Spirit dwelling and acting in
us, and is accepted of God. Of this our text speaks. In which,

1. The connection is to be noticed, "likewise." This chapter is
an inventory of the privileges of believers. (1.) Freedom from condemnation, ver. 1, " There is therefore now no condemnation to them
which are in Christ Jesus." (2.) Sanctification, ver. 5, " They that
are after the Spirit, do mind the things of the Spirit." (3.) Comfort against death, ver. 10, " If Christ be in you, the body is dead,
because of sin ; but the Spirit is life, because of righteousness.'
(4.) Sonship to God, ver. 14, " As many as are led by the Spirit of
God, they are the sons of God." (5.) Glorification abiding them,
ver. 18, " For I reckon, that the sufferings of this present time, are

---

* Several Sermons preached at Etterick, in the year 1727.

not worthy to be compared with the glory which shall be revealed in us." From this high privilege the apostle looks down on the cross and afflictions here laid on believers, and shews there is no comparison betwixt these afflictions and that glory, they being but like a prick with a pin received by one in his way to a crown. And this is a first grand consolation against the cross laid on believers. (6.) The help of the Spirit for the present, in the text. And this is the second grand consolation of believers under the cross. They have not only, under all their afflictions, eternal glory made sure to them in end; but for the present time, while they are going under their burden, they have the Spirit of the Lord helping them, and particularly in prayer, the noted relief of the distressed, " Likewise the Spirit also helpeth our infirmities," &c. And that is a great consolation under the cross.

2. The words themselves, in which we may observe two things :—

1*st*, A general assertion of the Spirit's assisting of believers in the midst of their infirmities. And here, (1.) There is something supposed, namely, That they are compassed with infirmities while here. They are recovered of their deadly sickness of sin, but they are still weak; they are restored to life, but they have as yet little strength, and are much bowed down with pressures on them. (2.) Something expressed, namely, the Spirit's helping of them in that case. Weak people need help, especially under heavy burdens. And believers want not help under theirs; they have the best of help, the help of God himself, the eternal Spirit of the Father and the Son, the third person of the glorious Trinity, by whom the Father and the Son do act in them. He "helps our infirmities," *i. e.* helps us in our infirmities, to whatsoever we have to do or bear.

This help of the Spirit is a joint action, as the word imports. *Q. d.* He " together over-against" takes a lift of our burden. Where the Spirit helps, the man is not idle; but while the believer is going under his burden, he lifts the heavy end of it, and makes it the lighter to us; he does as the nurse with the child learning to go; the child moves his feet, but she holds him up and helps him, holding it by the arms.

2*dly*, A particular condescension, namely, his helping them in prayer, which brings great relief under the cross. And here,

(1.) We have a general infirmity that believers labour under, and that is little skill of praying. Whenever the grace of God touches their hearts, they are set a-praying; however, they are in it but like children beginning to speak; while unbelievers meanwhile are but like dumb people making a roar. Their weakness and unskilfulness in praying lies in two things.

[1.] In the matter of prayer, "We know not what we should pray for." We are apt, instead of bread, to ask a stone; instead of a fish, a scorpion; to pray for what would do us ill, and against what is for our good.

[2.] In the manner of prayer, "We know not what we should pray for as we ought." We cannot put our prayers in right shape, even when we are right as to the matter of them. We cannot put our petitions in form, in the style of the court of heaven.

(2.) The Spirit's help afforded them in this case: "But the Spirit itself maketh intercession for us," &c. Where we may notice,

[1.] The agent in this help, "the Spirit itself," rather "the Spirit himself;" the meaning certainly is so, for the Spirit here spoken of is a person, not a thing; though, by reason of the language the apostle wrote in, it is expressed neutrally.

[2.] The help itself, He "maketh intercession for us." Christ intercedes for us in heaven; the Spirit intercedes in us, by his effectual working in us, helping us to pray aright, and make intercession for ourselves. He forms our petitions for the court of heaven. No gifts could avail to this end. If the best gift without the Spirit were bestowed on a man, he could not make a prayer that would be acceptable to God, though it might be much admired of men.

[3.] An instance of a particular, whereto the Spirit helps in prayer "with groanings." Not that the Spirit's help in prayer appears in these only; but that even these groanings for divine aid, which believers have in their prayer, though they may be reckoned small things, yet are really great and prevalent with God, as proceeding from and produced in them by his own Spirit; and they are more forcible and expressive of the desires of the soul than any words; so they are "groanings which cannot be uttered." It is evident, that the Spirit of God in himself doth not groan; but groanings are attributed to him, so far as he causes us to groan, by exciting our affections. Therefore his intercession is to be understood of his causing and helping us to intercede in prayer for ourselves.

The following doctrines may be observed from the words thus explained.

DOCTRINE I. It is a comfortable case under affliction, where the party is helped from heaven to pray under their burden.

DOCTRINE II. It is the privilege of believers to have the help of the Holy Spirit, under the infirmities with which they are compassed while here.

Doctrine III. Such is the weakness of God's own children, that they have not skill to manage even their addresses to God by prayer aright, without the Spirit.

Doctrine IV. All our praying aright is so far done by the help of the Spirit, that it is justly reckoned his work, his making intercession for us.

Doctrine V. ult. The Spirit helps believers to pray, particularly causing in them gracious groanings, which cannot be uttered.

Doct. I. It is a comfortable case under affliction, where the party is helped from heaven to pray under their burden. This doctrine arises from the connection and scope of the words.

In discoursing from it, I shall consider,

I. What is the help from heaven to pray under a burden.

II. The comfort that is in this case.

III. Make improvement.

I. What is the help from heaven to pray under a burden. I take it up in these two particulars.

1. Help to lay the case before the Lord, and to table petitions before the throne of grace upon the case. If any are thus helped it is a token for good, they may take comfort of it; Psalm lxvi. 16, 17, "Come and hear, all ye that fear God, and I will declare what he hath done for my soul. I cried unto him with my mouth, and he was extolled with my tongue." Little do we know how to table petitions on our case at the court of heaven; but if a shower of trouble should fall on us, and withal the spirit of prayer be poured on us, we would have no cause to complain. Though the Lord press down a person with the one hand, and stir him up to the exercise of prayer with the other, it is a hopeful case, as was that of Jonah, chap. ii. 1.

2. Help to insist and resolutely to hang on and not faint, however longsome the hearing may be, Col. i. 11. Thus the Spirit helps the children of God in prayer; Psalm cxxxviii. 3, " In the day when I cried thou answeredst me; and strengthenedst me with strength in my soul;" 2 Cor. xii. 9, "And he said unto me, My grace is sufficient for thee; for my strength is made perfect in weakness." The patience of others in applications to the throne of grace will soon be tired out; they cannot wait, so they drop the matter, Job xxvii. 10, and go to another door. But those in whom the Spirit dwells see no other door, John vi. 68, and the Spirit is a spring of living water in them, which causes them to hold on.

II. What is the comfort that is in this case. It is manifold. I instance in the following particulars.

1. That is comfortable in it, that the native effect of affliction is stopped in such a person by influence from heaven. Affliction in its own nature is a whip, a brier, a thorn; and the native effect of it is, to drive the sinner away from God, to harden his heart, irritate his corruption, and make his heart a hell; Job xxxvi. 13, " The hypocrites in heart heap up wrath; they cry not when he bindeth them." But, by divine institution, it is a medicine, having a promise annexed to it; Isa. xxvi. 9, " When thy judgments are in the earth, the inhabitants of the world will learn righteousness ;" and so it brings the believing sinner to God, as the bitter potion causes the sick man turn to his physician, who would all he could keep himself out of the way of an enemy that had given him such a bitter draught, Rom. x. 14.

2. It is comfortable, even that the party gets a vent to his full heart. Those in a trouble find a kind of relief in pouring out their heart into the bosom of a sympathising friend; and it is an aggravation of affliction, when the fire must burn in the bosom, and there is no access to give it a vent. How much more is it a solid comfort, to be helped to pour out one's heart unto a gracious God, able and willing to help in due time ? Micah resolved to take comfort this way; Micah vii. 7, " I will look unto the Lord; I will wait for the God of my salvation; my God will hear me." And Hannah got it; 1 Sam. i. 15, 16, " And Hannah answered and said, No, my lord, I am a woman of a sorrowful spirit; I have drunk neither wine nor strong drink, but have poured out my soul before the Lord. Count not thine handmaid for a daughter of Belial; for out of the abundance of my complaint and grief have I spoken hitherto." Ver. 18, " And she said, Let thine handmaid find grace in thy sight. So the woman went her way, and did eat, and her countenance was no more sad."

3. It is comfortable that the Lord takes that way to draw the sinner to him, and keep him about his hand, and it is effectual; Hos. v. ult., " I will go and return to my place, till they acknowledge their offence, and seek my face; in their affliction they will seek me early." We reckon in the world, that they are in the best case that hold all within themselves; but in respect of spiritual thriving, they are fairest for that who are kept from hand to mouth, and never want a new errand to God's door. The Lord loves to have his children always about his hand, but they would be like children at their play about meal-time, that would never mind home if hunger did not bite them; and so in effect it fares with many.

4. That is comfortable in it, that it is a sign of eternal good-will and everlasting love to such persons; Luke xviii. 7, " And shall not God avenge his own elect, which cry day and night unto him, though

he bear long with them ?" They would be tired out, if they were not God's chosen, possessed by his Spirit. Do ye see a place which is always full of water, summer and winter, in the greatest drought? ye may be sure that is no pool, but a spring, John iv. 14. The man prays and wrestles against a body of death, cries and goes on under a weight of trials; he holds on notwithstanding of seeming fruitlessness. See the verdict; Matth. xxiv. 13, "He that shall endure unto the end the same shall be saved."

5. That is comfortable in it, that his prayers shall be heard at length to his heart's content, if it should not be till he get into heaven; Luke xviii. 8, "I tell you that he will avenge them speedily." The help of the Spirit in prayer is a certain pledge of the hearing of prayer, Jam. v. 18. If a poor man were to petition the king, but had no skill to draw his petition; and the king should send one from about his hand to help that poor man, and draw his petition for him; would not that be a sign that the king had a good mind to grant it? So it is equally a certain sign of God's good-will to the praying person, and a certain token that his prayers shall be heard to his full satisfaction at length, that the Spirit now helps him in prayer, and, as it were, draws his petitions for him.

6. It is comfortable, that the party is now and then getting some off-fallings about the Lord's hand; otherwise he would give over. In the way of duty, wherein people are not formal, but truly serious, there is a concomitant reward; Psalm xix. 11, "In keeping of them there is great reward;" and particularly in prayer; Isa. xlv. 19, "I said not unto the seed of Jacob, seek ye me in vain." Though the Lord does not give the main request for the time, yet he gives something that keeps the heart from fainting; Lam. iii. 57, "Thou drewest near in the day that I called upon thee; thou saidst, Fear not." So we find it happened to Paul; 2 Cor. xii. 8, 9, " For this thing I besought the Lord thrice that it might depart from me. And he said unto me my grace is sufficient for thee; for my strength is made perfect in weakness. Most gladly, therefore, will I rather glory in my infirmities, that the power of Christ may rest upon me."

From what is said on this doctrine, the following things may be shortly observed for improvement.

1. The Lord's cross on his people's back, is better than the world's crown on the head of his enemies. For there is more comfort in the one's being helped from heaven to commit their case to the Lord, and depend on him for it, than in all the prosperity of the wicked. For all is well that ends well; and the former will have a joyful end, the latter a sad one, Prov. i. 32, 33.

2. They are doubly to be pitied, who are under an afflicted lot,

and withal strangers to the duty and comfort of prayer. This world is a place wherein neither good nor bad will miss their share of crosses. But to see this world frowning on a man, and in the meantime him not seeking his comfort from heaven ; to see a person full of matter of complaints, and yet having no heart to pour them out into the bosom of our heavenly Father, is a sad sight.

3. Let praying people beware of afflictions deadening them, and taking heart and hand from them in prayer. Satan will do his utmost to work up afflictions to this pitch ; and when he has got it done, he has what he would wish, he has an envenomed arrow sticking in their flesh. Let them haste to get it away, as ever they would cast a coal of hell out of their bosom ; and remember that " God is love ; and he that dwelleth in love, dwelleth in God, and God in him," 1 John iv. 16 ; that " the Lord doth not afflict willingly, nor grieve the children of men," Lam. iii. 33 ; and that " all things work together for good, to them that love God, to them who are the called according to his purpose," Rom. viii. 28.

4. *Lastly,* Let those who are helped to pray under their affliction be thankful, and acknowledge God has not forgotten them. When the Lord's people have plied the throne of grace long for a mercy, and yet it comes not, they are ready to think that the Lord regards them not. But if ye be helped still to hang on, that very thing is an evidence that it is not true ; and is a token for good in your case.

DOCTRINE II. It is the privilege of believers to have the help of the Holy Spirit, under the infirmities with which they are compassed while here.

Here I shall shew,

I. What are the infirmities believers are compassed with here.

II. Why in the depth of sovereign wisdom, believers are left compassed so with infirmities while here.

III. Consider the Spirit's helping believers under these infirmities.

IV. Make some practical improvement.

I. I am to shew what are the infirmities believers are compassed with here.

First, They are always compassed with natural infirmities.

1. Pure natural infirmities, which though they be their weights and burdens, yet are not their sins. There is a natural weakness inwrought with human flesh, though at its prime of vigour, Isa. xl. 6, so that it was found even in the man Christ, 2 Cor. xiii. 4. This makes God's children objects of their Father's pity, Psalm ciii. 13, 14, " Like as a Father pitieth his children : so the Lord pitieth them

that fear him. For he knoweth our frame : he remembereth that we are dust." Such are the need of meat, drink, sleep, &c., whereby the tabernacle must be daily underpropped, Matth. xxvi. 41. Even Samson was sore pressed with such infirmity, Judges xv. 18, " He was sore athirst."

2. Sinful natural infirmities, which are both pressures on them, and defilements of them, wounding and polluting.

(1.) Common to them all, namely, the remains of the corruption of nature, which makes them all a company of poor weaklings, groaning under their infirmities, Rom. vii. 24. Their sanctification is imperfect ; every grace in them has the contrary weed of corruption growing by the side of it. Grace indeed has got the house, but dwells not alone in it ; the Canaanites are left in the land, and they cannot quite drive them out. Hence is the struggle not only with those without, but those within.

(2.) Peculiar to every one of them, namely, the particular bias of corrupt nature in each of them, arising from their natural constitution and temper ; and this is a cast of disposition to some particular evil, commonly called " the predominant sin, the sin which doth so easily beset us," Heb. xii. 1. Thus the peculiar infirmity of some is passion, of others vanity, worldliness, &c. Every one will know their own, for it will be that which costs more struggle than anything else, and in which they will find need of the peculiar help of the Spirit.

Secondly, They are often compassed with accidental infirmities.

1. Sinless ones. Such are afflictions, trials, and temptations, which though not their sins, yet are heavy weights to them, causing them much need of help, as in Paul's case, 2 Cor. xii. 7, 8, 9. Thus diseases and ailments of whatsoever nature go under the name of infirmities, as weakening body or spirit, Luke v. 15. Timothy had frequent attacks by them, 1 Tim. v. 23. And in the road to heaven such weights and pressures one way or other will not be missed, Acts xiv. 22.

2. Sinful ones, being wrong casts of spirit, arising from education or other circumstances, giving them as it were a second nature. Such was the infirmity of the disciples, whereby they were ready on all occasions to mind a temporal kingdom of Christ, and to be stumbled at his sufferings ; and the bias towards the ceremonial law, which the believing Jews had remaining with them ; Rom. xv. 1.

Hence the infirmities of believers may be taken up in the following particulars :—

1. They have weak heads for discerning and understanding sin and duty, snares, temptations, and proper means for eviting the one, and compassing the other, Jer. x. 23, " It is not in man that walk-

eth to direct his steps." The subtle enemy is ready to outwit them, and by his devices to triumph over their weakness. Therefore we are warned not to trust our own understanding, Prov. iii. 5.

2. They have weak hearts for venturing on difficulties, which make them ready to faint at the appearance of them, Isa. xxxv. 4. And the formidable enemy is ready to damp them, and discourage them. They know themselves how little strength they have ; and their faith being weak withal, they are apt to sink in their courage for doing and suffering.

3. They have weak hands for doing of duties in the right manner, Isa. xxxv. 3. They are not in themselves man enough for the most ordinary duties of religion, and therefore being left to themselves, they quite mismanage them, John xv. 5, 2 Cor. iii. 5. And sometimes the Lord calls them to extraordinary duties.

4. *Lastly*, They have weak backs for bearing burdens, so that they are easily bowed down, yea and foundered under them, 2 Cor. ii. 16. Their suffering strength is small, considering the weak frame of their bodies, and the remaining distempers in their souls.

II. I come now to show why, in the depth of sovereign wisdom, believers are left compassed so with infirmities while here. Surely it is not for want of power in their Father to deliver them : for he is almighty, and in the moment he gave them grace, could have perfected them in soul and body. Neither is it for want of love to and concern for them ; for he has the bowels of a Father, and gave them his own Son, which was more than all that. But so it is ordered,

1. That the members may be conformed to the head, Rom. viii. 29. Our Lord Jesus did not enter to his glory, but after a long track of sufferings, Heb. ii. 10. This was necessary in the case of Christ the head, for the purchasing of our salvation, Matth. viii. 17 ; Luke xxiv. 26. And it is necessary in the case of believers, that they may be conformed to him, bearing the image of his sufferings, for his glory.

2. That the emptiness of the creature may be discovered, and the pride of all created glory stained, and that the crown may be put on the head of free grace only ; so that we may say, "The Lord of hosts hath purposed it, to stain the pride of all glory, and to bring into contempt all the honourable of the earth," Isa. xxiii. 9. Therein a scene is opened, wherein there is a full display of the nothingness of the creature, that heaven may appear to be peopled with those that could have no pretensions to it, but on the score of mere free grace.

3. That all the graces of the Spirit in believers may be brought

forth into the field of battle, and exert themselves, 1 Pet. i. 6, 7. There are some graces whose exercise is to be eternal, as love, reverential fear, &c. these will be exerted in heaven as well as here. But there are others that are occasional in their exercise, such as faith, hope, patience, watchfulness, &c. which agree only to a state of imperfection: and there they have occasion to shew themselves. So, for the exercise of these, and trial of both sorts, the Canaanites are left in the land. And therefore some are loaded with peculiar infirmities.

4. That the power of the grace of Christ may be magnified. The infirmities wherewith believers are compassed, make a scene wherein the power of Christ is signally displayed, as, says the apostle, 2 Cor. xii. 9, " Most gladly therefore will I rather glory in my infirmities, that the power of Christ may rest upon me." God could have seated Israel in Canaan, without stroke of sword; but then Joshua's valour, which appeared in the conquest of that land, had lain hid. Believers are committed into Christ's hand, as the great Pilot, to guide them through the sea of this world, to the shore of Immanuel's land: and it will magnify the power of his grace, that by his conduct so many broken ships are brought safe ashore, through so many rocks and shelves, and suffering so many storms.

5. That the bruised serpent may be beat the more shamefully, and Christ's victory and triumph over him may be the more signal. He encountered Christ in person on the cross; and there he was overcome, the Son of God being an overmatch for all the powers of hell. But that his defeat may be more shameful, he is yoked with poor believers with a heap of infirmities about them; and by them too, after he has done his worst, he is baffled at length, Rom. xvi. 20. " The God of peace shall bruise Satan under your feet shortly.

And here it is worth observing, that our Lord Jesus singles out some of his people to combat with Satan, loaded with some uncommon infirmity, whereby he has a peculiar advantage against them, that he has not against others: and all to make that malicious spirit's defeat yet more shameful. As if one, to pour contempt on his enemy, should say, I will take such an one of my children that are not quite recovered out of their sickness, and I will bind one of his arms behind his back, and yet make him throw you down, and tread on you. Thus Job was stript of all his comforts, his children, wealth, and health; nothing left him but his life, and his unkind wife that Satan had use for; and Satan makes a furious attack on him to blaspheme, when he had him at all this disadvantage. And yet he was baffled in the end, Jam. v. 11, " Ye have heard of the patience of Job, and have seen the end of the Lord; that the Lord is very pitiful and of tender mercy. And when the gospel was to be spread in the world, Satan had the power of the sword and the learning in the world engaged in the defence of his kingdom; and Christ singles out a few fishermen, neither swordsmen nor bookmen, Paul excepted, and they pull it down; notwithstanding all the magistrates could do by their force, and they learned by their subtilty to support it.

6. *Lastly,* To screw up the glory of the exceeding riches of grace to a height, Eph. ii. 7, " That in the ages to come he might shew the exceeding riches of his grace, in his kindness towards us, through Christ Jesus." According to this dispensation, believers are drowned deeper in the debt of free grace, than otherwise they would have been, Rom. v. 20. By these infirmities wherewith they are compassed, it comes to pass that their accounts of pardoning and supporting grace are swelled with many items; the view of which will make them sing the praises of God in heaven, on a higher key than innocent Adam would have done.

III. We shall consider the Spirit's helping believers under those infirmities they are compassed with. And here I shall shew,

1. The import of this.

2. How the Spirit helps them under their infirmities.

First, I am to shew the import of the Spirit's helping believers under their infirmities. It imports in it,

1. A bent of heart in the believer toward his work and duty, set him by the great Master, Rom. vii. 22; for what people have no mind to, they need no help for. The heart of every child of God is reconciled to the whole law, Heb. viii. 10. And what God carves out for him either to do or suffer, he would fain come up to, Matth. xxvi. 41. Even when there is a felt averseness to it, this bent in the renewed part remains with him, to which that averseness is a burden, Rom. vii. 22, 23.

2. The infirmities hanging about the believer, make duty difficult to him: if it were not so, what need would he have of help? Matth. xxvi. 40, 41. These hang like weights on him, and draw him down, when he would mount upwards; so his executive powers cannot answer his will. He is at best like a bird flying with a stone tied to its foot; whereby it comes to pass, that it cannot fly far till it light, and the short way it flies is with difficulty.

3. The believer is sensible of his infirmities, for it is supposed that he is wrestling under them, Rom. vii. 23, 24, He sees, he feels, that he is not man enough for his work; that his own hands are not sufficient for him, nor his own back for his burden; this is what drives him out of himself to the grace that is in Christ Jesus, 2 Cor.

iii. 5. And thus he lies open to the help of the Spirit, while proud nature in unbelievers is left helpless, 1 Pet. v. 5, " God resisteth the proud, and giveth grace to the humble." Isa. xl. 4, " Every valley shall be exalted, and every mountain and hill shall be made low."

4. The believer aims at and attempts to do his duty, over the belly of his infirmities. For helping is a joint action, Phil. iii. 14, " I press towards the mark." Many feel a difficulty in the weightiest parts of religion, that makes them at length to give them over. They neither have ability in themselves to master such a lust, nor have the grace to betake themselves to Christ for the help of his Spirit. But they sit down contented under it, soothing themselves with this, that every one has his infirmity, and that is theirs ; and so they discover their hypocrisy. But real saints wrestle with their infirmities, sit not down, but go on though they go halting.

5. *Lastly,* The spirit of the Lord comes in to the believer's help in this case, so as the work and duty is got done. " For the Spirit helpeth our infirmities." As the nurse helps the child attempting to go, or one helps a man attempting to lift up a weighty burden ; so the Spirit helps the weak believer essaying his duty, to perform it. He stretches out the withered hand, and with the aiming to stretch it out, power is sent in from above.

Secondly, I am next to show how the Spirit helps believers under their infirmities.

1. He helps them by his influence in gifts. Here he does two things.

1*st,* He bestows on them gifts necessary for the performance of what the Lord calls them to, of whatever nature that be, temporal or spiritual, 1 Cor. xii. 8 —11, " To one is given by the Spirit, the word of wisdom ; to another the word of knowledge by the same Spirit ; to another faith by the same Spirit ; to another the gifts of healing by the same Spirit ; to another the working of miracles ; to another prophecy ; to another discerning of spirits ; to another divers kinds of tongues ; to another the interpretation of tongues. But all these worketh that one and the self-same Spirit, dividing to every man severally as he will." The gifts of believers are various, according to the variety of their stations in life, and the respective particular duties required of them in their stations. Every one has not all, nor will ever have all ; because there are many of them which they have no necessity for, in respect of what God calls them to. But there are two things I would have you advert to.

(1.) Whatever good gift a child of God has, he will get use for it, for God, soon or late, 1 Cor. xii. 7 ; though for a time he may have little or none for it. For in that case the Spirit lays in aforehand for their help. David had the gift of music in his younger years; the use of it for God appeared afterwards, when on that account he was sent for to Saul's court, and afterwards he ordered the temple service in that point. Paul had a gift of human learning; he got use for it afterwards, when he fought those at Athens with their own weapons, Acts xvii. 28. Moses had a gift of extraordinary meekness of temper, and Job of extraordinary patience; each got as much ado with them for God.

An unbeliever indeed may have a gift, which he never has any use for, for God. For he always does one of two things with it; either he hides it in the earth, and makes no use of it all, Matth. xxv. 25; or else he uses it to the service of his own lusts, Jam. iv. 3, 4. But God will not let any good gift in his own people lie by useless.

(2.) Whatever duty, in temporal or spiritual things, God calls a believer to, he will, in a way of believing, get the gift from God necessary for it, Prov. x. 29, "The way of the Lord is strength to the upright:" and iii. 6, " In all thy ways acknowledge him, and he shall direct thy paths." For it is the office of the Spirit to help his people's infirmities. And so a call from the Lord to any piece of work, imports a promise of a gift of ability for it, the sap of which promise is to be sucked by believing it; and it is withal a call to look to the Lord for the help of his Spirit. For the Lord treats not his children as the Egyptian taskmasters did, who would have the Israelites make brick without giving them straw. Moses is called to go Jehovah's ambassador to the court of Egypt; he is sensible of an infirmity, but the Spirit's help is secured to him, Exod. iv. 10, 12. Bezaleel and Aholiab must work the curious work of the tabernacle. Where should they have learned it, when they were slaves in Egypt at the brick-kilns? But the Spirit helps their infirmity, bestowing on them necessary gifts, Exod. xxxi. 2, &c.

But in case the believer do not go to God for the gift, in the way of believing, no wonder he want it. For is it anything strange that the help of the Spirit is not given a man, in a particular, wherein he does not look for it? as he is commanded to do, Prov. iii. 6.

2dly, He influences them to the exercise of these gifts, Matth. x. 19, 20, "But when they deliver you up, take no thought how or what ye shall speak, for it shall be given you in that same hour what ye shall speak. For it is not ye that speak, but the Spirit of your Father which speaketh in you. As every good gift is from the Spirit, so the same Spirit has not given them away so to any, but that he has still lock and key on them, opening them out, and shutting them up as he will, Isa. xxix. 14. Therefore there ought to be a dependance on the Lord, for the help of his Spirit, to the exercise of any gift necessary for what the Lord calls one to. That unbelievers have a common influence of the Spirit, in the way of common providence, to the exercise of their gifts, though they look not to the hand it comes from, is for the benefit of human society; but even the Spirit's influence on gifts, coming to believers in the channel of the covenant, their blunders and mismanagements in the exercise of their gifts, are rebukes to them for their not looking more to the help of the Spirit therein, and to bring them to their duty.

2. He helps them by his influence in grace. Here he helps their infirmities three ways.

1st, He preserves the grace he has planted in believers, so as it never dies out; 1 John ii. 27, "The anointing which ye have received of him, abideth in you; and ye need not that any man teach you; but, as the same anointing teacheth you of all things, and is truth, and is no lie; and even as it hath taught you, ye shall abide in him." The quickening spirit of Christ being communicated to the dead elect in the time of loves, they are made to live and believe in Christ, and so are united to him; upon which union the same Spirit takes of the treasure of grace in Christ, and plants in the believer grace for grace in Christ Jesus, Eph. i. 13, with John i. 16. And this for all time after he preserves; 2 Tim. i. 14, "That good thing which was committed unto thee, keep by the Holy Ghost which dwelleth in us. John x. 28, "I give unto them eternal life, and they shall never perish, neither shall any pluck them out of my hand." Deut. xxxiii. 3, "All his saints are in thy hand; and they sat down at thy feet; every one shall receive of thy words," i.e. thy Spirit. Luke xi. 20; with Matth. xii. 28. Now, this is a great helping of their infirmities, if ye consider jointly these four things.

(1.) That holy quality called grace, is in its own nature a thing liable to be lost. Adam at his creation was endowed with a far greater measure of it than any believer has in this world; yet that holy fire in him was quite extinguished; that heavenly plant, by one bite of the venomous teeth of the old serpent, died out quite, and withered away. How then is it preserved in believers compassed with infirmities, but by the help of the Spirit? Free-will in Adam lost it, but the free grace of the free Spirit preserves it in weak ones of his family.

(2.) It dwells with an ill neighbour, even the corruption of nature, that is quite opposite to it. The old man of sin had the first possession, the new man of grace is brought in upon him, and meets with a continual resistance, yet is preserved. There is the weight of a body of sin and death pressing grace in the believer, yet is it not crushed to death.   Whoso looks into his own heart, and sees what powerful lusts are there, must needs wonder to see the pearl kept in such a dung-hill, and the spark of holy fire kept in the midst of an ocean of corruption; and must own it to be entirely owing to the help of the Spirit; Gal. v. 17, "The flesh lusteth against the Spirit, and the Spirit against the flesh, and these are contrary the one to the other, so that ye cannot do the things that ye would."

(3.) The whole force of hell is bent for its extinction; 1 Pet. v. 8, "Your adversary the devil, as a roaring lion, walketh about seeking whom he may devour."   The image of God repaired in a believer, though but in part, is an eye-sore to Satan, he cannot endure to look at it.   Therefore he uses all his subtilty, power, and unwearied diligence to rase it.   He works against it incessantly, turns himself into all shapes that he may overturn it; employs his friends within and his friends without to the same purpose, yet it is preserved. How? but by the help of the Spirit; 1 John iv. 4, "Ye are of God, little children, and have overcome them; because greater is he that is in you than he that is in the world.

(4.) *Lastly*, The believer in himself is but a weak creature; he has a weak head, heart, hands, and back; is easily outwitted by a subtle enemy, discouraged, overthrown, and bowed down.   Innocent Adam's strength and skill failed in preserving the grace received in his creation; yet the believer's grace received in his new creation is never lost; though of itself it is a perishing quality, is surrounded with corruption, and the whole force of hell is employed to extinguish it.   For why? the almighty Spirit helps their infirmities.

2dly, He excites grace in them, and brings it forth into exercise; Phil. ii. 13, "For it is God which worketh in you, both to will and to do of his good pleasure."   If the exercise of gifts depends on a common operation of the Spirit, surely the exercise of grace on a special operation of the same Spirit.   As the fire buried under the ashes will not serve the purposes of the family's provision, nor the tree with its sap retired into the heart and root bring forth fruit; so grace in the habit only is not sufficient for duty.   The holy fire must be blown up, and through the return of the sap to the branches they must bud and blossom.   And this is the work of the Spirit, Cant. iv. ult., "Awake, O north wind, and come, thou south, blow upon my garden, that the spices thereof may flow out; let my Beloved come into his garden, and eat his pleasant fruits."   Now the Spirit excites grace in believers,

(1.) Presenting objects to their minds fit to rouse it up; and so he acts as a teaching Spirit; John xiv. 26, "He shall teach you all

things, and bring all things to your remembrance, whatsoever I have
said unto you." Corruption thrives most in darkness, because it
belongs to the kingdom of darkness. But light let into the soul
stirs up grace, therefore it is called the light of life, John viii. 12.
Thus the Spirit presenting a man's sin to him in its ugly colours,
stirs up the grace of repentance, Psalm li. 3; discovering the glory
of God in the face of Jesus Christ, it excites love; and discovering
the creature in its emptiness, excites contempt of the world. And
this is a great help, for,

(1.) We are apt to forget these things when we have most need to
mind them; as to forget human frailty and divine might, when there
is greatest need of confidence in the Lord, against the terror of man;
and the Spirit in that case is the believer's remembrancer, and so
excites grace; Isa. li. 12, 13, "I, even I, am he that comforteth
you; who art thou, that thou shouldst be afraid of a man that shall
die, and of the son of man which shall be made as grass? and for-
gettest the Lord thy maker, that hath stretched forth the heavens
and laid the foundations of the earth? and hast feared continually
every day, because of the fury of the oppressor as if he were ready
to destroy? And where is the fury of the oppressor?" Our weakness in such points makes us need a monitor, being often like Hagar,
whose eyes saw not the well, though it was very near by, until God
opened them, Gen. xxi. 19. So that when such a thing is suggested,
one is often made to wonder how they saw it not.

(2.) When we do mind them, we cannot command a lively sight
of them, without the blowing of the Spirit, Hos. viii. 12. They lie
before our eyes as so many dry bones, till the Spirit set them in motion, by setting them in a due light. Joseph's brethren could not
forget that they had been guilty concerning him, nor David that he
had sinned in the matter of Uriah; but till the Spirit set these
things in another light to them, they were not moved to repent.

(2.) By touching their hearts and affections, and immediately
bringing them forth into exercise. Thus the sleeping spouse was
awakened; Cant. v. 4, "My Beloved put in his hand by the hole of
the door, and my bowels were moved for him." And so he acts as
a quickening Spirit. The hearts of men are in the hand of the
Lord, to turn them what way he will; and so he moves them by a
touch in common things, as he did the band of men that went with
Saul to Gibeah, "whose hearts God had touched," 1 Sam. x. 26; and
he also moves them by a touch in gracious actions, as the spouse
found; Cant. vi. 12, "Or ever I was aware, my soul made me like
the chariots of Ammi-nadib. As the thaw wind makes the frozen
waters to flow amain, and the air in the bellows blows up the fire;
so there is an influence of the Spirit on the hearts of believers, open-

ing them in the exercise of grace, Phil. ii. 13.   This is a great help
to believers; for,

(1.) Their hearts are oft-times very dead within them, when called to
duty, either doing or suffering, Cant. v. 2, 3, " I sleep, but my heart
waketh : it is the voice of my Beloved that knocketh, saying, Open
to me, my sister, my love, my dove, my undefiled : for my head is
filled with dew, and my locks with the drops of the night.   I have
put off my coat, how shall I put it on !   I have washed my feet, how
shall I defile them ?"   Their affections are flat, and their souls indis-
posed for spiritual action.   But when the Spirit touches their hearts,
they are fitted for duty; their spiritual life is brought forth into
liveliness and activity, Psalm lxxx. 18, " Quicken us, and we will
call upon thy name.

[2.] They can by no art of theirs remove their deadness of
heart and affections, 2 Cor. iii. 5, but they will lie windbound
in the harbour, till the Spirit blow.   They may be long toil-
ing in rowing in the use of means, and yet be still but where they
were, for all they can do.   But the influences of the Spirit rising and
filling their sails, they will presently make way, Cant. vi. 12.

Now, this double action of presenting to their minds, and touching
their hearts, whereby the Spirit excites grace, is signified to us by
comparing the Spirit to fire, which has both light and heat with it,
Matth. iii. 11.   And there is a twofold mean the Spirit makes use of
for that purpose, viz. the word and providence, of which afterwards.

3dly, He strengthens and increases grace in them, Eph. iii. 16,
" That he would grant you, according to the riches of his glory, to
be strengthened with might, by his Spirit in the inner man."   Grace
is a heavenly seed capable of growth, 2 Pet. iii. ult., and so admits
of various degrees of strength, not only in different persons, in respect of which some are little children, others youths, others fathers,
1 John ii. but in the same person at different times, Is. xl. ult, " They
that wait upon the Lord shall renew their strength."   And indeed
of its own nature it is a growing thing, as a seed; grace hath a
seminal virtue in it, that fits it for growing and receiving more
strength, John iv. 14.   Meanwhile the seed will not grow unless it
be watered from above ; so grace grows not, but by the influence of
the Spirit, Hos. xiv. 5, " I will be as the dew unto Israel : he shall
grow as the lily, and cast forth his roots as Lebanon."   Now the
Spirit doth strengthen and increase grace,

(1.) By frequent exciting it into action.   The habits of grace, as
well as others, are strengthened by the repeated exercise of them.
The more it shines, it shines the brighter, Prov. iv. 18.   It is for

this cause that God has bound converts also to the hearing of the word, whereby their graces are brought forth into one act after another, as the object is still anew proposed ; and for this cause he trysts his people with a variety of incidents, afflictions, and trials, which bring their graces into frequent exercise, whereby at length they become strong.

(2.) By bringing forth into exercise one grace, he strengthens the rest, 2 Pet. i. 5, 8, " And besides this, giving all diligence, add to your faith, virtue ; and to virtue, knowledge ; and to knowledge, temperance : and to temperance, patience ; and to patience, godliness ; and to godliness, brotherly kindness ; and to brotherly kindness, charity. For if these things be in you, and abound, they make you that ye shall neither be barren, nor unfruitful in the knowledge of our Lord Jesus Christ." As a mason by laying on a new stone in his wall, fastens the rest under it ; or the sheaves of corn stand the more firmly, that one is set at the side of another ; so one grace is still the better of another joined to it in the exercise thereof. So humility strengthens meekness and patience, love strengthens obedience in all points, and faith strengthens altogether ; like a band or keystone in an arch, the more firm it is, the firmer is the whole arch ; so the Spirit, by bringing forth one grace in the believer's heart after another, strengthens the whole collection, and makes it the more firm and steady.

(3.) By affording them Christian experiences, whereby they find the truth and reality of what they have believed, and the blessed sensible advantage of the exercise of grace, Rom. v. 3, 4, 5, " We glory in tribulations also, knowing that tribulation worketh patience ; and patience, experience ; and experience, hope ; and hope maketh not ashamed, because the love of God is shed abroad in our hearts, by the Holy Ghost which is given unto us." Experienced Christians are therefore always the strongest Christians, even as the spoil got in one battle helps the soldier to fight the more stoutly in the next, 1 Sam. xvii. 36, 2 Tim. iv. 17, 18. Former experiences are the traveller to Zion's way-marks in dark steps, and his cordials in difficult ascents. Every taste of divine goodness and grace refreshes and strengthens. Now it is the Spirit that gives these experiences, John xvi. 14, " He shall receive of mine, and shall show it unto you."

(4.) By immediate supplies of grace, Phil. i. 19, " I know that this shall turn to my salvation through your prayer, and the supply of the Spirit of Jesus Christ." As the lamp is preserved from going out, and is caused to burn more vigorously, by new oil poured in ; so grace is strengthened by the Spirit giving new supplies thereof, Isa. xliv. 3, 4. Hence the Spirit is said to " build us for an habitation to God," Eph. ii. ult. He works the first grace; and all the intermediate supplies of it, and the perfecting of it, are his, Psalm cxxxviii. ult. "The Lord will perfect that which concerneth me." Now, this is a great help; for,

[1.] Weighty is the work that lies to the believer's hand; doing work, suffering work. The Christian life is no easy life, however men that go no further than the outside of it, may make it so to themselves. It is a striving, taking by force, running, labouring, fighting, &c. How could it be managed, without the helps of the Spirit?

[2.] Great is the opposition that they must work against, Eph. vi. 12, "For we wrestle not against flesh and blood, but against principalities, against powers, against the rulers of the darkness of this world, against spiritual wickedness in high places." The wind will be blowing in their face from hell at all times; and sometimes they will meet with violent storms. How could they stand against it, if the Spirit did not help?

[3.] Weak are the hands that work is put into, that has all that opposition. There is a feebleness natural to them, that makes them oft hang down. How could they ever do that work maugre so much opposition, without the helps of the Spirit?

The means which the Spirit of God makes use of to preserve, excite, and strengthen grace in believers, and so to help them, are two.

1. Providences; Psalm xcii. 4, "For thou, Lord, hast made me glad through thy work; I will triumph in the works of thy hands." The kingdom of providence is put into the hand of the Mediator, for the behoof of the kingdom of grace; and he guides it by his Spirit. The wheels of providence are managed by the Spirit; Ezek. i. 20, and so managed as to help believers in their infirmities. And here two things are especially to be noticed,

(1.) Seasonable turns of the wheel of providence, whereby the believer's wain is often kept up when it is at the oversetting; 1 Cor. x. 13, "God is faithful, who will not suffer you to be tempted above that ye are able; but will with the temptation also make a way to escape, that ye may be able to bear it." Psalm xciv. 18, "When I said, My foot slippeth; thy mercy, O Lord, held me up." Thus many times the believer is brought to an extremity, as Isaac when the knife was at his throat, when providence seasonably interposes for his relief and outgate; Psalm cxxv. 3.

(2.) Seasonable intermixtures of providence. Thus the Spirit intermixes encouraging dispensations with difficult duties, Judg. vii. 13, 14., merciful incidents with their sharp afflictions; and, on the other hand, afflicting incidents with their prosperity; and all that they may neither be swallowed up with adversity, nor destroyed with prosperity.

2. Ordinances, Isa. xii. 3, "Therefore with joy shall ye draw water out of the wells of salvation." These are instituted by the King of Zion, for the special means of grace, whereby his Spirit is to work, and to render them effectual. And the experience believers have of the Spirit's helping their infirmities by these, makes them very precious in their sight. And among these there are two especially used for this end.

1*st*, The sacraments. They are exciting and strengthening ordinances particularly, and consequently preservative of grace. The eunuch's experience witnesseth this as to baptism, Acts viii. 39, he "went on his way rejoicing." And the Lord's supper is "the communion of the body and blood of Christ," 1 Cor. x. 16., which, by the Spirit's working, has been to the experience of many a great help.

2*dly*, The word. This is the most special mean. Providence has its efficacy from the word, and so have the sacraments. It is their continual mean of help, their every-day's meal, which they can go to when providence is most lowring, and sacramental occasions offer not. And the Spirit uses it for their help three ways.

(1.) Preached, 1 Cor. i. 21, "It pleased God by the foolishness of preaching to save them that believe." This affords to the attentive believer a continued occasion of the exercise of his faith and love, while a variety of spiritual truths and objects are represented to him, in their turn; which the Spirit makes use of to draw forth his graces into exercise. Whence believers go away instructed, warmed, strengthened, in a word, edified, by reason of so many actings of grace, during their hearing, like the two disciples going to Emmaus, when they said, "Did not our heart burn within us, while he talked with us by the way, and while he opened to us the scriptures?" Luke xxiv. 32.

(2.) Read, 1 Tim. iv. 13, "Till I come, give attendance to reading." This has the same advantages attending it. Thereby the Spirit of God speaks immediately to the believer by his own word in his own express terms. And the experience of the usefulness of this mean has made saints prize their Bibles as their life.

(3.) Suggested, John xiv. 26, "He shall bring all things to your remembrance, whatsoever I have said unto you." The bringing of the word to mind with a man is the office of the Spirit; and by that means he helps believers' infirmities, bringing a word suitable to their case, into their remembrance, whether to clear them in doubts, comfort them under pressures, direct them in difficulties, or check them for their debordings, &c. And herein he uses often the very words of the Bible, always what is the sense and doctrine of the Bible. And,

[1.] Sometimes the Spirit barely suggests the word to the mind without any peculiar light about it, or power impressing it, John xiv. 26, just cited. Thus it is presented as an object for the believer to act faith on, and is a call to look up to the Spirit to enlighten it and help to believe it, Acts viii. 30. 31. And thus a word at first coming in this way, comes afterwards to be illuminated by the Spirit's shining on it to the man.

[2.] Sometimes there is a peculiar light and power that comes along with it at the very first, clearly holding out the meaning of it, and impressing it so on their hearts, that they must needs believe and embrace it, John ii. 17, "And his disciples remembered that it was written, The zeal of thine house hath eaten me up." There were many Old Testament passages speaking more clearly of Christ which they understood not, but the Spirit thus suggested this to them.

Meanwhile it is to be observed, that all suggestions of the word are not from the Spirit of God. That Satan may suggest scripture to a man, is evident from Matth. iv. 6. Therefore is that warning, 1 John iv. 1, "Beloved, believe not every spirit, but try the spirits whether they are of God; because many false prophets are gone out into the world." But the cloven foot may be discerned in such cases two ways.

[1.] They are always of a tendency to drive sinners away from Christ, 1 John iv. 2, 3, "Hereby know ye the Spirit of God: every spirit that confesseth that Jesus Christ is come in the flesh, is of God. And every spirit that confesseth not that Jesus Christ is come in the flesh, is not of God. And they tend to drive out of the road of duty, Matth. iv. 6, "And saith unto him, If thou be the Son of God, cast thyself down: for it is written, He shall give his angels charge concerning thee, and in their hands they shall bear thee up, lest at any time thou dash thy foot against a stone." This was the design of the testimony he gave to Christ, and to his apostles; while the testimony was indeed true in itself, he gave it maliciously for an ill end. Therefore mark the tendency of suggestions of the word. Whatever tends to carry off from faith in Christ, or from any point of commanded duty, is not from the Spirit. For his work tends to faith and sanctification. Hence,

[2.] They are always applied by him contrary to their true sense and scope, forasmuch as the Lord's word cannot serve an ill purpose, unless it is wrested; as is evident from what the devil says to Christ, Matth. iv. 6, above cited, compared with Psalm xci. 11, 12, "For he shall give his angels charge over thee, to keep thee in all thy ways. They shall bear thee up in their hands, lest thou dash thy foot against a stone." And therefore the scripture-passage is to be considered, and how it agrees with other scriptures as to the sense and scope in which it is suggested, Matth. iv. 7, " Jesus said unto him, It is written again, Thou shalt not tempt the Lord thy God." The Holy Spirit is the Spirit of truth, and leads to the true sense and scope of scripture, John xvi. 13.

I add one observe more on the means, namely, that sometimes the Spirit helps believers' infirmities, by a particular providence trysting the word to their case. This often comes to pass in hearing the word preached, while the word in its ordinary course is brought directly to what is their case in the time; so that it is like the Midianite's telling his dream, Judg. vii. 13, while Gideon, unknown to him, was overhearing; or they are providentially led to such a place, where such a word suitable to their case is handled, Cant iii. 3. The same particular providence appears often in the reading of the word, whether at family worship, or in secret, or by some providential casting of it in one's way.* I think it dangerous to make a fortune-book of the Bible, as some under temptation have opened the Bible, to know their case by the first word that should cast up to them. This is an unwarrantable and dangerous practice, though a merciful God may sometimes condescend to outshoot the devil in his own bow as in the case of her who threw the glass at the wall, and it broke not. But when people are thus met in the way of their duty, or surprised, with a word suited to their case, the work of the Spirit is to be owned in it, as an accomplishment of the promise, Isa. xxx. 21, " Thine ear shall hear a word behind thee, saying, This is the way, walk ye in it, when ye turn to the right hand, and when ye turn to the left." Certainly the Spirit gives instruction, reproof, invitations, to unbelievers this way; and much more helps the infirmities of his people the same way, for so the word is in its true use, 2 Tim. iii. 16, 17, " All scripture is given by inspiration of God, and is profitable for doctrine, for reproof, for correction, for instruction in righteousness: that the man of God may be perfect, throughly furnished unto all good works. And this should recommend the reading of the word of God in an ordinary.

I shall now make some short improvement of this doctrine.

USE 1. Of information. This teaches us and shews,

1. That believers owe their spiritual strength and comfort to the same hand that they owe their spiritual life to. As the mother who

---

* Many instances of this are to be found in the author's own experience, in his Memoirs.

brought forth the child nurses it with her own breasts; so the Spirit, who is to the elect the Spirit of life to quicken them lying dead in sin, is likewise the Comforter to strengthen them under their infirmities when spiritually alive, John vi. 63, and xvi. 13; compare Psalm cxxxviii., ult.

2. The Lord calls none of his people to any duty, but they may get it done acceptably, however difficult it is. For the help of his own Spirit is their allowance; Phil. iv. 13, "I can do all things through Christ which strengtheneth me." Here is the great difference betwixt those under the law and under grace. The law or covenant of works exacts duty rigidly, but affords no help; the covenant of grace affords the promise of help with the command; for the latter is, but the former is not, the ministration of the Spirit, 2 Cor. iii. 8.

3. How that gospel-paradox; 2 Cor. xii. 10, "When I am weak, then am I strong," is so often verified in the experience of the saints. Many a time when they are strong and well buckled in all appearance for a work, it miscarries; why, they do not go out of themselves in a way of believing, and so the Spirit withdraws. At other times they see themselves quite out of case and ability to manage such a work, and yet it succeeds; why, the Spirit comes in to their help, while they are sensible of need.

USE II. Of reproof. It may reach a reproof,

1. To believers sometimes venturing on duties, more in confidence of their own abilities, than of the Spirit's help, as Peter did when he said, "Though all men shall be offended because of thee, yet will I never be offended," Matth. xxvi. 33. This is the cause that the duty is marred; the bow so bended cannot miss to break. It is sometimes marred as to the very getting it done, and always as to its acceptance with God.

2. To unbelievers, who neither have the Spirit, nor are careful to have him dwelling in them, and influencing them. Their best works are dead works, having nothing of the quickening and sanctifying Spirit in them; and they themselves are but natural men spiritually dead, Jude 19. Whatever flourish they make with their gifts in duties, their best duties will no more be accepted of God than carrion, or a beast that died of itself would have been accepted on the altar.

3. To those who press on men still this and the other duty, without leading them to Jesus Christ for his Spirit and grace. This is another gospel, that will never make men holy, Gal. iii. 2, for it is not the ministration of the Spirit. And the same veil they cast over the Spirit and grace of Christ, they will always be found to cast

over the corruption of man's nature too, that they may with some decency say to every man, Physician, heal thyself.

USE III. Of exhortation. And, 1. To natural men void of the Spirit. Be concerned to get the Spirit first to quicken you, and then to assist and help you. Ye can do nothing acceptable to God in that state; and no wonder, for ye have not the gracious help of the Spirit, without which ye can have no access to God, Eph. ii. 18. So ye and your works are both dead carcases before him.

Therefore come to Christ in the way of believing; for the fulness of the Spirit is lodged in him to be communicated, Rev. iii. 1. So uniting with him, ye shall receive the Spirit. The fire that was set to the incense, was brought from the altar of burnt-offering. See John xx. 22, and Gen. ii. 7.

2. To believers. (1.) Let this comfort you under, and reconcile you to, the state of infirmities, wherewith ye are compassed; 2 Cor. xii. 9, 10. Though sinless infirmities are not to be desired, and sinful ones are much to be lamented; yet it is matter of rejoicing, that in these the Spirit gives sweet experience of his help.

(2.) Learn to look habitually for the help of the Spirit under your infirmities. While ye consider what ye have to do or bear, it is reasonable you cast one eye on your infirmity, but another eye upward for the Spirit's help. And by this means you will get his help. Luke xi. 13, "If ye being evil, know how to give good gifts unto your children; how much more shall your heavenly. Father give the Holy Spirit to them that ask him?"

DOCTRINE III. Such is the weakness of God's own children, that they have not skill to manage even their addresses to God by prayer aright, without the Spirit. For we know not what we should pray for as we ought; but the Spirit itself maketh intercession for us." They are like children putting their hand to a work, but with so little skill, that they must needs have one to stand over them, and direct them at every turn.

In discoursing from this point, I shall shew,

I. What is implied in this truth.

II. Wherein believers are ready, through their weakness, to mistake, go wrong, and mismanage in their prayers.

III. *Lastly*, Apply.

I. I shall shew what is implied in this truth. It implies,

1. That they are not of themselves able for what is to be done and borne in the Christian life; 2 Cor. iii. 5. So far from it, that they do not well know what is necessary for their help, what to seek of God for that end, and how to seek it. If a duty is to be done, a

cross to be borne, they are at a loss there through weakness and infirmity; that sets them to their prayers : but then they are at a loss there again, they know not what, and how to ask.

2. That the children of God are all praying persons; Zech. xii. 10. If they can speak at all, they will speak to God by prayer; and even when they either cannot speak, or have no access to speak, if they have the exercise of judgment, they will pray in their hearts; 1 Cor. xiv. 15. So the habitual neglect of prayer is none of the spots of God's people. There is no child so unnatural, as to be still in his father's presence, and never to converse with him.

3. A gift of prayer, without the Spirit of prayer, cannot be sufficient to make one right prayer, that will be acceptable to God; John iv. 24. Gifts of prayer are bestowed on believers, as well as others; but still they know not what to pray for as they ought, without the Spirit prompting them. The prayer that is the mere exercise of a gift, may indeed be edifying to the hearers, but cannot be acceptable to God.

4. Nay, habitual grace is not sufficient for praying aright; for still there is a necessity of actual assistance from the Spirit; Psalm lxxx. 18, "Quicken us, and we will call upon thy name." Life is not sufficient for making a discourse to our prince; a man may have life, and yet not be able to speak a word; but some vigour and liveliness is necessary to such a purpose. So spiritual life never departs wholly from the believer; 1 John iii. 9, but it must be breathed on anew to fit him for praying; Cant. iv. ult. New influences are still necessary; hence is the promise; Isa. xxvii. 3, "I will water it every moment."

5. *Lastly*, Prayers are marred so far as the Spirit of God does not assist the party in them; they are marred so far in point of acceptance with God; Eph. ii. 18. As no prayer can be accepted but through Christ's intercession, so none will be offered to God by the Intercessor farther than it is the product of the influence of his own Spirit. Nadab and Abihu's hearth-fire offered with the incense, was a costly lesson of this; Lev. x. 1, 2, 3. So if, through the whole prayer, the Spirit's assistance is wanting, the whole will be unaccepted; if in any of it, that wherein it is wanting will be so.

II. The next head is to show, wherein believers are ready, through their weakness, to mistake, go wrong, and mismanage in their prayers. They are ready to do so both in the matter and manner of them.

First, In the matter of prayer, " We know not what to pray for." Even the things to be prayed for, they are not so well versed in them, but they are ready to go wrong therein. So that they need the

Spirit's teaching, to tell them and make them take up their errand, when they are going and come to God in prayer; they need to be set right, and kept right in the very matter of prayer. Their weakness in this point appears, in that,

1. They are apt to pray against their own mercy. Thus did Job, chap. vi. 8, 9, "O that I might have my request; and that God would grant me the thing that I long for! even that it would please God to destroy me; that he would let loose his hand, and cut me off." When Satan was permitted to take all from him, there was an express reserve of his life as the greatest mercy; but he prays very earnestly against it, though no doubt at long-run Job blessed God from his heart that he did not hear him in that. We are so weak, that in God's dispensations many times we take our friends for our foes, and call what is for our good, evil, as Jacob did when he said, "All these things are against me," Gen. xlii. 36.

2. They are apt to seek what is not so good as God has a mind to give them; 2 Cor. xii. 8, 9, "For this thing I besought the Lord thrice, that it might depart from me. And he said unto me, My grace is sufficient for thee." To be freed from the messenger of Satan was good, but to have God's grace poured in sufficiently to maintain the combat, was better. And therefore Paul upon reflection takes God's way to have been better than what he himself proposed, ver. 9, "Most gladly therefore will I rather glory in my infirmities, that the power of Christ may rest upon me." Narrow asking ofttimes makes narrow receiving. It fares with believers sometimes as with Joash; 2 Kings xiii. 18, 19, "Elisha said unto him, Take the arrows; and he took them. And he said unto the king of Israel, Smite upon the ground; and he smote thrice, and stayed. And the man of God was wroth with him, and said, Thou shouldst have smitten five or six times, then hadst thou smitten Syria till thou hadst consumed it; whereas now thou shalt smite Syria but thrice." They are straitened in their own bowels in asking, and therefore they come not speed.

3. They are apt to seek what would be for their hurt. So did Jonah, when he wished in himself to die, and said, it is better for me to die than to live; chap iv. 8. It would have been very ill for Jonah to have died in such a bad frame and temper of spirit, as he was then in. And if God had struck him immediately, it is like he would immediately have changed his note. David prayed for the life of the child, 2 Sam. xii. 16, but God took it away, for it would have been a living blot upon him. As a foolish child seeks a knife to play with, which he can do nothing with, but hurt himself; so we are apt to seek from God, what in mercy he keeps from us.

4. They are apt to seek food for their corrupt lusts and affections;

Matth. xx. 20, 21, " Then came to him the mother of Zebedee's children, with her sons, worshipping him, and desiring a certain thing of him And he said unto her, What wilt thou ? She saith unto him, Grant that these my two sons may sit, the one on thy right hand, and the other on the left in thy kingdom." James and John were tickled with a lust of ambition, and they seek honour to satisfy it. And it is God's goodness to his people in such a case, not to do with them as he did with the lusting Israelites; Psalm cvi. 15, " He gave them their request, but sent leanness into their soul." Men may go wrong here, and not see their error, till the Lord correct it; for they may take lust for love; Luke ix. 54, 55, and so seek to feed their enemies whom they should starve.

5. They are apt, through ignorance or inadvertency, not to pray for what they really need for their case ; as the children of Israel, when they " went up to the house of God, and asked counsel of God, and said, which of us shall go up first to the battle against the children of Benjamin ?" Judg. xx. 18. To pray for God's presence with them, was not in their head ; but that they really needed it, they afterwards felt to their cost. Many sad experiences praying people may have of this, which may shew the need of the Spirit's assistance. Hence general and formal prayers, little suited to the particular cases and exigences of the party ; which is but trifling in so solemn and serious a matter as prayer to God.

6. Though they do know and advert to it before they go to prayer, they are ready to forget it in the time. There is a forgetting of particular petitions designed or coming of course, which is an effect of the Spirit's influence ; in that case the forgotten petition is from one's own spirit, not from the Spirit of God, as in the instance of the prodigal son, Luke xv., what he designed to say to his father, ver. 19, " Make me as one of thy hired servants," when he came to him, he forgets, ver. 21. There is such a forgetting which is an effect of our own weakness ; in that case the petition forgotten is from the Spirit of God, the forgetting it from ourselves, Heb. ii. 1.

Thus going to God sometimes, we forget much of our errand, whether by wandering of heart or being left to ourselves in the matter. In a word,

7. *Lastly*, They are apt to pray for things not agreeable to the will of God, that there is neither precept nor promise for. The many petitions in which they are not heard evince this ; because " if we ask anything according to his will he heareth us," 1 John v. 14. There is so much remains of corruption in the best, that it is hard even in our prayers to keep within the compass of what is agreeable to his will.

I shall now endeavour to assign the reasons why God's own children are so apt to mistake and go wrong, even in the matter of prayer.

The great reason is, the remains of darkness that are on the minds of the best, while here; Job xxxvii. 19, " Teach us what we shall say unto him; for we cannot order our speech by reason of darkness." It is true, God's children are not in midnight darkness, but their light is but a twilight, in which they are apt to mistake their way. And the more sensible they are of this, the more need they will find of the Spirit's help in prayer. More particularly, we know not what we should pray for, but are ready to go wrong in the matter of prayer,

1. Because we have at best but little knowledge of our own case ; and no wonder that they who are not thoroughly acquainted with the nature of the disease mistake as to the remedy. The blind man, Mark viii. 22—25, is an emblem of the natural man, the true convert, and the glorified saint. The child of God while here, " sees but in part," 1 Cor. xiii. 12. Every believer is a mystery, Cant. iii. 6, a mystery to the world, a mystery to himself. There are many folds and plies in his case, which he himself cannot unfold; plies of grace, sin, temptation, danger, &c.

2. Little knowledge of what is good and best for us, Gen. xlii. 36. We see the weakness of understanding in children makes them often to desire of parents what really is not for them ; even so it is with God's children, and therefore it is fatherly love that denies some of their petitions ; as in the case of Job, Jonah, and others. We are apt to think that that is best for us that is most pleasant and most easy, but that is often a very deceitful rule.

3. Little acquaintance with the word, particularly the commands and the promises, the measure of our petitions. There is much need of the Spirit's help in that matter, John xiv. 26. We are ready to measure our petitions rather by our own inclinations than by the word ; and many read the Bible often, that have but very little skill of making a practical improvement thereof in their prayers, Mark x. 35, 37.

4. We are apt to take the subtle cravings of lust for the cravings of grace or innocent affection, Luke ix. 54, 55. And thence good people unwittingly are made intercessors for their spiritual enemies; which, if they did discern, they would confess their error, and retract their request. Sin dwells in the believer together with grace, and that so closely that the language of the one is often taken for that of the other.

5. Believers are liable to prejudices and wrong notions of things,

which they have drunk in from their education, manner of life in the world, &c. Such was the disciples' notion of the temporal kingdom of Christ, that was the spring of that rash petition of James and John ; Mark x. 37, " Grant unto us that we may sit, one on thy right hand, and the other on thy left hand in thy glory." Such was that of the case of Gentiles among the believing Jews, that was the spring of the offence taken at Peter ; Acts xi. 2, 3, " They that were of the circumcision contended with him, saying, Thou wentest in to men uncircumcised, and didst eat with them." An erring conscience will mislead men under pretence of divine authority, John xvi. 2 ; Acts xxvi. 9. No wonder then it form wrong requests in prayer, Luke ix. 54.

6. *Lastly*, They are subject to much confusion in prayer, both through natural and spiritual indisposition, Psalm lxxvii. 4. Hence they are ready as Job did, chap. xxxviii. 2, " to darken counsel by words without knowledge." The exercise of their very gift is not always ready at hand with them, far less the exercise of their grace. An influence of the Spirit is necessary both for the one and the other. And when it is wanting, so that they are in no case for praying, no wonder they know not what to pray for.

Secondly, Believers are ready to go wrong in the manner of prayer ; " We know not what we should pray for as we ought." It is not in vain our Lord gave his disciples a direction in that point ; Matth. vi. 9, "After this manner pray ye," &c. The prayer may be right as to the matter, that yet may be mismanaged in the manner of performance, 1 Chron. xv. 13. And therefore there is need of the Spirit's help in this point too ; not only to teach us what, but how to pray. Their weakness in this point appears, in that,

1. They are apt to slip the best season for managing their address before the throne. Thomas missed an opportunity of communion with Christ, that left him under the feet of unbelief, while the rest were delivered from theirs, John xx. 24, 25. The best season is, when the signal is given from heaven to the petitioner, to come forward ; sometimes the door is as it were cast open to him, and there is a sign given by some inward motion of the Spirit, or some providential call moving him to come forward. The spouse missed this ; Cant. v. 2, 3, " I sleep, but my heart waketh," &c., and she smarted for it ; ver. 6, " I opened to my Beloved, but my Beloved had withdrawn himself, and was gone ; my soul failed when he spoke : I sought him but I could not find him ; I called him, but he gave me no answer."

Moses was very careful to fall in with it immediately ; Exod. xxxiv. 8, 9, " And Moses made haste, and bowed his head toward the earth, and worshipped. And he said, If now I have found grace

in thy sight, O Lord, let my Lord, I pray thee, go amongst us (for
it is a stiff-necked people) and pardon our iniquity and our sin, and
take us for thine inheritance."

2. They are apt to enter on prayer with a temper of spirit very
unfit for such a holy exercise; being either entangled with worldly
cares, or discomposed with unruly passions, Luke xxi. 34; 1 Tim.
ii. 8. They both make the Spirit of a man like troubled water, unfit to
receive the image of the sun, unfit for divine communications. Jonah's prayer behoved to be marred when he was in a fret. Therefore
the apostle exhorts married persons to take heed to their behaviour
one towards another, that their prayers might not be hindered, 1 Pet.
iii. 7, nothing being more apt to do it than domestic jars, Mal. ii. 13.

3. They are apt to be formal, lifeless, and coldrife in prayer, Cant.
iii. 1; Rev. iii. 2. We are called to be "fervent in spirit, serving
the Lord." But even where the fire of grace is in the hearth, unless
it be blown up by the influence of the Spirit of God, the prayers will be mismanaged, Psalm lxxx. 18. There will be bands of
iniquity on the heart which they will not be able to loose, more than
to dissolve the ice with their breath; but "where the Spirit of the
Lord is, there is the liberty."

4. Their hearts are apt to wander in duty, and will do so if the
Spirit fix them not. Therefore David prays, "Unite my heart to
fear thy name," Psalm lxxxvi. 11. When Abraham had divided
the carcases, the fowls came down on them; so when one is conversing with God, evil spirits will be at work, to cast in something that
may divert him from the present duty, Rom. vii. 21. Many a prayer
is lost this way, while the heart steals away after some other thing
than what it should then be on.

5. They are apt to content themselves with exercising their gift,
without exercising their grace. Therefore Paul warns the Ephe-
sians, chap. vi. 18, "to pray always with all prayer and supplication
in the Spirit, and to watch thereunto with all perseverance." Hence
many petitions, confessions, thanksgivings, all of them just; yet lost
for want of suitable affections coming along with them. For it is
the exercise of praying graces, reverence, faith, love, humility, &c.,
and not the exercise of praying gifts without them, that is pleasing
to God.

6. They are apt to disproportion their concern to the weight of
the matters they pray for. This is carefully guarded against in the
Lord's prayer, Matth. vi. 9, &c., where the glory of God has the first
place, and there is but one petition for temporals, and two for spirituals. But how ready are we to be more concerned for our own
interest, than for the honour of God; more fervent for temporal

than for spiritual mercies ? This makes the prayers like the legs of the lame that are not equal, the affection being disproportioned to the matter.

7. They are apt to be too peremptory in circumstances, without leaving a due latitude to sovereignty. That is limiting the holy One of Israel. This is often done as to time, the timing of mercies, in which we are too apt to take upon us to prescribe to the sovereign manager, John ii. 3, 4, as to the manner of bringing about a mercy, which, short-sighted as we are, we are very ready to determine. And the same may be said as to the measure of mercies.

8. They are apt to mix their own wild fire with the holy fire in prayer. So did the disciples, Mark iv. 38, when they say, " Master, carest thou not that we perish ?" The language of passion is sometimes mixed with the language of grace in the prayers of saints; which when they discern, they will be ready to correct, Psalm lxxvii. 7—10. Hence there are expressions of saints unto God, recorded in scripture, not for our imitation, but for our warning of this corrupt bias of the heart; as Job xxx. 21, " Thou art become cruel to me; with thy strong hand thou opposest thyself against me." Jer. xv. 18, " Why is my pain perpetual ? and my wound incurable, which refuseth to be healed ? wilt thou be altogether unto me as a liar, and as waters that fail ?" These he looks on as the ravings of his sick children.

9. They are apt to lay too much weight of their acceptance in their prayers, on what will bear none of it. It is certain, that there is nothing will bear any weight of that, but the merit and intercession of Jesus Christ; Rev. viii. 4. But the natural bias of the heart lies another way, to lay weight on the very performance of the duty, and the way how it is performed, as with such affection, pointedness, length, nay the very voice, as insignificant a thing as it is before the Lord. Hence our Lord cautions against "using vain repetitions" in prayer, "as the Heathen do; for they think (says he) that they shall be heard for their much speaking ;" Matth. vi. 7. And that the Heathen laid much stress on a loud voice in prayer, appears from what Pharaoh says to Moses ; Exod. ix. 28, (Heb.) Make ye supplication to the Lord, and much, i. e. Make much supplication. Compare 1 Kings xviii. 28, where it is said of Baal's prophets, that " they cried aloud." There are remains of that legal bias in the hearts of God's own children ; Matth. xix. 27. And it is only by the Spirit that saints are brought to lay their whole weight on Jesus Christ; Eph. ii. 18; Phil. iii. 3. Otherwise their deceitful hearts will be found disposed to slip aside that way, they being very ready to believe the acceptance of some fluent prayer of theirs, and hard

to believe the acceptance of one that goes not so fluently though seriously; yet the blood of Jesus is still the same security.

10. *Lastly*, They are apt to faint and give over, upon the Lord's delaying to answer; whereas it is a chief piece of right management of business at the court of heaven, resolutely to insist and hang on, Luke xviii. 1, 8. We are naturally hasty, and long trials are apt to run us out of breath. There is need of much faith, that patience may have her perfect work; and that is not to be reached without the help of the Spirit; Rom. xv. 13.

I shall now give the reasons why believers are so apt to go wrong in the manner of prayer. They are the following:—

1. Because of the sublimity of the work, that is so far above our reach, that we can by no means know how to manage it, but as we are taught by him with whom we have to do in it. To say a prayer in a formal uttering of words, is no such hard work indeed. But rightly to manage an address at the throne of heaven, on which sits the Sovereign Majesty; and that about the weightiest of all concerns, is such sublime work, that it passes the skill of the greatest orator on earth to do it without the Spirit; Eccl. v. 1, 2. Were any of us to go on business to our earthly king, would we not need to be directed by some knowing the way of the court? How much more do we need direction from the Holy Spirit in our addresses to the throne of grace?

2. Because of the remains of corruption that yet hang about them; Rom, vii. 24. This is a clog at their heels at all times, and will not miss to exert itself in holy duties, ver. 21, " When I would do good, evil is present with me." There is much darkness yet in the minds of the best, as to spiritual things; no wonder they know not how to pray as they ought. Much perverseness there is in the will, both with respect to God's precepts and providences. There is much carnality and disorder in the affections, as they all soundly feel, that are concerned to get the heart fit for praying, kept right in it, and kept right after it.

3. Because there is a subtile adversary busy to mar them in that their work; Zech. iii. 1. He well knows that all the hope in their case is from the divine help; and therefore while they are before the throne of mercy, he will bestir himself effectually to mar their application. He is an enemy to prayer, and therefore he will keep back from it if he can; if he cannot, he will do his utmost to mar it.

4. *Lastly*, Because of the weakness of grace in them. Grace disposes men to pray; Zech xii. 10. But the weakness of that grace leaves them in hazard of mismanaging in it. Sometimes it is not in exercise; at best it is but weak, and mixed with corruption, in

the struggle with which it will be overcome, if the spirit come not in to its help.

I shall now make some practical improvement.

This doctrine may be of use, both unto strangers to God, and to his own children. And,

FIRST, Ye that are strangers to God, yet in your natural state, without the Spirit, and therefore children of Satan, we may take you up in these two sorts to be spoken to, viz. prayerless natural persons, and praying natural persons.

First, Prayerless natural unconverted persons, such as are living in the state they were born in, and withal living without praying to the God that made them. I have two things to say to you from this doctrine.

1. Learn from it, that this prayerless life of yours declares your case a very sad one. It declares you,

(1.) None of God's children; for whatever mismanagements of it they fall into, they all practise the duty of prayer. So of you that is verified : Deut. xxxii. 5, "Their spot is not the spot of his children." And if so, ye are the children of the devil; John viii. 44, of the family of hell. And his possession of you remains undisturbed to this day, since ye have never been so far awakened, as to set you to, and keep you at prayer.

(2.) Without the Spirit of God; Jude 19. And being without the Spirit, ye are spiritually dead in sin; for so are all naturally ; Eph. ii. 1, and it is "the Spirit that quickeneth ;" John vi. 63. So that whosoever are without the Spirit are dead still. You are then dead souls in living bodies. It is plain you are dead, for your speech is laid, your senses are gone, there is no moving nor breathing towards God in you, and the Spirit of life is departed from you.

2. Be exhorted from it to reform. And,

(1.) Set about prayer, 1 Thess. v. 17. Remember ye are God's creatures, and therefore obliged to worship him. Ye are men, and not beasts, and therefore should distinguish yourselves from them by religion, Isa. xlvi. 8. Ye have souls that will not die, and therefore ye should be concerned to pray for them, that ye live not in eternal misery.

(2.) Be concerned to partake of the Spirit, and come to Christ for that end, who "hath the seven Spirits of God," Rev. iii. 1. Ye say ye cannot pray. If the Spirit of Christ were in you, it would not be so, Zech. xii. 10, Gal. iv. 6. Ye say ye have no time for prayer, or ye have no place to pray in. If the Spirit of Christ were in you, ye would have a heart to pray; and if ye had the heart for it, ye would find both time and place.

Secondly, Praying natural unconverted persons. People may be praying persons, and yet in the gall of bitterness, and none of God's children; praying persons, and yet profane, Isa. i. 15, 16; formal hypocrites, Matth. xxiii. 14, 27, 28. They may have a gift of prayer, that are void of the spirit and grace of prayer. To such I would say from this doctrine, Then,

1. Certainly ye can pray none at all aright; an evidence of which is, All your prayers are rejected of God, Prov. xv. 8, John ix. 31. If God's own children cannot pray aright without the Spirit, how is it possible ye should do so, who neither have the Spirit, nor yet are children of God? If the weak man cannot go without help, sure the man void of life cannot move at all. View your own case in the case of the true saint, and think, if it be so in the green tree, what must it be in the dry? They are God's children, yet cannot pray aright to their Father without the Spirit; how much less can ye who are none of his family, and therefore never have the Spirit? They always have the Spirit dwelling in them as a Spirit of life, yet cannot pray aright without actual influence from him; how, then, can ye ever pray aright, who are so far from his actual influence, that he is not so much as in you, since ye are not in Christ? Hence,

(1.) Your praying, though continued never so many years, without coming to Christ by faith, is but like so many ciphers, which being without a figure at their head, the value is just nought. There is never one right or acceptable prayer among them all, Heb. xi. 6. They are all lost labour. And such a life of duties is but a wandering in the wilderness of duties, like Israel's wandering forty years in the wilderness, where they died at length, and never entered Canaan.

(2.) All your prayers are turned to sin, Psalm cix. 7. If ye have never prayed aright, ye have always prayed wrong, spilled and marred that duty, profaned that holy ordinance. And so what ye reckon so much praying to God, God will reckon so much taking of his name in vain, for which he will not hold you guiltless. Wherefore let praying persons look well to their state.

2. Think not much of your gifts of prayer, for a gift of prayer will go short way before God. If it were never such a ready, full, and taking gift, it cannot make a man pray one petition aright without the Spirit, John iv. 24. Yet how are men puffed up with such a gift, that have it, and have not grace to keep them humble under it? They think themselves something on account of their gift, while God knows they are nothing, as being without the Spirit; for they see wherein they excel others, but see not wherein

they come short of true prayer in the sight of God, Gal. vi. 3, 4.

I have four things to say of a gift of prayer without the spirit of prayer.

(1.) It is a "good gift" of God indeed, James i. 17. But it is a left hand gift, which may be lost and taken away from him that has it now; Zech. xi. ult., "Wo to the idol shepherd that leaveth the flock : the sword shall be upon his arm, and upon his right eye : his arm shall be clean dried up, and his right eye shall be utterly darkened ;" compared with John x. 12, for the prophecy relates to the Scribes and Pharisees. It is of that sort that is common to Christ's sheep and the devil's goats. The spirit of prayer is a grace-gift, a right hand gift, which can never be quite lost ; Rom. xi. 29, "For the gifts and calling of God are without repentance."

(2.) It may be useful to others for the profit of their souls, but in that respect it is useless to yourselves, 1 Cor. xiii. 1, 2, 3. Others may have communion with God in your exercise of your gift, but you yourself can have none, Prov. xv. 8. Gifts are bestowed on hypocrites for the good and behoof of the saints, as the purse bearer to a young prince gets his purse filled for the needs of the prince, 1 Cor. iii. 21—23. The raven, though an unclean creature, was employed to feed Elijah. The gift the carpenters had that built the ark, was of use to the saving of Noah and his family, but they themselves perished in the deluge, for all their skill of ark-building.

(3.) It cannot but be hurtful to your own souls ; which hurtfulness is not from the good gift itself, but from the light and foolish heart it is lodged in, Prov. i. 32. The very gospel, 2 Cor. ii. 16, is hurtful that way ; yea Christ himself is a stumbling-block by that means. A man with a gift of prayer, without the Spirit, is like a ship without ballast ; the more sail she has, she is in the greater danger of being overwhelmed.

(4.) You may perish for ever, for all that gift. Judas had a gift of praying doubtless given him with the gift of preaching ; yet for all it he fell from his ministry, and is gone to his own place, Acts i. 25. The light of a gift without the warmth of the Spirit of grace, serves to show the way to outer darkness. And such a gift will aggravate the condemnation of the possessor, being like a bag of gold on a drowning man, that makes him only to sink the sooner and the deeper.

3. *Lastly*, Come forward then another step in religion, and be concerned for a higher attainment in it, than ye have yet reached. Ye have come the length of praying, that is good, but it is not all ; if ye stick there, ye perish ; come forward to Christ, out of all confidence in your prayers, by believing, uniting with the Son of

God. Ye have attained to the gift of prayer; come forward till ye reach the Spirit of prayer, which Christ communicates to all his members, John i. 12; with Gal. iv. 6.

Secondly, Ye that are God's own children, to you I would say,

1. Surely many a mismanaged prayer hath gone through your mouths, so that ye may say, "We are all as an unclean thing, and all our righteousnesses are as filthy rags," Isa. lxiv. 6. So much prayer as has been made by you without the Spirit, so much mismanaged unacceptable prayer has there been, for which ye need pardon. Ye may here view,

(1.) The many prayers of yours, that have been the mere lifeless exercise of a gift without the Spirit from the beginning of them to the end. All which have been lost prayers by the lump. Since ye were acquainted with Christ, ye have kept a constant course of praying daily; but at this rate it will be found there have been many days, and perhaps weeks and months, wherein ye have prayed none at all aright and acceptably. So that if ye seek your prayers in heaven, which ye think ye have sent thither, it will be found that many of them never came there; they wanted the wings of the Spirit's influences, and so fell upon the earth, and are lost.

(2.) The many parts of some of your prayers, and some parts of the best of them, that have been the mere product of your own spirits, and not of the Spirit of God. How much of the prayer has been over many times, ere your lips have been touched with the live coal? And perhaps ere ye have done, ye have quenched the coal, provoked the Spirit to depart. And when it has been best with you, the deceitful heart has made a sinful mixture in it. At this rate seeking many a long prayer before the throne, ye would find that but a short part of it came thither; perhaps but a few sentences. For alas! the skin and dung of our sacrifices are often more bulk, than the flesh that comes on the altar.

2. Be humbled under a sense of your mismanagements in the prayers ye have prayed all along to this day; "for in many things we offend all," Jam. iii. 2. See the need ye have of the blood of Christ to purge away the guilt of your prayers, and apply it by faith for that end, Rev. vii. 14. Lament the too little concern ye have had to get the Spirit's help to your praying, and see for the pardon thereof.

3. *Lastly,* Learn that praying is a more solemn serious work than it is generally looked on to be; and that it is not such an easy thing to pray to purpose, as we are apt to imagine. Take these three warnings then.

(1.) Trust not to your gift of prayer, neither be vain of it, Prov.

iii. 5; 1 Cor. i. ult. Oh! it is sad to think of that vanity, and airiness, and self-seeking that is to be found in some people's exercise of their praying gift. It is an argument that the person forgets both God and himself. And nothing can be more contrary to the help of the Spirit in prayer. The heart is deceitful in this point, and we have need to watch it.

(2,) Trust not to your frame. One may have a good frame before he go to prayer, and yet when he comes to the work, may not find his hands; hence often least is got when most is expected; because it is expected rather on what we have, than what we look for from the Spirit. A person may have a good frame in prayer, that may quickly leave him; the wheels of the soul in swift motion may suddenly stop, 2 Tim. ii. 1; Prov. xxviii. 26.

(3.) When ye go to prayer, be impressed with a sense of your inability to manage it aright, Josh. xxiv. 19; and then, and all along in prayer, lay yourselves open, and look for the help of the Spirit. Lay the sacrifice on the altar, and look to the Lord for fire from heaven to consume it, as Elijah did, 1 Kings xviii. 33, 37, 38. The Spirit is that fire.

I proceed to another doctrine from the text.

DOCTRINE IV. All our praying aright is so far done by the help of the Spirit, that it is justly reckoned his work, his making intercession for us.

In handling this point, I shall shew,

I. What is to be understood by praying aright.

II. That all our praying aright is done by the help of the Spirit.

III. In what respects our praying aright is so far done by the help of the Spirit, that it is justly reckoned his work.

IV. What is the Spirit's work in our praying aright, or what his making intercession for us is.

V. *Lastly*, Apply the whole.

I. I am to shew what is to be understood by praying aright.

Negatively, 1. It is not praying aright in a legal sense, without any imperfection in the eye of the law, attending the prayer. There was never a prayer in the world of that sort since Adam's fall, except the prayers of the man Christ. The best prayers of the best saints have always been attended with blemishes visible to the eyes of God, though not to ours, Isa. lxiv. 6. Such praying is our duty indeed, Matth. v. ult., but the attainment of none in this life, by any measure of grace to be expected, Phil. iii. 12.

2. It is not praying aright in a moral sense, wherein the most rigid hearer can discern nothing contrary to the precepts of morality.

A prayer may be so far right as no unlawful thing may be prayed for in it, and yet may be naught, Luke xviii. 11. The matter may be very good, where the manner of praying spoils all. If that were enough, the book-prayers of formalists would be sufficient help, in some cases, to pray aright.

3. It is not praying aright in a rhetorical sense, a well-worded prayer, with a suitable delivery. Words, voice, and gesture are of little moment before God, 1 Sam. xvi. 7; 1 Cor. ii. 4. It may be a right prayer, where the expression is far from being polite, where sentences are broken off before they make a complete sense; as in Psalm vi. 3, "My soul is also sore vexed; but thou, O Lord, how long?" The Lord himself knows what is the mind of the Spirit, though the words do not fully express it. And where all these things are accurate and exact, the prayer may be all wrong before God: where there is not a wrong word, there may not be one right affection.

Positively, It is praying aright in an evangelical sense, so that in the eye of the gospel it passes as acceptable prayer before the throne. This implies two things.

1. Sincerity in prayer, 1 Chron. xxix. 17, in opposition to formality and hypocrisy, 2 Tim. iii. 5; Psalm xvii. 1. The righteous God loveth uprightness of heart in duty, Prov. xv. 8; and though there may be many blemishes in the duty, where the man is sincere in it, the Lord will regard it, notwithstanding of these blemishes. Hereby the heart is really for God as the chief good, and goes along with the tongue in prayer.

2. A perfection of parts in prayer, though not of degrees. That is to say, praying aright is,

(1.) Praying for things agreeable to God's will revealed in his word of command or promise, 1 John v. 14. Nothing can make praying for things without the compass of the command and promise, to be praying aright. For there faith has nothing to bottom itself upon, and "without faith it is impossible to please God." Heb. xi. 6.

(2.) Praying in a right manner in a gospel-sense, Jer. xxxix. 13, "Ye shall seek me, and find me, when ye shall search for me with all your heart." Hereunto are required praying graces and affections in exercise, as faith, fervency, humility, reverence and the like. These are the soul and life of prayer, whereas the expressions of the lips are but the body of it. Where these are wanting, the duty will be reckoned but bodily exercise, 1 Tim. iv. 8.

Such praying is right in so far as it is acceptable in the sight of God, i. e. capable of being accepted according to the rule of the gospel. It is a sacrifice fit to be laid on God's altar; a prayer which may be put in the Mediator's hand, that through his intercession it may be actually accepted. For it is not anything in our prayers themselves for which they are accepted, but only the intercession of Christ, for the best things in them are mixed with sin. Only such prayers are fit to be put in the Mediator's hands, and he will take them off the sinner's hand to present them to the Father, and the Father will accept them at his hand; whereas other sorts of prayer, wherein the petitioner is not sincere, or where they are wrong as to the matter of them, or are not made in the right manner, they cannot come into the Mediator's hand, he will never present them for acceptance; and so it is impossible they can be accepted.

Hence it is evident that none who are out of Christ, unregenerate, unconverted, can at all pray aright, or pray as they ought. For what sincerity can be there, where converting grace has never touched? What faith, fervency, or humility can be exercised by unbelievers dead in sin, whose stony heart is not yet removed? Therefore the form of prayer, Matth. vi. begins, "Our Father," &c., shewing that none can pray aright or acceptably but God's own children, or those who have an interest in him as their Father; and it is the Spirit that teaches them so, Gal. iv. 6.

II. I am next to shew that all our praying aright is done by the help of the Spirit. This is to be understood as comprehending these two things.

1. It is done by the help of the Spirit dwelling in us, Gal. iv. 6. Ye are not to think that the Spirit as an external agent helps us to pray aright; nay, but the Spirit helping to pray is as a Spirit of life, dwelling in the man as a member of Christ, 1 John ii. 27. So that till we have the Spirit dwelling in us we can never pray aright.

2. It is done by the help of the indwelling Spirit actually influencing us, Gal. iv. 6, "Crying, Abba, Father," i. e. so influencing us as to make us cry. Even the indwelling of the Spirit is not enough for that effect; but there is requisite an agency of the Spirit in us, whereby we may be acted in prayer, which is called "the blowing of the wind," John iii. 8, Cant. iv. ult.

Now that all our praying aright is done by the help of the Spirit indwelling and influencing, is clear,

1. From scripture-testimony. The Spirit is the author of our whole sanctification, whereof praying aright is a part, 2 Thess. ii. 13, particularly of all our acceptable worship, Phil. iii. 3. It is by him we have access to God in worship, Eph. ii. 18. And prayer by name, if of the right sort, is owing to his help, Eph. vi. 18, and that

as an indwelling Spirit, a Spirit of adoption, Rom. viii. 15, with Gal. iv. 6, and an influencing Spirit, 1 Thess. v. 17, 18, 19.

2. We are spiritually dead without the Spirit indwelling, and spiritually asleep without the Spirit influencing, Eph. ii. 1, Cant. v. 2. Neither a dead man, nor a sleeping man is fit to present a supplication to the king; so neither is a dead sinner, nor a sleeping saint capable to pray aright. The former, praying, is like a ghost walking and talking; the latter, like a man speaking through his sleep. It is the Spirit that quickens the dead soul, John vi. 63, who coming to dwell in the heart makes the first resurrection; and it is he also who awakens the sleeping saint, Cant. v. 4.

3. There is no praying aright without sanctifying grace, nor without that grace in exercise, John ix. 31, Cant. iii. 1. Where sanctifying grace is not, the filth and pollution of sin remains, and defiles all, Tit. i. 15. So that such a man's praying is like the opening of an unripe grave, Rom. iii. 13. Accordingly the praying Pharisees are called " whited sepulchres," Matth. xxiii. 27. Where grace is not in exercise, there is incense indeed, but no pillar of smoke ascending from it to heaven; spikenard indeed, but no smell thereof. Now it is the indwelling Spirit that works sanctifying grace, 2 Thess. ii. 13, puts that grace in exercise, Cant. iv. 16, and so fits men to pray, Zech. xii. 10.

4. *Lastly*, To praying aright is required light and warmth, a light of the mind, and warmth of affections; the former for the matter, the latter for the manner. And it is a false light and warmth that makes some natural men think that sometimes they pray aright, Isa. lviii. 2. But all genuine light, and vital warmth comes from the Spirit, Eph. i. 17, 18; 2 Tim. i. 7. Hence the emblem of the virtue of the Holy Spirit was " cloven tongues, like as of fire," Acts ii. 3, 4. And the effect thereof is someway compared with that of drunkenness (which excuses it no more than Christ's being compared to a thief excuses stealing, Rev. xvi. 15); for as the liquor being received to excess, influences the man, so that things come in his head which otherwise would not, and the affections and passions are wrought up by it, Prov. xxiii. 33, so the Spirit indwelling and influencing, presents to the mind matter of prayer, and works up the affetcions suitable thereto, Eph. v. 18, 19, Cant. vii. 9.

III. I shall shew in what respects our praying aright is so far done by the help of the Spirit, that it is justly reckoned his work. That it is so reckoned in scripture, is evident from the text, where his interceding for us with groanings cannot be understood of himself as the subject, but of us according to the analogy of faith. It is plain also from Gal. iv. 6, " Because ye are sons, God hath sent

forth the Spirit of his Son into your hearts, crying Abba, Father."
Now the Spirit's crying Abba, Father, is meant certainly of our crying so, by the help of the Spirit, not of a crying whereof the Spirit
is the subject; for God is not the Father of the Spirit, because it is
the second person, and not the third, who is the Son of God; and
Father and Son are the relatives.   And thus the apostle explains it,
Rom. viii. 15, "Ye have received the Spirit of adoption, whereby we
cry, Abba, Father."   Now the reasons of this are,

1. Because all that is right in our prayers is from the Spirit, and
all that is wrong in them from ourselves, either as to matter or manner, 1 Cor. xii. 11; 1 Pet. i. 22 ; with 2 Cor. iii. 5.   In the incense of
our prayers there is smoke that goes up towards heaven, ashes that
remain behind on the earth; it is the fire from the altar that sends
up the smoke, it is the earthly nature of the incense that occasions
the ashes.   The flesh of any such spiritual sacrifice is wholly owing
to the Spirit, the skin and dung is our own, and ours only.   Therefore all our right praying is justly reckoned the Spirit's work.

2. None pray aright but as they are members of Christ, and children of God, Gal. iv. 6, Rom. viii. 15, John xv. 5.   Now it is the
Holy Spirit of the Head that dwells in and actuates all the members
acting as members, 1 Cor. xii. 11, 12.   Therefore as the soul sees by
the eye, and hears by the ear ; so whatsoever the members of Christ
do aright as members, is justly ascribed to the Spirit that actuates
the mystical body, and is the Spirit of adoption.   But there may be
a defect in seeing by the eye, and hearing by the ear ; these are not
to be ascribed to the soul, but to some disease in the eye or ear.   So
whatever defects may be in the members of Christ, these are not to
be ascribed to the Spirit, but to the remains of corruption in them,
and their state of imperfection while here.

3. The Spirit is the principal cause of our praying aright, we are
but the instrumental causes of it.   The act of praying in heart and
expression is done by us; but the grace, ability, frame for prayer,
and the exciting and bringing forth into exercise that grace and
ability, is from the Spirit, Phil. ii. 12, 13.   Hence prayer is said to
be inwrought in us, Jam. v. 16.   If the wind blow not, the spices
send not forth their pleasant smell, Cant. iv. 16.   As the sound of
the horn ceases as soon as one ceases to wind it, so does our praying
aright on the withdrawing of the Spirit, 2 Cor. iii. 5.

4. *Lastly,* All our praying graces, as all others, are in their exercise
the product of the Spirit, and his work in us, Gal. v. 22, 23.   There
is a root and stock of grace in the believer, implanted and preserved
by the Spirit, 1 John iii. 9.   In prayer these are brought forth into
exercise, the man acts faith, love, &c., and therein the soul of prayer

lies; but look on them as they are so brought forth from the stock, and they are the fruit of the Spirit, though the believer is the tree they hang on. For the Spirit is the vital fructifying sap of the trees of righteousness, Isa. xliv. 3, 4. Thus the holy lustings, longings, and desires of a believer against sin, are called "the Spirit's lusting," Gal. v. 17 (compare ver. 16, 18), in the same sense as the groanings in our text. See 1 John iv. 4.

OBJECT. If our praying aright is the work of the Spirit, what need have we of the intercession of Christ, for the acceptance of our prayers? Surely the Spirit needs no intercessor betwixt him and the Father. ANSW. Though it is the Spirit's work, it is not his work separately by himself without us; but it is his work in us, and so our work too, Gal. iv. 6, with Rom. viii. 15. And so far as it is done by us, we groaning, lusting, crying in prayer, every thing has a sinful mixture from us at best; so there is need of Christ's intercession still. The water comes pure from the fountain, the Spirit; but running through a muddy channel, such as every saint here is, it cannot be accepted in heaven, but as purified and sweetened by the intercession of Christ.

IV. I come now to consider, what is the Spirit's work in our praying aright, or what his making intercession for us is. And here I shall shew,

1. The difference betwixt Christ's intercession and the Spirit's.

2. The help of the Spirit in prayer.

FIRST, I am to shew what is the difference betwixt Christ's intercession and the Spirit's.

1. Christ intercedes for us in heaven at the Father's right hand; Rom. viii. 34. The Spirit intercedes in our hearts, upon earth; Gal. iv. 6. We have no intercession made for us in heaven, but by Christ the only intercessor there.

2. Christ's intercession is a mediatory intercession, wherein he mediates or goes between God and us; an office peculiar to him alone; 1 Tim. ii. 5. But the Spirit's intercession is an auxiliary intercession to us, whereby he helps us to go to God in a right manner, prompting us to intercede for ourselves aright.

3. The Spirit's intercession is the fruit of Christ's intercession, and what is done by the sinner through the Spirit's intercession, is accepted of God through the intercession of Christ. Christ by his death purchased the Spirit for his people, and through his intercession the Spirit is sent into their hearts, where he helps them to pray for themselves; and these prayers are accepted of God by means of the Mediator's intercession, John xiv. 16, and xvi. 7, 13; Rev. viii. 4. In a word,

The difference is such as is between one who draws a poor man's petition for him, and another who presents it to the king, and gets it granted. The Spirit does the former, and Christ does the latter, for us.

SECONDLY, I shall consider the help of the Spirit in prayer, which is his making intercession for us, in the style of the scripture. We shall view this work of the Spirit, more generally, and more particularly.

FIRST, More generally, and that in two things. He acts in it,

1. As a teaching Spirit; John xiv. 26. It is our infirmity in point of prayer, "We know not what we should pray for as we ought." He enlightens our minds, and helps our ignorance as to the matter and manner of prayer, 1 John ii. 27. He is the great Teacher of the church, and none teacheth like him. He will teach them who are so weak that no other can teach them; so that hearing some of God's weak children pray, one must needs say, "This is the finger of God."

2. As a quickening Spirit; Psalm lxxx. 18. Therefore the Spirit is compared to fire, which gives both light and heat. He removes spiritual deadness, and stirs up praying graces in the heart; whence his influences are compared to the blowing of the wind, that puts things that were at rest in motion. Thus he is said to "make intercession with groanings which cannot be uttered," setting the gracious heart a labouring and working towards God, with the utmost earnestness, as one groaning.

SECONDLY, More particularly, the work of the Spirit in our prayers lies here.

First, He excites us to pray, Rom. viii. 15, "Ye have received the Spirit of adoption, whereby we cry Abba, Father." He prompteth us to go to the throne of grace, who otherwise would be negligent of it, and backward to it; Cant. v. 2, 3, 4, "I sleep, but my heart waketh, &c. My beloved put in his hand by the hole of the door, and my bowels were moved for him." Thus he leads us to God (Eph. ii. 18, *Gr.*) as an internal moving principle. This lies in two things,

1. He impresses our spirits with a sense of a divine call to it, and so binds it on our consciences as duty to God, Psalm xxvii. 8. *Heb.* "My heart said unto thee, Let my face seek thy face, when thou saidst, Seek ye my face." Thus he applies the general command for praying to particular times, that the man is made in effect to say, now God is calling me to this duty; and so he sees he cannot slight it without disobedience, but must go to it from conscience of duty. This cuts off the low motives to prayer, of custom, credit, regard to the commands of men, &c.

2. He disposes our hearts for it, inclines us to the duty, that we willingly comply with it. "When thou saidst, Seek ye my my face; my heart said unto thee, Thy face, Lord, will I seek," Psalm

xxvii. 8. Men may have a sense of the command on them, who for want of a disposition to the duty commanded, either neglect the command, or else are but dragged to obey it. But the Spirit powerfully inclines the will to the duty, so that the man obeys out of choice, Psalm cx. 3; Cant. vi. 12. This cuts off the low motives of fear of man, and slavish fear of God too, which move many.

Secondly, He gives us a view of God as a gracious and merciful Father in Christ; Gal. iv. 6. Without this there can be no acceptable prayer. Where there is no spiritual view of God at all in prayer, we worship we know not what. Where we view him as an absolute God out of Christ, we may be filled with terror of him, but can have no true confidence in him. But by the Spirit viewing him in Christ, we have at once the sight of majesty and mercy. And hereby he works in us,

1. A holy reverence of God, to whom we pray, which is necessary in acceptable prayer, Heb. xii. 28. By this view he strikes us with a holy dread and awe of the majesty of God, whereby is banished that lightness and vanity of heart, that makes such flaunting in the prayers of some, as if they were set down on their knees to shew their gift, and commend themselves.

2. A holy confidence in him, Eph. iii. 12, " Abba, Father," speaks both reverence and confidence, whereof the Spirit is the author, Rom. viii. 15. This confidence respects both his ability and willingness to help us, Matth. vii. 11. Without this there can be no acceptable prayer, Heb. xi. 6; Jam. i. 6. This is it that makes prayer an ease to a troubled heart, the Spirit exciting in us holy confidence in God as a Father. Hence the soul, though not presently eased, draws these conclusions. (1.) He designs my good by all the hardships I am under, Rom. viii. 28. (2.) He pities me under them, Psalm ciii. 13. (3.) He knows the best time for removing them, and will do it, when that comes, 1 Sam. ii. 3.

Hereby is cut off that unbelieving formality, whereby some expect nothing by prayer, and get as little ; as also the despondency, wherewith others are struck, from the sense of God's justice, and their own sinfulness.

Thirdly, He gives us a view of ourselves in our own sinfulness and unworthiness, John xvi. 8. This always accompanies the view the Spirit gives of God, Isa. vi. 5, " Wo is me, for I am undone, because I am a man of unclean lips, and I dwell in the midst of a people of unclean lips ; for mine eyes have seen the King, the Lord of hosts." We are very ready to become strangers to ourselves, and to lose sight of our sinfulness. But the Spirit of prayer, according to the measure of his influence, opens out the man before his own eyes, casts abroad the many foul plies of his heart and life, Luke xviii. 13 ; Isa. lxiv. 6. Hereby he works in us,

1. Humiliation of heart before the Lord, fills us with low thoughts of ourselves before him, Gen xviii. 27; makes us see ourselves unworthy of the mercies, that either we have got, or desire to have, Gen. xxxii. 10 ; fills us with holy shame, and self-loathing, Luke xviii. 13 ; Ezek. xxxvi. 31. This fits us for the receipt of mercies of free grace ; and the want of it makes sinners to be in their prayers, as if they came to buy of God, and not to beg, and so to be sent empty away.

2. Cordial confession, that comes away natively from seen and felt sinfulness, Psalm lxii. 8. Thus the influence of the Spirit in prayer causes full and free confession of sin with the mouth, to the honour of God, and our own shame. And the things thus being impressed on the heart, there follow natively words to express them by; and where they fail, groans do well compensate them before the throne. This cuts off the formal, hale-hearted confessions of sin, wherewith prayers are often vitiated.

3. Hearty thanksgiving for mercies received, Psalm cxvi. 11, 12. Hereby the smallest mercies appear very big ; and the sinner, that wondered at other times how he came not to get more mercies, begins to wonder he has any at all left him, Lam. iii. 22. But without a discovery of our sinfulness by the Spirit, all our thanksgivings for mercies are but empty compliment, like the Pharisee's, Luke xviii. 11.

4. A high value for the Mediator, and his righteousness, which lies out of the view of the unhumbled heart, Phil. iii. 9. As the stars are best seen from the bottom of a deep and narrow pit, so Christ crucified is best discovered in his excellency and suitableness, by the humbled soul. The lower the soul is in its own eyes, the higher will the Mediator be in its eyes; and the higher the Mediator is, the more fit one is to pray.

Fourthly, He gives us a view of our wants, and the need we have of the supply of them, Luke xv. 17. This may be seen, comparing the Pharisee's and Publican's prayers, Luke xviii. 11, 12, 13. The Spirit taught the one, and not the other. The want of this mars prayer, Luke i. 53, " He hath filled the hungry with good things, and the rich he hath sent empty away." Here he acts,

1. As an enlightener, opening the eyes of the mind, to discern the wants and needs we are compassed with, Eph. i. 17, 18. The Spirit's shining in on the soul, as the sun on a moth-eaten garment holden up betwixt us and it, the soul gets a broad sight of its wants ; whence it is made to say, as Isa. lxiv. 6, " We are all as an unclean

thing, and all our righteousnesses are as filthy rags." Luke xviii. 13, " God be merciful to me a sinner." Psalm xix. 12, " Who can understand his errors ?" This the Spirit doth by opening up the law in its spirituality, and giving us a view of our own circumstances in a present evil ensnaring world.

2. As a remembrancer, bringing seasonably to mind the wants we have, or might have adverted to, John xiv. 26. To everything there is a season ; but ofttimes in the season of getting supply at the throne of grace, our wants and needs escape us, they come not in mind, till the market is over. The Spirit is a remembrancer in this case, seasonably suggesting to us our needs for ourselves or others. So he sets things before us in time of prayer.

3. As a forewarner of what we may need, John xvi. 13. So we find Job not only offering sacrifice, with a view to what he could not know, chap. i. 5 ; but also possessed with a fear of a trial before it came, chap. iii. 25. Thus men are led to lay up for what they may meet with, and in prayer to have a view to the grace that may be needful in such and such emergents. Hereby he helps us,

(1.) To matter of prayer, sets before us things to be prayed for. Where the Spirit is thus at work in the soul, persons will be taught to pray, and it will supply the want of a form ; and therefore they that soothe themselves with that, they cannot pray, do but bewray themselves to be void of the Spirit of God.

(2.) To the right manner of praying ; for hereby he,

[1.] Impresses us with a sense of need, that we are made to pray feelingly, that the tongue does but express what the heart feels, Luke xv. 17, 18, 19. Insensibleness of our needs makes us formal in prayer, and therefore to be sent empty away. A mere rational sight of our wants will not cure it ; but the light of the Spirit is the light of life, John viii. 12 ; that will not miss to affect the heart.

[2.] Hereby we are rendered sincere in our addresses to God, Psalm xvii. 1. Feigned lips in prayer proceed from a dark and insensible heart. He that really sees his disease, and is persuaded of the need of the Physician, there is no doubt of his being in earnest for his help.

[3.] Hereby we are made importunate in prayer. Necessity has no law, and hunger breaks through stone walls, as we see in the woman of Canaan, who did hang on, over the belly of discouragement, and would take no refusal. Importunate praying is prevailing, Luke xi. 8 ; and felt-need that one cannot bear without relief, makes importunity.

[4.] Hereby we are made particular in prayer, laying our hand on our sores, and laying out our particular wants before the Lord, Luke

xviii. 41. General prayers, like general preaching, have little of the Spirit in them. They that go where help is to be found, being indeed pinched, will readily tell where they are pinched.

Fifthly, He gives us a view of the grace and promises of the covenant, Psalm, xxv. 14; John xiv. 26. Without this, the sinner, pressed with a sense of need, has nothing to support him, and therefore cannot pray in faith. Our Lord Jesus Christ has purchased all the grace and promises of the covenant for his people, and there is enough there for all they can need. It is the office of the Spirit to open them out before their eyes, and apply them. And here the Spirit,

1. Brings to their remembrance the grace and promises suited to their case, Gen. xxxii. 11, 12. The promises are the rule and encouragement of prayer; but while they lie out of our sight, we can neither have suitable direction nor encouragement from them; but when the Spirit draws near with the promise to us, there is help at hand in prayer.

2. He unfolds that grace and these promises, causing to understand them in a spiritual and saving manner, 1 Cor. ii. 12. The letter of the promise can only help to words in prayer; but the Spirit shining on the promise, will help to pray in a gracious manner, for the demonstration of the Spirit is always with power. Hereby,

(1.) The Spirit teaches what to pray for, according to the will of God. While the promises rightly understood regulate our prayers, and they are agreeable to the grace of the covenant, we may be sure we do not err in the matter, 2 Sam. vii. 28, 29. These are God's bills and bonds to his people, and by them he shows what he allows us to ask of him. What he is debtor to his faithfulness for, we may crave.

(2.) In what terms to pray for it, the terms of the promise, terms agreeable to the grace of the covenant. And this is the rise of some expressions of God's children in prayer, which may seem strange and uncouth to others, that have not their view of the grace of the covenant, which want makes them appear unseemly to them; yea, they may seem strange to themselves. And hence also is the agreement to a nicety, that is sometimes to be found betwixt the answer of prayer, and their expression in prayer.

(3.) Hereby he fills our mouths with arguments, helping us to plead and pray, Job xxiii. 3, 4. The grace and promises of the covenant, held before the eyes by the Spirit shining on them to the soul in prayer, is such a fountain of heavenly oratory that will make a weak and unlearned Christian plead and pray at the rate that others are strangers to, and which themselves at another time are quite unable to reach.

(4.) Hereby he stirs up in us a faith of particular confidence as to the thing prayed for, so that we are helped to pray believingly, and not doubtingly and distrustfully. The necessity of this faith in prayer is evident from the scriptures, Matth. xxi. 22; Mark xi. 24; 1 Tim. ii. 8; James i. 6; and the Spirit is the author of it, 2 Cor. iv. 13. He gives a view of the promise and grace of the covenant with relation to that thing, and helps to regulate the prayer thereby, strengthens to believe the accomplishment of the promise in that particular for the Mediator's sake, and consequently the hearing of prayer in that particular. Hereby it appears what this faith is, namely, a confidence agreeable to the promise as demonstrated by the Spirit; absolute as to the particular thing, where the promise is demonstrated absolute, or by the Spirit particularly applied to the thing, Psalm cxix. 49, which may be in things not absolutely necessary, as Mark v. 27, 28, 34. Or indefinite, where the promise is left so by the Spirit, that is to say, a confidence of the thing itself, or of what is as good. And hereby also this faith is distinguished from presumption, in that it is founded on a word of God, and the merit of Christ.

(5.) *Lastly*, Hereby he works in us a holy boldness in prayer, Eph. iii. 12. Faith coming before the throne, and spreading out the word of promise with the grace of the covenant, makes bold there for a gracious answer. How bold was Jacob in that case, "I will not let thee go, except thou bless me?" Gen xxxii. 26. Foolish men have ignorantly censured this boldness in the prayers of God's children, but God is well pleased with it, when he says, "Ask me of things to come concerning my sons, and concerning the work of my hands command ye me, Isa. xlv. 11; though the counterfeiting of this holy oil must needs be dangerous. It is distinguished by its attending humility, as in Jacob, Gen. xxxii. 10, "I am not worthy of the least of all the mercies, and of all the truth which thou hast shewed unto thy servant."

Sixthly, He raiseth in us holy desires for the supply of our wants; "groanings which cannot be uttered." The Spirit working as fire, fires the heart in prayer, sets it in motion, Cant. v. 4, a lusting, longing, panting for what may tend to the perfection of the new creature, either removing the impediments of its growth, or supplying it with fresh incomes of grace for its growth. Of this more afterwards. But thus we are made to pray fervently, Jam. v. 16; Rom. xii. 11.

Seventhly, He gives us a view of the merit and intercession of the Mediator, Eph. i. 17. This is the work of the Holy Spirit, without whose illumination Christ will be a hidden beauty to us. He shewed Zechariah the intercessor, at his work, Zech. i. 12, and Stephen,

Acts vii. 56, and he shews believers the same sight for substance by the eye of faith, 1 Cor. ii. 12. Hereby,

1. He points us to the only way of acceptance of our prayers, John xiv. 6 ; while hypocrites overlooking Christ lose all their requests. He teaches us to pray as we ought, and so to pray in the name of Jesus Christ, depending on his merit and intercession allenarly.

2. He lays before us a firm foundation of confidence before the Lord ; 1 John ii. 1, " If any man sin, we have an advocate with the Father, Jesus Christ the righteous ;" an Advocate who never loses the plea he takes in hand, John xi. 42, having an undisputable ground to go upon, namely, the purchase of his own blood. A fresh view of this makes faith in prayer renew its strength, and fills with confidence ; Eph. iii. 12, " In whom we have boldness and access with confidence by the faith of him."

3. *Lastly*, He furnishes us with an answer to all objections, that an unbelieving heart and a subtile devil can muster up against us, in prayer ; Rom. viii. 33, 34, " Who shall lay anything to the charge of God's elect ? It is God that justifieth : who is he that condemneth ? It is Christ that died, yea, rather that is risen again, who is even at the right hand of God, who also maketh intercession for us." Are we sinful and vile ? The merit of Christ is of infinite value. Are we unworthy for whom God should do such a thing ? Yet the Mediator is worthy. Can our prayers, smelling so rank of sinful imperfections, not be accepted at our polluted hands ? Yet being perfumed with his merit, they can be accepted at his hand, Rev. viii. 4.

Eighthly, He manages the heart and spirit in prayer, which every serious soul will own to be a hard task ; Jer. x. 23, " O Lord, I know that the way of man is not in himself ; it is not in man that walketh to direct his steps." Gal. v. 16. Therefore the psalmist says, Psalm xxxi. 5, " Into thine hand I commit my spirit." And,

1. He composes it for prayer ; Psalm lxxxvi. 11, " Unite my heart to fear thy name." He frames the heart, that is out of frame for it ; commands a heavenly calm in the soul, whereby it may be fitted for divine communications ; saying to the heart tossed with temptations, troubles, and risings of corruption, " Peace and be still ; and he blows up the fire of grace into a flame, 2 Tim. i. 7. So the preparation of the heart is owing to him ; Psalm x. 17, " Lord, thou hast heard the desire of the humble ; thou wilt prepare their heart, thou wilt cause thine ear to hear."

2. He fixes it in prayer, that it wander not away in the duty ; Ezek. xxxvi. 27, " I will put my Spirit within you, and cause you to walk in my statutes, and ye shall keep my judgments, and do them."

There is need not only of quickening grace in duty, but of establishing grace ; for the heart itself is apt to wander off from the serious purpose, and the powers of hell exert themselves to divert from it. But the supply of the Spirit in prayer keeps the heart fixed. And, in the case of wandering,

3. He reduces it from its wanderings in prayer; Psalm xxiii. 3, "He restoreth my soul; he leadeth me in the paths of righteousness for his name's sake." It will always cost a struggle to hedge in the heart in duty, and the help of the Spirit is necessary to maintain the struggle, Rom. vii. 21 ; Gal. v. 17. But sometimes the heart is quite carried off by its wandering disposition, that the prayer is quite marred, the heart leaving the tongue. In this case the Spirit convinces and humbles the soul under the sense of that sin, and so makes it more serious than before, from thence shewing the corruption of nature, Rom. viii. 37.

Ninthly, and *Lastly*, The Spirit causes us to continue in prayer from time to time, till we obtain a gracious answer ; and so makes us pray perseveringly, Eph. vi. 18. The Lord may keep his people long hanging on for an answer ere they get it. The promise may be big with the mercy prayed for, and yet it be not only many months but years ere it bring forth, as in the case of Abraham and David. This is a sore trial, and there would be no keeping from fainting if the Spirit did not help our infirmity. But he helps to hang on,

1. By accounting for the delay of our answer, in a way consistent with God's honour and our good, and so satisfying us in that point; Psalm xxii. 2, 3, "O my God, I cry in the day-time but thou hearest not ; and in the night season and am not silent. But thou art holy O thou that inhabitest the praises of Israel." He helps to discern the unsoundness of the subtile reasonings of unbelief, tending to despondency, and so hinders from making rash conclusions ; Psalm lxxvii. 10, "I said, this is my infirmity ; but I will remember the years of the right hand of the Most High." And so he keeps up in us kind thoughts of God's dispensations.

2. By strengthening faith and hope, which have the battle to fight in this case, Eph. iii. 16. Hangers on at the throne of grace may get a long stand, but they will get their strength renewed, Psalm xxvii. 13, 14. This the Spirit does, by shining anew on the promise ; adding other promises to it tending to the same scope ; giving some present experience and off-fallings from the Lord's hand, whereby the soul is refreshed in the time ; and helping to observe the signs of the approaching day while yet the night continues.

3. *Lastly*, Continuing and reviving on our spirits the sense of our need, which, pinching us anew, obliges to renew our suit for relief

until the time we get it, 2 Cor. xii. 8, "For this thing I besought the Lord thrice, that it might depart from me." If in this case we were left to our own spirits, we would seek our help from another quarter, than hanging on about the Lord's hand, and our sense of need would wear off, and we would drop our petition. But the Spirit perfects what he begins; Psalm cxxxviii. ult., "The Lord will perfect that which concerneth me."

I shall now make some practical improvement of this subject.

USE I. Of information. This may let us see,

1. That men in this world are under the influence of that part of the other world which they are in the road to. If ye are in the road to the happy part of the other world, ye are under the conduct and influence of the Holy Spirit, prompting and helping you to do your duty to God. Whence ye may gather, that they are in the road to destruction, who are under the conduct and influence of the spirit of the world, prompting and helping them to a course of sin. Consider the prevailing course of your lives, and trace it to the spring, and ye will find it is the spirit ye are acted by, 1 John iv. 4. One part of men is led by the Spirit of God, and they are holy, heavenly, and spiritual; another by the evil spirit, and they are unholy, hellish, and carnal. He is a spirit of covetousness in some, of uncleanness in others, &c.

2. Praying is another thing than men generally take it to be. It is not the exercise of a gift, but of grace; not a piece of task laid on men, but a privilege they are advanced to; not a work to be done in our own strength, but by help from heaven; not a piece of the form of religion, but of experimental religion. Consider prayer in this scripture view of it, and among many that bow their knees in prayer to God, there will be found few really praying persons; many whose hearts must say on what they have heard of it, Ezek. xx. 49, "Doth he not speak parables?"

3. True praying will always make people holy and humble; for the Spirit by which it is done is the Spirit of holiness and light, Matth. iii. 11. Does a man value himself upon, and appear proud and conceited of himself on the account of his good praying? still continue in his profane, untender, unholy course? His prayers are his own, they are not by the help of the Spirit in him. God regards them not.

4. Great is the encouragement that poor sinners have to apply themselves to serious and spiritual praying. The weakest are left inexcusable, if they neglect prayer still; and the formal professor, if he continue with his formal task-work of praying still. We have the Hearer of prayer to go to, the Father of our Lord Jesus, with

our petitions; an Intercessor in heaven, to present them; and an Intercessor on earth, to draw them for us, and help us to make our petitions. This is the office of the Holy Spirit. Therefore,

USE II. Of exhortation. Set yourselves for praying in the Spirit, Eph. vi. 18. Prayerless persons, give yourselves to praying, and to this kind of praying. Praying persons, satisfy not yourselves without this kind of praying. Stand not still in the outer court of prayer, with hypocrites and formalists; come in to the inner court, with God's own children. Look for the help of the Spirit, employ the Spirit in all your duties, and particularly your prayers. Remember that all the prayers are lost that are not done in the Spirit.

I shall give you some advices, how to get the help of the Spirit in prayer.

1. Come to Christ in the way of believing the gospel. The fulness of the Spirit is lodged in Christ, Rev. iii. 1. He communicates the Spirit to dead sinners, 1 Cor. xv. 45, with John xx. 22, and this in the word of the gospel, Gal. iii. 2. It is vain to expect the help of the Spirit in prayer, till once we have received the Spirit to dwell in us, Eph. iii. 17, with 1 John iii. ult. To receive the word of the gospel as an engrafted, quickening word, whereby we close with Christ for all, is the necessary foundation for all this.

2. Beware of maltreating the Spirit. And so,

(1.) Resist not the Spirit, Acts vii. 51. Do not stave off convictions, and awakenings out of a state or course of sin. Beware of sinning over the belly of light, and persisting in sin against calls to repentance. That is to resist the Spirit, and so to provoke him to leave you.

(2.) Quench not the Spirit, 1 Thess v. 19. If this holy fire begin to burn at any time, so as you see the light and feel the heat of it, do not withdraw fuel from it by neglecting the motions and operations of it, not taking care to cherish them; do not smother them; by not giving them vent in prayer: far less drown it out, by taking your swing in any sinful course; Luke xxi. 34, "Take heed to yourselves, lest at any time your hearts be overcharged with surfeiting, and drunkenness, and cares of this life."

(3.) Grieve not the Spirit, Eph. iv. 30. The Spirit is grieved by undervaluing his graces, comforts, influences, and his means of communicating them; by sins gross in their nature or aggravations, whereby the conscience is wasted and signally defiled, whereby some have quite withered away, the Spirit leaving them.

(4.) Vex not the Spirit; Isa. lxiii. 10. Vex him not by your still relapsing into the same sins; Numb. xiv. 22, especially after convictions of the ill of them, confessions thereof, resolutions against them, and smarting for them. This is the great trial of the divine patience, whereby men are in hazard of being given up of God, Numb. xiv. 27.

(5.) Blaspheme not the Spirit in his operations, particularly praying in the Spirit. Take heed of making a mock of religion, preaching, praying, seriousness, talking slightingly of these things, and of making persons the objects of your derision and spite on these accounts. Sometime these things were only to be found among malignants and persecutors; but now they are to be found among people that pray themselves, and partake of the Lord's table. These Satan is training up for greater service, when such times shall come again. But take heed, it is a dangerous course, as these young blasphemers of the Spirit in his operations felt; 2 Kings ii. 23, 24, " As Elisha was going up by the way, there came forth little children out of the city, and mocked him, and said unto him, Go up, thou bald head; go up, thou bald head. And he turned back, and looked on them, and cursed them in the name of the Lord; and there came forth two she-bears out of the wood, and tare forty and two children of them."

3. Walk tenderly and circumspectly; Eph. v. 15. A loose and untender walk, wherein people let down their watch over the frame of their heart, and the course of their life in words and actions, provokes the Spirit to withdraw; when a tender walk is followed with the tokens of his favour; John xiv. 21, "He that hath my commandments, and keepeth them, he it is that loveth me, and he that loveth me, shall be loved of my Father, and I will love him, and will manifest myself to him."

4. When ye go to prayer, be convinced of your absolute need of the Spirit. Look for him, and wait, and lay yourselves open to his influences; Luke xi. 13. Labour to revive that conviction at every occasion of prayer, and to keep it up throughout it. Look for the Spirit in the promise, believing it with application; Ezek. xxxvi. 27, " I will put my Spirit within you," &c. Lay yourselves down at his feet, to be enlightened, quickened, &c., Jer. xxxi. 18, as one lays open himself to receive the fresh air.

5. Be habitually concerned for answers of prayer. They that are in good earnest to have their petitions granted, will be careful to have them right drawn; but they that are indifferent in the one, will be so in the other too; Psalm v. 3, " In the morning will I direct my prayer unto thee," says David, " and will look up." If ye be concerned for Christ's intercession for you in heaven, so will ye be for that of the Spirit in your own heart.

6. Let the Bible be dear to you, and look on it as God's word to you in particular, Rom. xv. 4, " For whatsoever things were written aforetime, were written for our learning ; that we through patience and comfort of the scriptures might have hope." Rev. iii. ult., " He that hath an ear, let him hear what the Spirit saith unto the churches." The word is the vehicle wherein the Spirit is conveyed to us; it is the channel of communicating his influences to us ; and the instrument he works by in us, in all the parts of his working in us, exciting, enlightening, &c. Isa. lix. ult, " As for me, this is my covenant with them, saith the Lord, My Spirit that is upon thee, and my words which I have put in thy mouth, shall not depart out of thy mouth, nor out of the mouth of thy seed, nor out of the mouth of thy seed's seed, saith the Lord, from henceforth and for ever."

7. Be careful observers of providence, Psalm cvii. ult., " Whoso is wise, and will observe these things, even they shall understand the loving kindness of the Lord." The spirit is in these wheels ; and the more people are set to observe their motions, the more they will readily get to observe. This is a way to carry you off formality in prayer, and give you an errand in good earnest to the throne of grace, whether in the way of petition, confession, or thanksgiving.

8. *Lastly*, Be watchful in prayer, Eph. vi. 18. The evil spirit watches against us at all times, and in a special manner the fowls come down on the carcases of our spiritual sacrifices. When ye sit down on your knees, the heart will be apt to fall a-wandering, and it will be much if before the end it do not give the slip. The Spirit of the Lord only can manage our spirits, and he will be provoked by our wanderings to withdraw. Therefore take that watchword, Prov. iv. 23, " Keep thy heart with all diligence ; for out of it are the issues of life."

I shall now proceed to the last doctrine observable from the text.

DOCTRINE V. ult. The Spirit helps believers to pray, particularly, causing in them gracious groanings, which cannot be uttered.

In discoursing this point, I shall,

I. Consider the nature of these groanings caused by the Spirit in believers.

II. Shew how the Spirit makes intercession for believers with groanings.

III. In what respects these groaning are groanings that cannot be uttered.

IV. Conclude with two or three reflections.

I. We shall consider the nature of these groanings caused by the Spirit in believers. And here I shall shew,

1. Of what kind they are.

2. The moving causes of them.

FIRST, I am to shew of what kind these groanings are. There is a twofold groaning.

First, A natural groaning, the effect of pain, and any heavy pressure that lies on men's spirits, Jer. li. 52, " Through all her land the wounded shall groan." This is common to men with beasts, Joel i. 18, " How do the beasts groan ?" And men may groan so, without any gracious movings of heart towards God ; therefore they are none of the groanings in the text, Job xxxv. 9, 10, " By reason of the multitude of oppressions, they make the oppressed to cry ; they cry out by reason of the arm of the mighty. But none saith, Where is God my maker, who giveth songs in the night ?"

Secondly, Spiritual and gracious groanings, whereby the gracious soul natively expresses its movings towards God under some heavy pressure, 2 Cor. v. 4, " We that are in this tabernacle do groan, being burdened." These are they with which the Spirit helps believers, and which he causes in them. When men are in a swoon, they groan none ; but when they are recovering, they will discover it by groaning ; an argument that their sense and feeling is returned. So by these groanings believers are distinguished from the dead in sin.

These spiritual groanings of believers speak,

1. Their feeling of a weight and pressure upon them, 2 Cor. v. 4, above cited. Such is the imperfection of our state in this life, that if there is life in a soul, it must groan, because there is no escaping of pressures, from an evil world without, and an evil heart within. And the easy jovial life that men lead without these groanings, they owe it to spiritual death, which has taken away their feeling, Eph. iv. 18, 19.

2. Their labouring under these pressures, like one under a burden, Psalm vi. 6, " I am weary with my groaning, (*Heb.*) " Laboured to weariness in my groaning." This imports,

(1.) An earnest endeavour to get them off, or to bear them while they are kept on. The new creature is surrounded with weights of various kinds, which in their own nature tend to hinder its growth, and coming to perfection ; and there are mighty labourings and workings of it against them, that it may get forward to its desired perfection ; Phil. iii. 14.

(2.) Great difficulty in that labouring, so that the man is as it were out of breath wrestling with his burden which natively issues in a groan, Eph vi. 12. There is difficulty in the Christian life, that will try what metal men are of, and will put them to the exerting of their utmost vigour ; and therefore it is compared to the exercise of wrestlers and runners.

3. The working of their affections under them ; especially,

(1.) Grief of heart, Jer. xlv. 3. Groaning is the natural expression of sorrow : and sighs, sobs, and groans, are what a heart pierced and weighed down with grief naturally vents itself in. Christ was " a man of sorrows, and so we find him groaning, John xi. 38 ; and true Christians, whatever their natural temper is, will be found to resound as an echo to a groaning Saviour.

Particularly, groans are the more heavy, when they arise from a double grief, a grief for such a thing, and a grief that it is beyond our power to help it ; and of this sort mostly are the groans of believers, Rom. vii. 24.

(2.) Earnest desire of help and relief, 2 Cor. v. 2. Here the heart of the believer in these groanings moves directly towards God, with eyes lifted up to heaven. And hence these groanings are prayers in effect, and are so reckoned before God, Rom. viii. 27. Whence it appears how the Spirit makes intercession for us with groanings, that helping to groan before the Lord, he helps to pray. These groanings may be considered two ways.

[1.] As they are joined with solemn prayer. When a Christian is seriously praying, and is so weighted, that his prayers are here and there interrupted with groanings ; these groanings which the prayers are interspersed with, are in God's account parts of the prayer, and as acceptable parts as are in it all ; whether they come in when a sentence is closed, or come in before it be perfected, Psalm vi, 3, " My soul is sore vexed ; but thou, O Lord, how long ?" Men know not distinctly the meaning of such groans, but the Lord sees it as plain as if expressed by words.

[2.] As they are separate from solemn vocal prayer. And thus we may also consider them two ways.

(1.) As they come in the room and stead of vocal prayer intended.

I believe it is very possible, that a child of God may go to his knees to pray, and may rise again without having been able to speak a word, but only to groan ; and though he thinks he could pray none at all, he is mistaken ; as far as the Spirit helped him to groan, he helped him to pray, though none could understand that prayer of his but God himself who searcheth the heart, Rom. viii. 27. As a full bottle does not orderly empty itself, so a heart may be too full to empty itself by words, but by groans, Psalm lxxvii.

4, "Thou holdest mine eyes waking; I am so troubled that I cannot speak."

(2.) As they are without any design of solemn prayer. When a man is walking or sitting, musing on the sinfulness of his own heart and life, or on the wickedness that is done in the world, with the dishonour that comes on the holy name of God thereby; till his heart, swelling with grief, natively vents itself in a groan; that groaning is in God's account a prayer, and a prayer that shall be heard at length, as proceeding from the influence of his own Spirit. What was it that set the wheel of providence in motion, to stop the wicked career the Egyptians were in, Exod. ii. 24? Why, God heard the groaning of the children of Israel.

SECONDLY, I come now to shew the moving causes of these groanings of believers. Believers by the Spirit, have their groanings unto the Lord,

1. Under a pressure of trouble. While they are here, they cannot miss so much of a suffering lot, as will make them groan; Rom. viii. 18, 23; and by the Spirit, these groans are directed towards God, as those of a child, under the difficulties of the way, are directed to his father.

(1.) Sometimes they are groaning to him under outward troubles. So Israel groaned under the Egyptian bondage; Exod ii. 23, 24; yea Christ himself; John xi. 33, 38. These are weights that press their spirits, make them to groan, and look upward for relief; Rom. viii. 23, longing for the day when they shall be beyond them.

(2.) Sometimes they are groaning under inward troubles; Psalm xxx. 7, "Thou didst hide thy face, and I was troubled." While here they are liable to spiritual desertions, wounds in their spirits under the apprehensions of the Lord's anger against them. And they groan out their case towards the hand that smites them. Both outward and inward troubles often meet together, as in the case of David; Psalm vi. 2, 3, 6, "Have mercy upon me, O Lord, for I am weak; O Lord, heal me, for my bones are vexed. My soul is also sore vexed; but thou, O Lord, how long? I am weary with my groaning, all the night make I my bed to swim; I water my couch with my tears;" and in that of Job: chap. xxiii. 2, "Even to-day is my complaint bitter; my stroke is heavier than my groaning."

2. Under a pressure of temptations. These are a heavy weight to a gracious soul; they made Paul to go groaning to God again and again; 2 Cor. xii. 7, 8. Our Lord Christ had experience of an hour of the power of darkness; Luke xxii. 53, "When I was daily with you in the temple, ye stretched forth no hands against me; but this is your hour, and the power of darkness." And his followers

will not want experience of the same, wherein temptations come on thick and vigorous. These cause groanings,

(1.) Because of their disturbing the peace of the soul; they turn the calm into a storm, that the soul is tossed thereby as on a raging sea, which makes them cry, " Lead us not into temptation."

(2.) Because of the difficulty of one's keeping his ground against them; Eph. vi. 12, 16. Every temptation has a friend within us, and men's nature is unto temptation as tinder to sparks of fire, apt to take fire; so that it requires hard wrestling to keep our ground.

(3.) Because of the danger of falling thereby into sin. Temptation is the precipice, and sin is the devouring gulf; and they who have a sense of their danger, no wonder they groan, groan under the pressure, and groan for relief.

3. Under the pressure of sin. This is a light burden to the most part of mankind, but it is the heaviest burden to a child of God, and causes in him, through the Spirit, the heaviest groans. For it is of all things the most contrary and opposite to the new nature in him, whence are these continued strugglings; Gal. v. 17, " The flesh lusteth against the Spirit, and the Spirit against the flesh; and these are contrary the one to the other; so that ye cannot do the things that ye would." Many troubles Paul met with; but did any of them all ever cause in him such an exclamation as that; Rom. vii. 24, " O wretched man that I am! who shall deliver me from the body of this death ?" Now the children of God groan,

1st, Under the weight and pressure of their own sin, the sin of their nature, and the sin of their life; Psalm li. 3, 5, " I acknowledge my transgressions; and my sin is ever before me. Behold, I was shapen in iniquity; and in sin did my mother conceive me." It lies on them heavy as a body of death, while others being dead in sin, it is no burden to them; no burden to their heart, though sometimes it may be to their conscience. And there are three things in their sin that press them sore.

(1.) The filthiness of it, that deformity that is in it, being the quite contrary of the holiness of God expressed in his law. The soul seeing the glory of the holiness of God, and how its sin is the very reverse of that glory; that fills it with shame; Ezra ix. 6, and self-loathing; Ezek. xxxvi. 31. Beholding itself in the glass of the pure and holy law, as a polluted and defiled creature, it groans under it as one pressed down to the earth with a burden; Jer. iii. ult., " We lie down in our shame, and our confusion covereth us; for we have sinned against the Lord our God."

(2.) The prevailing power of it; Psalm lxv. 3, " Iniquities prevail against me, (*Heb.*) Have been mightier than I." The new na-

ture struggles against sin; Gal. v. 17. The new man of grace and
the old man of sin are engaged in combat; and ofttimes the old man
prevails, and the new man is cast down. Now the believer taking
part with grace against corruption, groans under this prevailing
power of corruption (Rom. vii. 23, 24,) as an insupportable tyranny
that he longs to be rid of.

(3.) The guilt of it; Psalm li. 4, "Against thee, thee only have I
sinned, and done this evil in thy sight." In the eyes of a believer,
life lies in the favour of God, the shinings of his countenance; but
their guilt binds them over to his anger, and overclouds his countenance. And that is a weight that makes them groan; that when
it is removed, they rejoice as one that has got a burden taken off
his back; Psalm xxxviii. 4, " Mine iniquities are gone over mine
head; as an heavy burden they are too heavy for me." Compared
with Hos. xiv. 2, "take away all iniquity, and receive us graciously; so will we render the calves of our lips."

2dly, Under the weight and pressure of the sin of others; Ezek.
ix. 4, " Go through the midst of the city, through the midst of Jerusalem, and set a mark upon the foreheads of the men that sigh
and that cry for all the abominations that be done in the midst
thereof." As one cannot but loath an abominable thing on another
as well as on himself; so sin, wherever it appears, on others, as well
as on ourselves, will be a burden to a gracious soul, that will make
it groan; Isa. vi. 5, "Wo is me, for I am undone, because I am a
man of unclean lips, and I dwell in the midst of a people of unclean
lips." Thus Lot was under a continued burden in Sodom, while he
was among them; 2 Pet ii. 7, 8. And none groan spiritually under
their own sin, that do not groan also under the sins of others
amongst whom they live. There are three things in the sins of
others that make them groan.

(1.) The dishonour to the holy name of God that is in them;
Rom. ii. 23, 24. To see men trampling under foot the holy laws of
God, and, by their profane courses, affronting the God that made
them, and walking after their own lusts, cannot but be a burden to
any who truly love the Lord, and are concerned for the honour of
his name; Psalm cxix. 136, " Rivers of waters run down mine eyes,"
says David, "because they keep not thy law." Zeal for the honour
of God, as it is native to his children; so, where it cannot prevail
against sin, natively vents itself in groaning under the burden;
Psalm lxix. 9.

(2.) The ruin to the sinner's own soul that is wrapt up in it; Jer.
xiii. 17. There needs no prophetical eye, but an eye of faith in the
Lord's word, to foresee the ruin of those that go on impenitently in

their sinful course; Rom. vi. 21. When sinners are fighting against God, by going on in their trespasses; it is easy to see whose head must be wounded in the encounter; Psalm lxviii. 21, and who must fall at length, however long they keep foot; Deut. xxxii. 35. Now the prospect of this is enough to make a gracious soul groan for those that cannot groan for themselves; Psalm cxix. 119, 120, "Thou puttest away all the wicked of the earth like dross; therefore I love thy testimonies. My flesh trembleth for fear of thee, and I am afraid of thy judgments." So Hab. iii. 16.

(3.) The hurt that is in it to others. It is Solomon's observation that "one sinner destroyeth much good," Eccl. ix. ult. And there is a woe pronounced on the world, because of offences, Matth. xviii. 7. Sin is a noxious vapour, spreading its infection over many; wounding some, and killing others; grieving to the godly, and hardening to the wicked. And a serious view of the mischief it does to others, beside the sinner himself, makes the godly groan.

From what is said it appears that sin is the fundamental and chief cause of the believer's groaning. Troubles outward and inward rise from it, temptations lead to it. That is it within them, and that is it without them that makes them groan. That is the burden to the Spirit of God that grieves him, as one groaning under a burden, Amos ii. 13; Isa. i. 24. That is it that makes the whole creation groan, Rom. viii. 22. And it is that which makes the believer groan.

II. The second general head is to shew how the Spirit makes intercession for believers with groanings.

1. He works in them a spiritual feeling of their burdens; Rom. viii. 23, "And not only they, but ourselves also, which have the first fruits of the Spirit, even we ourselves groan within ourselves." The time was, when they lay with the rest of the world without sense or feeling of the burden on them, and he gave them life; and sometimes spiritual life in them has been so low, that they could have but little true feeling of their own case; and it was a burden to them to bestir themselves to rid themselves; Cant. v. 3, "I have put off my coat; how shall I put it on? I have washed my feet; how shall I defile them?" But the Spirit excites grace, and gives them a lively feeling of their spiritual case; ver. 4, "My Beloved put in his hand by the hole of the door and my bowels were moved for him."

2. He gives them a view of the free and unburdened state wherein mortality is swallowed up of life, 2 Cor. v. 4. There is such a state, it is represented in the word of truth. The Spirit strengthens the eye of faith, whereby the soul sees it clearly, though afar off; a

state wherein there is an eternal putting off of the burden of trouble, temptation, and sin.

3. He excites in them ardent desires of riddance from their burden, and of arriving at the unburdened state; 2 Cor. v. 2, "For in this we groan, earnestly desiring to be clothed upon with our house which is from heaven." Rom. viii. 23, "Even we ourselves groan within ourselves, waiting for the adoption, to wit, the redemption of our body." What ardent desire of deliverance would a man have who was kept lying among dead corpses, rotting and sending forth their stench into his nostrils ? Such ardent desire will a Christian have, when, through the Spirit, grace is put in lively and vigorous exercise, while the dead world without him, and the body of death within him, conspire to annoy him with their savour of death, Rom. vii. 24. Hence,

4. He engages them in earnest wrestling with their burden, in order to get clear of it, that the new creature of grace may get up its back, and run the way of God's commandments, Gal. v. 17. Here grace has a mighty struggle with its enemy, longing and panting for the victory, and pressing towards a state of perfection, Phil. iii. 14.

5. *Lastly*, Finding themselves still entangled with their burden, notwithstanding of all their wrestling, he helps them to groan out their case before the Lord, as a case that is beyond their reach to help; Rom. vii. 23, 24, "I see another law in my members, warring against the law of my mind, and bringing me into captivity to the law of sin which is in my members. O wretched man that I am! who shall deliver me from the body of this death ?" But the groaning through the Spirit's aid is not groaning and dying, but,

(1.) Groaning and looking to the Lord for help; Psalm cxxiii. 1, "Unto thee lift I up mine eyes, O thou that dwellest in the heavens." The believer groans and looks upward to God for relief. His burden of trouble, he will lie under it, till the Lord take it off, and will not take any sinistrous course for his deliverance; Isa. xxviii. 16, "He that believeth shall not make haste." The burden of sin, he is never to be reconciled with that, but however long he wrestles with it without the desired success, he will ever be looking and longing for deliverance, Phil. iii. 13, 14.

(2.) Groaning and waiting for relief, Rom. viii. 23. Unbelief makes one to groan and despair of deliverance, either in temporals or spirituals, Jer. ii. 25. But the Spirit makes the believer to groan and wait in hope, Gal. v. 5. Though the eyes fail while they wait for their God, yet still they will wait in hope of the promise, Luke xviii. 1.

III. I come now to shew in what respects these groanings are groanings that cannot be uttered.

1. The working of their affections, thus set in motion by the Spirit, is sometimes such as stops the course of the words. This is often seen in the workings of natural affections, how that either joy or grief filling the heart, mars the ordinary course of words; the heart being too full, to be vented easily in expression. It is not then to be thought strange, that it so falls out in the case of spiritual affections put in mighty motion by the Spirit. Yea they do,

(1.) Sometimes interrupt the expression, and the groaning fills up what is wanting in the words, Psalm vi. 3. Even as a hurt and pained child tells his case to his mother, in imperfect expressions, filling up the want with tears, sighs, and sobs; so that she may have difficulty to understand what ails him; but our Father in heaven has no difficulty in coming at the meaning of his children so expressed, Rom. viii. 27, "He that searcheth the hearts, knoweth what is the mind of the Spirit." Our elder Brother sometimes spoke by broken sentences from the same cause, Luke xix. 41, 42, "And when he was come near, he beheld the city, and wept over it, saying, If thou hadst known, even thou, at least in this thy day, the things which belong unto thy peace! but now they are hid from thine eyes." So Gen. iii. 22.

(2.) Sometimes stop the expression altogether, like as a multitude of people rushing all together to a door, they all stick, and none can get out, Psalm lxxvii. 4, "I am so troubled that I cannot speak." So a child of God may go to prayer, and not be able to speak a word. But let them go to their knees before the Lord for all that; and if they cannot speak a word, let them groan their case before the Lord. That is a proper way of praying in the Spirit, and God will certainly hear and accept that kind of praying, though there be nothing but groaning in it. Do ye put away dumb people without an alms, because they cannot speak? are ye not more moved with their signs and humming noise, than with the cries of common beggars? Do not the sighs and sobs of your frighted or hurt children move you more than their complaints formed in words? And do ye think that God will disregard the groans and sighs of his people, when they cannot speak a word to him? No, surely; he will hear the groaning of the prisoner, Psalm cii. 20.

2. What they feel and see in this case, by the Spirit, is always beyond what they can express in words. I own that what a child of God sometimes feels and sees in prayer, is so small, that their words may sufficiently express it; but when the Spirit helpeth them to these groanings, it is quite otherwise, their words cannot come up to their affections. When the Spirit gives a Christian an experimental feeling of the burden of sin, realizes to him the glory of the

unburdened state, and makes him groan between the two, there is something there that is truly unspeakable. As the gift of Christ is unspeakable to those who truly see it, 2 Cor. ix. 15, and the joy in the Holy Ghost to those that feel it, 1 Pet. i. 8, so are the groanings by the Spirit unutterable to the groaners.

I conclude with two or three reflc. .ions.

1. God's people are a groaning people. For they have the Spirit of Christ, and he makes intercession for them with groanings; they have put on Christ, and he was a groaner. And those that are strangers to these groanings, their groaning time is coming; walking now in the vanity of your minds, will make eternal groaning.

QUEST. How are God's people regarded when they get leave to groan on? ANSW. They must abide the trial of their graces, and be conformed to the image of a groaning Saviour. In due time their burden will be taken off, and they will groan no more.

2. Prayer is a business of great weight and seriousness. It is one thing to say a prayer, another thing to pray indeed acceptably. Wherefore from this, and all that has been said,

3. *Lastly*, Learn to pray by the help of the Spirit, for no other praying is acceptable to God; look to him in all your addresses to the throne, and depend upon his guiding and influence; that through Christ Jesus ye may have access by one Spirit unto the Father, Eph. ii. 18.

OF PRAYING IN THE NAME OF JESUS CHRIST.*

JOHN xvi. 23,

Whatsoever ye shall ask the Father in my name, he will give it you.

OUR Lord Jesus is here comforting his disciples under the want of his bodily presence which they had so long enjoyed, showing them that it should be well made up to them. They should see him again after his resurrection, though not to return to that familiarity with them as before; they should see him by the Spirit, in his exalted state; and should find God so reconciled to them by his sacrifice of himself, that they should have a boldness of access to the throne in heaven, which they had not before; that in that day they should ask him nothing in that manner they used while he was with them in the days of his flesh; but in a manner more to his honour and their comfort. Here he declares,

* The substance of some Sermons preached at Etterick in the year 1728.

1. What that manner is, and that in two things. (1.) They should apply themselves, in asking or petitioning, directly to the Father as their God and Father allowing them access to him, for the supply of all their needs. (2.) They should apply to him in the name of the Son, the exalted Redeemer, expressly, seeing more clearly the way of sinners trea_ng with God through the Mediator, than either the Jewish church had done, or they themselves while they had his bodily presence with them.

2. The success of that manner of applying to God. It should be successful in all points. Whatsoever, in spiritual or temporal things, they should petition the Father in the name of Christ, he should give it them for his sake.

The following doctrine arises from the words.

DOCTRINE.—Whosoever would pray to God acceptably, must pray to him in the name of Jesus Christ.

In treating this point, I shall,

I. Shew what it is to pray in the name of Jesus Christ.

II. Give the reasons why acceptable prayer must be in the name of Christ.

III. *Lastly*, Apply.

I. I am to shew what it is to pray in the name of Jesus Christ. That this takes in whatever is necessary in prayer, both as to matter and manner, is evident from the text, " Whatsoever ye shall ask in my name," &c. And no man can thus pray but by the Spirit, 1 Cor. xii. 13.

Negatively, It is not a bare mentioning his name, in prayer, and concluding our prayers therewith, Matth. vii. 21, " Not every one that saith unto me Lord, Lord, shall enter into the kingdom of heaven." We must begin, carry on, and conclude our prayers in the name of Christ, Col. iii. 17, " Whatsoever ye do in word or deed, do all in the name of the Lord Jesus, giving thanks to God and the Father by him." The saints use the words, " through Jesus Christ our Lord," 1 Cor. xv. 57; but the virtue is not in the words, but in the faith wherewith they are used. But alas! these are often produced as an empty scabbard, while the sword is away.

Positively, we may take it up in these four things.

FIRST, We must go to God at Christ's command, and by order from him. This is the import of the phrase " in his name," Matth. xviii. 20, " Where two or three are gathered together in my name, there am I in the midst of them." If a poor body can get a recommendation from a friend to one that is able to help him, he comes with confidence and tells, such a one has sent me to you. Our Lord

Christ is the friend of poor sinners, and he sends them to his Father to ask supply of their wants; and allows them to tell that he sent them; John xvi. 24. And coming that way, in faith, they will not be refused. This implies,

1. The soul's being come to Christ in the first place; John xv. 7, "If ye abide in me, and my words abide in you, ye shall ask what ye will, and it shall be done unto you." Sense of need brings the soul to Christ, as the poor man's friend, who has the favour of the court of heaven, that through his means the soul may get its wants supplied there. See Acts xii. 20. We must first come to Christ by faith, ere we can make one acceptable prayer to God.

2. That however believers in Christ are relieved of the burden of total indigence; John iv. 14, yet while they are in the world, they are still compassed with wants. God will have them to live from hand to mouth, and so to honour him by hanging on daily about his hand for their supply from time to time. In heaven they shall be set down at the fountain; but now the law of the house is, "Ask, and ye shall receive;" Matth. vii. 7.

3. That Christ sends his people to God by prayer, for the supply of their wants. This he does by his word, commanding them to go, and by his Spirit inclining them to go. For thus the whole Trinity is glorified by the praying believers, the Father as the Hearer of prayer, the Son as the Advocate and Intercessor presenting their prayers to the Father, and the Spirit as the Author of their prayers; Eph. ii. 18, "For through him we both have an access by one Spirit unto the Father."

4. That acceptable prayer is performed under the sense of the command of a God in Christ; Isa. xxxiii. 22, "For the Lord is our judge, the Lord is our lawgiver, the Lord is our king, he will save us." Men may pray, though not acceptably, with little or no sense of the command of God on their consciences; that is, not serving God, but themselves. They may pray under the sense of the command of an absolute God out of Christ; that is but slavish service to God. But the believer has the sense of the command, as from Jesus Christ, where majesty and mercy are mixed in it; and that is son-like service.

5. *Lastly*, That the acceptable petitioner's encouragement to pray is from Jesus Christ; Heb. iv. 14—16, "Seeing then that we have a great High Priest, that is passed into the heavens, Jesus the Son of God, let us hold fast our profession. For we have not an High Priest which cannot be touched with the feeling of our infirmities; but was in all points tempted like as we are, yet without sin. Let us therefore come boldly unto the throne of grace, that we may obtain mercy, and find grace to help in time of need." It is Christ's

token that he has given them to carry with them, that affords them all their confidence with God; that is the promises of the covenant sealed with his own blood. Faith laying hold on these, carries them as Christ's token to the Father, upon which a poor criminal may expect to find acceptance and supply.

SECONDLY. We must pray for Christ's sake, as our motive to the duty. This also is imported in the phrase, "in his name;" Mark ix. 41, "Whosoever shall give you a cup of water to drink, in my name, because ye belong to Christ,—he shall not lose his reward." As we must be influenced by his command, as the reason of our praying, so with regard to him as our motive. As there is no coming to God but by him; so there is no kindly drawing of us to God, but by the allurement of the glory of God in the face of Jesus; 2 Cor. iv. 6. Any other sight of the glory of God would fright the sinner away from him, as from a consuming fire. So we must behold God in Christ, and go to him as the object of our love and adoration. This implies,

1. An high esteem of Christ in the acceptable petitioner; 1 Pet. ii. 7, "Unto you which believe, he is precious." No man's prayer will be acceptable to God, who wants a transcendent esteem of the Lord Christ; for God is honoured in his Son; John v. 23. And the more the esteem of Christ has place in one's heart, the more it will be found, he will give himself to prayer.

2. Complying with the duty out of love to Christ; Heb. vi. 10, "God is not unrighteous, to forget your work and labour of love." The soul must discern Christ's stamp on every duty, and so embrace it for his sake. The duty of prayer some embrace and use, because of the usefulness of it to themselves; but God's children embrace it for the sake of Christ; 2 Cor v. 14, "For the love of Christ constraineth us." Love natively leads to desire communion with the party beloved; and love to Christ recommends prayer to a holy heart, as a means of communion with God in Christ.

3. Complying with the duty out of respect to his honour and glory; Phil. i. 21, "For to me to live is Christ." Christ humbled himself, and therefore the Father has glorified him; chap. ii. 9—11. And every act of praying in his name glorifies him, being an acknowledgment before God of the unspeakable dignity of his merit and intercession, as procuring that access for sinners unto God, that no other way could have been obtained.

4. *Lastly*, Doing it with heart and good-will; for what is done for Christ's sake by a gracious soul, must needs be so done; Isa. lxiv. 5, "Thou meetest him that rejoiceth, and worketh righteousness, those that remember thee in thy ways." One praying indeed in the name of Christ, is acted by a principle of love to him, which,

oiling the wheels of the soul, sets all in motion, so that the heart is poured out like water before the Lord. And where that principle is wanting, there is acting by constraint.

THIRDLY. We must in praying to God act in the strength of Christ. This also is imported in the phrase; Luke x. 17, " And the seventy returned again with joy, saying, Lord, even the devils are subject unto us through thy name." So Zech. x. ult., " I will strengthen them in the Lord, and they shall walk up and down in his name." We must go to prayer, as David went against Goliath; 1 Sam. xvii. 45, " I come to thee in the name of the Lord of hosts." And here consider,

1. What this pre-supposes.

2. Wherein it lies.

FIRST, Let us consider what this acting in prayer in the strength of Christ pre-supposes. It pre-supposes,

1. That praying acceptably is a work quite beyond any power in us; 2 Cor. iii. 5, " Not that we are sufficient of ourselves to think any thing as of ourselves." The want of this persuasion mars many a prayer, and makes many a rash and inconsiderate approach unto God. To manage aright an address to God on his throne of glory, cannot miss to appear such a work in the eyes of all, who have due thoughts of God's majesty, or of their own ignorance and weakness.

2. That there is a stock of grace and strength in Jesus Christ, for our help, as to other duties, so for this duty of prayer; 2 Cor. xii. 9, " My grace is sufficient for thee." Man at first had his stock of grace in his own hand, and he made a sad account of it. Now the Lord has lodged it in the Mediator, as the head of believers; Col. i. 19, " For it pleased the Father, that in him should all fulness dwell." In him there is not only a fulness of sufficiency for himself, but of abundance for his people, as of water in a fountain, or of sap in the stock of a tree; John iii. 34, " God giveth not the Spirit by measure unto him."

3. Sinners are welcome to partake of this stock of grace and strength in Christ; 2 Tim. ii. 1. For it is lodged in him as a store-house, to be communicated. The fountain stands open, and whosoever will may come and take; Zech. xiii. 1. They are very welcome; as it is an ease and pleasure for the mother to have the full breast sucked by her babe, so it is a pleasure to Christ to communicate of his fulness; Isa. lxvi. 12, 13, " For thus saith the Lord, Behold, I will extend peace to her like a river, and the glory of the Gentiles like a flowing stream; then shall ye suck, ye shall be borne upon her sides, and be dandled upon her knees. As one whom his mother comforteth, so will I comfort you; and ye shall be comforted in Jerusalem."

4. We must be united to Christ, as members to the head, and branches to the vine, if we would act in prayer or any other duty in the strength of Christ; John xv. 5, " I am the vine ye are the branches; he that abideth in me, and I in him, the same bringeth forth much fruit; for without me ye can do nothing." We cannot partake of the stock of grace and strength for duty in Christ, without partaking of himself; Rom. viii. 32. As the soul in a separate state doth not quicken the body, so the soul not united to Christ cannot be fitted for duty by strength derived from him. The graft must knit with the stock, ere it can partake of the sap.

SECONDLY. I am to shew wherein acting in prayer in the strength of Christ lies. It lies in two things :—

1. The soul's going out of itself for strength to the duty; that is, renouncing all confidence in itself for the right management of it; 2 Cor. iii. 5, forecited. Every duty is to be undertaken, begun, and carried on, under a sense of utter weakness and insufficiency for it in ourselves.

(1.) Gifts are not to be trusted to; Prov. iii. 5. That is the way to get gifts blasted, for they are but an arm of flesh; Jer. xvii. 5, 6. And though ye should have the free exercise of your gift; yet a bare gift can never make a man do a duty graciously. The work will still be but a dead work, without the life of grace derived from Christ the Lord of life.

(2.) Nay grace received and implanted in us is not to be trusted to for this end. Learn ye, that even of our gracious selves we can do nothing; 2 Cor. iii. 4, 5. There must be continued supplies of grace from Christ unto us, else we will bring forth no fruit; John xv. 5. It is true, grace is a seed that in its nature tends to fruit; but what will come of the seed, if the showers, and dew, and heat of the sun be withheld ?

2. The soul's going to Christ for strength to duty, by trusting on him for it; Isa. xxvi. 4, " Trust ye in the Lord for ever; for in the Lord Jehovah is everlasting strength." This is the exercising of faith, by which the saints live; Gal. ii. 20, and derive grace and strength from Christ their head; John i. 16. Faith is that grace by which the weak soul fetches in strength and grace from the fountain of it in Christ. So he prays in the name of Christ, in this respect, who goes about the duty in confidence of, and trusting in Christ for, strength and ability to manage it acceptably; Psalm lxxi. 16, " I will go in the strength of the Lord God; I will make mention of thy righteousness, even of thine only." To make this more plain, consider,

(1.) By faith a Christian sees, in the glass of the word, an utter inability for duty in himself, believing, on the testimony of the word, that of himself he is unable to work any good work, Isa. xxvi. 12; nay, not to begin it well; Phil. i. 6, to will it; chap. ii. 13, nor so much as to think it; 2 Cor. iii. 5. In all which the Christian's faith is strengthened by experience.

(2.) By faith he sees also a fulness of grace and strength treasured up in Christ the head, to be communicated to the members of his body; 2 Cor. xii. 9, " And he said unto me, My grace is sufficient for thee; for my strength is made perfect in weakness." Col. i. 19, " It pleased the Father, that in him should all fulness dwell." And he beholds the promises he has made of it, as the conduit pipes by which it is conveyed unto them; 2 Pet. i. 4, " Whereby are given unto us exceeding great and precious promises; that by these you might be partakers of the divine nature." These things the Christian believes on the testimony of the same word of God; and thus he sees a sufficiency to oppose to his own emptiness, and a fulness of strength to remedy his own weakness.

(3.) By faith he trusts that this fulness in Christ shall be made forthcoming to him, in a measure of it, for the duty, according to the promise; Psalm xviii. 2, " The Lord is—my God, my strength, in whom I will trust." Hab. iii. 19, " The Lord God is my strength, and he will make my feet like hinds' feet, and he will make me to walk upon mine high places." Thus there is a particular application in faith, that the Christian trusts in the word of promise, that grace and strength shall be given to him. So the word holds it out for particular application by faith; 2 Cor. xii. 9, " My grace is sufficient for thee;" and this is the way to bring in strength, as the Psalmist's experience testifies; Psalm xxviii. 7, " The Lord is my strength and my shield, my heart trusted in him, and I am helped;" and so the promise secures it; Jer. xvii. 7, 8, " Blessed is the man that trusteth in the Lord, and whose hope the Lord is. For he shall be as a tree planted by the waters, and that spreadeth out her roots by the river, and shall not see when heat cometh, but her leaf shall be green, and shall not be careful in the year of drought, neither shall cease from yielding fruit." Take away that trust, that particular application, the soul is left helpless, having nothing to gripe to, and the communication of strength is blocked up; according to what the apostle James says, chap. i. 6, 7, " Let him ask in faith, nothing wavering; for he that wavereth is like a wave of the sea, driven with the wind, and tossed. For let not that man think that he shall receive any thing of the Lord."

FOURTHLY. We must in praying to God pray for Christ's sake, as the only procuring cause of the success of our prayers; Dan. ix. 17,

" Now therefore, O our God, hear the prayer of thy servant, and his supplications, and cause thy face to shine upon thy sanctuary that is desolate, for the Lord's sake." Going to God in prayer, we must as it were put off our own persons, as not worth noticing in the sight of God, and put on the Lord Jesus Christ ; come and receive the blessing in the elder Brother's clothes, having all our hope from the Lord's looking on the face of his Anointed. This is the main thing in the text, a relying on the Lord Jesus for the success of our prayers in heaven. Here I shall shew,

1. What is pre-supposed in this.

2. Wherein it consists.

FIRST. I am to shew what is pre-supposed in praying to God for Christ's sake. It pre-supposes,

1. That sinners in themselves are quite unacceptable in heaven, even in their religious duties. Not only are the wicked so; Prov. xv. 8, but even the saints considered in themselves ; Isa. lxiv. 6. The reason is plain, God is holy, we are impure and defiled. There is such a rank smell of sinful pollution about us, that the opening of a sinner's mouth in prayer is like the opening of an unripe grave ; Rom. iii. 13. It is too strong, that we cannot sweeten ourselves. The loathsome savour of the sins about the best, cannot be mastered by any sweet savour of their duties, but only by the sweet savour of the sacrifice of Christ ; 2 Cor. ii. 15, with Eph. v. 2.

2. Christ is most acceptable there ; he is the darling of heaven, the prime favourite there ; Matth. iii. ult., " This is my beloved Son, in whom I am well pleased." He is acceptable there as God, the only begotten of the Father from eternity ; but that is not it. He is acceptable as God-man, Mediator, who has in our flesh fulfilled his Father's will, by his obedience and death ; Eph. v. 2, " Christ— hath given himself for us, an offering and a sacrifice to God for a sweet-smelling savour. And he is acceptable to the Father,

(1.) In himself; Matth. iii. ult., above cited. The Father is well pleased with his person, and delights in him, as the brightness of his own glory, and his own express image. He is well pleased with his undertaking the work of our redemption, and his management of that work; he is pleased with his holy birth, righteous life, and complete satisfaction ; so pleased with his humbling himself, that he has " highly exalted him ;" Phil. ii. 9.

(2.) He is so well pleased with him, that he accepts sinners for his sake ; Eph. i. 6, " He hath made us accepted in the Beloved." For his sake rebel sinners are accepted to peace and favour, criminals, to eternal life, their performances, mixed with much sinful imperfections, are accepted as pleasing in his sight. The sweet smell of his sacrifice so masters the rank savour of sin about them, that they are for his sake brought into his presence and made near. The Father knows not to refuse him any request; John xi. 42, "I knew that thou hearest me always."

3. Sinners are warranted to come to the throne of grace in his name; Heb. iv. 15, 16, "We have not an High Priest which cannot be touched with the feeling of our infirmities; but was in all points tempted like as we are, yet without sin. Let us therefore come boldly unto the throne of grace, that we may obtain mercy, and find grace to help in time of need." It is sinners of mankind, not of the angel tribe; chap. ii. 16, "For verily he took not on him the nature of angels: but he took on him the seed of Abraham." Whatever be our case, he will do for us to the uttermost; Heb. vii. 25. He is an Advocate that will take our most desperate causes in hand, carry them through, and that in a way agreeable to justice; 1 John ii. 1, "If any man sin, we have an Advocate with the Father, Jesus Christ the righteous." The petitions put into his hand cannot miscarry.

SECONDLY, I am now to shew wherein this praying to God for Christ's sake consists. And,

First, In general, it consists in our relying on the Lord Jesus only, for the success of our prayers in heaven. And,

I. Consider what we are in this matter to rely on him only for.

(1.) We are to rely on him only, for access to God in our prayers; Eph. iii. 12, "In whom we have boldness and access with confidence by the faith of him." In vain do we pray, if we get no access to the prayer-hearing God; and there is no access to him, but through Christ; John xiv. 6. Whoever attempt to draw near to God otherwise, will get the door of heaven cast in their face; but we must take hold of the Mediator, and come in at his back, who is Heaven's favourite and the sinner's friend.

(2.) For acceptance of our prayers; Eph. i. 6, forecited. Our Lord Christ is the only altar that can sanctify our gift; Heb. xiii. 10, 15. If we lay the stress of our acceptance on any person or thing, but Jesus Christ, the crucified Saviour, we cannot be accepted. For our best duties being mixed with sinful imperfections, cannot be accepted of a holy God but through a Mediator; and there is no Mediator but he; 1 Tim. ii. 5.

(3.) For the gracious answer of prayer in granting our petitions. So the text, "Whatsoever ye shall ask the Father in my name, he will give it you." We have forfeited all other pleas for Heaven's favours, by Adam's fall. And now no prayers can be heard and answered in heaven; but for Christ the second Adam's sake. A sinner cannot have the least favourable glance from the throne of God, but what is given for Christ's sake. What men get otherwise, they get with a vengeance, an impression of wrath on it; Hos. xiii. 11; Psalm lxxviii. 29.

2. Consider how we are to eye Christ as the object of this reliance. We are to eye him in it as our great High Priest; Heb. iv. 15, 16, forecited. A believer is to eye Christ in his prayers, in all his offices. We are to eye him as our Prophet, teaching us by his Spirit how and what to pray for; as our King, having the office of distributing Heaven's favours to poor sinners; but in point of our access, acceptance, and hearing, we are to eye him as a Priest; for it is in that office only we can find what to rely on before God, for these ends. And here we find,

(1.) The infinite merit of his sacrifice to rely on; Rom. iii. 25, " Whom God hath set forth to be a propitiation, through faith in his blood." Man by sin lost himself, and all Heaven's favours from the greatest to the least, from heaven's happiness to the least drop of water to refresh him. Accordingly Christ redeeming sinners by his blood, paid the ransom not only for their persons, but for all Heaven's favours to them, from the greatest to the least. Therefore he says, "Incline your ear, and come unto me; hear, and your soul shall live, and I will make an everlasting covenant with you, even the sure mercies of David; Isa. lv. 3. He bought their seat in heaven, their peace, and pardon, yea and their seat on earth, their bread, and their water; Isa. xxxiii. 16, " He shall dwell on high; his place of defence shall be the munitions of rocks, bread shall be given him, his waters shall be sure." Now, would we pray in his name?

Then in prayer eye Christ on the cross, bleeding, dying, and by his bloody death and sufferings paying for the mercy thou art seeking. Is it a spiritual mercy, or a temporal mercy? It is a purchased mercy, the purchase of the blood of Christ; seek it of God as such, as the purchase of the blood of Jesus.

(2.) His never-failing intercession to rely on; Heb. vii. 25, " Wherefore he is able also to save them to the uttermost, that come unto God by him, seeing he ever liveth to make intercession for them." Our great High Priest having offered his sacrifice on earth, is now gone into the heavens, presenting there the blood of his sacrifice in the infinite merit thereof before his Father; that he may obtain the purchased mercies for his people. So that the supply of the needs of his people, is his business in heaven, as well as it is theirs on earth. And he offers their prayers to his Father; Rev. viii. 4. Therefore if ye would pray in his name,

In prayer eye Christ as your Intercessor at the right hand of God,

Rom. viii. 34. If the price of his blood was extended to the purchasing of all the mercies we need; surely his intercession extends from the greatest to the least of them also. And therefore we need not stick to put our petitions for any mercy we need, in his hand. Hence it may appear,

Secondly, More particularly, wherein praying in the name of Christ, and for his sake consists,

1. Renouncing all merit and worth in ourselves, in point of access, acceptance, and gracious answer, saying with Jacob, Gen. xxxii. 10, "I am not worthy of the least of all the mercies, and of all the truth, which thou hast shewed unto thy servant." If we stand on personal worth, from the consideration of our doings or sufferings, or any thing in or about ourselves, we pray in our own name, and will speed accordingly. Self-denial is absolutely necessary to this kind of praying, that stopping our eyes to all excellencies in ourselves or duties, we may betake ourselves to free grace only.

2. Believing that however great the mercies are, and however unworthy we are, yet we may obtain them from God through Jesus Christ; Heb. iv. 15, 16. There can be no praying in faith without this. If we do not believe this, we dishonour his name, whether our unbelief of it arise from the greatness of the mercy needed, or from our own unworthiness, or both. For nothing can be beyond the reach of his infinite merit and never-failing intercession.

3. Seeking in prayer the mercies we need of God, for Christ's sake accordingly. So we present our petitions "in his name;" John xvi. 24. We are to be ashamed before God in prayer, ashamed of ourselves, but not ashamed to beg in the name of his Son. Our holy shame respects our unworthiness; but Christ's merit and intercession are set before us, as a ground of confidence.

4. Pleading on his merit and intercession; Psalm lxxxiv. 9, "Behold, O God our shield, and look upon the face of thine Anointed." We are not only to seek, but to plead in prayer, as needy petitioners whose pinching necessity makes them fill their mouths with arguments; Job xxiii. 3, 4. Christ's merit and intercession is the fountain of these arguments; and to plead on mere mercy, mercy for mere mercy's sake, is too weak a plea. But faith founding its plea on Christ's merit, urges God's covenant and promise made thereupon; Psalm lxxiv. 20, his glorious perfections shining in the face of Jesus, the honour of his name manifested in Christ.

5. *Lastly,* Trusting that we shall obtain a gracious answer for his sake; Mark xi. 24, "What things soever ye desire when ye pray, believe that ye receive them, and ye shall have them." The

soul praying according to the will of God, is to exercise a faith of particular confidence in God through Christ, which is not only warrantable, but necessary; Jam. i. 6, 7. This glorifies the Mediator, and glorifies the faithfulness of God in the promise; and the want of it casts dishonour on both.

II. The second general head is, to give reasons why acceptable prayer must be in the name of Christ. I offer the following :—

1. Because sinners can have no access to God without a Mediator, and there is no other Mediator but he ; Isa. lix. 2 ; 1 Tim. ii. 5. Innocent Adam might have come to God immediately in prayer, and been accepted; for while there was no sin, there was no need of a Mediator. But now the justice of God bars the access of sinners to him ; and there is none to mediate a peace betwixt God and the sinner but Christ ; John xiv. 6.

2. Because the promises of the covenant were all made to Jesus Christ, as the party who fulfilled the condition of the covenant; Gal. iii. 16. The promises are the measure of acceptable prayer ; what God has not promised, we cannot warrantably pray for. In prayer we come to God to claim the promises ; and we cannot claim them, but in the right of Christ the head of the covenant, to whom they were made ; that is to say, we cannot pray acceptably but in his name.

3. Because our praying in the name of Christ is a part of the reward of Christ's voluntary humiliation for God's glory and the salvation of sinners ; Phil. ii. 9, 10. He gave his life a ransom for sinners, and a price of redemption of their forfeited mercies ; therefore God has statuted and ordained, that sinners shall crave and receive all their mercies in his name, that they shall kneel in him to receive the blessing, as his members.

4. Because it is not consistent with the honour of God, to give sinners a favourable hearing otherwise ; John ix. 31, with 2 Cor. v. 19, 21. Where is the honour of God's justice, if Heaven's favours be bestowed on sinners otherwise than on the account of a satisfaction ? —the honour of his holiness, if they may have communion with him as they are in themselves ?—of his law, if they may get their petitions of mercy answered, but in the name of one who has answered its demands ? They dishonour God, his Son, and his mercies, that ask any thing but in the name of Christ.

5. Nothing can savour with God, that comes from a sinner, but what is perfumed with the merit and intercession of Christ ; 2 Cor. ii. 15 ; Eph. i. 6. It is not the inward excellency of the prayers of the saints, that makes them acceptable in God's sight; but the righteousness of Christ, which is by faith on the praying saint praying in faith ; Heb. xi. 4. The merit of his righteousness, presented

in his intercession, with the prayer, makes it acceptable; Rev. viii. 4. It savours in heaven out of his mouth.

6. *Lastly,* The stated way of all gracious communication between heaven and earth, is through Jesus Christ, who opened a communication between them by his blood, when it was blocked up by the breach of the first covenant; John xiv. 6. Whatever favour is conveyed to us from heaven in a way of grace and love, whatever we offer to God in a way of duty or desire, must go through him. This was represented in Jacob's ladder; Gen. xxviii. If we would come to God, or present a petition to him, it must be through Christ; Heb. x. 19, 20. If the Lord comes to us, or sends us a gracious answer, it is through him; 2 Cor. v. 19.

I shall now make some practical improvement of this subject.

USE I. Of information. From this doctrine we learn,

1. What a holy God we have to do with in prayer, who hath said, " I will be sanctified in them that come nigh me, and before all the people I will be glorified; Lev. x. 3. He sits on his throne of majesty, and we can have no access to him, being sinners, but through Christ. His very throne of grace, from which he breathes love and good-will to sinners, is founded on justice and judgment; Psalm lxxxix. 14. We must come to him under the covert of the Mediator's broad righteousness and efficacious blood; otherwise we cannot stand before his spotless holiness.

2. Let us prize the love of Christ, in making an entrance for us into the holy place, through the vail of his flesh; Heb. x. 20. The flaming sword of justice, which guarded the way to the tree of life, was bathed in his blood, to procure us access to God. He bought again the estate that Adam forfeited for us, and he bought it with his precious blood; that since we could not have it again in our own name, we might have it in his.

3. There can be no acceptable praying to God but by believers united to Christ, having on the garment of his righteousness; John ix. 31, "God heareth not sinners." An unregenerate man, living in his natural state, may pray; but can never pray acceptably, while in that state; for he cannot pray in the name of Christ, which is not the work of the tongue using these words, but the work of the heart by faith relying on Christ, his merit and intercession.

4. Even believers cannot pray in the name of Christ, and so not acceptably, without faith in exercise. It is not enough for this end, that one have faith in the root and principle; but faith must be exercised in every duty; Gal. ii. 20, " The life which I now live in the flesh," says Paul, " I live by the faith of the Son of God." It is as necessary to every acceptable performance, as breathing to the common actions of life; John xv. 5.

5. *Lastly,* We have great need not to be rash in our approaches to God in prayer, but that we prepare our hearts and compose them aforehand for such a solemn duty; Eccl. v. 1. We should beware lest custom in these things, and particularly in the more frequent and less solemn approaches to God in prayer, at our meals, turn us to formality; but should labour to impress our hearts with the holiness of God, the necessity of a Mediator, and stir up grace in our hearts.

USE II. Of reproof to all those who approach unto God in prayer, otherwise than by and in the name of Jesus Christ. The idolatrous Papists allow other mediators of intercession, besides the one only Mediator; and pray to, employ, and rely on saints and angels, to intercede in heaven for them, though religious worshipping of the creature is directly forbidden; Matth. iv. 10, and angel-worship; Rev. xix. 10, and the saints departed are not acquainted with our particular cases; Isa. lxiii. 16. But those also among us are to be reproved, as approaching to God in prayer otherwise than in Christ's name,

1. Who make approach unto God in prayer, as an absolute God, without consideration of the Mediator. This is the effect of the natural blindness and ignorance of men's minds; not knowing God, nor discerning the flaming sword of justice guarding the tree of life, they rush forward on the point thereof to pull the fruits. Let such consider their dangerous rashness, and reform; Heb. xii. ult., " For our God is a consuming fire;" knowing they can never worship God acceptably in that way; John v. 23, " He that honoureth not the Son, honoureth not the Father which hath sent him." Hence the knowledge and belief of the doctrine of the Trinity is the foundation of all acceptable worship, without which it cannot subsist; Eph. ii. 18, " For through him we both have an access by one Spirit unto the Father;" and the Christian church is thereby distinguished from the rejected Jews; 1 Thess. i. 1, and it must be practically improved in every piece of true worship.

2. Those who, in their approaches to God, put other things in the room of the Mediator, or join other things with him. For as there is no access to God without a Mediator, so there is none but by the one Mediator only; John xiv. 6, " No man cometh unto the Father, but by me." But who do that? Even all those who in their approaches by prayer, lay the stress of their access and acceptance with God, in whole or in part, on any thing but Christ. Whatever thou reliest on for these ends, besides Christ, has his room, and so mars the duty; Phil. iii. 3, and provokes God; Jer. xvii. 5, 6. There is a bias in the hearts of the best this way.

There are four things which men are apt to put thus in the room of Christ, in whole or in part,

(1.) Their own worth, in respect of their qualifications and good things done by them; Judg. xvii. ult. This the proud Pharisee relied on in his approach; Luke xviii. 11, 12, " God, I thank thee," says he, " that I am not as other men are, extortioners, unjust, adulterers, or even as this publican. I fast twice in the week, I give tithes of all that I possess." So proud and conceited professors go to their prayers, and with their money in their hand miss the opened market of free grace. They say they beg for Christ's sake, but yet in reality they have more expectation from their own personal worth, than from the merit of Christ's blood. Their want of a humbling work of the Spirit raises the value they have for themselves ; and the want of saving illumination sinks the value of Christ's merit with them.

(2.) The mercy of an unatoned God, that is, mercy considered in God without a view to the satisfaction of his justice by the Mediator. This the ignorant and profane are apt to stumble on, whose eyes are open to the mercy of God, but blind to his justice, which therefore they are in no concern about the satisfaction of. It never enters into their hearts, to question, how it is consistent with the honour and justice of God to accept them; but the notion they have framed of the mercy of God answers all their difficulties. Howbeit, no such mercy is proposed to sinners in the gospel; Isa. xxvii. 11 ; Psalm lxxxv. 10. It is true, it was a good prayer of the publican, Luke xviii. 13, " God be merciful to me a sinner ;" but his words bear an eye to mercy through a propitiation ; and so was the mercy of God held forth to the Old Testament church in the mercy-seat, as well as to the New.

(3.) The manner of their performing the duty itself. Great weight is laid here, as if a well-said prayer were sufficient to recommend itself and the petitioner too. Cain laid such weight on his sacrifice; Gen. iv. 4, 5. A flash of affections and seeming tenderness in prayer, is in the eyes of many a prayer that cannot be rejected ; Isa. lviii. 3, " Wherefore have we fasted, say they, and thou seest not ? wherefore have we afflicted our soul, and thou takest no knowledge ?" Enlargement in duty raises the value of it so in their own eyes, that they cannot think but it must be valuable in the eyes of God too. So in the earnestness of the prayer, and many words used; Matth. vi. 7. Let men examine their expectations, and they will be fair to find more weight laid there than on the merit of Christ, though this only can bear weight.

(4.) Their own necessity ; Hos. vii. 14, " They have not cried unto me with their heart, when they howled upon their beds; they assemble themselves for corn and wine, and they rebel against me." Sense of need is a necessary qualification in acceptable prayer; but pinching necessity, where the heart is unhumbled, is apt to be set in a room higher than becomes it, as if of itself it were a sufficient plea. When it is thus abused, may be known by this, That on the not hearing of the prayer, the heart riseth against God; a sign that the petitioner is not as a needy beggar craving an alms, but a needy creditor craving his own. Our necessity should quicken us to seek, but it is the merit and intercession of Christ alone that is to be relied on for our access.

Use III. Wherefore rely on Christ, and on him only, for access to God in, and acceptance of, your prayers; that is, pray in the name of Christ.

Mot. 1. In this way of praying ye may obtain any thing ye really need. So says the text, "Whatsoever ye shall ask the Father in my name, he will give it you." There is no mercy so great, nor any sinner so unworthy, but he may have it, coming to God this way; Heb. vii. 25, with John xi. 42. God can bestow it in that way with the safety of his honour, the sinner may confidently expect it on good grounds. For Christ's merit is infinite, his intercession always prevalent.

2. There is no access to God, nor acceptance of prayer another way; John xiv. 6. It is through him our persons can be accepted, Eph. i. 6; and through him our duties can be so; Heb. xi. 4. Every sacrifice not offered on this altar, however valuable it seems, will be rejected. There is no return of prayer in a gracious manner otherwise.

I conclude with giving you a few directions for praying in the name of Christ.

1. Labour to impress your hearts with a sense of the spotless holiness and exact justice of God, Psalm lxxxix. 7. This will shew the necessity of a Mediator to interpose, as in Israel's case.

2. Be sensible of your need of, and look for, the help of the Spirit in every approach, Rom. viii. 26. As the sending of the Spirit is the fruit of Christ's merit and intercession; so the Spirit being come leads back to the Mediator, Eph. ii. 18.

3. Shake off all confidence in yourselves, and see your utter unworthiness of the least mercies, how great soever your need of them be, Gen. xxxii. 10. As Jacob put off his own raiment to put on his elder brother's for the blessing, so do ye cast off your own filthy rags, and put on the Lord Jesus Christ.

4. Satisfy not yourselves with bare seeking for Christ's sake; that

is not enough : but be confident that ye shall get access, acceptance, and a gracious return for his sake, Mark xi. 24. Raise a believing expectation in him.

QUESTION, How may one reach that ? ANSWER, (1.) By a believing view of Christ on the cross purchasing, and at the Father's right hand, interceding for, our mercies; and particularly eying his sufferings, agreeable to your wants, as in the case of your want of light, the darkness came on him ; in the case of your want of bread, his hunger, &c. (2.) By a believing application of the promises suitable to your needs. (3.) Considering this as God's ordinance for communication between heaven and earth, Gal. iii. 8.

5. *Lastly,* Watch against your hearts going off to any confidence in the duty itself ; for that is to dishonour the name of Christ, and will provoke the Spirit of the Lord to depart from you.

OF GOD'S HEARING OF PRAYER.*

PSALM lxv. 2,

O thou that hearest prayer, unto thee shall all flesh come.

WHAT avails prayer, if it be not heard ? But God's people need not lay it aside on that score. Our text bears two things with respect to that matter.

1. A comfortable title ascribed to God, with the unanimous consent of all the sons of Zion, who are all praying persons, "O thou that hearest prayer." He speaks to God in Zion, or Zion's God, that is, in New Testament language, to God in Christ. An absolute God thundereth on sinners from Sinai, there can be no comfortable intercourse betwixt God and them, by the law ; but in Zion from the mercy-seat in Christ, he is the hearer of prayer ; they give in their supplications, and he graciously hears them. Such faith of it they have, that praise waits there for the prayer-hearing God.

2. The effect of the savour of this title of God, spread abroad in the world, "Unto thee shall all flesh come ;" not only Jews, but Gentiles. The poor Gentiles, who have long in vain implored the aid of their idols, hearing and believing that God is the hearer of prayer, will flock to him, and present their petitions. They will throng in about his door, where by the gospel they understand beggars are so well served. They will " come in even unto thee," (Heb.) They will come in even to thy seat, thy throne of grace, even unto thee thyself, through the Mediator.

---

* The substance of some Sermons preached at Etterick in the year 1728.

The doctrine I chiefly propose speaking to, is,

DOCTRINE, God in Christ is the hearer of prayer.

In handling this doctrine, I shall shew,
I. Wherein God's hearing of prayer lies.
II. The import of his being the hearer of prayer.
III. What prayers they are that God hears.
IV. More particularly consider the hearing and answering of prayer.
V. *Lastly*, Apply.

1. I am to shew wherein God's hearing of prayer lies. God being omniscient and every where present, there can nothing be said or done in the world, but he hears or discerns it. But the hearing of prayer in the sense of the scripture is a peculiar privilege of the Lord's people, and lies in the following things.

1. God's accepting of one's prayer, Psalm cxli. 2, " Let my prayer be set forth before thee as incense; and the lifting up of my hands as the evening-sacrifice. Many prayers are said in the world, that are so far from being accepted of God, that they are an abomination to him, Prov. xxviii. 9. God turns them away from him, as one flings a petition over the bar, that he is displeased with, Psalm lxvi. ult. But the prayers that he hears, he is well pleased with them, he approves of them. Hence he is said to attend, hearken to the voice, and consider prayer, as one listens to a sound that pleases him, and dwells on a pleasing thought, Psalm lxvi. 19, " Verily God hath heard me; he hath attended to the voice of my prayer." He delights in the petition, Prov. xv. 8, " The prayer of the upright is his delight." He loves to hear the petitioner's voice, Cant. ii. 14, " Let me hear thy voice; for sweet is thy voice." He accepts the petitioner's person, and his petition too, as the angel said unto Lot, Gen. xix. 21, " See I have accepted thee concerning this thing also, that I will not overthrow this city, for the which thou hast spoken." For where prayer is heard, the person is accepted too, as Gen. iv. 4, " The Lord had respect unto Abel, and to his offering; Job xlii. 9, " The Lord also accepted Job."

2. His granting the request, Psalm xx. 1, 4, " The Lord hear thee in the day of trouble ;—grant thee according to thine own heart, and fulfil all thy counsel." The sinner coming to God with a petition, lays it before him, and his desire is granted. God wills it to be unto him accordingly, Matth xv. 28, " O woman," said Christ to the woman of Canaan, " great is thy faith; be it unto thee even as thou wilt." The mercy prayed for is ordered for the sinner, in kind or equivalent. Thus prayer is heard in heaven, heard and granted.

3, His answering of prayer, Psalm cii. 2, " In the day when I call answer me speedily." This is more than granting the request, being a giving unto the petitioner's hand what is desired. It is an answer not in word to the believer's faith only, but in deed to the believer's sense and feeling. Thus Hannah prayed for a child, and she got one; Paul prayed for the removal of a temptation, and he got grace sufficient to bear him out against it. Thus prayer heard in heaven comes back like the dove with the olive-branch of peace in her mouth.

II. I shall shew the import of God's being the hearer of prayer. These comfortable truths are imported in it.

1. God in Christ is accessible to poor sinners, 2 Cor. v. 19, " God was in Christ, reconciling the world unto himself, not imputing their trespasses unto them." Though he sits on the throne of glory, and we are guilty before him ; yet he is on a throne of grace, so as we may have access to him with our supplications. The flaming sword of justice guards the tree of life, on the side of the law ; so that on that part our God is a consuming fire, which sinners are not able to dwell with ; yet behold him in Christ, and through the vail of his flesh he is accessible to the worst of sinners.

2. He is a sin-pardoning God, Exod. xxxiv. 6, 7, " And the Lord passed by before him, and proclaimed, The Lord, The Lord God, merciful and gracious, long suffering, and abundant in goodness and truth, keeping mercy for thousands, forgiving iniquity, and transgression, and sin." Prayer is made particularly for the pardon of sin ; the daily cry at the throne is, " Forgive us our debts." If then he is the hearer of prayer, he is a sin-pardoning God. We cannot pay our debt, but God can forgive it, and will forgive it to all that come to him in Christ for forgiveness. All kinds of sin he forgives freely, Micah vii. 18 ; Isa. i. 18. There is no exception, but of the sin against the Holy Ghost, which in its own nature makes the guilty refuse pardon, Matth. xii. 31. The pardon is proclaimed in the gospel, Acts xiii. 38 ; not to encourage presumption in any, but to prevent despondency in all, Psalm cxxx. 4, " There is forgiveness with thee ; that thou mayest be feared."

3. He is an all-sufficient God, Gen. xvii. 1, " I am the Almighty God, (*Heb.*) " All sufficient." He is self-sufficient for himself, and all-sufficient for his creatures. If he were not so, he could not be the hearer of prayer ; the needs of praying persons would soon exhaust his treasure. But though all flesh come to him for supply of their various wants, he is the hearer of prayer ; he has enough for them all, to answer all their needs, come as oft as they will. He is a fountain of goodness, that never runs dry, but is ever full.

4. He is a bountiful and compassionate God, Psalm lxxxvi. 5,

"Thou, Lord, art good, and ready to forgive; and plenteous in mercy unto all them that call upon thee." He is willing and ready to communicate of his goodness and mercy to poor sinners for the supply of all their needs. He is more ready to give, than we to ask; we are not straitened in him, for he is the hearer of prayer; but in our own bowels. He has laid down a method, how we are to ask; and in that method, it is ask and have, James i. 5, 6, 7, "If any of you lack wisdom, let him ask of God, that giveth to all men liberally, and upbraideth not; and it shall be given him. But let him ask in faith, nothing wavering; for he that wavereth is like a wave of the sea, driven with the wind, and tossed. For let not that man think that he shall receive anything of the Lord." The faith of this is necessary to acceptable prayer, Heb. xi. 6. "For he that cometh to God, must believe that he is, and that he is a rewarder of them that diligently seek him."

5. He is an omnipresent and omniscient God, Psalm cxxxix. 7, "Whither shall I go from thy Spirit; or whither shall I flee from thy presence?" Heb. iv. 13, "Neither is there any creature that is not manifest in his sight; but all things are naked, and opened unto the eyes of him with whom we have to do." How else could he be the hearer of prayer? What part of the world soever the petitioner is in, whether he prays with the voice or with the heart only, God is the hearer of prayer. Idolaters might choose high places to worship their idols in; but it is all one to the hearer of prayer, whether the petitioner be on the top of the highest mountain, or as low as the centre of the earth. Jonah was heard out of the whale's belly. Though thousands of voices be going in prayer to the throne at the same time, the infinite mind comprehends them all, and every one, as easily as if there were but one at once.

6, *Lastly*, He is a God of infinite power, Rev. iv. 8, "They rest not day and night, saying, Holy, holy, holy, Lord God Almighty." —While there is such a variety of cases, that the creatures have to lay before him in prayer, he could not be the hearer of prayer, if there were anything too hard for him to do. But nothing is impossible with him; he calleth things that are not to be as if they were, at the voice of prayer.

III. I proceed to show what prayers they are that God hears. It is not every prayer, nor every one's prayer that God hears. But it is the prayers of his children, for things agreeable to his will, made by the assistance of his Spirit, and offered through Christ.

1. They are the prayers of his own children, who are justified by faith, and reconciled to him, James v. 16, "The effectual fervent

prayer of a righteous man availeth much." Our Lord teaching how to pray, teaches us to call God " our Father ;" which can be only through faith. Our persons must be accepted in justification, ere any work of ours can be so. Where there is no peace betwixt God and the sinner, what communion can be there ? Amos iii. 3, " Can two walk together, except they be agreed ?" The scripture is plain, " God heareth not sinners," John ix. 31. God's way of giving graciously, is to give other things with Christ, Rom. viii. 32, " He that spared not his own Son, but delivered him up for us all, how shall he not with him also freely give us all things ?" It is in the covenant only that one can have a bottom for acceptance of his prayers.

OBJECTION. Then it is in vain for any to pray, but true believers. ANSW. There is less evil in praying by an unbeliever, than in his omitting it; and consequently less punishment will be. But going to pray, go to Christ by faith, and so your prayer shall be accepted ; and no otherwise.

2. They are such prayers of theirs as are for things agreeable to God's will, 1 John v. 14, " This is the confidence that we have in him, that if we ask anything according to his will, he heareth us." Even in saints there are remains of a corrupt will, and so it is not left to them to pray for what they please ; not what is the choice of their corruption, but what is the choice of their grace. When James and John would have prayed for fire from heaven to consume the Samaritans, Christ rebuked them, and said, " Ye know not what manner of spirit ye are of," Luke ix. 54, 55. Elias did it, but they might not, not having his spirit.

3. They are prayers made by the assistance of the Holy Spirit, hence called " inwrought," (Gr.) Jam. v. 16. No language is acceptable in heaven, but what is learned from thence. It is not the art of payer, but the Spirit of prayer, that is pleasing in the sight of God. The former may be reached by God's enemies, whose false heart may vent itself by a flattering tongue, as Israel did, Psalm lxxviii. 36, 37, " Nevertheless, they did flatter him with their mouth, and they lied unto him with their tongues. For their heart was not right with him, neither were they stedfast in his covenant." The latter is the peculiar privilege of God's children, yet common to them all; Gal. iv. 6, " Because ye are sons, God hath sent forth the Spirit of his Son into your hearts, crying, Abba, Father."

4. Lastly, They are prayers offered to God through Christ the Mediator, the soul trusting on his merit and intercession alone for the hearing of them, Dan. ix. 17, " Now therefore, O our God, hear the prayer of thy servant, and his supplications, and cause thy

face to shine upon thy sanctuary that is desolate, for the Lord's sake." John xiv. 14, "If ye shall ask anything in my name, I will do it." Christ is the altar on which our spiritual sacrifices can be accepted; and it is not consistent with the honour of God, to hear the prayers of sinners otherwise.

The doctrine being thus explained in the general, I come in the next place more particularly,

1. To confirm it, and shew that there is such a thing as hearing of prayer, the privilege of the Lord's people in this lower world.

2. To shew in what manner the Lord hears prayer.

FIRST, I am to confirm it, and shew that there is such a thing as hearing of prayer, the privilege of the Lord's people in this lower world, God is in heaven, they are on the earth; voices from heaven, or angel-messengers to report the acceptance of prayers there, are not to be expected. Nevertheless we are sure there is such a thing still in being, and it is necessary to prove it.

1. For the sake of a profane generation, who, as they are strangers to, so they are despisers of, communion with God.

2. For the sake of formalists, who go about the duty of prayer as a task, but are in no concern for the fruit of it; send away the messenger, but look for no report.

* 3. For the sake of discouraged Christians who go bowed down, because they cannot perceive it as they desire.

That God is the hearer of prayer, and will hear the prayers of his people, is evident from these considerations.

First, The supernatural instinct of praying that is found in all that are born of God, Gal. iv. 6, forecited. It is as natural for them to pray, to fall a praying when the grace of God has touched their hearts, as for children when they are born into the world to cry, or to desire the breasts; Zech. xii. 10, "I will pour upon the house of David, and upon the inhabitants of Jerusalem the spirit of grace and of supplications." Compared with Acts ix. 11, where, in the account that is given of Paul, at his conversion, it is particularly noticed, "Behold he prayeth." Hence the whole saving change on a soul comes under the character of this instinct; Jer. iii. 4, 19, "Wilt thou not from this time cry unto me, My Father, thou art the guide of my youth? I said, Thou shalt call me, My Father, and shalt not turn away from me." This supernatural instinct being the work of God in the new nature, cannot be in vain. Accordingly it is determined; Isa. xlv. 19, "I said not unto the seed of Jacob, Seek ye me in vain." But it would be a vain appetite, if it were not to be satisfied by hearing.

Secondly, The intercession of Christ; Rom. viii. 34, "It is Christ that died, yea rather, that is risen again, who is even at the right hand of God, who also maketh intercession for us." It is a great part of the work of Christ's intercession, to present the prayers of his people before his Father, Rev. viii. 4, to take their causes in hand contained in their supplications, 1 John ii. 1. So we find him interceding for his church of old in her low condition, Zech. i., and in the New Testament, John xvii. He is ever at the work, and cannot neglect it, Heb. vii. 25, and it cannot be without effect; John xi. 42, "I knew that thou hearest me always," said Jesus to his Father.

Thirdly, The promises of the covenant, whereby God's faithfulness is impawned for the hearing of prayer; as Matth. vii. 7, "Ask, and it shall be given you; seek, and ye shall find; knock, and it shall be opened unto you." Isa. lxv. 24, "And it shall come to pass, that before they call, I will answer, and whiles they are yet speaking, I will hear." Psalm cxlv. 19, "He will fulfil the desire of them that fear him; he also will hear their cry, and will save them." The promise of hearing of prayer, is one of the great lines of the covenant; Hos. ii. 20, 21, "I will even betroth thee unto me in faithfulness, and thou shalt know the Lord. And it shall come to pass in that day, I will hear, saith the Lord, I will hear the heavens," &c. ; and it is so proposed with his being his people's God; Zech. x. 6, "I am the Lord their God, and will hear them."

Fourthly, The many encouragements given in the word to the people of God, to come with their cases unto the Lord by prayer. He invites them to his throne of grace with their petitions for supply of their needs; Cant. ii. 14, "O my dove that art in the clefts of the rock, in the secret places of the stairs, let me see thy countenance, let me hear thy voice; for sweet is thy voice, and thy countenance is comely." He sends afflictions for to press them to come; Hos. v. ult, "I will go and return to my place, till they acknowledge their offence, and seek my face; in their affliction they will seek me early." He gives them ground of hope of success, Psalm l. 15, whatever extremity their case is brought to; Isa. xli. 17, "When the poor and needy seek water and there is none, and their tongue faileth for thirst, I the Lord will hear them, I the God of Israel will not forsake them." He shews them, that however long he may delay for their trial, yet praying and not fainting shall be successful at length; Luke xviii. 8, "I tell you that he will avenge them speedily."

Fifthly, The gracious nature of God, with the endearing relations he stands in to his people; Exod. xxii. 27, "And it shall come to pass, when he crieth unto me, that I will hear; for I am gracious."

Matth. vii. 9—11, " What man is there of you, whom if his son ask bread, will he give him a stone ? or if he ask a fish, will he give him a serpent ? If ye then being evil, know how to give good gifts unto your children, how much more shall your Father which is in heaven give good things to them that ask him ?" He wants not power and ability to fulfil the holy desires of his people ; he is gracious, and will withhold no good from them that they really need. He has the bowels of a Father to pity them, the bowels of a mother to her sucking child. He has a most tender sympathy with them in all their afflictions, the touches on them are as on the apple of his eye ; and he never refuses them a request, but for their good ; Rom. viii. 28.

Sixthly, The experiences which the saints of all ages have had of the answer of prayer. The faith of it brings them to God at first in conversion, as the text intimates ; and they that believe cannot be disappointed. Abraham, Moses, David's and Job's experiences of this kind are in record, with many others, Paul's, &c. The Psalmist sets up his case as a way-mark to all the travellers to Zion ; Psalm xxxiv. 6, " This poor man cried, and the Lord heard him ; and saved him out of all his troubles." And to this day the saints' experience seals the truth thereof.

Lastly, The present ease and relief that prayer sometimes gives to the saints, while yet the full answer of prayer is not come ; Psalm cxxxviii. 3, " In the day when I cried, thou answeredst me ; and strengthenedst me with strength in my soul." The unbosoming of themselves to the Lord in prayer, comforts and strengthens the heart ; 1 Sam. i. 18. This is on the faith of the Lord's hearing of prayer ; Micah vii. 7, " I will look unto the Lord ; I will wait for the God of my salvation ; my God will hear me."

SECONDLY, I come to shew in what manner the Lord hears prayer. For clearing of this, I lay down the following observations thereon,

FIRST, A thing desired of God may be obtained, and yet the prayer not heard and accepted, as in Israel's case ; Psalm lxxviii. 29, " So they did eat, and were well filled ; for he gave them their own desire." For as it is plain on the one hand, that sinners out of Christ may sometimes obtain a thing they pray for, as in the case of the Ninevites, it is as plain on the other, that no prayer of theirs can be accepted of God, according to John ix. 31, " God heareth not sinners." It is one thing to get a thing prayed for, another to get it as an answer of accepted prayer ; Psalm lxxviii. 34—38. Now this falls out in two cases,

1. When the thing prayed for is given downright in wrath, as it was in the case of the Israelites seeking a king ; Hos. xiii. 11, " I

gave thee a king in mine anger." Men often need no more to ruin them, but to get their will; and God may give it them with a vengeance. They get their desire, but it is far from being accepted; for it is in anger it comes to them.

2. When it is given in the way of uncovenanted condescendence. Thus sinners out of Christ may get particular requests of theirs answered, as Ahab; 1 Kings xxi. 29. For though God does not accept their persons, nor any performance of theirs; yet he may shew regard to his own ordinance of prayer, and therefore make it not fruitless even to them. And thus the Lord does to train sinners to the yielding themselves to him, and to depending on him by faith and prayer; Hos. xi. 3, "I taught Ephraim also to go, taking them by their arms."

Answers of accepted prayer come in the way of the covenant of grace, but these in the way of common providence. And they may be discerned by these attending signs.

(1.) Wilfulness and unhumbledness of spirit in asking; 1 Sam. viii. 19, "Nevertheless the people refused to obey the voice of Samuel; and they said, Nay, but we will have a king over us." When one's will is peremptory, and is not brought to a holy submission to God in the matter, but they will wring the mercy out of God's hand, and have it at any rate, whether with or without his good will ; be sure that is what comes in the way of common providence only.

(2.) Strengthening and feeding of lusts by them when received, Psalm lxxviii. 29, 30. Hence on such receipts men commonly grow worse, and their mercies are short-lived; being greedily snatched off the tree of providence, ere they are ripe, their teeth are set on edge with them, vers. 30, 31.

(3) A frame of spirit, in asking and receiving, not of the mould of the gospel, but of the law; whereby more stress is laid upon our own necessity than on the intercession of Christ; there is much desire of the mercy, but no believing dependence on the Lord for it in the promise as a free promise through Christ; and ordinarily it leaves the heart fixed on the gift, and does not carry it back to the Giver.

Secondly, A prayer may be heard and accepted, and yet the desire of it not granted. That is to say, God may be pleased with, and accept of the prayer as service to him; and yet may see meet not to grant the thing prayed for. Even as a father going to correct one of his children, may be very well pleased with another child of his interposing for sparing, though he may not see it meet to forbear for all that.

The truth of this is put out of doubt, in the case of Jesus Christ himself, Matth. xxvi. 39, who prayed, saying, " O my Father, if it be possible, let this cup pass from me ; nevertheless, not as I will, but as thou wilt." Compare, Heb. v. 7, " Who in the days of his flesh, when he had offered up prayers and supplications, with strong crying and tears, unto him that was able to save him from death, and was heard, in that he feared." If it was so done with the Head, no wonder it be so with the members too, as David, 2 Chron. vi. 8, 9, " But the Lord said to David my father, Forasmuch as it was in thine heart to build an house for my name, thou didst well in that it was in thine heart ; notwithstanding, thou shalt not build the house, but thy son which shall come forth out of thy loins, he shall build the house for my name." A thing may be very agreeable to the command of God, to be prayed for, which yet may be otherwise ordered in the holy wise providence of God. It is one thing what he requires of us by his revealed will, another what in his secret will he minds to do, Deut. xxix. ult., " The secret things belong unto the Lord our God : but those things which are revealed, belong unto us, and to our children for ever, that we may do all the words of this law."

Now of prayers accepted and not granted, it is to be observed,

1. They are not absolute and peremptory, but with holy submission to the divine pleasure, as of our Lord's, Matth. xxvi. 39. If we pray absolutely, for what God has not so promised, and such a prayer is not granted, it is not accepted neither. So all that this amounts to is, that God sees meet to refuse what the petitioner did seek, but with submission to his will either to grant or refuse it.

2. Where a prayer is accepted and not granted, there is in the bosom of the denial an unseen greater mercy. Had that cup passed from Christ, where had been the glory of God the Father, Son, and Holy Ghost, in the salvation of an elect world, that was wrapt up in the denial of that sinless desire of Christ's holy human nature ? Had David's child lived for whom he prayed, he had been a lasting stain on his father's reputation ; but God refused David's petition in that, where the refusal was a greater mercy than the granting would have been.

3. Hence that treatment of such prayers is agreeable to the chief scope and aim of the petitioner, which is God's glory and his own good. This is the design of believers in all their accepted prayers, which, being agreeable to the promise, there is no jarring there betwixt God and them. Only, they in this case look on such a thing as they pray for to be the most proper mean for that end ; God sees it is not, and therefore refuses it. So all that this amounts to is, as if one should desire one to lead him such a way to such a place ; he refuses not to lead him to the place, but he will not lead him that way, but a nearer and better way.

QUESTION. How may I know such prayers of mine to be accepted, when they are not granted ?

ANSWER 1. When the heart is brought to submit to the denial as a holy and righteous dispensation; Psalm xxii. 2, 3, " O my God, I cry in the day time, but thou hearest not; and in the night season, and am not silent. But thou art holy, O thou that inhabitest the praises of Israel." When the sinner from his heart clears the Hearer of prayer, leaving his complaint on his unworthy self, such an effect is an argument of prayer accepted, though not granted.

2. When though the thing be denied, yet divine support under the denial is granted, and made forthcoming, Luke xxii. 42, 43. Christ having prayed, saying, " Father, if thou be willing, remove this cup from me; nevertheless, not my will, but thine be done; there appeared an angel unto him from heaven, strengthening him." And he was carried through all his sufferings by his Father, so that he was victorious over death itself. Thus often God, denying the petitions of his children, with respect to temptations, troubles, &c., yet testifies his acceptance of their prayers by the supports given under the same ; Psalm cxxxviii. 3, " In the day when I cried," says David, " thou answeredst me ; and strengthenedst me with strength in my soul."

3. *Lastly,* When such a soul is helped to go back to the same God with new petitions in faith and hope of hearing; 2 Sam xii. 20, " Then David arose from the earth, and washed, and anointed himself, and changed his apparel, and came into the house of the Lord and worshipped." This argues a faith of the promise of all things working together for good, Rom. viii. 28, a leaving a latitude of dispensation to sovereignty, well becoming a submissive and resigned petitioner.

Thirdly, The desire of a prayer may be heard and granted, and yet it may be long ere it be answered. That is to say, all prayers not answered to our sense and feeling, are not lost; they may stand granted in heaven, and yet it may be many a day ere the answer of them come to us. A prayer may be granted, and yet the mercy prayed for be still withheld, so that the petitioner may be obliged to send new petitions day by day for it still.

I shall first confirm this, and then shew why it may be so ordered.

First, To confirm the truth of this, consider,

1. Scripture instances. Abraham prayed for an heir, it was granted, Gen. xv. 3, 4, yet it was more than thirteen years before that prayer was answered, in the birth of Isaac, Gen. xvii. 25. So the Israelites in Egypt, Exod. ii. 23, 24 ; and Daniel, chap. ix. 23. Such instances are recorded for our learning.

2. There is a difference betwixt the granting of a petition, and the intimation of that grant to us; betwixt Heaven's order for our getting of the mercy, and the execution of it. The one is the hearing and grant of prayer, the other is the answer; and though these sometimes may come both in one instant, as Matth. xv. 28, " Jesus answered and said unto her, O woman, great is thy faith; be it unto thee even as thou wilt; and her daughter was made whole from that very hour;" yet often they are at a great distance of time, as in Abraham's case.

3. The hearing and granting of prayer is an object of faith, the answer of prayer an object of sense and feeling, 1 John v. 14, 15; Matth. xv. 28. A prayer made through the assistance of the Spirit, according to the will of God, and offered to God through Christ, is heard and granted in that instant wherein it is made; and this is what we are to believe, on the ground of the faithfulness of God in the promise, before we get the answer to our sense and feeling; for " faith is the substance of things not seen, and we walk by faith not by sight;" and therefore this is the ordinary way to put the grant and answer at some distance of time, though not always, Isa. lxv. 24.

Secondly, I shall shew why the answers of prayers heard and granted, are kept up for a time, and may be for a long time.

1. To keep the petitioners hanging on about the throne of grace; Prov. xv. 8, " The prayer of the upright is his delight." The Lord by this means gives them many errands to the throne, so that they must always be going back again, and renewing their suits. So fathers make their little children follow them, and hang about them, and speak to them as they can; and no father has such delight in the company and converse of his children, as God has in his, Cant. ii. 14.

2. For the trial of their graces; Jam. i. 12, " Blessed is the man that endureth temptation; for when he is tried, he shall receive the crown of life, which the Lord hath promised to them that love him." This life is the time of trial, and God's withholding for a time the answers of granted prayers, is a piece of trial that will go in through and out through the child of God. It tries their sincerity and earnestness for an answer, Job xxvii. 10; with Luke xviii. 7; their patience and disposition to wait on God, Hab. ii. 3; their hope in God, Psalm cxlvii. 11; and xlii. 5; especially it tries their faith in the word of promise, and that is a trial of great estimation in the sight of God; 1 Pet. i. 6, 7, " Wherein ye greatly rejoice, though now for a season (if need be) ye are in heaviness through manifold temptations. That the trial of your faith being much more precious

than of gold that perisheth, though it be tried with fire, might be found unto praise, and honour, and glory at the appearing of Jesus Christ. Every new act of faith in the word, is more valuable than all the famed exploits of carnal, selfish men; especially when faith keeps hold of the promise like a rope in the water, while providence is bringing one wave after another over the man's head, Psalm lvi. 10. So Matth. xv. 21—28.

3. Till they be prepared and fitted for receiving the answer; Psalm x. 17, "Lord, thou hast heard the desire of the humble; thou wilt prepare their heart, thou wilt cause thine ear to hear." Mercies we need, but we are not at all times meet to receive them. God gives his left-hand gifts to strangers, in the way of common providence, whether they be prepared for them or not; and hence many are ruined getting much laid to their hand before they have the grace or wisdom to manage it, for God's honour and their own good. But his right-hand gifts to his children, in the way of the covenant, though they be ready for them, yet he will keep them back till they be made ready and prepared for them too. So he is at pains to humble them, and work them for that thing. Saul was brought to the kingdom easily, but David not so.

4. *Lastly*, Till the best time come, for their getting it, when it may come to them with the greatest advantage; Eccl. iii. 14, "I know that whatsoever God doth, it shall be for ever; nothing can be put to it, nor any thing taken from it; and God doth it, that men should fear before him." There is much in the timing of a favour; the same thing may be worth double to a man at one time, beyond what it will be at another. And be sure, if God is keeping back the answer of a granted prayer, he is only reserving till the best time of bestowing it; John xi. 14, 15, and ii. 4.

QUEST. How may a Christian know his prayer is heard and granted, while yet it is not answered?

ANSW. 1. If ye have prayed in faith, no doubt your petition is heard and granted, though it should not be answered for ever so long after; Matth. xxi. 22, "All things whatsoever ye shall ask in prayer, believing, ye shall receive." God refuses not, nor rejects any prayer for things agreeable to his will, made in faith of the promise, through the assistance of the Spirit, and offered to him through his Son. And ye ought to believe, that such prayers are granted, but that God for holy wise ends delays the answer.

2. If ye are strengthened to hang on about the Lord's hand for the answer, hoping and waiting for the Lord; Psalm cxxxviii 3. It is a certain truth, which ye may build upon; Gal. vi. 9, "In due season we shall reap, if we faint not." This is the very character

of an elect believer, on his trials for glory; Luke xviii. 7, " Shall
not God avenge his own elect, which cry day and night unto him,
though he bear long with them ?"   Granted prayer brings something
in hand, namely, grace to wait on; Psalm xxvii. ult., " Wait on the
Lord; be of good courage, and he shall strengthen thine heart;
wait I say on the Lord."   Compare ver. 13, " I had fainted, unless
I had believed to see the goodness of the Lord in the land of the
living."

3. *Lastly*, It is a good sign when ye are encouraged to wait for
the desired answer, by the Lord's answering you in other things
that fall out in the meantime of the delay.   For the Lord lays these
to your hand to support your faith and hope in point of the delayed
answer.   How was David's faith of the promise of the kingdom kept
up, so many years during Saul's reign ?   Why, David in that time
had many experiences of answers of prayer, and fulfilling of promises in other things, as Psalm xxxiv. 6, " This poor man cried, and
the Lord heard him ; and saved him out of all his troubles."

FOURTHLY, Prayers accepted and granted, shall certainly be
answered to the believer's sense and feeling at length.   The answer
may be delayed, but it cannot be forgotten nor miscarried.   Such
prayers will surely be turned into praise at long-run ; and faith
will bring in sense and feeling, when it is tried a while.

I shall first confirm the truth of this, and then shew when they
shall be so answered to their sense and feeling.

First, To confirm this, consider,

1. The interest the Mediator has in the matter, which secures and
puts it beyond doubt.   It is upon his merit that the prayer is accepted, on his intercession that it is granted ; so that he is nearly
concerned in the obtaining of the answer; and then he is the
great Steward in heaven, into whose hands the whole fulness of co-
venant-benefits for sinners' supply is put.   How then can it fail,
when the mercy petitioned for is lodged in the hand of our Intercessor ?

2. The faithfulness of God in his word; Psalm lxxxix. 8, " O
Lord God of hosts, who is a strong Lord like unto thee ? or to thy
faithfulness round about thee ?"   This stands as a rock immoveable
in all the changes that befall his people.   His word must be accomplished, and his promise fulfilled, whatever stand in the way of
it.   Heaven and earth shall rather be removed than it fail, or fall a
minute behind the set time of its bringing forth ; Hab. ii. 3, " For
the vision is yet for an appointed time, but at the end it shall speak,
and not lie; though it tarry, wait for it, because it will surely come,
it will not tarry."

3. The love and pity God has to his children that cry to him. " His ears are open to their cry; Psalm xxxiv. 15. He forgets it not; Psalm ix. 12. As he is their God, so he will be " a God to them," as the expression is; 1 Chron. xvii. 24, namely, to do the part of a God to them; that is, to hear and answer their prayers.

4. *Lastly,* Such prayers are the product of his own Spirit in them; Rom. viii. 26. And be sure, the mouths that he opens, he will fill; the holy appetite and desires that he creates in them, he will satisfy.

Secondly, I shall shew when they shall be answered to their sense and feeling. There are two periods in general, wherein God gives answers of prayers accepted and granted. Answers of prayer are given,

1. In time, during the petitioner's life in this world; Psalm lviii. ult., " Verily there is a reward for the righteous; verily he is a God that judgeth in the earth." Believers in this life have communion with God, and do get answers of prayer, as provision allowed them of their Father, for their journey through the wilderness. But one may wait a long time of his life for an answer of some prayers, and ere he go off be made to say, " Lord, now lettest thou thy servant depart in peace, according to thy word; for mine eyes have seen thy salvation;" Luke ii. 29, 30.

Of the seasons of life for answers of prayer, we may say in the general, there are four seasons thereof.

(1.) A time of the Lord's return to a church and people from whom he had hid his face; Psalm cii. 16, 17, " When the Lord shall build up Zion, he shall appear in his glory. He will regard the prayer of the destitute, and not despise their prayer." The children may cry long to their Father, ere he let on he notices them, when he is angry with their mother; but when he is pleased with her, they get speedy answers from him; Dan. ix. 1, 2, 23. Times of reformation, and outpouring of the Spirit on a land, are times of answers of prayer to particular persons; which should move us to carry along the public case, with our private cases, as David did; Psalm li. 18, 19, " Do good in thy good pleasure unto Zion; build thou the walls of Jerusalem;" &c.

(2.) A time of greatest extremity, when matters are carried to the utmost point of hopelessness; Deut. xxxii. 36, " For the Lord shall judge his people, and repent himself for his servants; when he seeth that their power is gone, and there is none shut up, or left." When God's people are brought to that, they can do no more, then is the special season of God's doing for them; Isa. xli. 17, " When the poor and needy seek water, and there is none, and their tongue faileth for thirst, I the Lord will hear them, I the God of Israel will not forsake them." When the child was laid by for dead, the well was discovered. When the knife was at Isaac's throat, the answer comes from heaven, " Stay thine hand." A sentence of death is often passed on all probable means, the thing is put as it were in the grave, and the stone sealed; and then comes the resurrection of it; 2 Cor. i. 8—10. Psalm cxxvi. 1, " When the Lord turned again the captivity of Zion, we were like them that dream."

(3.) A time of the petitioner's deepest humiliation, when he is beat down from all his heights, and brought as low as the dust of the Lord's feet, as in Job's case; chap. xlii. 6, 7, &c., and the woman of Canaan's; Matth. xv. 27, 28. It is the Lord's way with his children to lay them very low, before he raise them up; to empty them soundly of themselves, before he fill them. They must be made to see their own utter unworthiness, that God is no debtor to them, be wholly resigned to the divine pleasure, and become as a weaned child. And that may cost much hewing; but it is the way they are prepared for mercy; Psalm x. 17.

(4.) *Lastly*, A time wherein the mercy may come most seasonably for God's honour and their comfort, Gal. vi. 9, " In due season we shall reap, if we faint not," The husbandman expects to reap his crop in the harvest, for that is the most proper season. Our God is the best judge of time for this or that purpose, and he does all in judgment, Deut. xxxii. 4. So that the petitioner shall be fully satisfied as to the delay of the answer, and the whole steps of providence in the matter, and be made to sing as Rev. xv. 3, saying " Great and marvellous are thy works, Lord God Almighty; just and true are thy ways, thou King of saints.

2. In eternity, when the believing petitioner is got into another world, then will be a season of answers of prayer, Mal. iii. 17, 18, " They shall be mine, saith the Lord of hosts, in that day when I make up my jewels, and I will spare them as a man spareth his own son that serveth him. Then shall ye return and discern between the righteous and the wicked; between him that serveth God, and him that serveth him not." I do not say, they will pray in another world, but prayers poured out in this world will be answered in another world, partly after death, and fully and completely at the resurrection. For consider,

(1.) There are accepted and granted prayers that are never answered on this side of time; yet they cannot miss to be answered, Psalm ix. 18, " For the needy shall not alway be forgotten; the expectation of the poor shall not perish for ever." Therefore they are answered in eternity. Such is that prayer of all the children of God, Rom. vii. 24, " O wretched man that I am, who shall deliver me from the body of this death? The complete victory over all their enemies, and being set beyond their reach, which is delayed till the resurrection, 1 Cor. xv. 26, "The last enemy that shall be destroyed, is death."

(2.) There are prayers that are answered here in part, but are not fully answered till the petitioner comes into another world. The prayers for the coming of Christ's kingdom are begun to be answered now, but they will not be fully answered till the last day. Petitions for deliverance from temptation, the power of lusts and corruptions, are answered so as an earnest is given, but the full answer is till then in reserve, Rom. xvi. 20, "The God of peace shall bruise Satan under your feet shortly."

(3) *Lastly*, All the accepted prayers of those that wait for the Lord, whether for their souls or their bodies, will be at once answered in heaven fully ; there the promises will be told out to them for ever in full tale. There are many prayers for deliverance from temptations, trials, and troubles, which God sees not meet to answer now ; but they will be all answered at once then, Rev. xxi. 4, "God shall wipe away all tears from their eyes ; and there shall be no more death, neither sorrow, nor crying, neither shall there be any more pain ; for the former things are passed away."

Therefore, let none think that all the prayers are lost that are not answered during this life ; for prayers here made in faith, may be delayed as to their answer, till the petitioner come home to his Father's house; and there will be a second crop there of prayers here answered.

QUEST. When an answer of prayer comes, how shall it be known to be an answer of accepted and granted prayer, and not come in the way of common providence?

ANSW. 1. Mercies that come so make the soul more holy, tender, and watchful, whereas others prove snares and fuel to men's lusts, Psalm vi. 8, "Depart from me, all ye workers of iniquity ; for the Lord hath heard the voice of my weeping." Common providence filled the rich man's barns, then said he, "Soul take thine ease."

2. They enlarge the soul in thankfulness to God, Psalm cxvi. 1, 12, "I love the Lord, because he hath heard my voice, and my supplications. What shall I render unto the Lord, for all his benefits towards me?" And they make it to rejoice more in the Giver, than in the gifts, 1 Sam. ii. 1, "My heart rejoiceth in the Lord." The signature of God's good will that is upon the mercy, makes it of a great bulk, though it may be a small thing in itself, Gen. xxxiii. 10, "I have seen thy face, said Jacob to Esau, as though I had seen

the face of God, and thou wast pleased with me." Thus coming from God in the way of the covenant, it leads back to God; but others not so.

3. *Lastly*, They come seasonably, the heart being in some measure prepared for the receipt, Psalm x. 17, when the soul is moulded in a submissive disposition. Exercised souls will be afraid of a mercy coming too soon.

Fifthly, God answers prayer, either by giving the very thing itself asked, or the equivalent of it. As a man may pay his bond, either in money, or money worth. So there are two ways of God's fulfilling his promises, and answering his people's prayers.

1. Sometimes God answers prayer by giving the very thing desired. So he answered Hannah's prayer for a child, and Solomon's prayer for wisdom. And what comes that way will bear much bulk in the eyes of a gracious soul, because of the good will of God that is stamped on it, whereby it is distinguished from what comes in the common road.

And what comes that way, readily comes with a good incast to it, especially if the petitioner has been kept long hanging on for it. Such an incast got Solomon, 2 Chron. i. 12, " Wisdom and knowledge is granted unto thee, and I will give thee riches, and wealth, and honour, such as none of the kings have had, that have been before thee, neither shall there any after thee have the like." They that wait long for their answer, ordinarily get as it were both the stock and interest together. So Abraham and Sarah waited long for the promised seed, even till they were come to extreme old age; and then they got it with a renewing of their age.

2. Sometimes by giving, though not the thing itself, yet the equivalent of it, that which is as good; as one may pay his bond, by giving, though not money, yet what is as good as money. Thus though God did not give David the child's life, yet he gave him a Solomon, a mercy as good and better. Paul, though he got not free of the temptation at his asking, yet he got grace sufficient to bear him up under it, 2 Cor. xii. 9.

And God's as-good that he gives his people, will readily be found better, all things considered. That is best which is best for God's honour and our good, and God knows better than we what is most suitable to these purposes. It would have been more easy for Paul, to have been freed from the messenger of Satan; but it was more for God's honour and his spiritual good, to be helped to fight that messenger and overcome.

Learn then, that your prayers may be answered, though ye get not the very thing ye ask. Though God answer you not in kind, if he answer you in kindness, you have no reason to say your prayer is not heard. If he take not off your burden, yet if he gives you support, he hears you, Psalm cxxxviii. 3. There are two ways how God gives his people as good.

(1.) Sometimes he gives them as good in the same kind : though he gives them not the same temporal mercy they would have had, he gives them another of the same kind as good as it. Though he gave not David the life of the child he asked, he gave him a Solomon. So God reserves to himself the choosing.

(2.) Sometimes he gives them as good in another kind ; as not giving them such a temporal mercy, he gives them a spiritual mercy and enjoyment in the room of it; and surely there is no loss there.

QUESTION, How may one know that God answers his prayer, by giving him the as-good.

ANSWER 1. When that which is given answers or serves the purpose as well as the thing desired would have done. David desired the child's life as a token of God's reconciliation with him; but Solomon's birth answered the same purpose, 2 Sam. xii. 24, 25. So there was no loss as to the main thing in view.

2 When the heart is brought to rest contented with what is given in the room of what was desired. So Moses was sufficed with a sight of the land from Pisgah, instead of entering into it. When the thing given takes the heart off what is withheld, it is a sign it comes as an answer of prayer by the way of an as-good.

3. When a person is to his own conviction a gainer by the choice God makes for him. Thus the Lord sometimes answers his people's prayers in trouble for deliverance, by giving them manifestations of his love and mercy, which they would not have gotten if the trouble had been removed, Lam. iii. 57, " Thou drewest near in the day that I called upon thee ; thou saidst, Fear not."

Sixthly, God's answer of prayer sometimes agrees with the expression used in prayer, though not with the preconceived design and desire of the petitioner. There is a special help of the Spirit allowed God's people in prayer, beyond what they have otherwise, Rom. viii. 26. Hence going to God on such a particular errand, they are sometimes carried so to express their desire, that the answer agrees exactly to the expression used in the petition, though the petition as expressed doth swerve somewhat from what they intended.

It will therefore be profitable on the receiving an answer of prayer, to compare it with the expression in which the petition was made ; and the harmony betwixt them being observed, will set the matter of the answer in a clear light.

Lastly, One mercy may be the answer of the prayers of many.

Whether it be a public mercy to a society, or a private mercy to a particular person, it may be given in answer to the prayers of many, and many may take the comfort of that answer. As when the prayers of a congregation are heard, or a mercy is given which many have privately prayed for, though the answer is one, it may belong to many.

QUESTION, How may one know that in such a case there has been any regard had to his prayer for the mercy?

ANSWER 1. If thy heart did join in prayer for the mercy, with others, thy affections being touched with earnest desire of the mercy, thy soul lifted up to depend on the merit and intercession of Christ for the granting it, thou needest not doubt but it is an answer to thy prayer as well as to others, Matth. xviii. 19, "I say unto you, that if two of you shall agree on earth, as touching any thing that they shall ask, it shall be done for them of my Father which is in heaven."

2. If thou findest thy heart enlarged in thankfulness to God for the mercy when it is obtained, that is another evidence that it is an answer to thy prayer as well as others, 2 Cor. iv. 15, "For all things are for your sakes, that the abundant grace might, through the thanksgiving of many, redound to the glory of God." Many a prayer had been put up for the coming of the Messiah; Simeon when he saw him is transported with thankfulness of heart, as having obtained his desire, Luke ii. 29.

I shall now shut up this subject with some practical improvement.

USE I. of information. Hence see,

1. How much we poor sinners stand indebted to free grace providing a Saviour for us. We could have had no access with our prayers to an absolute God; justice would have barred our acceptance. So fallen angels have no access to God allowed them; for Christ took not on their nature. But great is our privilege in this point; 1 John ii. 1, "For if any man sin, we have an Advocate with the Father, Jesus Christ the righteous.

2. The heinousness of the sin of neglecting prayer. A price is put in men's hands to get wisdom, but they have no heart to it. The door of mercy and grace stands open, but they will not come to it; God sits on a throne of grace, ready to answer petitions; but they have none to put in his hand.

3. The impiety and profaneness that is in abusing of prayer, making a scorn of it in ordinary conversation, as "God pity you, help you, bless us, save us," &c. How lamentable is it, that the name of God, and the ordinance of prayer, should be thus prostituted

to the lusts of men at every trifle! The day will come, when God's pity, help, &c., which ye make so light of now, will appear more valuable than ten thousand worlds, and ye shall not have them, if ye repent not of that contempt which ye now treat them with.

4. The folly of those who are in no concern for the hearing of their prayers. Surely, they forsake their own mercy. Ye would have little satisfaction in your meat, if it did not feed you; in your clothes, if they did not keep you warm. What satisfaction then can ye have in your praying, if ye cannot find it is heard?

5. *Lastly*, This shews why serious souls do so much value prayer, and betake themselves thereto in all their straits. Slight it who will, it will not be slighted by those who have experience of the Lord's hearing their prayers, Micah vii. 7, "I will look unto the Lord; I will wait for the God of my salvation; my God will hear me." Daniel was such a man; and he would rather venture on the den of lions, than forego his praying to God. The neglect of it, is a sign of unacquaintedness with that.

USE II. Of direction and comfort to the people of God, in all the trials and troubles they meet with in the world. Here is your course ye should take, go to God with your case, whatever it be, and make your prayer to him about it, Phil. iv. 6, " Be careful for nothing; but in everything by prayer and supplication with thanksgiving, let your requests be made known unto God." Here is your comfort, God is the hearer of prayer, Isa. xlv. 19, " I said not unto the seed of Jacob, Seek ye my face in vain." There are four things I would suggest to you here for your direction and comfort.

1. God has made the way to heaven lie through many tribulations, that his children might have the more errands to his throne of grace. That this is the path-road to the kingdom of God, is clear from scripture testimony, Acts xiv. 22, " we must through much tribulation enter into the kingdom of God; John xvi. ult, " In the world ye shall have tribulation;" and the experience of Christ the Head, and the saints in all ages. That this is the design of it, appears also from the word, Hos. v. ult. " I will go and return to my place, till they acknowledge their offence, and seek my face; in their affliction they will seek me early." Prosperity seldom fails to issue in forgetting of God, Deut. xxxii. 15. Adversity causes to feel a need of his help, Zeph. iii. 12. So God keeps the thorn of affliction at the breast of his people, to keep them waking, and sends the cross to invite them to the throne of grace.

2. The way to heaven in that respect never alters, though the external circumstances of the church in the world do alter. Sometimes there is persecution in the church; sometimes peace; but in the most peaceable time of the church, God's people shall go through

the world to the kingdom through much tribulation. The seed of the serpent will vent their enmity one way or other against the people of God, though they have not law on their side to bear them out in persecuting them. God will have his people tried, and caused to suffer in their bodies, goods, liberty, and life, if not by the hands of persecutors, yet by his own hand one way or other. For that is a perpetual rule, Matth. xvi. 24, " If any man will come after me, let him deny himself, and take up his cross, and follow me." Luke xiv. 26, " If any man come to me, and hate not his father, and mother, and wife, and children, and brethren, and sisters, yea, and his own life also, he cannot be my disciple." So there is no change, but only as to the means and instruments of trial.

3. Whatever be your trial, whether it be in temporal or spiritual things, ye are welcome to the throne of grace with it, Phil. iv. 6, forecited. Whether it come on you immediately from the hand of God, or men, ye may carry it to God by prayer, and pour out your heart before him as a prayer-hearing God, in confidence that he can help you, and will do it in due time.

4. The more trials and afflictions God's people meet with, the more experience readily they will be found to have of God's hearing prayer; Rom. v. 3, 4, " And not only so, but we glory in tribulations also, knowing that tribulation worketh patience, and patience experience; and experience, hope." Of all the patriarchs Jacob had the most trials, and accordingly was richest in experiences. The more battles the Christian soldier is engaged in, the more is he enriched with spoil. The Israelites had not sung that triumphant song recorded Exod. xv., had they not been in that great strait at the Red Sea.

Use last, of exhortation. Then,

1. Improve your privilege of access to God through Christ in prayer. Since God has cast open the gates of mercy, come enter in by them; since he is saying to you, " What is thy petition and it shall be granted thee?" slight not the golden season of petitioning. Consider,

(1.) Your need is great. Whatever ye have or want in temporals, surely ye need a resting place for your conscience and for your heart; you need something to make you happy in time and eternity.

(2.) The whole creation cannot answer your needs. There is an emptiness in every creature, that it cannot be a resting place to you, Isa. lv. 2. The soul is of such a make, that no less than an infinite good can satisfy it. Only God in Christ can make you happy.

(3.) He offers to supply all your needs; Psalm lxxxi. 10, " I am the Lord thy God; open thy mouth wide, and I will fill it." Ask in faith, and ye shall receive.

(4.) *Lastly,* This door of access will not always stand open; Matth. xxv. 10, 11, 12, "And while they went to buy, the bridegroom came, and they that were ready went in with him to the marriage, and the door was shut. Afterward came also the other virgins, saying, Lord, Lord, open to us. But he answered and said, Verily I say unto you, I know you not." Now is the accepted time.

2. Be concerned for God's hearing of your prayers; look after them and see what speed they come. There are two things wherein this concern should appear.

(1.) In making your addresses to the throne of grace, being careful so to manage that, as ye may be accepted. They who are rash in their approaches to God, and careless how their petitions are formed and presented, cannot be duly concerned for a hearing of them. Labour, therefore, so to pray, as your prayers may be heard and accepted.

(2.) In depending and waiting on after prayer for an answer; Psalm v. 3, "My voice shalt thou hear in the morning, O Lord; in the morning will I direct my prayer unto thee, and will look up." Do not drop your suits, but insist for an answer, depending for it on the promise of God in his word.

Thus far of God's hearing of prayer. I shall shut up this with a word to another doctrine for the use of the whole.

DOCTRINE. Such is the glory of God as the hearer of prayer in Christ, that it will make all flesh that discerns it come unto him.

Here I shall shew,

I. What is that glory of God as the hearer of prayer in Christ, that is so attractive.

II. How this glory of God in Christ is discerned by a sinner.

III. What that coming unto God is, that is the effect of discerning that glory.

IV. *Lastly,* Deduce an inference or two.

I. I am to shew what is that glory of God as the hearer of prayer in Christ, that is so attractive. It is twofold.

1. The glory of his all-sufficiency; Gen. xvii. 1, "I am God all-sufficient." He is not only all-sufficient for himself, but for his creatures; if he were not so, he could not be the hearer of prayer. But sinners in the darkness of their natural state discern it not; they cannot comprehend what way he can be so, and therefore they traverse the round of the creation, seeking in the creature that sufficiency; till the light of the glory of God's all-sufficiency shine into their

hearts in Christ. Then it shines unto them with a threefold ray of glory.

(1.) An absolute suitableness to their case, which must needs be very glorious in their eyes, since that is what they were always seeking, but could never find before, according to that; Isa. lv. 2, "Wherefore do ye spend money for that which is not bread? and your labour for that which satisfieth not? hearken diligently unto me, and eat ye that which is good, and let your soul delight itself in fatness." Therefore with the wise merchant they "sell all to buy the one pearl," Matth. xiii. 45, 46. The heart of man is an empty, hungry thing, going among the creatures seeking a match for itself, in which it may rest; but there they cannot find it; but discovering it in a God in Christ, they are attracted with the glory of that sight.

(2) A complete fulness for them; Col. i. 19, "For it pleased the Father, that in him should all fulness dwell." In his all-sufficiency the soul sees the fulness of a Godhead, an infinite boundless fulness, to answer and satisfy the boundless desires of an immortal soul. That is a fountain for the thirsty soul to drink at to the full; a treasure to enrich the soul oppressed with poverty; a salve for all its sores, and a remedy for all its wounds. So it cannot miss to attract.

(3.) An ability to help in all possible incidents, Heb. vii. 25, "Wherefore he is able also to save them to the uttermost, that come unto God by him, seeing he ever liveth to make intercession for them." The arm of the creature is weak in all cases, and quite too short in many cases; but so is not the arm of an all-sufficient God; Isa. lix 1, "Behold, the Lord's hand is not shortened, that it cannot save; neither his ear heavy, that it cannot hear." There is nothing too hard for him, there is nothing that Omnipotency can stick at. Who can but draw towards such a one for a Friend?

2. The glory of his free grace and good-will to poor sinners; hence the heavenly host sang; Luke ii. 14, "Glory to God in the highest, and on earth peace, good-will towards men." When the Lord would shew Moses his glory, he proclaimed the name of the Lord before him; Exod. xxxiv. 6, 7, "The Lord, the Lord God, merciful and gracious, long-suffering, and abundant in goodness and truth, keeping mercy for thousands, forgiving iniquity, and transgression, and sin." The glory of all-sufficiency may attract the desire of sinners; but the sinner cannot come to him, while that treasure appears to be locked up from him, a gulf fixed betwixt him and it. But when once an all-sufficient God appears in the glory of his free grace in Christ, the treasure appears open to the sinner, there is a bridge for him laid over the gulf; and so he comes freely away

to God in Christ. This shines to the coming sinner with a three-fold ray of glory.

(1.) Readiness to forgive sin; Psalm cxxx. 4, 7, 8, " But there is forgiveness with thee; that thou mayest be feared. Let Israel hope in the Lord; for with the Lord there is mercy, and with him is plenteous redemption. And he shall redeem Israel from all his iniquities." He is gracious to pardon the sins for which he might justly condemn the sinner; he is willing to be reconciled to offenders, and receive them into peace, 2 Cor. v. 19. This is an attractive glory where the conscience is awakened.

(2.) Willingness to give and communicate all that is needful to make the sinner happy; Rev. xxi. 7, " He that overcometh shall inherit all things, and I will be his God, and he shall be my son." He is gracious to give, as well as to forgive; Hos. xiv. 2; not only to lay by his wrath against the sinner, but to load him with benefits.

(3.) And all this freely, without any view to any worth in the creature, as Isa. lv. 1, " Ho, every one that thirsteth, come ye to the waters, and he that hath no money; come ye, buy and eat, yea, come, buy wine and milk without money, and without price." No condition, no qualification is required; only the sinner is welcome to take and have, whatever he has been.

II. The next thing is to shew, how this glory of God in Christ is discerned by a sinner.

1. The mean of discerning it is the gospel; 2 Cor. iii. ult., " Beholding as in a glass the glory of the Lord." As by means of light in the air we discern bodily objects, so by the means of the gospel we discern this glory of God, 2 Cor. iv. 4. By the law we discern the glory of an absolute God terrifying and confounding to a sinner, but by the gospel the glory of God as in Christ, attracting and refreshing to a sinner. It is as a looking-glass wherein we see the image of things; 2 Cor. iii. ult. It brings before us the lovely image of a God in Christ reconciling the world to himself.

2. The organ or instrument of discerning it is faith, Hab. iv. 2. Though there be full light in the air, and the looking-glass presenting the beautiful image of a person, be set before one's face, if the man's eyes be out, he cannot discern it. So the glory of God in Christ is held forth unto men in the gospel; but they are spiritually blind who are unbelievers, they perceive it not; 1 Cor. ii. 14, " The natural man receiveth not the things of the Spirit of God; for they are foolishness unto him; neither can he know them, because they are spiritually discerned." But faith sees the glory; John i. 14, " The Word was made flesh, and dwelt among us, (and we beheld

his glory, the glory as of the only-begotten of the Father) full of grace and truth."

3. The author of sinners discerning it is the Spirit, 2 Cor. iii. ult. It is he that illuminates the dark mind, that cures sinners of their natural blindness. He works faith in the soul, brings home the gospel-report to the sinner in particular, demonstrating it to be the word of God, and God's word to him in particular, and so makes the soul embrace it by believing it, Isa. liii. 1.

III. The third head is to shew what that coming unto God is, that is the effect of discerning that glory. The sinner discerning the glory of God in Christ as the hearer of prayer,

1. He comes away from all other doors, which before he used to hang about for supply. He despairs at length of coming speed there, Jer. iii. 22, 23, " Return ye backsliding children, and I will heal your backslidings ; behold, we come unto thee, for thou art the Lord our God. Truly in vain is salvation hoped for from the hills, and from the multitude of mountains ; truly in the Lord our God is the salvation of Israel." The light of the glory of God shining into his heart, discovers the emptiness of all the poor shifts the sinner makes to get supply in his natural state of blindness.

(1.) He comes away from the door of the empty creation, where he had long laboured to find a rest ; and despairs of finding it there any more. The profits, pleasures, comforts, and conveniencies of this world, appear lying vanities that can never give rest to the heart ; and they must have another portion ; Jer. xvi. 19, " O Lord, my strength and my fortress, and my refuge in the day of affliction, the Gentiles shall come unto thee from the ends of the earth, and shall say, Surely our fathers have inherited lies, vanity, and things wherein there is no profit."

(2.) From the door of sin, where he expected a satisfaction in the fulfilling of his lusts ; and he despairs of ever finding it there, Job xxxiii. 27. He finds that puddle-water will not quench his thirst, that the pleasure of it is but short, but the pain and sting of it lasting.

(3.) From out of the world lying in wickedness, 2 Cor. vi. 17, as he would escape away from lions' dens and mountains of leopards, Cant. iv. 8. He despairs of ever finding his account in the way of the world.

2. He comes away unto God in Christ, for all, and instead of all ; Jer. iii. 22, " Behold, we come unto thee, for thou art the Lord our God." And he comes unto him,

(1.) As a Saviour, that will save his submissive supplicants, Jer. iii. 22, 23. Faith apprehends him as God our Saviour, and so comes to him and trusts on him for salvation from sin and from wrath, Matth. i. 21, " Thou shalt call his name Jesus; for he shall save his people from their sins."

(2.) As a portion, that will eternally make up impoverished and ruined creatures, Psalm cxlii. 5, and in which the poor petitioner may find what he has so long sought for in vain, in the world and the way of sin.

(3.) As his resort for ever in all his needs, whatever they shall be, Psalm lxxi. 3. The soul coming unto God, comes to him as one that will never go back to another, but will hang on about his door, though he should die at it.

I conclude with an inference or two.

1. Whoso come not unto God in Christ, as a Saviour, &c., are certainly ignorant of him, and see him not in his glory; " For they that know thy name," says the psalmist, " will put their trust in thee," Psalm ix. 10.

2. Great and powerful must that glory be, which draws sinners from all other doors unto God. By nature we are backward to come unto God; it must be a very ravishing glory that has such an effect on perverse sinners.

3. *Lastly*, Be concerned to discern that glory ; to discern it by faith, and by experience, in order to your coming to him as your Saviour, portion, and continual resort.

ON ACCEPTANCE WITH GOD:—THE DOCTRINE OF THE ACCEPTANCE OF MEN'S WORKS EXPLAINED, AND A PRACTICAL REGARD THERETO IN ALL THE DUTIES OF LIFE INCULCATED.*

2 Cor. viii. 12,

For if there be first a willing mind, it is accepted according to that a man hath, and not according to that he hath not.

THE Christians in Judea being in much distress and poverty, there was a contribution through the churches of the Gentiles for them. The communion of saints extends not only to spiritual, but temporal things too ; that they be ready to help one another out of their substance. And this communication of worldly things to the supply of the saints, is not confined to those of our own church ; but is to be extended to strangers on occasion, at the greatest distance. The

---

* The substance of several sermons preached at Etterick in the year 1726.

gospel came from Judea to the Gentiles; and now money must go from the Gentiles for the relief of those of Judea. Hereby God took a trial of the Gentile churches, their love to, and esteem of, the gospel. Many will pretend to great esteem of the gospel, but they must have it for nothing. Any of their money that is desired for any public use, for the furtherance of the gospel, it is all accounted lost.

This contribution is here recommended to the Corinthians. They readily fell in with the proposal, ver. 11. Now they are desired to perform, each according to his ability.

In the text, an objection of the poorer sort is answered, who might fear that any thing they had to give was so little, that it would not be accepted. In answer thereto, they are told that God regards men's works rather by the quality than the quantity; by the mind it is given with, rather than by the thing given.

1. The case of acceptance is put, " If there be first a willing mind, it is accepted." The acceptance here is of a man's work, not of his person; though the former always presupposeth the latter, in the gospel way. And it refers to God, for he only can judge with what mind a thing is done. Now God accepts a man's service, if there be first a willing mind; that is, a readiness and good will to the work of his service. If the heart go before and lead the hand, it is accepted; otherwise it is not.

2. What regard is had in this acceptance of one's work to the quantity of it. (1.) That it be according to one's ability, that it be done to his power. Some are able to do more, and be more useful than others; but if men have a willingness to the work, and do what they are able accordingly, it is accepted through Christ; his that can do but little, as well as his that can do much. But this cuts off the pretences of those who content themselves with lazy wishes, and lay not out themselves to do what they may do. (2.) That want of power to do more, shall not mar the acceptance of what is done according to power with a willing mind, Mark xii. 43. The Lord will take the little piece of service off his people's hand, when the heart is right; as well as the great service of those of his that have great abilities. Not but that where the inability is brought on by people's own fault, it is their sin that they do not do more; but that sin shall be forgiven them, and what they do be accepted, " if there be first a willing mind."

The scope and substance of the text may be taken up in the following doctrines.

DOCTRINE I. Works may be done in service to God, that are not accepted of him.

DOCTRINE II. It should be our main concern in our works, that they may be accepted of God.

DOCTRINE III. Where there is a willing mind carrying out a man to do and serve the Lord to his ability, what is so done is accepted of God.

DOCTRINE IV. Want of power to do more, shall not mar the acceptance of what is done from a willing mind according to one's power. In that case, God will accept of his people's will for the deed.

I shall speak to each of these doctrines in order.

DOCTRINE I. Works may be done in service to God, that are not accepted of him.

In treating this point, I shall,

I. Confirm the doctrine.

II. Assign the reasons thereof.

III. Make some improvement.

1. In order to confirm the doctrine, consider,

1. Oft-times God hides his face from the man and his work too, and people have no communion with God in their services to him; Hos. v. 6, "They shall go with their flocks and with their herds to seek the Lord; but they shall not find him, he hath withdrawn himself from them." When a master will not look on his servant's work, it is an evidence he is not pleased with him, nor it, Isa. i. 15. This may be the case of the godly sometimes, and it is the case of the wicked always. O how many lost services are there this way.

2. Such services may be so far from being accepted, that they are really loathsome to a holy God; Prov. xv. 8, "The sacrifice of the wicked is an abomination to the Lord." He reckons them to be to no purpose, he is full of them, they are vain in his esteem, he cannot endure them, they are a trouble, a burden, and a weariness to him, Isa. i. 11—14. So it is often fulfilled in this case, "That which is highly esteemed amongst men, is abomination in the sight of God," Luke xvi. 15. The man thinks highly of his own work, and others do so too; but in the mean time God abhors it.

3. God may put such services out of the roll of services to him, and set them down in the roll of sins against him. That is a terrible word, Jer. vii. 21, "Thus saith the Lord of hosts, the God of Israel, put your burnt-offerings unto your sacrifices, and eat flesh;" i.e., Put your sacrifices that should be all burnt on the altar, to your other sacrifices, and eat all together as common flesh to fill your bellies; q.d., Let your prayers, and your common discourse, your hearing of sermons and your idle tales go together; I esteem the

one no more than the other. And that is another dreadful word; Amos iv. 4, " Come to Bethel and transgress, at Gilgal multiply transgression; and bring your sacrifices every morning, and your tithes after three years ;" *q.d.*, Go to your knees now, and take the name of God in vain; go to the church, and put off a little time of a Sabbath day.

4. They may bring a curse and a stroke on men, instead of a blessing and token of God's favour; Hos. viii. 13, " They sacrifice flesh for the sacrifices of mine offerings, and eat it; but the Lord accepteth them not; now will he remember their iniquity and visit their sins." Nadab and Abihu were consumed by a fire that came out from the altar they were serving at; Ananias and Sapphira were struck dead on occasion of selling their land for the service of the church; and men may be smothered with the dung of their sacrifices spread on their faces, Mal. ii. 3.

5. *Lastly*, This may take place while the service stands the man both cost and pains. The Israelites were at cost for spices for the altar, but all was rejected, Jer. vi. 20; they were at pains in attending ordinances, and endured a stress in fasting, but all to no purpose, Isa. lviii. 2, 3. Bodily exercise profiteth little before God, who is a Spirit, and must be worshipped in spirit and in truth.

II. I am next to render the reasons of the point, That works may be done in service to God, that are not accepted of him. God is no austere master, but very indulgent to his servants, and will take a very small service kindly off their hands; but men often serve him in a way that is provoking to him, and to his dishonour; and thence are the reasons why their services are not accepted.

1. Sometimes that is offered for service to God, that is forbidden by him, John xvi. 2, " They shall put you out of the synagogues : yea, the time cometh, that whosoever killeth you will think that he doth God service." A blinded conscience gets the leading of a man, and leads him out of the way of God; it dictates what is sin to be duty, and what is duty to be sin; so that the man thinks he is serving God, while he is really serving his own corruptions; and so instead of a " Well done, good and faithful servant," he meets with a " Wo unto them that call evil good, and good evil; that put darkness for light, and light for darkness," Isa. v. 20; and " lies down" at length " in sorrow," Isa. l. ult.

2. Sometimes that is offered that is not commanded or required; Matth. xv. 9, " In vain they do worship me, teaching for doctrines the commandments of men." Nothing can be acceptable to God, but what is required by some one or other command of his; " for whatsoever is not of faith, is sin," Rom. xiv. ult. See Isa. i. 12.

Horrid idolatry is condemned on that very ground, that it was uncommanded service, Jer. vii. 31. It is an affront to the sovereignty of God, and his mastership, for men to order his service according to the devices of their own hearts, and not to keep precisely to his orders. Hence are the superstitions of Popery, and the uninstituted ceremonies of the Church of England, which are the product of human device, without any countenance from the word of God.

3. Ofttimes, though the work be commanded of God, yet it is marred in the making. There is something about the person, or the work, that ruins all.

1st, About the person, that mars the acceptance. As,

(1.) He may be in a state of separation from Christ, not united to him by faith, and so not accepted of God, John xv. 5. No acceptable work can be done by any man while he is out of Christ; Eph. ii. 10. For a man's person must be accepted, before his work can be accepted, since his work being imperfect, cannot procure the acceptance of his person. Now no sinner's person is accepted but in Christ, Eph. i. 6, and we come to be in Christ by faith; therefore faith in Christ must go before acceptable obedience, Heb. xi. 6. Faith makes the tree good, ere it can bring forth good fruit, Matth. vii. 17. And no fruit of obedience is accepted of God, but what grows on a branch of Christ the true vine. The blasting curse lies on all other. See Gen. vi. 9.

(2.) He may be in a state of enmity with God; and as no man will like the services of his enemies, so God will not accept the services of one not reconciled to him; Amos iii. 3, " Can two walk together, except they be agreed?" Every unbeliever is an enemy to God, Rom. viii. 7, for his sin remains unpardoned, and his nature unchanged; and therefore his best works are but splendid sins, himself but a whited sepulchre; and when he speaks and acts fairest, there are seven abominations in his heart. How then can an allseeing God accept such services?

(3.) He may be an unregenerate man, and so like Simon "in the gall of bitterness, and in the bond of iniquity," Acts viii. 23. Whosoever are out of Christ, are unregenerate; for it is by being in him, and so partaking of his Spirit and fulness, that we become new creatures, 2 Cor. v. 17; Eph. i. 13. Now how can the corrupt tree bring forth good fruit? or the old nature acceptable obedience? If the fountain be poisoned, can the streams be wholesome? Could one like the best liquor in a vessel wherein there is no pleasure?

(4.) He may be habitually unholy or profane in his life, or as to the body of his conversation; Prov. xxviii. 9, " He that turneth away his ear from hearing the law, even his prayer shall be abomination."

So the Lord rejects the sacrifices of the Israelites, Isa. i. 15, 16 The Psalmist tells us, that "the man who shall ascend into the hill of the Lord, and stand in his holy place," must "have clean hands, and a pure heart," Psalm xxiv. 3, 4. The apostle wills to "lift up holy hands, without wrath and doubting ;" 1 Tim. ii. 8, if we would be accepted. Their conversation must be of a piece, whose works will be accepted ; for God will never accept the services of men, that for the most part serve the devil, the world, and their lusts. Many are like the harlot ; Prov. vii. 13, 14, as if they thought their duties would purge away their sins. Nay but their sinful courses otherwise will pollute and render abominable their duties, Hag. ii. 11—14.

2*dly*, About the work, that may mar its acceptance.

(1.) It may be none of the work of the Spirit of Christ in the man, but proceeding from a man's self allenarly. All good works accepted of God are the product of the Holy Spirit in believers, as the sap which the vine-stock communicates to the branches. Therefore to "the works of the flesh ;" Gal. v. 19, are opposed "the fruits of the Spirit ;" ver. 22. And "all goodness is the fruit of the Spirit ;" Eph. v. 9, and a Christian's life is "a walking after the Spirit ;" Rom. viii. 1, as a borrowed life. And as no common hearth-fire could be accepted at the altar, but only the holy fire that came from heaven ; so no work will be offered to the Father for acceptance by the Son, but what is the work of his own Spirit ; and no work will be accepted by the Father, but what is offered by the Son as intercessor. See Eph ii. 18. See what prayer is accepted, Jam. v. 16. Not the prayer of every one, but of a "righteous man ;" not every prayer of a righteous man neither, but "the inwrought" (*Gr.*) "prayer" of his, viz. that which is inwrought by the Spirit.

(2.) It may be no work of love to God, or of a willing mind ; but done awkwardly and against the grain ; 1 Tim i. 5 ; some bye-considerations moving the man to serve the Lord ; and no liking of him or his service. Forced service can never be accepted, that which people are constrained to. It is the obedience of slaves, not of sons, that natural men do perform ; and flows from a spirit of fear, more than a spirit of love ; 2 Tim. i. 7. See Isa. lxiv. 5.

(3.) It may be not done in faith, and so cannot be accepted ; Heb. xi. 6. Acceptable service is done in the faith of the command, having authority on the man's conscience ; and in the faith of the promise, the promise of strength to perform, and the faith of the reward of grace, believing the labour shall not be in vain in the Lord, 1 Cor. xv. ult. But instead of that, most of our good works are done without any regard to God's authority, without any dependence on him for strength, and without the true hope of the gratuitous reward of grace won by Christ to be communicated to us.

(4.) It may be done selfishly; men seeking their own profit in them, more than God's honour; seeking to please their own conscience that otherwise will not let them rest, rather than to please God; seeking a name to themselves, rather than to glorify his name; and to save their own souls from hell by them, rather than to testify their thankfulness to the Saviour, who has purchased salvation by his blood. This is to pervert the end of duties, to use them for unhallowed ends; in a word, to serve ourselves, and not God; and therefore no more to be accepted than a servant's working his own instead of his master's work, Hos. ix. 4; Zech. vii. 6. Yea good things may be done downright to serve a lust, or to satisfy a passion, Matth. xxiii. 14; 2 Sam. iii. 9.

(5.) It may be done by chance rather than design; Lev. xxvi. 21; (Heb.) There are who are chance-customers to religion, who fall in with a good work, rather because it falls in their way, than because God lays it in their way; as the Danites, Judg. xviii. 5. God looks to the heart, and undesigned service to him will be reckoned no serving of him, but serving one's own fancy. This is another thing than one's embracing an opportunity which the Lord puts in his hand; Gal. vi. 10, wherein one is glad of an occasion of serving God.

(6.) It may be done by the power of custom, rather than of conscience. Custom, fallen into by education, or otherwise, is the spring of many duties done by men; wherein men move, by that, as a clock by the weights; rather than from an inward principle; which can never be acceptable to the heart-searching God, who requires reasonable service.

(7.) It may be done in a slighting manner, dealing scrimply and grudgingly with God. As when there is no proportion between the work and one's ability, as in the rich men casting in their little piece of brass-money, Mark xii. 41; when men offer to God, not the best, but the most worthless they have; so did Cain, Gen. iv. 3, 4. Thus men by thinking any thing may serve in the service of God, pour contempt on the holy One, and bring on themselves a curse instead of a blessing; Mal. i. 14.

(8) Lastly, When it is not offered to God for acceptance through Christ. It is God's appointment; Col. iii. 17, " Whatsoever ye do in word or deed, do all in the name of the Lord Jesus." A young pigeon would have been accepted on the altar of Jerusalem, when a bullock would not have been accepted on the altar of Bethel. If the service of men be never so great and costly, if it is offered to God otherwise, and the acceptance of it looked for because of its own worth, it will be rejected, Rev. vii. 14. No works savour with God, but as they savour of Christ, 2 Cor. ii. 15.

I now proceed to make some short improvement of what has been said,

1. People may do much in the service of God, and yet do nothing to purpose, Eccl. x. 15. A man may go many a weary foot, and yet never come to the place he designed, while he wanders from the right way, 2 John 8. Such wanderers in religion are all unregenerate men, who set about duties; they are busy doing nothing. They do many good things like Herod, and yet they never do one thing acceptably. For their persons are not accepted; and so their works cannot be so.

2. Even among the duties of a godly man, there may be much refuse; many unaccepted duties. A believer's person is always accepted of God, Eph. i. 6, for the state of justification is perpetual. But such may be the prevalence of faithlessness, selfishness, &c., in some particular works of his, that they may never come to be accepted of God; for sanctification has its ups and downs, being liable to many changes.

3. How little reason is there to boast of our works! There is nothing we can do, can be accepted for its own worth. If it be accepted, the meanness of it is seen, the soul is humbled, and no acceptance of is looked for, but for the sake of Christ. If we be so conceited of our work, as to boast of it; it is an evidence that God accepts it not; hence said our Lord unto the Pharisees, Luke xvi. 15, "Ye are they which justify yourselves before men; but God knoweth your hearts; for that which is highly esteemed amongst men, is abomination in the sight of God."

4. What will come of them that do nothing in the service of God at all; but live in the habitual neglect of known duties, are prayerless, slighters of the means of grace, &c.? 1 Pet. iv. 18. If they that set off to the heavenly city may miss the way, and never reach it; sure those that sit still, and never move that way, will never see it. Many soothe themselves in the neglect of duties, because some that do them walk so unlike them; but the case of such is very dangerous; for no habitual neglecters of duties can be saved; and it is in vain for men to make the practice of others an excuse for evil doing.

5. *Lastly*, Take heed how ye perform duties, and satisfy not yourselves with the bare performance, without being solicitous as to the manner, Luke viii. 18. Better is one duty so managed as to be accepted than a hundred otherwise; as one piece of gold is more worth than a hundred counters. But this brings me to

DOCTRINE II. It should be our main concern in our works that they may be accepted of God.

In handling this point, I shall

I. Shew what is the acceptance of our works with God.

II. Give the reasons of the doctrine.

III. Make improvement.

I. I shall shew what is the acceptance of our works with God. It lies in these two things.

1. His being pleased with them; Col. i. 10, "That ye might walk worthy of the Lord unto all pleasing." The accepted work God approves of, and is well pleased with. Though the saints do no works that they are every way pleased with themselves; yet there are some works of theirs that are very pleasing to God. He delights in them, Prov. xv. 8. They are sweet to him, as honey to the mouth, Cant. v. 1. They are sweet as music to the ear, and as beauty to the eye, Cant. ii. 14.

This pre-supposeth them to be good, and agreeable to his will. For evil cannot be pleasing to him, Psalm v. 4. He who is goodness itself, can never be pleased but with what is good, Heb. xiii. 16. The unregenerate do nothing good, Psalm xiv. 2, 3, and so nothing they do is accepted, Heb. xi. 6. The saints do some things good, some things evil; the good is accepted, and the refuse is cast away.

2. His taking them off their hand, as service done to him. God testified his acceptance of the sacrifice by fire, Lev. ix. ult. for the fire made them go up in flames towards heaven, Judg. xiii. 20. See Psalm xx. 3, Gen. iv. 4, 5. So he received them off their hand. He reckons such a work a piece of service done to him, sets it down as it were in his book, in due time to give it a reward of grace, Lev. vii. 18, Mal. iii. 16.

Hence is the after-notice God takes of the good works of his people;—in time, as it fared with Moses, who, refusing to be called the son of Pharaoh's daughter, was afterwards advanced to be king in Jeshurun;—in eternity, as Matth. xxv. He will not forget any of them, Heb. vi. 10, but a plentiful sowing of them will have a plentiful reaping. So they are the surest riches, 1 Tim. vi. 18. Not that the reward is given for their sake, but for Christ's sake; and such is the covenant connection.

QUESTION. How can any of our works be accepted of a holy God, or he be well pleased with them, &c, since there is so much sinfulness attending the best of them?

ANSWER 1. In point of justification they are not, nor cannot be accepted; i. e. our persons cannot be accepted as righteous for our works, since they are not legally perfect, perfect in every point. In the way of the covenant of works, the work was first to be accepted for its own sake, as absolutely perfect; and then the person for the works' sake. So that whosoever seek by their works to be accepted of God, they go back to the covenant of works; and must either bring works every way perfect, or be rejected; and because they cannot do such works, "therefore by the works of the law shall no flesh be justified," Gal. ii. 16.

2. In point of sanctification the good works of the justified may be accepted; *i. e.* one's person being accepted, his works may be accepted, being evangelically perfect, though not legally; being perfect in parts, though not in degrees. For in the way of the covenant of grace, the person is first accepted in Christ, and then his work though imperfect. Hence it appears,

(1.) That to a person's being accepted of God in Christ, there is no working, but believing required; Mark v. 36. For till the person be accepted of God in Christ, he can do no acceptable work. He can yield no savoury fruit till he be ingrafted by faith in Christ.

(2.) That the way to bring sinners to good works, is to bring them to Christ in the first place by faith, that they may be justified and accepted in him. Men may be made proud legalists otherwise, but not evangelical Christians; whited sepulchres, but still full of rottenness.

(3.) That there is very good reason why the good works of unbelievers are rejected, because they are imperfect; and yet the good works of believers are accepted, though they be imperfect. For besides that the principle, motives, and ends of their works are vastly different, there is a great odds between,

[1.] Their states. The one is the King's friend, the other an enemy; the one the King's son, the other but his hired servant. If a man is pleased with a little piece of service that his own child does him, can the hired servant expect that as little will be taken off his hand? Can our enemy expect the same acceptance of his service, as our friend?

[2.] The desired acceptance. The unbeliever desires his work may be accepted for his salvation; but the believer desires his work may be accepted as only a token of his gratitude to his Saviour, who has saved him already. Can any man rationally think, that as little can be accepted at his hand, for the price of salvation, as may be accepted for an acknowledgment of salvation received?

But further to clear this question, consider,

1. Even the acceptance in point of sanctification, is not for the sake of the work itself, nor for the worker's sake neither; but for Christ's sake, and by the means of his intercession. This is clear from the necessity of Christ's intercession to the acceptance of our

works; and that intercession being a pleading of the merit of his own obedience and death; Col. iii. 17; Rev. vii. 14, and viii. 3. It is for the same merit of Christ, that first the believer himself, and then his imperfect works are accepted of God.

2. The sinfulness and imperfections that attend the works of the believer, are not, nor cannot be ever accepted. God is displeased and angry with the dross of sin that cleaves to the believer's best performances; and he never is so well pleased with the good in them, as to accept the ill too. Yea, he may write his indignation against these, when he is pleased with the substance of the work.

3. The main of the accepted work is good, however sinfulness attends it. For the matter of it, it is commanded; for the form of it, it proceeds from a right principle, the love of God; it is done in faith, and to the glory of God. And this is the work of God's own Spirit in the believer; the weaknesses that attend it, proceed from the believer himself. And such works as are good in the main, God will not reject, for the infirmities that attend them. As for those works even of believers that are not thus good in the main, they are not at all accepted.

4. Christ separates the precious from the vile part, and offers the former perfumed with his merit, unto the Father for acceptance, Heb. x. 21, 22; Rev. viii. 3. In every sacrifice there were two very different things, the flesh and the skin and dung. The former came to the altar, the latter never. So Christ separates in a believer's duties that which is from his own Spirit, and that which is from the believer himself puts away this, and presents that to his Father. This was lively represented in the burning of the incense, where the fire being set to it, the finer part went up in flame and smoke, towards heaven; and the gross part, the ashes, remained, and a priest came and carried them away in a golden dish. So is the case here,—the finer part in the saints' services, that which is done by the assistance of the Spirit and in faith, ascends to heaven for acceptance; and the ashes that remain are carried away, in virtue of the free promise, Ezek. xxxvi. 25.

5. *Lastly*, The Father then accepts the precious part for the Son's sake, and for the same sake pardons the guilt of the vile part, the infirmities attending it, Rev. viii. 4; Psalm cxli. 2. The accepted duties go through two hands, first the believer's, then Christ's; their prayers are first said on earth by themselves, then they are repeated in heaven by the Mediator. It is from the second hand only, and on the repetition only, that they are accepted, 1 Kings viii. 32; and in the second hand, and on the repetition, they are not so bulky, but better.

II. I shall next give the reasons of the point, That it should be our main concern in our works that they may be accepted of God. Because,

1. As God is the first cause, so he is the chief end of all things; Rom. xi. ult., "For of him, and through him, and to him are all things." So as we are his creatures, our chief end in all our duties should be to please him; as all the waters coming from the sea do return to it again. This was the duty of Adam in the covenant of works, as sure as he was not to have another God, as in the first command; though he was to gain life by his works, which we are not, and therefore it is surely ours much more.

2. Our duties are a matter of gratitude; we owe them to God, not only in point of justice, but thankfulness, for benefits received, creation, preservation, and redemption; Exod. xx. 2, "I am the Lord thy God, which have brought thee out of the land of Egypt, out of the house bondage." We are in debt to him, and we cannot pay, but only acknowledge by small tokens, Hos. xiv. 2. If we are to offer to a fellow creature a token of our obligation to him, the first question is, What is it that I can give that will be most acceptable to him? How much more should the first question be, What is it that I can give that will be most acceptable to God?

3. God looks mainly to the heart with which a duty is done, and knows whether he gets it or not, 1 Chron. xxviii. 9. Though a servant do well, yet if he hath no regard to his master's pleasure in what he does, it is disobliging; and whatever men do, if it is not their main aim to please God, it is provoking. Our aims may be hid from men; but they are as open to God as our overt actions.

4. *Lastly*, It is a necessary ingredient in a good work, so that a work cannot be good without it, 1 Cor. x. 31. For such a work is pointed wrong as to the end of it, Zech. vii. 5. It is a sacrifice wanting the heart, the thing that God mainly requires and delights in, Prov. xxiii. 26. So whatever we may account it, God will not account it a good work.

I come now to the practical improvement of this doctrine, which I shall discuss in a twofold use, viz., of conviction, and of exhortation.

USE I. This doctrine may serve for conviction, humiliation, and reproof to men, who generally are strangers to it, and at best very defective in it. It may convict men,

1. In point of ill works. These are fruitful in the world, things that are altogether evil, and cannot be good, Gal. v. 19. In the midst of gospel-light they overflow, and there is no true repentance for them, because there is no reformation. To such workers I would say,

(1.) How far are ye from regarding at all God's acceptance of your works, who take the liberty to do against the letter of his law, what ye know his soul abhors ?   The drunkard, swearer, sabbath-breaker, or unclean person, is not so abandoned as to think that these his actions can please God.   But the truth is, the pleasing of God is what he is not anxious about, but he is resolved to please himself in his lust, let his Maker take it as he will.   What must be the end of these things ? Rom. i. 18, " For the wrath of God is revealed from heaven against all ungodliness, and unrighteousness of men, who hold the truth in unrighteousness."

(2.) Ye thereby evidence, that it is not the pleasing of God, but yourselves, that ye seek in your good works ; and that therefore your ill works and your good works will all go one way, being rejected of God ; your swearing and your praying, &c. will be reckoned all one.   If it were your main design in one thing to please God, it would be so in all, Jam. ii. 10, 11 ; and therefore since ye do not endeavour to please him in all, know that ye can please him in nothing ; Psalm cxxv. ult., " As for such as turn aside unto their crooked ways, the Lord shall lead them forth with the workers of iniquity."

2. In point of good works, namely, those that for the matter of them are good, wherein men may be accepted of God, if they rightly manage them.   These are of three sorts :—

1st, Natural good works, such as eating and drinking, sleeping, &c.   I call them good works, because they are commanded of God, are necessary to be done, and it would be sin to omit them.   They are duties of the sixth command, the neglect whereof is sinful, Col. ii. ult., and one may be accepted of God in them, Rom. xiv. 3, or rejected of him, Zech. vii. 6.   Bring these works of ours to this rule, That it should be our main concern in our works, that they may be accepted of God ; and how may we stand convicted of,

(1.) Regardlessness of God's approbation and acceptance in these things ; having no eye to God in them, but going about them as men without God in the world, or as beasts, Matth. xxiv. 38, without any regard to God's command requiring our use of them, dependence on God for the benefit of them, or design to be strengthened by them for serving God in the duties of religion and our particular calling.

(2.) Dishonouring of God in them.   In the way of purchasing them, many an ill shift is made for the belly ; and if men can get it, to satisfy the appetite, they are not anxious about their right to it before God, whether it be with a good conscience their own bread, got with honest labour and industry, 2 Thess. iii. 12 ; or whether doing their utmost with their industry, they have a right to it as charitable supply.   In the way of using them, without conscientious moderation, by gluttony or drunkenness; a sinful eagerness to satisfy a lust for them; and unfitting themselves for the service of God by them.

It is but a little the time of eating and drinking will last; there is an eternity to be spent without them. If we endeavour to be accepted of God in them while they last, it will be our comfort when we shall for ever lay them aside; if not, the regardlessness and dishonouring of God in them, will be an eternal sting in the conscience.

2*dly*, Civil good works, which are the duties of men's station, in the common affairs of this life; such as the management of family affairs, the duties of service, of a man's lawful trade or employment. These are good works on the matter, being commanded of God, and in which one is to walk with God, 1 Cor. vii. 24; and therein one may be accepted, Eccl. ix. 7, or rejected, Prov. xxi. 4. Here again men may be convicted of,

(1.) Regardlessness of God's acceptance, Luke xvii. 28. These things mostly are managed without any eye to God, or to be accepted of him in them. His command and call by his providence unto them is not waited for; or if men have it, yet they do not regard it, to go about their business under a sense of God's command, Eph. vi. 7. The Lord is not looked to for direction, but men trust themselves for conduct in these matters, Prov. iii. 5, 6. He is not depended on for success, but men are either flushed with presumptuous confidence, or tormenting anxiety as to events, Psalm cxxvii. 1. And not God's word is the rule they act by in them, but their own worldly interest or ease.

(2.) Dishonouring God in them. As by pride, passion, and selfishness, which are to be found in people's managing of their family affairs; if they get their business done, there is no concern how their families should serve the Lord. He is dishonoured by the unfaithfulness, dishonesty, eye-service, and perverseness of servants; and dishonoured by the lying, cheating, and injustice used by men in their dealings in their several employments.

These things are but time things either; and all the hurry of worldly business will be hushed ere long; and death will draw the busiest man out of the throng, as clean as if he had never been in it, Eccl. ix. 6. It will be your interest to seek to be accepted of God in them; otherwise ye will lay up bitterness from them, that will be lasting when they are gone for ever.

3*dly*, Religious good works, the duties whether of the first or second table, which are duties of our Christian calling, such as prayer, giving alms, &c. In them also men may here be convicted of,

(1.) Regardlessness of God's acceptance in them. Men proclaim this by their rash approaching to them, without considering what they are to be about, Eccl. v. 1 ; by their formality in them, satisfying themselves with the doing of the thing, without any anxiety to get their hearts up to the duty, to do it in a right manner, which is mere bodily exercise, 1 Tim. iv. 8; and their carelessness after them, unconcernedness as to their success, when once the task is off their hand, Psalm v. 3.

(2.) Making other things our main concern in them : As, [1.] A name for religion, Matth. vi. 2. An unholy heart, that is an enemy to religion at bottom, may be very fond of a name for it. And to advance this empty name, many times good gifts are prostituted, and enlargements in duty, and great performances for God ; all of them running in that channel of ambition, to be highly esteemed of men as religious. [2.] Some worldly interest, John vi. 26, 27. So it was with Jehu. They will please men for their carnal interest, and do religious duties to please men. Often doth the fear of men go deeper here than the fear of God; and the loss of some worldly interest deeper than the loss of the soul. [3.] Peace in their own minds. There is a conscience within men that will drive to duty, when there is no love to God drawing; so men by such duties rather seek to please themselves than to please God. And, (1.) To keep conscience quiet, while it is quiet ; so duties are made a bribe to cause conscience hold its tongue. And certain it is, that many could not live so quietly in their sins as they do, were it not for their duties, as appears from the case of the adulterous whore, Prov. vii. 14, 15. This is the reason that publicans and harlots enter into the kingdom of heaven before Pharisees ; and Laodicea's case was the most hopeless of all the seven churches. (2.) To still it again when it is roused, Psalm lxxviii. 34. Men may be very anxious for comfort by duty, that have no concern for sanctification thereby. [4.] Salvation from hell and wrath, Matth. xix. 16—20. One may follow duties on this account, without any love to God, as appears ver. 22, " But when the young man heard that saying, he went away sorrowful : for he had great possessions." Self is a strong motive, and heaven and hell are strong arguments for duty ; but the misery is, they seek not God for himself, but for themselves, and so are rejected, 2 Tim. i. 7.

In these duties we are now on our trials for heaven; in a little the sentence will be passed, according to our works. And those who are not now accepted of God in their duties, will then be rejected of God for ever.

Use II. Let it be your main concern in your works, that they may be accepted of God ; whether they be natural, civil, or religious. For motives, consider,

1. This is a distinguishing character of one's state, whereby ye will prove yourselves either gracious or graceless. It is a native result of justification and acceptance of one's person with God, to be mainly concerned for God's acceptance of them in their work, 2 Cor. v. 9. So Noah's integrity and uprightness is traced to his justification as the source, Gen. vi. 9. For so the love of Christ constrains. Whereas the soul being in a state of enmity with God, natively issues in no concern to please him.

2. God is a great God and King, infinitely above the greatest on earth ; he cannot be profited by our services, but requires us to labour to please him in them, Mal. i. 14. He gave us our being, and hath put each of us in our station, and carved out our work for us ; whence it necessarily follows, that it should be our main concern to please him, 2 Tim. ii. 4. And would men more narrowly consider this, that it is God that has set them their business and station, and consequently, that he will call for the account of our work, it would stir them up to make it their main care in their works, that they may be accepted of him.

3. There is a costly provision of an altar on which our sacrifices of praise may be accepted, Heb. xiii. 10, 15. There was nothing a sinner could have done, that could have been accepted; had there not been an altar to sanctify the gift. Now it is provided, a crucified Christ is that altar ; he by his death has become a proper intercessor for acceptance, both of our persons and our works. How heinous will our sin be, if we seek not to bring our gift to this altar, for acceptance with God ?

4. Whatever good work, natural, civil, or religious, we do, may be accepted of God, as pleasing service to him through Christ, Heb. xiii. 15, 16. Men are hugely mistaken to think that it is only works strictly called religious, that God accepts as service to him ; nay, whatever God calls for at thy hand, as to tend the sheep, as well as to attend his worship, if thou act in it to please him, and offer it to him for acceptance through Christ, it will be accepted, Col. iii. 23, 24. It is observable, that the apostle having given that general direction, ver. 17, " Whatsoever ye do in word or deed, do all in the name of the Lord Jesus," &c. falls immediately on relative duties, ver. 18, " Wives, submit yourselves unto your own husbands," &c.

5. The example of Christ may be very moving here, Rom. xv. 3, "For even Christ pleased not himself." His work was heavy work, but to please his Father he undertook it, set about it, and went through

with it, John viii. 29, Psalm xl. and John iv. 34. And shall not we be concerned to please him in our imperfect works, to please whom Christ laid down his life?

6. If ye be mainly concerned for acceptance with God in your work, ye may expect help from the Lord in it. The waters and rivers run all to the sea, and so they are fed again by the sea, that they never run dry. That work that has God's pleasure for its end will get God's hand to it for its help, Phil. ii. 12, 13, Prov. iii. 6. The man that slights God in his natural and civil actions, provokes God to leave him in them, Josh. ix. 14, and then his own understanding that he leaned to, proves folly. And he that slights God in his religious duties does the same, and his gifts prove a broken reed.

7. Whatever be the success of your work, ye will have solid peace, satisfaction, and comfort, in your having been mainly concerned in your works for God's acceptance, Isa. xlix. 4. Men are great fools, to promise themselves success on their own wise management of their natural and civil actions. It has been a truth from the beginning, and will be to the end of the world, that "the race is not to the swift, nor the battle to the strong, neither yet bread to the wise, nor yet riches to men of understanding, nor yet favour to men of skill, Eccl. ix. 11. And it is equally foolish to expect the world's thanks for doing them a good turn; for ye will be fair to be disappointed, 2 Tim. iii. 1, 2, and look blunt on the disappointment. Nay, such an ill-natured world it is, that it is one to a thousand if they be not heavy on you for it. For, says Solomon, Eccl. iv. 4, "I considered all travel, and every right work, that for this a man is envied of his neighbour." But when this is one's main concern, he has what he looked for; 2 Cor. i. 12, "For our rejoicing is this, the testimony of our conscience, that in simplicity and godly sincerity, not with fleshly wisdom, but by the grace of God, we have had our conversation in the world, and more abundantly to you-wards."

8. If ye do not thus, your works will be lost; lost with God, and lost for eternity; and if that be, all that ye will find of them in the world, will be little worth, Matth. vi. 2. This is our sowing time, good works are the seed; will it not be sad to lose all, so as in the harvest ye have nothing to reap? So it will be, if in this your sowing time ye do not throw in the seeds of good works, and make it your principal concern to look for acceptance with God in them; all ye do will be lost for ever, ye will have nothing to reap in the harvest at the last day.

9. *Lastly*, If ye do not, your best works will be turned to sin, Prov. xv. 8, and ye will be surprised to find so many actions of

yours that ye set down in the roll of good works, appear in God's book in the roll of sins; as cockle instead of barley. There is such a thing, Psalm cix. 7, " Let his prayer become sin."

For direction in this point, we proceed to

DOCTRINE III. Where there is a willing mind carrying out a man to do and serve the Lord, to his ability, what is so done is accepted of God.

Here I shall shew,

I. What sort of works they are that are accepted of God.

II. How or in what respect they are accepted.

III. Why they are so.

IV. *Lastly,* Apply.

I. I am to shew what sort of works they are that are accepted of God.

FIRST, They are works done with a willing mind. Wherein we are to consider,

1. What this willingness relates to.

2. What it is.

First, Let us consider what this willingness relates to. This willingness of the soul respects the will of God, as that which the soul is willing to comply with. The will of God is contained in his commands, summed up in a word, 1 Thess. iv. 3, " This is the will of God, even your sanctification ;" and it is the duty of all of us to be willing to that will of God, 1 Chron. xxviii. 9, and to say as Psalm xl. 8, " I delight to do thy will, O my God." Hence,

1. A work accepted of God is a commanded work, required of us by God himself, and not an unrequired work, Rev. xxii. 14, " Blessed are they that do his commandments." Matth. xv. 9, " In vain they do worship me, teaching for doctrines the commandments of men." Therefore,

(1.) Nothing in itself sinful can ever be accepted of God ; though people may pretend they have no ill in their mind against God in doing it ; yea though they may have a good intention in it to serve God by it, John xvi. 2. Yet how many do, on these pretences, lie without any check, and do other ill things ? Prov. xxvi. 18, 19, " As a madman who casteth firebrands, arrows, and death ; so is the man that deceiveth his neighbour, and saith, Am not I in sport ?"

(2.) Nothing, that is not required of God, though it be not in itself sinful, can be accepted of him, Matth. xv. 9. For there can be no obedience, where there is not a command ; these are relatives. If God command us not, we cannot be said to obey him, nor be accepted of him. Hence, [1.] Will-worship is false worship, and service to God just of men's own devising is not, nor can be accepted ; Col. ii. 21—23, " Devised of one's own heart," is a brand of rejection fixed on a work, that is not in itself evil, 1 Kings xii. ult. And Saul lost the kingdom on such a work, 1 Sam. xv. 21. [2.] Doing a duty not the duty of one's station cannot be accepted, 1 Cor. vii. 24. It was a duty to sacrifice, and to burn incense; yet Saul provoked the Lord by his doing the one, and Uzziah was smitten with leprosy for doing the other; because though they were duties, yet they belonged not to their stations. In a well-ordered family, one servant must not take his neighbour's work and post.

2. The command of God requiring the work must be known to the doer; for otherwise men serve the Lord but at a venture, not knowing whether it be his will or no, which can never be accepted, Lev. xxvi. 21. The acceptable work must be done in faith, faith of the command of God, implying knowledge of it, Rom. xiv. ult.

The sum of the whole lies here. If ye would have your work accepted of God, ye must (1.) Know it to be a commanded duty. (2.) Commanded to you. The want of either will mar the acceptance, as a duty not proceeding from a willing mind.

Secondly, Let us consider what this willingness of mind is. It is twofold, habitual and actual.

1. Habitual; which is a disposition of the soul to comply with the will of God's commands, arising from the new nature given in regeneration or the saving change; Heb. viii. 10, " I will put my laws into their mind, and write them in their hearts." Psalm cx. 3, " Thy people shall be willing in the day of thy power, in the beauties of holiness from the womb of the morning." The carnal unrenewed mind is enmity against God and his law, Rom. viii. 7. And while that corrupt set abides on the heart predominant, as in all natural men, there can be no true willingness to comply with the will of God. Hence, that any work of ours may be accepted of God, we must be,

(1.) United to Christ by faith, John xv. 5. While we continue in our natural state, growing on the old stock of the first Adam, we can bring forth no fruit acceptable to God; for the whole nature is corrupt according to the stock, and so must the fruit be, Rom. vii. 5. Particularly there is a reigning refractoriness in the will, whereby the soul is as a bullock unaccustomed to the yoke of God's will. Whereas the soul being in Christ is changed, according to the nature of the new stock, and made willing, 2 Cor. v. 17, and gets his image, opposed to Adam's, 1 Cor. xv. 49.

(2.) We must be regenerated, and have our nature changed. The tree must be made good, before the fruit can be so, Ezek. xxxvi. 26, 27. How can there be a willing mind for duty, while the will is unrenewed? How can there be new obedience, while one is not partaker of the new nature? The dark mind, the perverse will, and disorderly affections, not rectified by regenerating grace, being all of them opposite to good, shew the want of a willing mind.

(3.) We must have a predominant love to God, 1 Tim. i. 5. This disposeth the soul, by a constraining force, to fall in with whatsoever the Lord requires; and constitutes one's obedience labour of love. And where it is wanting, good things may indeed be done, for some by-ends, and from some by-principles; but there is not first a willing mind.

This is the habitual willing mind, whereby the soul being in Christ, regenerated, and having the love of God dwelling in it, is in such a disposition to fall in with the will of God, that getting a touch of a particular command, it readily complies therewith in obedience.

2. Actual; which is an actual compliance of the heart, with such and such a particular duty, laid before one at such a time and in such a place; and ariseth from the habitual disposition. The one looks to the whole law; the other to particular commands requiring such and such a particular duty, as of the Corinthians to help the poor saints of Judea. And it implies,

(1.) An approbation of the command of God for the duty. What the Lord by his word and providence requires of the man as duty, he has a love and liking of it from the heart, Rom. vii. 12. The carnal heart rises against this and the other command laying such a duty on the man; and he takes it on as a slave does his burden, because he cannot help it. But the willing mind has a liking of it, 1 John v. 3, as the little child has a liking of being bid do any little piece of service for his father.

(2.) A sincere resolution to set to the work in the season thereof, Josh. xxiv. 15; Psalm cxix. 106. The willing mind goes not about to seek how to shift obedience to the divine call; nor does it seek offputs and delays, till the season of the duty is away; nor does it muster up difficulties, saying, "There is a lion in the way," to palliate disobedience; but resolves to put to hand timely; Psalm cxix. 60, "I made haste, and delayed not to keep thy commandments."

(3.) A compliance of the heart with the command to the duty, because it is God's command, Psalm cxix. 4. The authority of God has weight with the man's conscience; and the love of God inclines his heart to obey. So the will of God is the reason, as well as the rule, of his obedience. As he believes the promise, because God has said it; so he obeys the command, because God has bid it. So the man's great aim is to answer the call of God, and please him.

(4.) A delight and cheerfulness in the duty, Isa. lxiv. 5; 2 Cor.

ix. 7. Love to the Lord oils the wheels of the soul, and the work goes on, not as of necessity, but as of choice, 1 John v. 3. The awfulness of the command is vailed with prevailing love; take off the threatening of wrath from the command, and the willing soul would not stop for all that; for the love of God in the heart is a law, and a powerful one too, Cant. viii. 6. Terror drives to duty, but weakens; love draws to duty, and strengthens, 2 Tim. i. 7. Terror will make men find their hands, but they lose heart; but love gives heart and hand too.

(5.) A design to honour God by the duty. The general direction is plain; 1 Cor. x. 31, " Whether ye eat or drink, or whatsoever ye do, do all to the glory of God;" and thereto the willing mind echoes back, " To me to live is Christ, Phil. i. 21. The willing mind is not obtained but by faith, whereby the conscience is made good, and the soul put in a state of salvation; hence natively follows the design of glorifying God by good works, and by them adorning the doctrine of God our Saviour, 1 Pet. ii. 9. The faith of Christ's salvation makes a powerful impression of gratitude on the soul, that it is glad of an occasion to glorify him, and express its love; Psalm cxvi. 12, " What shall I render unto the Lord, for all his benefits towards me ?"

(6.) *Lastly*, A looking-out for promised help to the duty, by faith, Heb. xii. 1, 2. The willing mind is not blind to its own weakness, but sees that better than others. But what one is really willing and hearty for the doing of, he will use all means for reaching his end. Carnal men say they are willing but they cannot; in that they deceive themselves, for if they were really willing they would go to the fountain of strength for help. So do they with whom is first a willing mind, they set about the duty in the faith of the promise. Hence they will go forward on God's call, however difficult the work be, and get through too; as the women came to the sepulchre, though not knowing how the stone would be rolled away.

Secondly, They are works that from a willing mind are done to their ability. We may take up this in these four things.

1. They are works which people having ability for, are done; they are not merely wished and woulded to be done, as the sluggard uses to wish well with folded hands, Prov. xxi. 25. For where the heart is to a work, the hand will be put to it, so far as in them lies. Men do but deceive themselves, who please themselves with good desires and wishes, without endeavours backing them; Matth. vii. 21, " Not every one that saith unto me, Lord, Lord, shall enter into the kingdom of heaven; but he that doth the will of my Father which is in heaven." Jam. i. 22, " But be ye doers of the word, and not hearers only, deceiving your own selves."

2. They are done according to the ability they could get in. That is, not only according to the ability in hand, but the man labours to get more ability for the work, whereby he may be fitted for it. We are naturally impotent for any good work; but there is a store-house of strength opened to us in Christ, to be brought in by faith, Isa. xlv. 24. Wherefore they that are not concerned to fetch in strength for duty, but are unable for duty, and hold themselves so, will not be accepted; for there is no willing mind there.

3. They are not done quite below what they might have done, and was in the power of their hand, Isa. xxxii. 5. Where there is an utter disproportion betwixt one's ability and service, it cannot be accepted but that service brings a curse instead of a blessing, Prov. xi. 24. Hence a certain quantity of service may be accepted off one's hand that will not be accepted off another's, Luke xii. 48. Where God gives much, he requires the greater returns.

4. *Lastly*, They are works wherein the willingness of the mind carries out the hand to do, as far as it can reach, 2 Cor. viii. 3. The willing mind loves to serve the Lord, and to serve him liberally; and so carries a man to do to his power.

II. The next general head is to shew how or in what respect such a work is accepted. God accepts such works,

1. As obedience to him and a doing of his will, Matth. xxv. 21. As the willing mind is peculiar to those within the covenant of grace, so it is the privilege of those in that covenant to have their works so done, accepted, though imperfect. There is not one piece of obedience they can do that is perfect, or could be sustained as obedience according to the covenant of works; but God in Christ, in virtue of the covenant of grace, accepts such imperfect works as obedience pleasing to him, Acts xiii. 22.

2. As a token of their love to God, Heb. vi. 10. A love-token is accepted, though not great, if according to the ability of the giver; especially with God, who looks more to the heart it is given with, than the gift. Some offered gold and precious stones for the service of the tabernacle; some but goats' hair and rams' skins; the latter as well as the former was accepted, where they gave according to their ability with willingness.

3. So as to be rewarded, 1 Cor. xv. ult. As believers' good works are tokens of their love to God, so God gives them tokens of his good pleasure with their works, not of debt, but of grace. To those that improve the abilities they have, he oft-times gives more ability, "To him that hath shall be given." However, accepted good works are a seed that will never miss a rich harvest sooner or later.

III. I proceed to shew why such works are accepted. It is not for their own worth; for the best works of the saints are attended with such sinfulness, that they could not be accepted in the eye of the law; but have in them more than sufficient matter of condemnation, Isa. lxiv. 6. But they are accepted through special privilege.

1. Being sanctified through the Spirit, Rom. xv. 16. Every work of ours is defiled by us, being in ourselves unclean creatures; but the Spirit works in believers, sanctifying them and their works. And he sanctifies their works, by influencing them to work, and in their work exciting them, giving gracious abilities; particularly working in them that approbation and liking of the command, that resolution to set about the work, that compliance of the heart with it, that delight and cheerfulness in the duty, that design to honour God by it, and that looking out for promised help, which I have spoken of before, and causing them to offer their works to God through Christ.

2. They are presented for acceptance, by the Mediator to the Father. Christ is the believers' resident in the court of heaven, managing all their matters there by his intercession, Heb. vii. 25. He takes their imperfect works, perfumes them with the merit of his obedience and death, and gains their acceptance with the Father, according to the covenant of grace, Rev. viii. 3, 4. The sum of the matter lies here; they are the work of his own Spirit in his children, presented for acceptance by the Son, and so they are accepted of the Father, Eph. ii. 18.

Use. From what is said, we may draw the two following inferences :—

1. See here of what concern it is to get the heart up to every duty, 1 Chron. xxviii. 9. The doing of the bare work is of small account with God; and where there is not a heart to it, God regards it not. A good work done grudgingly, whatever use it may be for among men, is an ill work in God's sight.

Question. How may one get up his heart to every duty?

Answer (1.) Accept of Christ's free salvation by faith, that ye may be brought into a state of salvation. We have a spirit of slaves, a backwardness to good, derived from Adam. It is from Christ we must get the spirit of sons, and the willing mind, uniting with him by faith, John i. 16. Faith trusting on Christ for salvation to be received freely, works that willingness of mind.

(2.) Exercise faith for every duty anew. Believe the promise, [1.] Of assistance by the Spirit, Ezek xxxvi. 26, 27. In the covenant of grace commands are turned to promises, as Deut. x. 16, " Circumcise the foreskin of your heart." Compare Deut. xxx. 6, " The Lord thy God will circumcise thine heart." Every call to duty implies a promise of assistance. The belief of this makes willing, Phil. ii. 12, 13. [2.] Of acceptance through Christ. The apostles' work was heavy, but that made them willing, 2 Cor. ii. 15, "For we are unto God a sweet savour of Christ, in them that are saved, and in them that perish." It is hard to be willing to a work, which one does not believe will be accepted.

2. See of what concern it is to put hand to every duty commanded us, and to do in it according to one's power ; and not to content ourselves with lazy wishes as some do, and slack and scrimp performances as others, Eccl. ix. 10. Neither will to wish and do nothing be accepted ; nor to do, but do niggardly. It is not in every case that God will accept the will for the deed.

1st, God will not accept the natural or unregenerate man's will for the deed, in any case. For such a one is under the covenant of works, and no less than works every way perfect can be accepted off his hand, Gal. iii. 10. But this is a privilege of the covenant of grace, which they are not under, not being in Christ. It is the privilege of sons, but they are but at best hired servants, working for hire, nay slaves, as under the curse. Their persons are not accepted ; therefore nothing they are, have, or can do, can be accepted. Therefore deceive not yourselves, looking for this benefit, while ye are out of Christ.

2dly, God will accept no man's will for the deed,

(1.) When they content themselves with wishing only they could do a duty commanded them, but yet never essay it, nor put hand to it, Prov. xxi. 25. The sluggard unwilling to obey, makes a cover for his sloth, of the difficulty and his inability for duty, Prov. xxii. 13. But God will rend off that cover, and shew them in their own colours, Matth. xxv. 24—30. Men cannot deny but that such a thing is their duty, and they wish they could, but that is all.

(2.) When they do not what is really in their power to do, Rom. i. 20, 21. Men's power is indeed little, but their doing is far less. Men are not as stocks and stones, but there are many things acts of moral discipline, that they may and can do, but they will not. But they grasp at the principle, that they can do nothing, and so fold their hands, sitting down contented. They cannot do all, therefore they will do nothing. But will that be accepted ? No, Exod. xiv. 15. The women did not so, Mark xvi. 2, 4.

(3.) Lastly, When they do not by faith fetch in grace from the Lord Jesus to strengthen them to duty, 2 Tim. ii. 1, compared with John v. 40. Many a good work is laid by, because of inability, and marred because we can carry it no further; but God will take notice what course is taken for getting in strength for duty. There are full promises lying between us and the full fountain, as the conduit-pipes at which faith is to suck and draw, Isa. xl. 29—31. Assure yourselves that the will will not be accepted for the deed, while this is neglected. And why should it? Is that man willing to pay his debt, who though he has nothing in hand, yet has a gift lying in a rich friend's hand, but he will not lift it? See the decision; Matth. xxv. 27, "Thou oughtest to have put my money to the exchangers, and then at my coming I should have received mine own with usury."

I shall now consider in a few words the last doctrine I offered from the text, viz.

DOCTRINE IV. Want of power to do more, shall not mar the acceptance of what is done from a willing mind according to power. In that case, God will accept of his people's will for the deed.

Here I shall shew,

I. In what particular cases God accepts his people's will for the deed.

II. Why he does so.

III. Apply.

I. I am to shew in what particular cases God accepts his people's will for the deed.

1. Where there is a sincere will to serve him in a piece of work, requiring some external abilities which are wanting. If it be hindered only by such want, the will is accepted. The disciples would fain have watched more, but the weak body could not bear up with their mind; and Christ kindly takes notice of it; Matth. xxvi. 41, "Watch and pray, that ye enter not into temptation; the Spirit indeed is willing, but the flesh is weak." Sometimes Satan makes a rack here to God's children; such a duty they would do, but bodily strength will not answer, and hereupon they are disquieted; but that is from Satan, and their own weakness; for God does not require that external duty from us, that we have no bodily strength for. That is a sweet word, 1 Cor. vi. 13, "The body is—for the Lord, and the Lord for the body." Peter would fain have given to the poor man, but had it not, and it was accepted in the will, Acts iii. 6.

2. When doing the best we can through grace, our work after all is attended with many blemishes; the Lord will not reject it for these blemishes, but accepts the will to do better for the deed, Cant. v. 1. There is a broad cover of Christ's righteousness cast over the believer's spots, that they appear not, Cant. iv. 7; and the Lord accepts of the will to that perfection they would be at.

3. Going as far as we have access in a work, but meeting with a

providential stop, the will to complete it is accepted for the deed, as if it had been fully done, as in the case of Abraham's offering up Isaac, Heb. xi. 17. There is a great difference betwixt the stops men make in these, and those which God makes ; the former argues an unwilling mind, but the latter not so.

4. Services that one really desires, and fain would perform for God, but have not opportunity ; the will to them is accepted for the deed, as in the case of David's purposing to build a house for the Lord, 2 Chron. vi. 8 ; and the Philippians care about supplying Paul's wants, Philip. iv. 10. Some have opportunities of usefulness, but slight them ; that is their sin ; others may have a heart to be so and so useful, but they cannot have the opportunity ; this God accepts.

5. *Lastly*, In services performed with a real desire of success for God's honour and men's good ; the Lord accepts the good will to the success denied, as if it had succeeded according to their wish, Isa. xlix. 4; 2 Cor. ii. 15. The want of success may mar their present comfort, but neither the acceptance nor reward.

II. Why does God accept such will for the deed ?

1. The sincere will to a work is present, which God mainly regards. The person sincerely aims at doing such a piece of service for God, but not attaining what he really desires, his good will thereto being present before the Lord, it is accepted, as if the work had been done.

2. We have a merciful High Priest to present that will for acceptance, notwithstanding all the weaknesses, blemishes, providential hindrances, want of opportunity, and failure of success, that it may be attended with, Heb. iv. 15, 16.

3. We have a merciful Father to deal with, Psalm ciii. 13, 14, who pities the weaknesses and infirmities of his people, and graciously accepts of their upright designs to serve and honour him.

Use 1. If the Lord accepts the will for the deed in his own people, then men must answer for the ill they had a will to have done, as if they had done it, Numb. xiv. 42—45. A will and intention to do an evil action, though it be not actually done, is in God's account the same thing with doing it, and will be resented and punished accordingly.

2. God is a gracious master to his servants, taking kindly off their hands through Christ their sincere will to his service, giving them ample testimonies of his regard in all circumstances, and bestowing upon them the special comforts of his grace here, as pledges of the full reward laid up for them in glory hereafter.

JESUS CHRIST THE BELOVED ONE, AND SINNERS ACCEPTED OF
GOD FREELY IN HIM.*

EPH. i. 6,

His grace, wherein he hath made us accepted in the Beloved.

BEFORE our works can be accepted, our persons must; and how that
is attained is here declared.

The apostle taking a view of the state of salvation that believers
are brought into, in the fulness of it, ver. 3; runs it up unto the
prime author of it, the Father, *ib.* the eternal plan of it in the decree of election, ver. 4; whereof the great design to be accomplished on them, their true sanctification, *ib.* to be begun here, and perfected in glory; the reason of this design, that they were predesti-
nated to adoption into his family, for it was inconsistent with the
honour of a holy God, to have unholy children, ver. 5. In this
verse are two things.

1. The great end of God's predestinating the elect to be his own
children; "the praise of the glory of his grace." It was a display
of his free grace that he aimed at. Grace is love and favour freely
flowing, without anything in the object to draw it out. This grace
shown to sinners is glorious grace, like a shining sun, casting such a
lustre, as is most admirable and attractive. And it is to be praised
by the sons of men; but they that do not see, and do not feel the
glory of it, cannot praise it, more than the blind the light of the
sun. But God purposed to bring the elect out of the devil's family, and make them his own children freely; that they seeing,
tasting, and feeling this glorious grace, might raise a song of praise
of it here, and joining voices in heaven, might carry it on in the
highest strain there for ever, praising the glorious grace appearing
in their adoption; opening the various folds of it, and admiring the
glories of free grace, for ever and ever. It is dangerous then to cast
a veil over it, doctrinally or practically.

2. A particular fruit of this glorious grace; "Wherein he hath
made us accepted in the Beloved." Where we have,

(1.) The fruit itself, the acceptance of the persons of believers
with God; "He hath made us accepted." The acceptor is the Father, vers. 3, 5. The accepted are us, believers, who are "blessed
with all spiritual blessings in heavenly places in Christ," ver. 3.
The acceptance is emphatically expressed. The word is, as if he had

---

* The substance of several sermons preached at Etterick in the year 1726.

said, he hath graced us; and imports not only that he hath accepted us, but freely accepted us, without anything in us to render us acceptable; and bears not only free love and favour, but also all kinds of real benefits and favours flowing therefrom, Luke i. 28.

(2.) The way and manner of the acceptance. How can a sinner be accepted of a holy God? "In the Beloved," that is, Christ. It is not only for his sake, but God looking on the sinner in Christ, united to him, accepts him. He calls Christ here "the Beloved," to intimate that the accepting love and favour of God is first pitched on him, and then for his sake comes down on his members; so he is the Beloved by way of eminency. He saith not, "his Beloved," though doubtless he mainly aims at that, but "the Beloved," that he might give a vent to that love to Christ that his heart swelled with on the mention of this; and so uses a general term, whereby Christ might be pointed out as the object whereon the loves of heaven and earth meet together.

(3.) The original spring and source of this acceptance, intimated by the relative wherein. It refers not only to the word grace, but to "the glory of his grace," q. d. From, through, and by which glorious grace and free favour, he hath freely accepted us undeserving and ill-deserving creatures; that glorious grace finding a way to accept the sinner, with the good leave of justice, in Christ.

From the text, thus explained, ariseth the following savoury points of doctrine.

DOCT. I. Jesus Christ is the beloved, the eminently beloved One.

DOCT. II. The way how a sinner comes to be accepted of God, is freely, in Christ.

DOCT. III. Glorious free grace shines forth in the acceptance of sinners in the beloved Jesus.

DOCT. I. Jesus Christ is the beloved, the eminently beloved One.

In discoursing from this doctrine, I shall,

I. Shew in what respects Christ is the eminently beloved One.

II. Make some improvement.

I. I am to shew in what respects Christ is the eminently beloved One.

First, He is the beloved of the excellent ones of the earth. Who these are, ye may see, Psalm xvi. 3. They are "the saints." Him all the saints love with a love above all persons and all things, Luke xiv. 26. And,

1. They meet altogether in him in love, however they are scattered through the world; hence is he called, "the desire of all nations," Hag. ii. 7. So that lovers of Christ and saints are of equal latitude; Eph. vi. 24, "Grace be with all them that love our Lord

Jesus Christ in sincerity." The American saints and the European saints take him all for their Beloved. As it is the same sun in the firmament that warms all their bodies, it is the same Sun of righteousness, Christ, that warms all their hearts in love. They differ vastly in their languages, customs, and particular dispositions; but they perfectly agree in their love of one beloved Jesus; Gen. xlix. 10, "Unto him shall the gathering of the people be." And so they are knit as one body, whereof Christ is the beloved head.

2. Each one of them loves him with a superlative and transcendent love; Psalm lxxiii. 25, "Whom have I in heaven but thee? and there is none upon earth that I desire besides thee." They have a general love to mankind, a special love to their respective countries, a more special love to their relations, but the most special and peculiar love, leaving all the rest behind, is to Christ, Luke xiv. 26. In the other they are divided, but in this they meet in one; their beloved ones are very different, but their beloved One is one and the same.

3. They love other persons and things for his sake, Rom. xv. 2, 3; Tit. iii. 3—5. When the soul is in its natural state, other persons and things have the man's love, but Christ has none of it; when Christ discovers himself in his glory to the soul, then the man hates all in comparison of him; but Christ regulates the soul's love to other things, and takes it not away, but makes it run in another channel, springing from himself. Now other things being loved for him, himself is the best beloved.

4. The liker any thing is to him, they love it the more. Hence the godly that bear his image, are therefore beloved by them; and the more godly they are, the more beloved are they, 1 John iii. 14. They love his ordinances, because they bear the impress of his authority, his law as the image of his nature; his way and example, because of the tread of his steps therein to be seen. All which bear him to be their eminently beloved. And,

1st, They love him with a love of good-will; and vent it in prayer and praise; Psalm lxxii. 15, "Prayer also shall be made for him continually, and daily shall he be praised." It is not in their power to profit him, and he needs nothing at the creature's hand, being completely happy in his Father; but they shew good-will to him, in concern for his glory in the world, that his kingdom may prosper, his name spread far and wide, and be perpetuated to all generations.

2dly, They love him with a love of delight and complacency, 1 Pet. ii. 7, "Unto you which believe he is precious." His name and every letter of it is sweet to them, Cant. i. 3. They delight in him as a sister in a brother, a child in a father, and a spouse in a husband. Everything in Christ is sweet to a believer; therefore they are said to eat his flesh, and drink his blood : for as by eating one finds the sweetness of the meat, and every bit of it, so by faith the soul finds the sweetness of Christ and every thing in Christ. And,

(1.) They love him for what he is in himself, Cant. v. 10—16. The glorious excellencies of his person and natures, his attributes and perfections, make him the object of their love. Their hearts are framed to the love of God : so they love him for himself, they love him for that holiness and purity for which carnal men hate him, as the owl doth the sun, Psalm xxx. 4.

(2.) They love him for what he is to them, Cant. v. 16. And as he is best in himself, he is the best to them. They love him for all his offices ; for what he has done for them, and for what he will do for them. They love him as the foundation of all their hopes, the scope of all their desires, and the spring of all their joys. And fitly does he go under the name, " the Beloved," even in respect of the saints : for,

[1.] They profess him to be the beloved of their souls; they are not ashamed of their choice. So the spouse calls him, Cant. *per tot.* See chap. iii. 3, " Saw ye him whom my soul loveth ?" as if she would have all to know him by that name, " her Beloved;" supposing there is none so but he.

[2.] They show him to be so, by their life and actions before the world, Cant. viii. 6, 7. Where love to Christ is, it will discover itself by the soul's preferring Christ to all persons and things, so as to part with any thing when it comes in competition with him.

Secondly, Christ is the beloved of the glorious ones in heaven. All eyes are upon him there, for he is there the light of the pleasant land, Rev. xxi. 23, as the sun is in this world. And he is there,

1. The beloved of the glorified saints, who now love him in perfection, Rev. vii. 10. Their love to him is now perfected, and they love him with a pure and ardent love. They see him now no more through a glass, but face to face ; they behold the glories of his person, the glories of his actings and sufferings for them ; his eternal undertaking, his going through with his undertaking in his birth, life, and death ; and the glory he now hath from his Father as the reward. So their love to him is in a continual flame.

2. The beloved of the holy angels, Rev. v. 11, 12. In the temple the cherubims were posted, looking towards the ark or mercy-seat, a type of Christ; which signified the angels looking to Jesus with love and admiration, 1 Pet. i. 12. They behold his glory, and cannot but love him. They love him as the brightness of the Father's glory, as the elder Brother of the family, the heir of all things, and

their Lord, Heb. i. 6, as the Saviour of sinners, and the head of angels, by whom they and all things do consist, Eph. i. 10.

3. The Father's beloved, Matth. xvii. 5. And here we may consider Christ two ways, as God, and as Mediator.

1*st*, As God, equal and co-eternal with the Father and Holy Spirit. He was the beloved of the Father and the Spirit. The Scripture teacheth that " God is love," 1 John iv. 8, and that love must be eminently among the persons of the glorious Trinity one towards another. Thus, Prov. viii. 30, he is held out as the Creator's delight. See John i. 18, Heb. i. 2. But what our text mainly aims at, is,

2*dly*, As Mediator, God-man, having a common relation to God and sinners of mankind, as the representative of an elect world, and the bond of union and communion betwixt God and sinners, for the glory of God and the salvation of sinners.

(1.) As such he is the Father's beloved, his prime favourite, and most accepted, his " well Beloved," Mark xii. 6, in whom he is " well pleased;" Matth. iii. ult., the perpetual rest of his eyes and heart, 2 Chron. vii. 16. And he is his beloved,

[1.] In respect of his person; John i. 18. He " is in the bosom of the Father." For he is "the brightness of his Father's glory," Heb. i. 2. The glory of God shines forth in his face, 2 Cor. iv. 6. He is " the image of God" in a peculiar manner, ver. 4. Therefore says he, John xiv. 9, " He that hath seen me, hath seen the Father." See Col. ii. 9, and i. 19. So he is the most beautiful object in the eyes of God, in heaven or in earth ; and accordingly has the highest place in his love, Heb. i. 13.

[2.] In respect of his office. The Father is well pleased with him in the character he took on. And,

(1.) He was well pleased with his undertaking for the great work of sinners' salvation. See with what satisfaction he speaks of it ; Psalm lxxxix. 19, " I have laid help upon one that is mighty ; I have exalted one chosen out of the people." He cordially accepted him as the sinners' surety, and took his single bond for all the elect's debt, and his security for the injured honour of his name. He was the Father's own choice, and he delighted in his choice, Isa. xlii. 1. He so loved the Undertaker, that,

[1.] He promised to be with him, and furnished him with all things necessary for the work, Isa. xlii. 6, and lxi. 1.

[2.] He bestowed eternal salvation on many, before the time the Saviour paid the ransom ; he set them free, and gave them their discharge, before the death of Christ. He rested in the Beloved's engagement.

(2.) He was well pleased with and accepted him in his carrying on the work that he had undertaken.—With his birth, therefore the angels were employed to carry the tidings of it, and sung solemnly on that occasion.—With his entering on his public work at his baptism, testified by a voice from heaven, Matth. iii. ult., and all along, testified by his being always with him, John viii. 29.

(3.) He was well-pleased with his perfecting of the work, by his death and burial. He did in it the most acceptable piece of service to God that ever was done, John x. 17. His sacrifice of himself was of a sweet savour unto God. He so loved him for it, that he raised him up, and set him on his right hand for ever for it, Phil. ii. 8, 9, and accepts the worst of sinners in him, for his sake.

(2.) As such he is the rest of the Holy Spirit, Isa. xi. 2. The Spirit came on the prophets, but he rested on Jesus as the beloved, Matth. iii. 16. All the saints as beloved ones have the Spirit in a measure; but he without measure as the Beloved, John iii. 34. The Spirit is in him as water in the fountain, to be communicated to others, Rev. iii. 1.

I shall conclude this point with a word of application.

Use. I. Hereby ye may try whether ye be saints or not, partakers of the divine nature. If so, Christ will be your Beloved, your eminently beloved One; for so he is to the saints, and so he is to God. And if he is your Beloved,

1. Ye will love him above all, Psalm lxxiii. 25, which will shew itself in desiring him above all, prizing him beyond all, rejoicing most in his favour, and sorrowing most for the want of him; and in loving other persons and things for his sake.

2. Ye will hate sin above all things, because it is most contrary to him, his nature and will, Gen. iii. 15. Ye will hate it universally, constantly as to the habitual bent of your heart, and irreconcilably.

Use II. Of reproof to those who love him not eminently, above all. It is an evidence, that,

1. Ye know him not, John iv. x. None can be let into a discovery of Christ in his glory but must love him, Matth. xiii. 44—46. It is to the blind world only there is no beauty in him for which he is to be desired.

2. That ye are in love with your sins and a vain world. For who would loath the physician but he that loves his disease and cannot part with it?

Use III. Let him be your Beloved then, and give him your heart.

1. He is best worth your love. None has done so much for sinners as Christ has, dying for them. None can do so much for you; he can satisfy the cravings of your souls, and make you happy.

2. If ye love him not, ye will be constructed haters of him, and

enemies to him; 1 Cor. xvi. 22, " If any man love not the Lord Jesus Christ, let him be anathema, maranatha.

DOCTRINE II, The way how a sinner comes to be accepted of God, is freely, in Christ.

In handling this doctrine, I shall,

I. Shew what is implied in it.

II. Consider the nature of a sinner's acceptance with God.

III. The way of it.

IV. Make some practical improvement.

I. I am to shew what is implied in the doctrine. And there are these things implied in it.

First, A state of non-acceptance, or unacceptableness with God, that sinners are in, while they are not in Christ. And we may take up this in these following things.

1. They are offenders ; they have sinned, and provoked him, Rom. iii. 23. Men's doing their duty, and men's misery, may make them unacceptable to men, yea, one may be unacceptable to another, who cannot shew wherefore, only they cannot endure them. But nothing can make us unacceptable to God but sin. So the unacceptable to God are undoubtedly sinners, offenders against him.

(1.) They are sinners in Adam, Rom. v. 12. The root was corrupted, and all the branches withered and rotted in him. So his guilt lies on us by nature, we are deprived of righteousness of nature, and instead of that we have derived a corrupt nature from him; all which makes us unacceptable to God by nature.

(2.) They are sinners in their own persons, who are capable of actual sinning, Gen. vi. 5. They imitate sinning Adam, as well as fall heirs to his offence. The debt left by him on their heads, they do not clear, but increase daily; they continue their rebellion while condemned for it. And so they are more and more unacceptable.

2. They are unpardoned offenders. All have sinned, but some are pardoned and accepted; but none are pardoned who are out of Christ, John iii. ult. The sentence of the broken law stands in force against all those who are not in him, who has fulfilled the law. Ho is " the end of the law for righteousness to every one that believeth," Rom. x. 4. And,

(1.) Their original guilt lies on them, unremoved, unforgiven, 1 Cor. xv. 22. God has never forgiven them their guilt of Adam's first sin, their want of original righteousness, and the corruption of their whole nature. The debt left on them by their father, they were never either able or willing to pay ; and though they may have forgot it, God has neither forgiven nor forgot it, but it lies on them still, to all effects and purposes of a dreadful pursuit for it.

(2.) The guilt of all their actual sins lies on them, Gal. iii. 10. All the sins they have been guilty of, from the first sproutings of corruption in their childhood to this day, are hard and fast on them. None of all their sins of omission or commission, of heart, lip, or life, are forgotten by God, Amos viii. 7, but the accounts are closely kept, Deut. xxxii. 34; Hos. xiii. 12. They may have made a fashion of repenting, and begging pardon, for some of their grosser sins; but since they are not in Christ, there is not one of them blotted out; for " without shedding of blood is no remission," Heb. ix. 22, and there is no saving benefit of Christ's blood, but by being in him, chap. xii. 24.

3. God is not pleased with them; for his being pleased with any of mankind is in his son Jesus Christ, and without him he can be pleased with none of them, Matth. iii. ult.; Heb. xi. 5, 6. He is not pleased with their persons nor with any of their works; because they themselves are not in Christ; but yet in the old stock, Rom. viii. 8, and their works are not wrought in him, John xv. 5. So the apostle teacheth, that it was faith that made the difference between Abel's offering and Cain's, Heb. xi. 4.

4. He is highly displeased with them. There is a cloud of divine displeasure ever upon them, John iii. ult. Whatever case they be in, rejoicing or weeping; whatever they be doing, serving God in their way, or serving their lusts, his countenance is never towards them, because they are not in Christ, Isa. lxvi. 2, 3. There is a displeasure conceived against them on the justest grounds, not to be removed till they be in Christ.

5. He cannot endure them to have any communion or intercourse with them, farther than in the way of common providence, Psalm v. 5. He and they are at enmity, he legally, they really; so there can be no communion, Amos iii. 3. And they cannot have it till they come to Christ, John xiv. 6. God may lay common favours to their hand, health, wealth, &c.; as the condemned man is allowed his meat till the execution; but he grants them no special saving favours, no peace, pardon, &c. He may allow them to come, and call them into the outer court of ordinances, and make them offers of grace; but they cannot come into the inner court, nor partake of grace, not being in Christ, John x. 9.

6. He loaths them, his soul abhors them, as abominable. They are abominable in their persons unto God, as wholly corrupt and defiled, Tit. i. 15, 16. The whole herd of them is so, Psalm xiv. 3. Their works are abominable, even the best of them, like precious liquor in a filthy vessel, Prov. xv. 8. Sin is the abominable thing unto God, Jer. xliv. 4. And all their sins lie on them, and there is

nothing on them to correct the abominable savour of the sinner by them. Sin is abominable in believers too; but the sacrifice of the sweet-smelling savour of Christ corrects it, and is a savour of rest, Gen. viii. 21.

7. *Lastly*, The wrath of God is upon them, and they lie under his curse, John iii. ult., Gal. iii. 10. They are "children of wrath," Eph. ii. 3. There is much wrath on them, and they are liable to more. There is wrath in God's heart against them, in his word, and in his providential dispensations. And if the thread of their life be cut while they are in that state of wrath, they are for ever undone without remedy.

Secondly, A way provided, how sinners may be accepted. The case is not hopeless, but he that is not, may be accepted. The acceptance of some with God is now secured, and cannot be lost. Believers on earth may fall under the frowns of a Father, but never out of the state of acceptance with him; being "accepted in the Beloved." The acceptance of the saints in glory is not liable to the least cloud. The acceptance of some, again, is absolutely hopeless. The fallen angels never can, nor could have been accepted: the damned sometimes might, but can no more now for ever be accepted; they sat their accepted time. But there is a way how sinners in life may be accepted.

1. God is ready to accept of them now, that will come to him in his own way; 2 Cor. v. 19. The Judge of all the earth is set down on a throne of grace, for receiving sinners into favour; and therefore we have now an "accepted time," and "day of salvation," chap. vi. 2.

2. There is ready for sinners what may procure them acceptance with a holy God, Matth. xxii. 4. There is a sacrifice slain and offered, that is of such a sweet-smelling savour, that the most loathsome sinner having the savour of it about him cannot miss to be accepted.

3. There is open proclamation made in the gospel, that all may have the benefit of that sacrifice, and be accepted of God, 2 Cor. v. 19, Matth. xxii. 4. Who they were whom the Father gave to the Son to be redeemed, is a secret; but the ransom is paid, the sacrifice is offered for you to lay hold on and be accepted by. And that is the voice of the gospel.

Thirdly, The sinner's bestirring himself for acceptance with God. There is a way to acceptance, but the sinner must take that way, else he will not get acceptance. He cannot sit still careless, and be accepted: he must be where he is not yet, that is, in Christ; otherwise he can have no acceptance. The sinner's bestirring himself in this matter, takes in these three things.

1. A conviction of unacceptableness to God, John xvi. 8. Men must be convinced of their being unacceptable to God, ere they will come to Christ. It is their not seeing their own loathsomeness, that makes them slight the sacrifice of sweet savour; and think to be accepted of God, while yet they are not in Christ. And for that cause it is needful they get a sight of God's holiness and their own vileness.

2. A weighty concern and uneasiness about it. They must not go on to be easy, whether they be accepted of God or not. As long as a man can live contented without it, he will never be accepted. But the soul shall be brought to that, that all shall be sapless without it.

3. Anxiety of heart for it, Acts ii. 37. There must be earnest longings to be accepted of him, yea the soul must be brought to esteem and so prize it, as to be content with it upon any terms, Acts ix. 6. Not as if these were required to qualify us for acceptance with God; but that without them we will never come into Christ to be accepted in him.

II. The next general head is to consider the nature of a sinner's acceptance with God; and this I shall do, 1. In itself, and 2. In its effects and consequents.

FIRST, I shall consider the nature of a sinner's acceptance with God in itself. And in itself it is a great and unspeakable benefit, and implies these following things.

First, In general, it implies an acceptance of the sinner with God, as a righteous person. A righteous God cannot accept a son of Adam, but as righteous, that is, as being really righteous before him. And so a believer in Christ indeed is, and by faith pleading Christ's righteousness for his righteousness in the sight of God, he is accepted accordingly. The Lord reputes, accounts, and accepts him into favour as a righteous person, 2 Cor. v. 21, Rom. iv. 6, and v. 19. So it stands in two things.

1. God's owning and sustaining a righteousness upon the believer, as answering the demands of the law fully, Rom. iii. 22, and holding him a righteous person thereupon. The sinner standing before him in the Beloved, pleading the Mediator's righteousness, the plea is sustained, and God saith, " Deliver him from going down to the pit, I have found a ransom," Job xxxiii. 24. The law gives in its demands against him, of holiness of nature, righteousness of life, and satisfaction for sin. And it is found that all these demands are satisfied, and that the righteousness upon him fully answers them all, that the law has no more to crave. And so in the very eye of the law, he is through grace held righteous.

2. On the account of that righteousness he is accepted into favour with God, Rom. iii. 24, 25. It was the sinner's unrighteousness that cast him out of God's favour, and held him out of it. Now that bar is taken away, and the righteousness upon him procures the favour of a righteous God, who loveth righteousness. God is perfectly pleased with that righteousness, as much as he ever was displeased with the party's sin; and he is so well pleased with it, that notwithstanding of all the sins the party ever committed, he accepts him into favour for its sake.

Secondly, More particularly, it implies,

1. The ceasing of wrath against the soul, Hos. xiv. 4. The wrath of God no more abides on the accepted person; that cloud clears. And it clears so, that that shower shall never come on again, nor one drop of it, of revenging wrath, for ever and ever, Isa. liv. 9. The small rain of fatherly anger may come on him for his after-miscarriages; but the great rain of his revenging wrath shall never return, Cant. ii. 10, 11.

2. The curse is removed, Gal. iii. 13. That is the sentence of the broken law, that lay on the sinner binding him over to revenging wrath; which seized all mankind in Adam, and which is fortified daily by actual sin, while the sinner is out of Christ. But being accepted in Christ, that is taken away, Rom. viii. 1. The sentence is reversed, ver. 33, 34, the cursed sinner is loosed from that dreadful stake to which he was tied as the mark for the arrows of God.

3. He is fully pardoned, Isa. xliii. 25. The accepted sinner gets the King of heaven's pardon, under his great seal; whereby his guilt of eternal wrath is for ever removed, as if he had never sinned. God takes the pen, dips it in the blood of the Beloved, and blots out his whole accounts. All his past and present sins are formally pardoned, and all his sins to come are secured not to be imputed to him, for guilt of revenging wrath, Rom. iv. 6—8.

4. He is reconciled to God, Rom. v. 1. The Lord lays down the legal enmity he bore against that person, never to take it up again; and he gives him peace through the Beloved, Eph. ii. 14. So that though all the world should be at red war with him, he has a firm peace with heaven, that he needs fear no hostilities from that quarter again for ever; which is enough to settle the heart amidst all troubles, Phil. iv. 7.

5. God is pleased with him, Heb. xi. 5. Still they are sinners indeed, and God can never be pleased with their sins; but their sins hinder not that he be pleased with their persons in Christ. The prodigal son returns to his father in rags, poverty, and want, with not a shoe on his foot; the father is not pleased with the rags on

his son, but natural affection embraces him notwithstanding of his rags, he being his own son. So God embraces the sinner in the Beloved, because he is in him.

6. He is highly pleased with him, Isa. xlii. 21. He is as much pleased with the believer's person, as ever he was displeased with him. He is pleased with him, as one is with his jewels, Mal. iii. 17; as if he saw no sin in them, Num. xxiii. 21; as if there were no spot on them, Cant. iv. 7. In a word, he is infinitely pleased with them, and can never cease to be so. For the only ground of his being pleased with them, is the Beloved in whom they are, his righteousness which is upon them; and he is infinitely pleased with the Beloved and his righteousness, and they are not liable to any alteration, John xvii. 21. Indeed, if their acceptance depended on what is wrought by them, or in them, it could not be so; but it is not set in such a slippery foundation. He is displeased with their sins, and they may smart for them; but the pleasedness with their persons in Christ is not alterable, Col. ii. 10.

7. He admits them into communion with him, 1 John i. 3. The person is let into the inner court, into the chambers of the King, Cant. i. 4. The Lord treats him as a friend, and not as a mere servant, John xv. 15. They are now agreed, and so walk together; and not only agreed, but received into special favour; and are made God's favourites, courtiers of heaven in the Beloved, in the court kept below, Isa. lvii. 15. He dwells and walks in them, 2 Cor. vi. 16; and they dwell in him; 1 John iv. 15; Psalm xc. 1.

8. *Lastly,* God hath a delight and complacency in them, Isa. lxii. 4. He looks on them in his own Son, and takes pleasure in them, as covered with his righteousness. As Isaac smelling the smell of the elder brother's garments on Jacob; so believers are to God a sweet savour of Christ, 2 Cor. ii. 15; and therefore he delights in them, whom before he loathed.

Secondly, Let us consider this acceptance in its effects and consequents. It is in these an unspeakable privilege. By means of it,

1. The springs of mercy are opened to the sinner, that rivers of compassion may flow towards him, Rom. v. 1, &c. Many look for mercy while unaccepted; but the unsatisfied law will draw a bar betwixt all saving mercy and them. But the believer being accepted, the law's mouth is stopt, and mercy may flow freely.

2. He is adjudged to eternal life, 2 Thess. i. 6, 7; Acts xxvi. 18. Life was promised in the first covenant, upon the fulfilling of the law; now the believer being accepted of God as a righteous person, for whom the law is fulfilled, is accordingly adjudged to live for ever.

3. The channel of sanctification is cleared for him, and the do-

minion of sin is broken in him, Rom. vi. 14. While the sinner is unaccepted, and under the curse, communion with God is stopt, and death preys on his soul; for "the sting of death is sin, and the strength of sin is the law," 1 Cor. xv, 56. As long as the law has a cursing and condemning power over a man, sin reigns in him, like briers and thorns in the cursed ground; but these being removed, sin loseth its strength, and the blessing coming in their room makes him fruitful. So faith sanctifies.

4. He is privileged with peace of conscience. Peace with God makes peace within one's breast, Phil. iv. 7. While one is unaccepted of God, guilt lies on the conscience, which makes a foul and condemning one, that will gnaw like a worm, and blast all outward peace and prosperity; but being accepted, the conscience is cleansed, Heb. ix. 14, and turns a good conscience, that will make one rejoice in trouble, 2 Cor. i. 12.

5. Access to God with confidence, Eph. iii. 12; 1 John iii. 21. God allows them whom he accepts, access to him in duties, that they may come to him, as children to a father, with all their wants, complaints, &c. expecting all from him that is really good for them, Job xxxiii. 24, 26. They are privileged with the hearing of their prayers, communion with him in word and providences, receiving, by the means of grace, light in darkness, strength in weakness, health in sickness, &c.

6. Acceptance of their works, Prov. xv. 8. God accepting a man's person in Christ, does next accept his work, Gen. iv. 4. If it were never such a small work, a cup of cold water given one in name of a disciple, though attended with many imperfections, yet being fruit that grows on a branch ingrafted into Christ, it is accepted of God, as savouring of the stock.

7. The unstinging of afflictions and death, 1 Cor. xv. 55. It alters the very nature of these; afflictions are no more properly penal, but correctory and medicinal, Isa. xxvii. 9, and death perfects the cure. A bee-sting they may have, but the serpentine deadly sting is gone; for the curse is removed out of their crosses, and they are blessings.

8. *Lastly*, All things working for good, Rom. viii. 28. In a state of non-acceptance, all things work for evil to a man; his prosperity destroys him; the very gospel is a savour of death unto him, that he draws death out of what others get life. But being accepted, the worst of things tend to his profit, God being for him, nothing can be eventually against him; but whether the wind blow on his back or face, it drives him to the harbour.

III. I proceed to shew the way of a sinner's acceptance with God. *First*, It is "freely." There is nothing in the sinner himself to procure it, or move God to it, Rom. iii. 24, but as the sun shines without hire on the dung-hill, so God accepts sinners of mere grace. It is done freely, in that,

1. It is without respect to any work done by the sinner, Tit. iii. 5. Grace and works are inconsistent in this matter. Men may render themselves acceptable to men, by some work of theirs, that is profitable or pleasant to them; but no work of ours can render us acceptable to God. It is natural for men to think to gain acceptance with God, by their doing better; and when they have set themselves to do and work for that end, they please themselves that they are accepted. But mistake it not, that way of acceptance is blocked up· For,

(1.) All works of ours are excluded from our justification, whereof our acceptance is a part, Rom. iii. 20, and faith and works are opposed in that matter, ver. 28; Gal. ii. 16.

(2.) Our best works are attended with sinful imperfections, Isa. lxiv. 6, and mixed with many evil works, Jam. iii. 2. So in them there is ground for God's loathing and condemning us; how then can we be accepted for what is in itself loathsome and condemnable?

(3.) We can do no good works before we be accepted, John ix. 31; Heb. xi. 6. The tree must be good, ere the fruit can be so. The person out of Christ can work no works, but dead works, John xv. 5, for he is, while so, in the gall of bitterness, and in the bond of iniquity. And what is all that the man can do before he believe and be accepted in Christ, but a parcel of hypocritical works?

2. It is without respect to any good qualification or disposition wrought in the sinner; Rom. iv. 5, "To him that worketh not, but believeth on him that justifieth the ungodly, his faith is counted for righteousness." Men may be accepted of men, if though they have done nothing, they yet are well qualified for doing, or are agreeable in their disposition; but that is not the way of a sinner's acceptance` with God, though the bias of our nature lies that way to expect it. For,

(1.) The way of a sinner's acceptance with God excludes all boasting, Rom. iii. 27. And it is the design of the gospel to exclude it; but if there were a respect to any good qualities in the party accepted, there would be some ground for boasting.

(2.) What good qualities can there be in the sinner before he be accepted in Christ? Heb. xi. 6. It is true he may be touched with a sense of his sin, may be filled with sorrow and remorse for it, and desiring to be delivered; but all these are but legal and selfish dispositions, whereof not God, but self is the end. It is by union with him that gracious qualities must be wrought in the soul, Acts xxvi. 18.

(3.) When the man comes to be endued with gracious qualities, as he is by that time already accepted, so if his acceptance depended on them, he would come short; for still they are imperfect, having a great mixture of the contrary ill qualities, that need to be covered another way. And how can one expect acceptance on that, for which he needs a pardon?

Secondly, It is in Christ the sinner is accepted. It implies,

1. The cause of a sinner's acceptance with God. It is for Christ's sake; Rom. iii. 24, 25, "Being justified freely by his grace, through the redemption that is in Jesus Christ: whom God hath set forth to be a propitiation, through faith in his blood, to declare his righteousness for the remission of sins." And v. 19—"By the obedience of one, shall many be made righteous." He is the Beloved of the Father, so highly acceptable to him, that sinners are accepted for his sake, Matth iii. ult. The acceptance of the Mediator is so full, that like the oil on Aaron's head, it runs down to the skirts of his garments. He is the Mediator, that brings in the sinner to the throne of grace, mediates his peace, and procures his acceptance into favour with God. This is,

(1.) The sole cause of the sinner's acceptance with God, Rom. iii. 24. As in purchasing the sinner's acceptance, so in procuring it, he alone is the actor. No righteousness is mixed with his, no works with his works. God has an eye to none but him, and nothing but him, in accepting the sinner. Some are better than others indeed, before they are accepted, but both are absolutely free grace's debtors for acceptance.

(2.) The full cause, fully proportioned in its efficacy to the acceptance of the worst sinners, Heb. vii. 25. As there is nothing else that can procure our acceptance, so we need nothing else for that end. Corrupt nature reckons it is too great a venture, to lay our acceptance with God on Christ's righteousness alone; and therefore, to make sure work, requires such and such works to be done, and such and such good qualities the sinner is to be adorned with. But what needs wood, hay, and stubble, to be laid in with the Rock for a foundation.

2. The state of acceptableness of a sinner, wherein he may, and will be, and cannot but be accepted of God; it is being in Christ, united to him by faith. One must not think to be accepted for Christ's sake while out of Christ; no more than the branch of one tree can partake of the sap of another, while not ingrafted into it; or the slayer could be safe, while he was not yet got within the gates of the city of refuge. For,

(1.) Where there is no union with Christ, there can be no communion with him; John xv. 6, "If a man abide not in me, he is cast forth as a branch, and is withered." Can a branch be nourished by the juice of a stock with which it is not knit? Neither can a man be accepted for the sake of Christ's righteousness, while he is not united to him. As it is the marriage with the woman that makes her portion the man's; so it is a spiritual marriage-union with Christ by faith that makes his righteousness actually ours, so as to be accepted for it.

(2.) Christ's salvation is in the event confined to his body, though in the offer it is extended to all. He is the Saviour of the world indeed, John iv. 42. But does he save all the world? No; thousands perish for all that, because they do not unite with him, are not in him. He is the Saviour of the body, Eph. v. 23. His body he actually saves, every member thereof, and none else. He is the Saviour of the world officially, of his body only eventually. An ark there was provided before the universal deluge, but none were saved that were not in it.

(3.) The Father's good pleasure with mankind-sinners goes not without him, Matth. iii. ult. As without the verge of the city of refuge the slayer could expect no protection; so without Christ there is nothing but the curse, wrath, and death. God cannot accept us as righteous, while he sees no righteousness on us; there can be no righteousness on us before God, but as we are in Christ, shaded with his righteousness, 2 Cor. v. 21. Therefore he cannot be pleased with a sinner out of Christ.

(4.) *Lastly,* The covenant of peace reaches not without him, Isa, xlix. 8, and there is no acceptance of a sinner but in it. He was the only party-contractor in it, and contracted only for his seed; and it is only by faith uniting with Christ that we are actually in it. Know then that the whole of your salvation lies here. Ye must be in Christ, or ye can have no saving benefit by him. For God will not accept you even for Christ's sake, if ye be not *in* him.

But in Christ the sinner is in a state of acceptableness to God. We take up this in these five things following:—

1. In Christ the sinner may be accepted of God; 2 Cor. v. 19, " God was in Christ, reconciling the world unto himself, not imputing their trespasses unto them." There God may, with safety of his honour, meet with the sinner, and receive him into favour. While the sinner is out of Christ, it is inconsistent with the honour of God to accept of him; where is the honour of his justice and holiness. and of his law, if that should be? But the sinner being in Christ, these bars are removed, Matth. xxii. 4.

REASON. Christ has fully satisfied the law, in the name and stead of all his, Rom. x. 4. The law can demand nothing of them, but what it has got of their Surety for them; so justice cannot hinder their acceptance. And it has got,

(1.) Holiness of nature. It is true, it is not in them in their own persons, in the eye of the law; but in Christ as a public person it is; for he was born perfectly holy, brought a holy spotless human nature into the world with him, which was never in the least stained, Luke i. 35; Heb. vii. 26.

(2.) Righteousness of life. They cannot pretend to it in their own persons; but Christ has furnished it for them; Phil. ii. 8, " He humbled himself, and became obedient unto death." All the ten commands had their due from him. His obedience was universal, constant without interruption, voluntary without constraint, and perfect without the least failure in degree or measure.

(3.) Satisfaction for sin. That is quite beyond their reach; but he has satisfied fully; Gal. iii. 13, " Christ hath redeemed us from the curse of the law, being made a curse for us." Death in all its shapes preyed on him. The forerunners of it met him, at his entrance into the world; it hung about him all his days; in end it came on him with all its joint forces, carried him to the dust of death, kept him in the prison of the grave, till the debt was declared to be completely paid.

2. In Christ the sinner will be accepted. Any, even the worst of sinners shall certainly be accepted in Christ; Acts xvi. 31, " Believe on the Lord Jesus Christ, and thou shalt be saved." Whosoever shall make their escape into this city of refuge shall be safe. Christ will refuse none that come to him; and God will reject none that are in Christ. Let this be secured, and all is safe.

REASON. The promise of the gospel ensures this. The truth of heaven is plighted for it, that sinners may have all encouragement to come to Christ; John iii. 16, " For God so loved the world, that he gave his only begotten Son, that whosoever believeth in him, should not perish, but have everlasting life." It is an unalterable statute, that "he that believeth shall be saved," Mark xvi. 16. The word is full of promises of this nature. See Isa. lv. 1, 2. So that as Christ's satisfaction shews it is in the power of a holy God, to accept sinners; the promise of the gospel ascertains it to be his will.

3. In Christ the sinner cannot but be accepted. It is impossible it should fail or miscarry; Heb. vi. 18, " That by two immutable things, in which it was impossible for God to lie, we might have a strong consolation, who have fled for refuge to lay hold upon the hope set before us." Heaven and earth may pass away sooner than a sinner in Christ should not be received into favour with God.

REASON. There is a right of a third party in this matter, which it is impossible to be baulked. It is not only God and the sinner that are here concerned, but the Mediator Christ appears for his interest. In the covenant that passed from eternity betwixt him and the Father, it was promised him, that on condition of his fulfilling all his righteousness, sinners should be accepted in him; he has fulfilled the condition, and so demands it as his own right, to whom the promises were made, Tit. i. 2.

4. That moment a sinner is in Christ, he is accepted, Rom. viii. 1, "There is therefore now no condemnation to them which are in Christ Jesus." No sooner does the soul come into Christ by faith, but all is safe; the man is in a state of favour with God, the day is risen with him, and the long and black night of the state of wrath is at an end. For then,

(1.) Heaven's offer is accepted as it was made. In the gospel there is an offer of Christ and his righteousness made to the sinner, Rom. i. 17; and of acceptance in him, Acts xiii. 38. The soul by faith coming to Christ, accepts the offer; so the acceptance with God offered, becomes actually his.

(2.) Faith uniting the soul to Christ, upon that union with him follows a communion with him in his righteousness, yea, in his fulness; as in marriage there is a communion of goods, 1 John i. 3. So the soul wants nothing to commend it to God for acceptance, having all in its head Christ, 1 Cor. i. 30; Col. ii. 10. The holiness and purity of his birth is theirs; all the good works he did during his life are theirs; and all that he suffered in life and death is theirs. All fullness being united to all emptiness, the empty creature is filled, and rendered accepted; the transcendent beauty of the Head casts a lustre on all the members.

(3.) The soul pleading Christ's righteousness, and Christ interceding for the soul on that ground, the imputation of it, and acceptance of the person upon it, must immediately ensue. Faith's plea is well bottomed, and cannot be refused: Christ's intercession is always effectual; so the righteousness that is theirs by faith, cannot miss to be reckoned theirs, and they accepted as righteous thereon, 2 Cor. v. 21.

5. *Lastly*, While they abide in Christ, they remain accepted; so their union with him being everlasting, the acceptance of their persons can never be interrupted; John x. 28, "I give unto them eternal life, and they shall never perish, neither shall any pluck them out of my hand;" Rom. viii. 1. It continues in their adversity, as well as prosperity, Job. xlii. 8. Their sins may bring them under heavy strokes, yet still their persons are accepted in Christ, Psalm lxxxix. 30—34. It continues in death, as well as in life, John xi.

11, and will continue through eternity, Heb. vii. 25, for that righteousness of Christ put on by faith will ever continue on them; their union with Christ can never be dissolved; and being in Christ, they can never be but accepted.

I come now to the improvement of this subject.

1. Then the door of acceptance with God is open to all; none are excluded, Isa. lv. 1, 2. What is given freely, one has access to, as well as another, whatever they have been. Not that God will accept of any who will continue in their sin, and will not come to Christ; but that none shall be refused, who will come for acceptance in the method God has laid down.

2. Seek then acceptance with God, that ye may find favour with him. This should be your main aim, 2 Cor. v. 9. Here your happiness lies in time and eternity; Psalm xxx. 5, "In his favour is life." The favour of the world is both insufficient and uncertain; it cannot satisfy in life, much less in death. God is the best friend, and the most terrible enemy; for he is an everlasting friend, and an everlasting enemy too.

3. Seek it freely, without pretending to anything in yourselves to recommend you to his acceptance or favour. Put no confidence in whole or in part, in your doings, sufferings, attainments, Phil. iii. 7, 8; otherwise ye do put a bar in your own way, and will meet with that, "Thy money perish with thyself." Mind that this may procure your rejection, and therefore not your acceptance.

4. Seek it through Jesus Christ only, that is, by faith in him, laying the whole stress of your acceptance on his righteousness. The Jews missed it, because they sought it not this way, Rom. ix. 32. No person nor thing else can procure you the favour of God; no righteousness else will cover you; nothing but the blood of the Redeemer can be a covert from revenging justice; nor will anything else purge the conscience. All other things will be but as a wall of dry boards betwixt you and the consuming fire.

5. *Lastly,* Therefore as ever ye would have acceptance or favour with God, seek to be in Christ; to be united to him. For as there is no acceptance with God, but for his sake; so there is no acceptance for his sake, but to those that are in him, Col. i. 27. There is salvation in Christ, but none partake of it that are not in him; a righteousness in him, but it covers none but the members of his body. And,

(1.) This is the only way to be safe in time; for it is the only way to be without the verge of wrath, John iii. ult. And they that are without it are safe, go times as they will, John xvi. ult. While the Lord is threatening a rousing stroke on the generation, the only safety will be in Christ, Micah v. 5.; Isa. viii. 14; and xxvi. 20.

(2.) It is the only way to be safe in eternity, Phil. iii. 9. We must launch out of time into eternity, and there is no escaping the gulf of eternal wrath, but in him. They that are not in him must depart from him; and departing from him, they must go into everlasting fire.

QUEST. How may we then get into Christ.

ANSW. 1. The only way to get into him is by faith, Eph. iii. 17. And faith is the convinced soul's renouncing all confidence in itself, and trusting on him entirely for salvation from sin and wrath, upon the ground of the faithfulness of God in the promise of the gospel. Hereby the soul knits with Christ, hangs on him, depends on him, wholly to stand or fall, according as he shall deal with them.

2. The only way to get that faith, is by his Spirit in us, 2 Cor. iv. 13. Christ communicating his quickening Spirit unto the dead soul, it believes; and believing is united to Christ, and accepted in him. Wherefore breathe, pant, and long for the Spirit of Christ, Luke xi. 13.

I shall now drop a word very briefly to the last doctrine, and so conclude this subject.

DOCT. III. ult. Glorious free grace shines forth in the acceptance of sinners in the beloved Jesus.

We shall consider, wherein it shines there. It shines,

1. In his admitting a Surety to mediate for the acceptance of sinners, when he might have insisted that the soul that sinned should die, Rom. v. 8, "God commendeth his love towards us, in that while we were yet sinners, Christ died for us." The necks of all the elect were on the block, and it was in the hand of spotless justice to reach them the fatal stroke. But glorious free grace admits a surety in their room.

2. He provided the Surety, John iii. 16; as he did the ram to come instead of Isaac lying bound on the altar. All the beasts of the field could not have afforded a sacrifice sufficient for the sinner's acceptance; nor the angels in heaven a cautioner; but glorious grace gave God's own Son; Psalm lxxxix. 19, "I have laid help upon one that is mighty; I have exalted one chosen out of the people." So the righteousness is the righteousness of God, not only of one who is God, but provided by God.

3. He demands nothing of us, to render us acceptable in whole or in part; but the cause of his accepting sinners is wholly without them; Rom. iii. 24, "Being justified freely by his grace, through the

redemption that is in Jesus Christ." To us it is in no wise, Give and get; but Take and have; Rom. iv. 16, "Therefore it is of faith, that it might be by grace; to the end the promise might be sure to all the seed." So nothing in us has any hand in it, but faith, as the hand whereby it is received.

4. The very hand of faith whereby it is received is God's free gift; Eph. ii. 8, "For by grace are ye saved through faith; and that not of yourselves; it is the gift of God." Philip. i. 29. That one believes while another doth not, is owing purely to free grace, which makes the difference; giving the quickening spirit to one, that is not communicated to another.

5. In its breaking over all impediments lying in its way, such as these in the case of the Corinthians, to whom the apostle says, "Know ye not that the unrighteous shall not inherit the kingdom of God? Be not deceived; neither fornicators, nor idolaters, nor adulterers, nor effeminate, nor abusers of themselves with mankind, nor thieves, nor covetous, nor drunkards, nor revilers, nor extortioners shall inherit the kingdom of God. And such were some of you: but ye are washed, but ye are sanctified, but ye are justified in the name of the Lord Jesus, and by the Spirit of our God," 1 Cor. vi. 9—11. In the best of sinners, there is that loathsomeness and unworthiness found, that proclaims a glory of grace in their acceptance; Jer. iii. 19, "I said, How shall I put thee among the children?" But in the worst of them there is nothing found but what glorious grace will break over, to accept them in Christ, as in Manasseh, Mary Magdalene, Paul, &c.

6. In the thoroughness of the acceptance; Isa. i. 18, "Come now, and let us reason together, saith the Lord; though your sins be as scarlet, they shall be as white as snow; though they be red like crimson, they shall be as wool." Acceptance among men is often coldrife, and by halves, so as the heart is not freely toward the pardoned offender. But God's acceptance of sinners in Christ is perfect the first moment; they are perfectly beloved in him, John xvii. 21.

7. *Lastly*, In the perpetuity and constancy of it; sinners are so accepted in Christ that they shall never be cast out of God's favour again; John x. 28, 29, "And I give unto them eternal life, and they shall never perish, neither shall any pluck them out of my hand. My Father which gave them me is greater than all; and none is able to pluck them out of my Father's hand." They are not put on their good behaviour as to the acceptance of their persons with God, but it is secured unalterably in Christ. The smiles and frowns of a Father will indeed be as they carry.

Use 1. Let us loath Popery then, as the smoke of the bottomless pit darkening the glory of grace in the acceptance of sinners, by their merit of works, and other corrupt doctrines and practices, laying another foundation than Christ. It is evident we are in danger of it, and it will be our wisdom to be on our guard, that we be not catched napping, come what will.

2. Let all be encouraged to come to God through Christ for acceptance, assuring themselves they may have it through him, God being well pleased with him, and with every one who believes in him for life, pardon and acceptance.

A VIEW

OF THE

COVENANT OF WORKS,

FROM THE

SACRED RECORDS.

WHEREIN

THE PARTIES IN
THAT COVENANT; THE REALITY OF IT; ITS PARTS,
CONDITIONARY, PROMISSORY, AND MINATORY; OUR FATHER
ADAM'S BREAKING OF IT; THE IMPUTATION OF THAT BREACH TO HIS
POSTERITY; AND THE STATE OF MAN UNDER THAT BROKEN CO-
VENANT, AND UNDER THE CURSE THEREOF, ARE DIS-
TINCTLY CONSIDERED:

TOGETHER WITH

A PARTICULAR APPLICATION OF THE SUBJECT, FOR THE CONVICTION
BOTH OF SAINTS AND SINNERS.

~~~~~~~~~~~~~~~~

" Earth felt the wound, and Nature from her seat
Sighing, through all her works, gave signs of woe,
That all was lost."—MILTON.

M 2

PREFACE.

THOUGH the doctrines and precepts of Christianity are unalterable in their nature, and must necessarily be the same in all ages and places; yet we find that the foolish caprice of men has made them appear in various shapes, in different periods and countries.

In the golden days of Christianity, before men had learned the art of making gain of godliness in a literal sense, and contracted the ridiculous humour of modelling religion according to their respective tastes and tempers, the religion of Jesus was then seen in its native simplicity, unadulterated with the unnatural additions and embellishments of human invention. In process of time, when it was found that religion was not unsubservient to worldly interest, some of its votaries, inclining to make the kingdom of Christ resemble the kingdoms of this world, stripped religion in a great measure of its native unadorned simplicity, and dressed it in garments of their own manufacture.

This dangerous spirit of innovating, when it once begins, knows no bounds or limits. It is like a river, or flood, whose current has been stopped, when once let loose it will disregard its proper channel, and carry every thing down with its impetuous torrent. The rapid progress which this wild spirit has made, is clearly seen in those enormous corruptions which gradually crept into the Church of Rome, until at length she arrived at the monstrous absurdity of a wafer god, created by the benediction of a priest.

It had not however been so fatal to the interests of true religion, if the inventions of men had been confined to circumstantials, or things of lesser importance. Had this been the case, the blessed religion of Jesus would not have had so much reason to put on her widow's weeds. The Christian world was pleased to indulge some ingenious triflers in forming refined theories of the creation of all things, and was not offended whether they chose a volcano or a long tailed comet for the instrument of their dissolution; nor has the

Christian denied the same gracious indulgence to such of the same kidney as have tried to lash their lingering " moments into speed," by attempting curious calculations with respect to the prophecies in the book of the Revelation, nor will he laugh, I am persuaded, when they out-live their calculations. A decent company will not readily quarrel with a conceited cook for garnishing the dishes with herbs that are not eatable ; but if he infuses these herbs into the sauce, every one who regards his life and health, will immediately take the alarm, and refuse to eat. In like manner the friends of Jesus, for the sake of peace, will be disposed to bear with men's foibles and humours, when they are, comparatively speaking, harmless, and do not alter the system, or affect the essentials of our holy religion ; but, on the other hand, if men take it into their heads to new-model the system of Christianity, and to prescribe a new plan of salvation, such criminal liberty can never be permitted, and those who regard the health and welfare of their souls, will neither taste, relish, nor digest such poisonous unwholesome food.

That such attempts have been made (and with considerable success too), the present state of the religious world is a sufficient proof. The rusty armour of Pelagius and Socinus has, with unparalleled effrontery, been buckled on, and the self-flattering doctrines of Arminius have, with sanguine hopes of success, been furbished up anew. Nor has the wild-fire stopt here. As Pelagius took away original sin, another adventurer, determined not to be out-done by the arch-heretic, at one blow rids us of actual transgression. Strange hypothesis! Sin, revelation as well as expereince and fact tell us, has an actual existence in the world. There are only two kinds of it, viz. original and actual; how then can any of these species of sin exist, if man is guilty of neither ?

One could scarce believe that such chimeras as these would ever enter into men's heads, to whom the uncorrupted sources of divine truth are accessible. But the truth is this :—Men have generally formed such conceptions of the present state of human nature, and the extent of its powers, as they wish to be true, and wishing them to be true, have asserted them to be so ; and after dressing her up in a gay attire of their own making, to complete her honour, and fix the crown of glory upon her head, have complacently enough given her salvation of her own working out. Hence it is, that human merit and personal righteousness pass so currently in this refined age as the only, conditions of our acceptance with God, and justification in his sight. The success of this modern method of Christian-making is easily accounted for. For as it ascribes the whole praise of his salvation to man himself, it is much more agreeable to the pride of the human heart, than the gospel method of salvation, which resolves the whole into the free grace of God in Christ Jesus. But though such a scheme of salvation is greedily swallowed by the human heart, yet if it has not the sanction of the infallible oracles of truth, it must be looked upon as " a cunningly devised fable."

Whilst such unscriptural principles as these, with respect to the way of access to the divine favour, are assiduously propagated by some, and greedily swallowed by others, the following publication cannot be deemed an unseasonable one. It turns upon a capital article in the Christian system, upon our notions of which all our views of the method of acceptance with God must depend. For if one man maintains that human nature, by proper culture and improvement, may acquire strength and integrity equal to that which it had in the days of primæval rectitude, salvation by works will to him appear quite practicable. But on the other hand, if another man, according to sacred writ, believes that the descendants of Adam are obnoxious to the curse of the law, and " dead in trespasses and sins," he will clearly see the necessity of Christ's satisfaction to remove the one, and the power of the Spirit to raise from the other.

As the following sheets therefore are designed to give us the scriptural account of the original transactions betwixt God and the first parent of the human race, to express the nature and extent of the effects of the fall, and consequently to lead us to right conceptions of the method of salvation prescribed in the gospel; they will not, the editor fondly hopes, be an unacceptable offering to the public.

As to the performance itself, the reader, when it comes into his hand, must judge of its merit. To attempt a character of it, would be too delicate a task for the pen of so near a relation as the author's grandson. He only begs leave to inform the public, that the work is genuine, and is printed from the author's manuscript, without any alterations or additions, but such as are merely verbal, and do not affect the sense. It was preached in a course of sermons to his own congregation by the worthy author, in the latter end of the year 1721, and in the beginning of the year 1722. And it appears from the following paragraph, extracted from his diary, that he was led to undertake the subject, on account of the controversy agitated before several General Assemblies of this National Church, concerning a book entitled " The Marrow of Modern Divinity." " I was now led," says the author, " for my ordinary, to treat of the two covenants, which lasted a long time.* I began on the covenant of works, August 27, this year [1721], and handling it at large from several texts, I insisted thereon till May in the following year. I studied it with considerable earnestness and application, being prompted thereto, as to the close consideration of the other covenant too, afterwards, by the state the doctrine in this church was then arrived at."—*N. B.* The author here alludes to the controversy above mentioned.

The Editor did not think himself at liberty to change its orignal form of sermons. He has, however, for the ease of the reader, divided the treatise into parts, and added general titles to them, as well as to the subdivisions of each part, which he thought himself sufficiently warranted to do, as the author himself has followed the same method in his " View of the Covenant of Grace."

The reader will find, in the book, several references to the celebrated Dr. Witsius' " Economy of the Covenants," which, though they are not in the original manuscript, the Editor has added, with a view of referring the reader to that great work, for a further illustration of some of the subjects of this essay.

It would be unnecessary to offer to the public the reasons why this

---

* The author's manuscript bears, that the sermons on this subject were begun August 27th, 1721, and ended May 6th, 1722, having preached on other subjects during that period. On the first of July that year he began his sermons on the covenant of grace, and ended them on the 14th of June, 1724. So that this important subject, the doctrine of the two covenants, employed his public labours a considerable part of near three years.

performance remained so long in manuscript, or why it now emerges from its obscurity so long after its rev. Author's death. Readers of a certain class will perhaps think that it has come to light soon enough, and those of another complexion will not relish it less because they have wanted it long. It now ventures out an orphan into the world; and as some of the same family ["The Fourfold State," &c., &c.], have met with a candid reception from the public, the orphan hopes, even under the disadvantages common to posthumous publications, that it will meet with some regard for its parent's sake.

MICHAEL BOSTON.

A VIEW

OF

THE COVENANT OF WORKS.

PART I.

OF THE TRUTH AND NATURE OF THE COVENANT OF WORKS.

GENESIS ii. 17,

But of the tree of the knowledge of good and evil, thou shalt not eat of it ; for in the day that thou eatest thereof thou shalt surely die.

INTRODUCTION.

My design is, under the divine conduct, to open up unto you the two covenants of works and grace ; and that because in the knowledge and right application of them the work of our salvation lies; the first covenant shewing us our lost state, and the second holding forth the remedy in Jesus Christ; the two things which, for the salvation of souls, I have always thought it necessary chiefly to inculcate. And I think it the more necessary to treat of these subjects, that, in these our declining days, the nature of both these covenants is so much perverted by some, and still like to be more so. And as I desire to lay a good foundation among you, while I have opportunity ; so I intreat all of you, and particularly the younger sort, to hearken and hear for the time to come. I begin with the first covenant to shew the nature of it from this text, " But of the tree of the knowledge," &c.

In which words we have an account of the original transaction between God and our first father Adam in paradise, while yet in the state of primitive integrity. In which the following things are to be remarked, being partly expressed and partly implied.

1. The Lord's making over to him a benefit by way of a conditional promise, which made the benefit a debt upon the performing of the condition. This promise is a promise of life, and is included in the threatening of death, thus; If thou eat not of the tree of the

knowledge, &c., thou shalt live ; even as in the sixth commandment, "Thou shalt not kill" is plainly implied, Thou shalt preserve thy own life and the life of others. And thus it is explained by Moses ; Rom. x. 5, "The man which doth those things shall live by them." Besides, the license given him to eat of all the other trees, and so of the tree of life, which had a sacramental use, imports this promise.

2. The condition required to entitle him to this benefit; namely, obedience. It is expressed in a prohibition of one particular, " Of the tree of the knowledge of good and evil, thou shalt not eat of it." There was a twofold law given to Adam ; the natural law, which was concreated with him, engraven on his heart in his creation. For it is said, Gen. i. 27, that " God created man in his own image ;" compared with Eph. iv. 24, "That ye put on the new man, which after God is created in righteousness and true holiness." This law was afterwards promulgated on Mount Sinai, being much obliterated by sin. Another law was the symbolical law, mentioned in the text, which, not being known by nature's light, was revealed to Adam, probably by an audible voice. By this God chose to try, and by an external action, exemplify his obedience to the natural law concreated with him. And this being a thing in its own nature altogether indifferent, the binding of it upon him by the mere will of the divine lawgiver, did clearly import the more strong tie of the natural law upon him in all the parts of it. Thus perfect obedience was the condition of this covenant.

3. The sanction, or penalty in case of the breach of the covenant, " In the day that thou eatest thereof thou shalt surely die." For if death was entailed on a doing of that which was only evil, because it was forbidden ; much more might Adam understand it to be entailed on his doing of anything forbidden, because evil, or contrary to the nature or will of God, the knowledge of which was impressed on his mind in his creation. The sanction is plainly expressed, not the promise; because the last was plainly enough signified to him in the tree of life, and he had ample discoveries of God's goodness and bounty, but none of his justice, at least to himself. And it does not appear that the angels were yet fallen ; or if they were, that Adam knew of it.

4. Adam's going into the proposal, and acceptance of those terms, is sufficiently intimated to us by his objecting nothing against it. Thus the Spirit of God teaches us Jonah's repentance and yielding at length to the Lord, after a long struggle, chap. iv. 11 ; as also Adam's own going into the covenant of grace, Gen. iii. 15. Besides, his knowledge could not but represent to him how beneficial a treaty this was ; his upright will could not but comply with what a bountiful

God laid on him; and he, by virtue of that treaty, claimed the privilege of eating of the other trees, and so of the tree of life, as appears from Eve's words, Gen. iii. 3, "But of the fruit of the tree which is in the midst of the garden, God hath said, Ye shall not eat of it, neither shall ye touch it, lest ye die."

Now it is true, we have not here the word *covenant ;* yet we must not hence infer, that there is no covenant in this passage, more than we may deny the doctrine of the Trinity and sacraments, because those words do not occur where these things are treated of in scripture, nay, are not to be found in the scripture at all. But as in those cases, so here we have the thing; for the making over of a benefit to one, upon a condition, with a penalty, gone into by the party it is proposed to, is a covenant, a proper covenant, call it as you will.

The Covenant of Works, between God and Adam, a proper covenant.

The truth deducible from the words is this :—

DOCT.—There was a covenant of works, a proper covenant, between God and Adam the father of mankind.

In handling this important point, I shall,

I. Confirm the great truth expressed in the doctrinal note, and evince the being of such a covenant.

II. Explain the nature of this covenant.

III. Conclude with practical uses.

The truth of the Covenant of Works confirmed.

1. I shall confirm this great truth, and evince the being of such a covenant. It is altogether denied by the Arminians that there was any such covenant, and amongst ourselves by Professor Simson,* that it was a proper covenant. The weight of this matter lies here, that if the covenant made with Adam was not a proper covenant, he could not be a proper representing head; and if he was not, then there cannot be a proper imputation of Adam's sin unto his

---

* Mr. John Simson was Professor of Divinity in the College of Glasgow, and was twice prosecuted before the judicatories of the church, first for Pelagian and Arminian errors, and lastly for Arianism. Among his Arminian and Pelagian errors, vented in his answers to the libel exhibited against him by the Rev. Mr. James Webster of Edinburgh, and in his letters to Mr. Rowan, he held, in express terms, "That there was no proper covenant made with Adam for himself and his posterity : That Adam was not a federal head to his posterity ; and that if Adam was made a federal head, it must be by divine command, which is not found in the Bible." These dangerous errors were solidly and judiciously refuted by the Rev. Messrs. James Flint and John Maclaren, both ministers of Edinburgh.

posterity. None could ever dream, but there must be a manifest difference betwixt covenants between God and man, and those between men and men. There is no manner of equality betwixt God and man; God could require all duty of men without any covenant; yea, they have nothing but what is from him, and so owe it to him. But those things do not hinder, that, upon God's condescending to enter into a covenant with man, there may be a proper covenant betwixt them. Though all similitudes here must halt; yet let us suppose a father to propose to his son, that if he will obey his orders, and especially in one point give him punctual obedience, for instance, labour his vineyard, he will give him a certain sum of money; and the son having nothing to labour it with, the father furnishes him with all things necessary thereto; the son accepts of this proposal. Can any man say that there is not a proper bargain, or covenant, in this case betwixt the father and his son, although the son was tied by the bond of nature to obey his father's commands in all this antecedently to the bargain, and though he has nothing to labour it with, but what he has from the father? Let him perform his father's orders now according to the covenant, and he can challenge the sum as a debt, which he could not do before. For proof of this, consider,

1. Here is a concurrence of all that is necessary to constitute a true and proper covenant of works. The parties contracting, God and man; God requiring obedience as the condition of life; a penalty fixed in case of breaking; and man acquiescing in the proposal. The force of this cannot be evaded, by comparing it with the consent of subjects to the laws of an absolute prince. For such a law proposed by a prince, promising a reward upon obedience to it, is indeed the proposing of a covenant, the which the subject consenting to for himself and his, and taking on him to obey, does indeed enter into a covenant with the prince, and having obeyed the law may claim the reward by virtue of paction. And so the covenant of works is ordinarily in scripture called "the law," being in its own nature a pactional law.

2. It is expressly called a covenant in scripture, Gal. iv. 24, "For these are the two covenants, the one from the Mount Sinai," &c. This covenant from Mount Sinai was the covenant of works as being opposed to the covenant of grace, namely, the law of the ten commandments, with promise and sanction, as before expressed. At Sinai it was renewed indeed, but that was not its first appearance in the world. For there being but two ways of life to be found in scripture, one by works, the other by grace; the latter hath no place, but where the first is rendered ineffectual; therefore the co-

venant of works was before the covenant of grace in the world; yet the covenant of grace was promulgated quickly after Adam's fall; therefore the covenant of works behoved to have been made with him before. And how can one imagine a covenant of works set before poor impotent sinners, if there had not been such a covenant with man in his state of integrity? Hos. vi. 7, "But as for them; like Adam, they have transgressed the covenant." Our translators set the word Adam on the margin. But in Job xxxi. 33, they translate the very same word, "as Adam." This word occurs but three times in scripture, and still in the same sense. Job xxxi. 33, "If I covered my transgressions, as Adam," Psalm lxxxii. 7, "But ye shall die like Adam." Compare ver. 6, "I have said, Ye are gods; and all of you are children of the Most High;" compared with Luke iii. 38, "Adam, which was the son of God." And also here, Hos. vi. 7. While Adam's hiding his sin, and his death are made an example, how natural is it that his transgression, that led the way to all, be made so too? This is the proper and literal sense of the words; it is so read by several, and is certainly the meaning of it.

3. We find a law of works opposed to the law of faith, Rom. iii. 27, "Where is boasting then? It is excluded. By what law? of works? Nay; but by the law of faith." This law of works is the covenant of works, requiring works, or obedience, as the condition pleadable for life; for otherwise the law as a rule of life requires works too. Again, it is a law that does not exclude boasting, which is the very nature of the covenant of works, that makes the reward to be of debt. And further, the law of faith is the covenant of grace; therefore the law of works is the covenant of works. So Rom. vi. 14, "Ye are not under the law, but under grace." And this was the way of life without question, which was given to Adam at first.

4. There were sacramental signs and seals of this transaction in paradise. As it has pleased the Lord still to deal with man in the way of a covenant, so to append seals to these covenants. God's covenant with Noah, that he would not destroy the earth again with water, had the rainbow as a sign of it to confirm it, Gen. ix. 12, 13. The covenant with Abraham had circumcision; that with the Israelites, circumcision and the passover; and the new covenant with the New Testament church, baptism and the Lord's supper. So to the covenant of works God appended the two trees; the tree of life, Gen. iii. 22, "And now lest he put forth his hand, and take also of the tree of life, and eat, and live for ever;" and the tree of the knowledge of good and evil, mentioned in the words of the text.

When we find then confirming seals of this transaction, we must own it to be a covenant.

5. *Lastly*, All mankind are by nature under the guilt of Adam's first sin; Rom. v. 12, "As by one man sin entered into the world, and death by sin, and so death passed upon all men, for that all have sinned." And they are under the curse of the law before they have committed actual sin: hence they are said to be "by nature children of wrath," Eph. ii. 3, which they must needs owe to Adam's sin, as imputed to them. This must be owing to a particular relation betwixt them and him; which must either be, that he is their natural head simply, from whence they derive their natural being; but then the sins of our immediate parents, and all other mediate ones too, behoved to be imputed rather than Adam's, because our relation to them is nearer; or because he is our federal head also, representing us in the first covenant. And that is the truth, and evidences the covenant of works made with Adam to have been a proper covenant.

The Nature of the Covenant of Works.

II. I shall explain the nature of the covenant of works. In order to this, I shall consider,

1. The parties contracting in this covenant.
2. The parts of the covenant; and,
3. The seals of it.

The parties in the Covenant of Works.

FIRST, I shall consider the parties contracting in this covenant. These were two.

God the first party in the covenant.

First, On the one hand God himself, the Father, Son, and Holy Ghost, Gen. ii. 16, "And the Lord God commanded the man, saying," &c. God, as Creator and Sovereign Lord of man, condescended to enter into a covenant with man, his own creature and subject, whom he might have governed by a simple law, without proposing to him the reward of life. Thus it was a covenant betwixt two very unequal parties. And here God shewed,

1. His supreme authority over the creature *man*, founded on man's natural dependence on him as his Creator, Rom. xi. 36, "For of him, and through him, and to him, are all things." He gave him a law which he was to obey, under the greatest penalty; not only the natural law, but that positive law depending on the mere will of the Lawgiver; Job xxv. 2, "Dominion and fear are with him." The

truth is, it is a flower of the imperial crown of heaven, due to him only who is absolutely supreme, to stamp mere will into a law binding men.

2. His abundant goodness, in annexing such a great reward to man's service, which it could never merit; Heb. xi. 6, "He is a rewarder of them that diligently seek him." Here was a full fountain of goodness opened afresh, after he had let out signal goodness to man in his creation and settlement in the world, after all appears a method how to make him eternally happy in another and better world.

3. His admirable condescension, in stooping to make a covenant with his own creature. It is true he was a holy creature, yet he was but a creature. What God might have exacted of him by mere authority, he is pleased to require by compact, so making himself debtor to man upon man's obedience, which without a covenant he could not have been.

Adam, as a public person, the other party in the Covenant.

Secondly, On the other hand was Adam, the father of all mankind. He must be considered here under a twofold notion.

1. As a righteous man, morally perfect, endued with sufficient power and abilities to believe and do whatever God should reveal to or require of him, fully able to keep the law. That Adam was thus furnished when the covenant was made with him,

1st, Appears from plain scripture; Eccl. vii. 29, " God hath made man upright." There was an agreeableness of the powers of his soul to the holy law of God, which is habitual righteousness, here asserted; and likewise, Gen. i. 31, " God saw everything that he had made, and behold it was very good." Not only were all things made good, but very good. Everything had the goodness agreeable to its nature; it was fit for the end God made it for; and so man, being made to serve God, was fitted for that service. So man was very good morally; for that is agreeable to his rational nature, without which he could not be reckoned very good.

2dly, Man was created in the image of God, Gen. i. 27. And so,

(1.) His mind was endowed with knowledge; for that is a part of the image of God in man, Col. iii. 10, where believers are said to " have put on the new man, which is renewed in knowledge after the image of him that created him." We have a most ample testimony of this, Gen. iii. 22, (*Heb.*), "Behold the man that was one of us, to know good and evil." He was sufficiently able to know good and evil; good, to follow it; and evil, to avoid it. He had a light of knowledge within him, which, rightly improved, might have directed his way, through all dangers, during the time of his trial.

(2.) His will was endowed with righteousness, Eph. iv. 24, where "the new man" is said to be "after God created in righteousness." It was, by its natural set received in creation, straight to the will of God. The holy law was not only written in his mind by the knowledge of it; but in his heart, by the inclinations of his will towards it. No contrary bent was in him, nor propensity to evil; that was inconsistent with the image of God in perfection, and would have been sin in him.

(3.) His affections were holy; hence, Eph. iv. 24, forecited, "the new man" is also said to be "after God created in true holiness." This speaks out the purity and orderliness of his affections. He was not created without passions and affections, as love, joy, delight, &c., for these belong to man's nature; Acts xiv. 15, where the apostles, Barnabas and Paul, said to the people at Lystra, "We are men of like passions with you." These affections are like winds to the ship at sea; but there were no poisonous blasts to be found among them; and no violent and impetuous blasts neither, as is the case since the fall. But there was a pleasant, regular gale of them, whereby he might have made way through all dangers.* .

(4.) He had an executive power, whereby he was capable to do what he knew to be his duty, and inclined to do. He was made very good, Gen. i. 31, forecited; which implies not only a power to do good, but a facility in doing it free from all clogs and hinderances. Now, the spirit may be willing, but the flesh is weak. But there was no such thing with Adam; there was no mixture of corruption in his soul, and nothing from the body to hinder his course of obedience.

3dly, and *Lastly*, If he had not been so, that covenant could not have been made with him. It was inconsistent with the justice and goodness of God to have required that of his creature, which he had not ability to perform given him by his Creator. Wherefore before Adam could be obliged to perfect obedience, he behoved to have ability competent for it; otherwise that saying of the wicked and slothful servant had been true; Matth. xxv. 24, "Lord, I knew thee that thou art an hard man, reaping where thou hast not sown, and gathering where thou hast not strawed." The case now is not the same with us, Adam having received and lost that power for himself and us. For although one cannot demand payment of a debt which he never lent or gave any manner of way; yet having

* The reader may see all the three preceding particulars more especially illustrated in our author's work, entitled, "Human Nature in its Fourfold State," State i., under the title, "Of man's original righteousness."

once lent the sum, he may require it of the debtor and his heirs, though they be not able to pay.

Thus was man perfectly furnished and fitted to enter into this covenant. Let me therefore improve this point in a very few words, before I proceed further.

Use 1. How low is man now brought, how unlike to what he was at his creation! Alas! man is now ruined, and sin is the cause of that fatal ruin.

2. What madness is it for men to look to that covenant for salvation, when they are nowise fit for the way of it, having lost all the furniture and ability proper for the observation thereof.

3. *Lastly*, See how ye stand with respect to this covenant; whether ye are discharged from it, and brought within the bond of the new covenant in Christ or not. But I proceed,

2. Adam, in the covenant of works, is to be considered as the first man, 1 Cor. xv. 47, in whom all mankind was included. And he was,

1*st*, The natural root of mankind, from which all the generations of men on the face of the earth spring. This is evident from Acts xvii. 26, "God hath made of one blood all nations of men for to dwell on all the face of the earth;" which determines all men to be of one stock, one original, or common parentage. And this also appears from Gen. iii. 20, "Adam called his wife's name Eve; because she was the mother of all living;" which determines that to be only Adam's family. And of him was also Eve, who was not only formed for him but of him, Gen. ii. 21, 22, 23. Thus Adam was the compend of the whole world.

2*dly*, The moral root, a public person, and representative of mankind. And as such the covenant of works was made with him. As to this representation by Adam, we may note,

(1.) That the man Christ was not included in it; Adam did not represent him, as he stood covenanting with God. This is manifest, in that Christ is opposed to Adam, as the last and second Adam to the first Adam, 1 Cor. xv. 45, one representative to another, ver. 48. And if that covenant had been kept, Christ had not come, whose work it is to repair the loss by the breach of the first covenant, by establishing another covenant for that end. Besides, Christ was not born, as all others are, by virtue of that blessing of fruitfulness given before the fall, under the covenant of works, while it yet remained unbroken; but by virtue of a special promise given after the fall, which promise was the erecting of another covenant, namely, the covenant of grace, whereof Christ was the head, Gen. iii. 15.

(2.) Whether Eve was included in this representation, is not so clear. I find she is excepted by some. It is plain, that Adam was the original whence she came, as he and she together are of all their posterity. He was her head, Eph. v. 23, "For the husband is the head of the wife." The thread of the history, Gen. ii., gives us the making of the covenant of works with Adam before the formation of Eve. The covenant itself runs in terms as delivered to one person, ver. 16, 17, "Thou mayest—Thou shalt." From whence it seems to me that she was included. It is true, she fell by her own transgression; and so might any of Adam's posterity have fallen to themselves, as she did to herself, during the time of probation in this covenant; but the ruin of mankind was not completed till he did eat. And therefore Adam is first convicted, though Eve was first in the transgression, Gen. iii. 9.

(3.) Without question, all his posterity by ordinary generation were included in it. He stood for them all in that covenant, and was their federal head, that covenant being made with him as a public person representing them all. For,

[1.] The relation which the scripture teaches betwixt Adam and Christ evinces this. The one is called the *first* Adam, the other the *last* Adam, 1 Cor. xv. 45; the one the *first* man, the other the *second* man, ver. 47. Now, Christ is not the second man, but as he is a public person, representing all his elect seed in the covenant of grace, being their federal head; therefore Adam was a public person representing all his natural seed in the covenant of works, being their federal head; for if there be a second man there must be a first man; if a second representative there must be a first. Again, Christ is not the last Adam, but as the federal head of the elect, bringing salvation to them by his covenant keeping; therefore the first Adam was the federal head of those whom he brought death upon by his covenant-breaking, and these are all, ver. 22, "For as in Adam all die, even so in Christ shall all be made alive." And therefore the apostle, Rom. v. 14, calls Adam a figure or type of Christ. Accordingly each of these representatives are held forth with their respective parties represented by them, being made like unto them, 1 Cor. xv. 48, "As is the earthly, such are they also that are earthly; and as is the heavenly, such are they also that are heavenly."

[2.] Adam's breaking of the covenant is in law their breaking of it; it is imputed to them by a holy God, whose judgment is according to truth, and therefore can never impute to men the sin of which they are not guilty. Rom. v. 12—" All have sinned." Now, if we enquire what is the particular sin here meant; the apostle makes it evident, that it is Adam's first sin, vers. 15, 19,—" If through the offence of one many be dead.—As by the offence of one judgment came upon all men." And that sin was the breaking of the cóvenant. Now, we could never be reckoned breakers of the covenant in him, if we were not reckoned first makers of it in him; that is, that Adam was our federal head in that covenant, so that it was made with us in him.

[3.] The ruins by the breach of that covenant fall on all mankind, not excepting those who are not guilty of actual sin. Hence believers are said to have been " the children of wrath, even as others," Eph. ii. 3, and that " death hath reigned over them that had not sinned after the similitude of Adam's transgression," Rom. v. 14. All were excluded from paradise, and from the tree of life, in the loins of Adam; the ground was cursed to them, as well as to him. Yea, all die spiritually, and that in him, 1 Cor. xv. 22, forecited. Yet it is only " the soul that sinneth, shall die," Ezek. xviii. 4. They thus die who are not chargeable with personal sins, Rom. v. 14, also above cited. It must be by virtue of that original threatening then, Gen. iii. 17,—" Dust thou art, and unto dust shalt thou return." And if they die by virtue of that threatening, they were under that law to which it was annexed; but they could no other way be under it, than as in Adam their federal head and representative.

[4.] *Lastly,* The sin and death we come under by Adam, is still restrained unto that sin of his by which he brake the covenant of works, Rom. v. 15—19, " Through the offence of one many be dead. The judgment was by one to condemnation.—By one man's offence death reigned by one.—By the offence of one judgment came upon all men to condemnation.—By one man's disobedience many were made sinners." As for Adam's after sins, the scripture takes no notice of them that way. If our communion with him in sin and death did depend merely on his natural relation to us, the conveyance of guilt from him unto us could not have ceased, till his whole guilt contracted all his life over had disburdened itself upon us; because the natural relation ceased not, but was still the same. It depended then upon some supervenient relation, the which could be no other but that he was constituted a public person, representing us in the first covenant; the which ceased, when he went in for himself into the second covenant. The ship whereof he was made steersman being split, the covenant of grace, as another ship came up, of which Christ was the steersman; and this covenant was let out as a rope to hale the passengers to land. This Adam laid hold on, and so quitted his first post, that his after mismanagement could no more harm as formerly.

The equity of this representation.

This representation was just and equal, though we did not make choice of Adam for that effect. The justice and equity of it appears, in that,

1. God made the choice; he pitched on Adam as a fit person to represent all mankind; and there is no mending of God's work, which is perfect, Eccl. iii. 14. There was infinite wisdom at making of it, and sovereign authority to establish it. The covenant proposed to Adam, could not but in duty be consented to by him; and there is the same obligation to his posterity. If judges on earth may name and give tutors to minors, might not the Judge of all the earth do the same to his own creatures?

2. Adam was undoubtedly the most fit choice. He was the common father of us all; so being our natural head, he was fittest to be our federal head. He was in case for managing the bargain to the common advantage, Eccl. vii. 29, being "made upright," and furnished with sufficient abilities. And his own interest was on the same bottom with that of his posterity. Thus his abilities, and natural affection concurring with his own interest, spoke him to be a fit person for that office.

3. *Lastly*, The choice was of a piece with the covenant. The covenant, in its own nature most advantageous for man, though it could not be profitable to God, Job xxxv. 7, was a free benefit and gift on God's part; for as much as man had not a claim to the life promised, but by the covenant. So that as the covenant owed its being, not to nature, but a positive constitution of God; so did the choice owe its being to the same. God joined the covenant and representation together; and so the consent of Adam or his posterity to the one, was a consenting to the other.

The parts of the Covenant of Works.

SECONDLY, I come now to discourse of the parts of the covenant. These are the things agreed upon betwixt God and man in this transaction; the which God proposed, and man assented to, which made it properly God's covenant. It was himself who settled and drew all the articles of it, by himself alone; Rom. xi. 34, "For who hath known the mind of the Lord? (says the apostle), or who hath been his counsellor?" Nothing was left to man, but to receive, acquiesce in, and consent to it, as is manifest from the text. This was becoming the inequality of the parties; suitable to God's sovereign authority over man, whose proposals to his creature are in effect laws; and suitable to the meanness of man in his best estate, who hath nothing but what he receives, and can never profit his Maker. Hence may be inferred,

1. That for a man's entering into the covenant of grace, there is no more required but the soul's hearty consent to the proposal of the covenant made to him in the gospel. For surely there is no more required of a sinner to instate him in the second covenant, a covenant of grace, than was required of Adam in innocence to instate him in the covenant of works; Isa. lv. 3, "Incline your ear, (says the Lord), and come unto me; hear, and your soul shall live; and I will make an everlasting covenant with you, even the sure mercies of David." Herein the two covenants are at least equal. What casts the balance on the side of the covenant of grace is, that it is an everlasting one, and a soul once in it can never fall out again, Cant iii. 10.

2. That surely God has made the second covenant himself; he proposes it to us, and requires us to embrace it; and has not left it to us to frame and mould it according to our mind, and then call on him to consent to the covenant we have framed. If he drew the whole of the first covenant to innocent man, much more has he drawn the whole of the second covenant for sinners. Let them know then, that it is their duty to study what God has proposed in his gospel, to examine themselves as to their liking of that way of salvation; and if their souls be content with it as it is laid down, let them embrace it.

3. Forasmuch as faith is the soul's assent to the covenant of grace, it cannot be the condition of that covenant properly so called. For consenting to a covenant is a consenting to the condition of it, and all the rest of the parts thereof; as we see in the first covenant, and may perceive in the second also in respect of Christ, where his doing and dying were the only proper conditions which he assented to; Psalm xl. 7, where he says, "Lo, I come; in the volume of the book it is written of me." But assenting to the condition of a covenant cannot be the condition itself properly speaking; otherwise we own faith to be the condition on our part, that is, the mean by which we are interested in Christ and the covenant, even as the woman's taking of the man may be called the condition of the marriage-covenant; which any may see is not the proper condition of it, but marriage faithfulness.

Now the parts of the covenant of works agreed upon by God and man were three; the condition to be performed by man, the promise to be accomplished to man upon his performance of the condition, and the penalty in case of man's breaking the covenant.

The Condition of the Covenant of Works.

FIRST, The first part is the condition to be performed; which was obedience to the law, fulfilling the commands God gave him, by doing what they required, Rom. x. 5, upon the doing of which he might claim the promised life in virtue of the compact. So this was a covenant, a covenant properly conditional. For understanding of this, we must consider,

1. What law he was by this covenant obliged to yield obedience to. And,

2. What kind of obedience he was obliged to yield thereto.

1st, Let us consider what law he was by this covenant obliged to yield obedience to.

Man under a twofold law, Natural and Symbolical.

1. The natural law, the law of the ten commandments, as the New Testament explains it, Gal. iii. 10, " Cursed is every one that continueth not in all things which are written in the book of the law to do them." The sum of this law is comprehended in what our Lord says ; Matth. xxii. 37—39, " Thou shalt love the Lord thy God with all thy heart, and with all thy soul, and with all thy mind. This is the first and great commandment. And the second is like unto it, Thou shalt love thy neighbour as thyself." That this law was given to Adam, is manifest, if it is considered that he was created righteous and holy, Gen. i. 27, compared with Eph. iv. 24. And all created righteousness and holiness is a conformity to the moral law, the perpetual rule of righteousness. And that he knew that law is evident, in that the knowledge of it is an essential part of righteousness and holiness, or the image of God, Col. iii. 10. Moreover, the remains of this law with the very heathens, Rom. ii. 15, are an evidence of its being given to Adam in perfection ; as the remains of a fallen house shew that sometime a house stood there.

If it be inquired, How that law was given him ? It was written on his mind and heart, Rom. ii. 15; and that in his creation, Eccl. vii. 29. Therefore it is called the natural law. He was no sooner a man than he was a righteous man, knowing the natural law he was under, and being conformed to it in the powers and faculties of his soul. That same law which God gave from Sinai with thunder and lightning, in all the precepts of it was breathed into Adam's soul, when God breathed into him the breath of life and he became a living soul.

This law was afterwards incorporated into the covenant of works, and was the chief matter of it. I say, afterwards ; for the covenant of works is not so ancient as the natural law. The natural law was in being when there was no covenant of works ; for the former was given to man in his creation, without paradise ; the latter was made with him after he was brought into paradise, Gen. ii. 7, 8, 15, 16, 17. The natural law had no promise of eternal life; for God might have annihilated his creature, though he had not sinned, till once the covenant of works was made. But then God put to the natural law a promise of eternal life, and a threatening of death, and so it became a covenant of works.

How then can men make such ado against believers being delivered from the law as it is the covenant of works, as if the law could no more be a rule of life to believers if that be so? It was a rule of life to Adam before the covenant of works, and it may, yea and must be a rule of life to believers, after the covenant of works is gone as to them. God made it once the matter of the covenant of works, and in that covenant a rule of life to Adam and all his natural seed; and why may it not be made the matter of the law of Christ, and therein be a rule of life to them that are his?

To shut up this point, see your deep concern in this covenant; and consider that your help is not therein, but in laying hold on Christ, the head of the second covenant.

2. Another law which Adam was obliged, by the covenant of works, to yield obedience to, was the positive symbolical law, forbidding him to eat of the tree of the knowledge of good and evil, recorded in the text. This law Adam had not, nor could have, but by revelation; for it was no part of the law of nature, being in its own nature indifferent, and altogether depending on the will of the Lawgiver, who, in a consistency with his own and man's nature too, might have appointed otherwise concerning it. But this law being once given, the natural law obliged him to the observation of it, inasmuch as it strictly bound him to obey his God and Creator in all things, binding him to love the Lord with all his heart, soul, mind, and strength. Hence it follows,

1st, That in as far as this law was obeyed, the natural law was obeyed; and the breaking of the former was the breaking of the latter also. They were but several links of one chain, constitutions of the Supreme Lawgiver, which, in point of obedience, stood and fell together.

2dly, That whatever is revealed by the Lord to be believed or to be done, the natural law of the ten commandments obliges to the believing or doing of it; Psalm xix. 7, "The law of the Lord is perfect." Hence faith is reckoned a duty of the first command. The gospel reveals the object of faith, and the natural law lays on the obligation to the duty of believing.

This law was not given, because of any evil that was in the fruit itself of that tree; for " God saw everything that he had made, and behold it was very good," Gen. i. 31. It was not forbidden because it was evil; but evil because forbidden. Yet was the giving of that law an action becoming the divine perfections, however small the matter seems to be in itself. In the most minute things God appears greatest.

(1.) Herein man's obedience was to turn upon the precise point of respect to the will of God, which was a trial of his obedience exactly suited to the state he was then in, and by which the most glaring evidence of true obedience would have been given. So this was a most fit probatory command. To love God and one's neighbour, nature itself taught Adam. Not to have another God, worship images, take God's name in vain; to keep the Sabbath, returning once a-week only; these could not have given such a demonstration of man's obedience to his Creator, having such affinity with the nature of God, in themselves, and with his own pure nature too. As little could the commands of the second table have been so, he having no neighbour then in the world with him, and Eve only his own flesh for a considerable time after.

(2.) Thus his obedience or disobedience behoved to be most clear, conspicuous, and undeniable, not only to himself, but to other creatures capable of observation; forasmuch as this law respected an external thing obvious to sense, and the discerning of any, who yet could not judge of internal acts of obedience or disobedience. So that God might be " clear in judging," Psalm li. 4; in the eyes of angels good and bad, and of man himself.

(3.) It was most proper for asserting God's dominion over man, being a visible badge of man's subjection to God. God had made him lord of the inferior world, set him down in paradise, a place furnished with all things for necessity and delight; so it was becoming the divine wisdom and sovereign dominion, to discharge him from meddling with one tree in the garden, as a testimony of his holding all of him as his great Landlord.

(4.) It was a most proper moral instrument, and suitable mean, to retain man in his integrity, who though a happy creature, was yet a changeable one. So far was it from being a bar to his further happiness, as Satan alleged, Gen. iii. 5. The tree of knowledge, as it stood under that prohibition, was a continual monitor to him to take heed to himself, a watchword to beware of the enemy; a plain lecture of his mutable state, wherein he might learn that he was yet but in favour on his good behaviour. Besides, it was a sign of emptiness hung at the door of the creation, with that inscription, "Here is not your rest;" so pointing him to God, as the alone fountain of happiness, forasmuch as there was a want even in paradise.

(5.) It was a compend of the law of nature. Love to God and one's neighbour was wrapt up in it; and all the ten commands were eminently comprehended therein. For in not eating thereof he would have testified his supreme love to God, and his due love to his posterity; and in eating thereof he cast off both, and so broke all the ten commandments.*

The nature of the Obedience due by man to the Law.

Secondly, Let us consider what kind of obedience to the law Adam was, by this covenant, obliged to yield, as the condition of it. To this twofold law he was to yield,

1. Perfect obedience. Imperfect obedience could not have been accepted under this covenant; neither for justification, for it would have condemned man, Gal. iii. 10, formerly cited; nor under the covenant of grace could it be accepted for that end neither, Matth. iii. 15 ; as it became the second Adam to fulfil all righteousness ; nor yet could it be accepted in point of justification under that covenant, though under the covenant of grace it is. The reason is, because under the first covenant the work must be accepted for its conformity to the law, and then the person for the work's sake ; but imperfect obedience could never be accepted of God for its own sake ; for God is "of purer eyes than to behold evil, and cannot look on iniquity," Hab. i. 13. But under the second covenant the persons of believers are first accepted for Christ's sake, Eph. i. 6; and then their works for the same Christ's sake, Heb. xi. 4. So then the condition of this covenant was perfect obedience, and that,

(1.) Perfect in respect of the principle of it. His nature, soul, and heart behoved always to be kept pure and untainted, as the principle of action. So the law is explained, Luke x. 25—28, "And behold, a certain lawyer stood up, and tempted him, saying Master, what shall I do to inherit eternal life ? He said unto him, What is written in the law ? how readest thou ? and he answering, said, thou shalt love the Lord thy God with all thy heart, and with all thy soul, and with all thy strength, and with all thy mind : and thy neighbour as thyself. And he said unto him, Thou has answered right; this do, and thou shalt live." Where the least blemish is in the soul, mind, will, or affections, it must needs make the actions sinful; "Who can bring a clean thing out of an unclean ?" Job xiv. 4 ; " A corrupt tree cannot bring forth good fruit," Matth. vii.

---

* How Adam, by eating the forbidden fruit, broke all the ten commandments, see proved in the Fourfold State, state 2, Head 1 ; under the title, " How man's nature was corrupted."

18. Where there is any indisposition for, or reluctancy to duty, there is a blemish in the frame of the soul. Therefore of necessity man behoved to retain a perfect purity in his soul, as the condition of that covenant. God gave man a heart perfectly pure, and commanded him to keep it from being in the least tainted; put on him a fair white garment of habitual inherent righteousness, and commanded it to be kept free from the least spot, under the pain of death.

(2.) Perfect in parts, nowise defective or lame, wanting any part necessary to its integrity; James i. 4. And it behoved to be thus perfect. [1.] In respect of the parts of the law, Gal. iii. 10. His obedience behoved to be as broad as the whole law, natural and positive; extending to all the commands thereof laid on him; nothing committed that the law forbade, nothing omitted that the law required. One link of this chain being broken, all was broke together; "For whosoever shall keep the whole law, and yet offend in one point, he is guilty of all," James ii. 10; [2.] in respect of the parts of the man, Luke x. 27, 28, forecited. His mind, will, and affections, his soul and his body, all of them behoved to be employed in obedience to the law; and it behoved to be the obedience, as of the whole law, so of the whole man. Thus was he bound to internal and external obedience in the whole compass of both, according to the law. [3.] In respect of the parts of every human action, Gal. iii. 10. The law requires in every such action, a goodness of the matter, manner, and end: a failure in any of these in any one action broke this covenant. So in every action what he did behoved to be good, well done; and all to the glory of God, as the chief end. The least mismanagement in any of these, the least squint look, would have marred all.

(3.) Perfect in degrees, Luke x. 27, 28, above cited. His obedience, as the condition of the covenant, was to be not only of equal breadth with the law, but of equal height with it, in every point. Every part of every action behoved to be screwed up to that pitch determined by the law; all that was lower than it was to be rejected as sinful.

2. Adam was obliged to perpetual obedience, Gal. iii. 10. Not that he was for ever to have been upon his trial; for that would have rendered the promise of life vain and fruitless, since he could never at that rate have attained the reward of his obedience. But it behoved to be perpetual, as a condition of the covenant, during the time set by God himself for the trial; which time God has not discovered in his word. The time of this life is now the time of trial. Our Lord Jesus Christ, in the room of the elect, obeyed the

law about the space of thirty-three years; for so long he lived. Whatever was the time appointed for man's trial, according to the covenant; his obedience behoved to be perpetual during that time, without interruption of the course of it, without defection and apostasy from it; till that time had expired in a course of continued obedience, he could not have claimed the final reward of his work. But that time being so expired, he would have been confirmed in goodness, so that he could no more fall away, as a part of the life promised. And the covenant of works would have for ever remained as man's eternal security for, and ground of his eternal life; but no longer as a rule of his obedience, for that would have been to reduce him to the state of trial he was in before, and to have set him anew to work as a title to what he already possessed, by virtue of his supposed keeping of that covenant. Yet man could be in no state, wherein he should not owe obedience to his Creator, no not in the state of glory; and if he owed obedience still, he behoved still to have a rule; and for that effect, the law of nature, which is perpetual, would have returned to its primitive constitution, the form of the covenant of works being done away from it; and so have been man's rule in the state of confirmation. Hence it follows,

(1.) That forasmuch as the Lord Jesus Christ has mended and perfected that work, which Adam marred; believers being united to him, are so confirmed in a state of grace, that they cannot but persevere, and that for ever. Hence it is observable, that the just by faith are declared to be entitled to that very benefit which Adam was by his obedience to have been entitled to; Hab. ii. 4, "The just shall live by his faith;" namely, a life which shall persevere and endure for ever. And therefore the apostle useth that scripture to prove the perseverance of believers, and the certainty of their eternal salvation; Heb. x. 38, 39, "Now the just shall live by faith; but if any man draw back, my soul shall have no pleasure in him. But we are not of them who draw back unto perdition; but of them that believe to the saving of the soul." And believers are declared actually to have eternal life, though that life is not yet come unto its full vigour, which is reserved for heaven, John xvii. 3, "This is life eternal, that they might know thee the only true God, and Jesus Christ whom thou hast sent." 1 John v. 13, "These things have I written unto you, that believe on the name of the Son of God; that ye may know that ye have eternal life."

(2.) As it is in vain for Christless sinners, utterly impotent for any good, to pretend to work that they may procure to themselves life; so believers ought not to work for life, or that they may, by their holiness and obedience, gain life. For believers in Christ have life already in him, by virtue of his working perfectly and perpetually in their room and stead ; and for them to pretend so to work for it, is to cast dishonour on Christ's perfect and perpetual obedience. The truth is, holiness is a main part of that life and salvation we have by Jesus Christ. " Of him [*i. e.* God] are ye in Christ Jesus, who of God is made unto us—sanctification," 1 Cor. i. 30. " Not by works of righteousness, which we have done, but according to his mercy he saved us by the washing of regeneration, and renewing of the Holy Ghost ;" Tit. iii. 5, " Who gave himself for us, that he might redeem us from all iniquity, and purify unto himself a peculiar people, zealous of good works," Tit. ii. 14. And were there more pressing of faith to obtain holiness, and less dividing of holiness from life and salvation, making the former the means to procure to ourselves the latter, there would be more true holiness in these dregs of time.

(3.) They that are not holy have no saving interest in Jesus Christ ; and while they continue so, shall never see the face of God in peace ; Heb. xii. 14, " Follow—holiness," says the apostle, " without which no man shall see the Lord." Where is the man that pretends to be in Christ, and to have faith, and yet makes no conscience of a holy life, of the duties of piety towards God, righteousness and mercy towards his neighbour ; but tramples on any of the ten commandments ; I say to him with confidence, as the apostle Peter said to Simon Magus, Acts viii. 21, " Thou hast neither part nor lot in this matter; for thy heart is not right in the sight of God." Has Christ fulfilled the covenant which Adam broke ; and are not all that are united to him made thereupon partakers of life ? How can it be otherwise according to the faithfulness of God ? Surely, then, thou who art living in sin, and so art dead while thou livest, hast no saving interest in him.

(4.) Though the believer is under the law of the ten commandments as a rule of life, he is not under the law as a covenant of works in any sense ; neither does the law he is under adjudge him to eternal life upon his obedience, nor lay him under the curse, and adjudge him to eternal death for his sins. But the law as to him is stript of its promise of eternal life to obedience, and of its threatening of eternal death to his sins. This is the apostle Paul's doctrine ; " Ye are become dead to the law by the body of Christ," Rom. vii. 4; " Ye are not under the law, but under grace," chap. vi. 14; " There is no condemnation to them that are in Christ Jesus," Rom. viii. 1 ; " That no man is justified by the law in the sight of God, it is evident: for, the just shall live by faith. And the law is not of faith; but the man that doth them, shall live in them. Christ hath redeemed us from the curse of the law, being made a curse for us," Gal. iii. 11, 12, 13. And how can it be otherwise, unless one will say that Christ, by his perfect and perpetual obedience, has not set his people beyond the reach of the curse, nor secured their life?

3. Adam was obliged to personal obedience. Hence says the Lord, " Ye shall keep my statutes and my judgments; which if a man do, he shall live in them," Lev. xviii. 5, which words the apostle Paul quotes; Rom. x. 5, " Moses describeth the righteousness which is of the law, That the man which doth these things shall live by them." It behoved to be personal obedience. Not that every person of Adam's race, according to the original constitution, behoved to yield this obedience for himself, in order to obtain the life promised. It is true, indeed, that all Adam's children, who should have been born and grown up, before the time of his trial was expired, would have been obliged, (it would seem) to that obedience for that end, in their own persons; and if they had failed in it, the loss would have been to themselves, and to themselves only. This may be learned from the case of Eve, noticed before. But that in case Adam had stood out the whole time of his trial, every one of his posterity after that should yet have been obliged to yield obedience for life in their own persons is what I cannot comprehend. For then, to what purpose was the representation of mankind by Adam? for what end was he constituted their federal head? It is plain, that by Adam's breaking of the covenant, death has come on them, who had no being in the world in Adam's time; and how this can be consistent with the goodness of God, and the equity of his proceedings, unless they were to have had the promised life upon running the set course of his obedience, I see not; and therefore must conclude, that after Adam's standing out the set time, all mankind then standing with him, would have been confirmed; and those who should afterwards have come into the world, would not only have had original righteousness conveyed to them from him, but have been confirmed too in holiness and happiness, so that they could not have fallen.

It is true, the covenant of works now proposes the same condition to every man under it, that it did to Adam, to be performed in his own person for himself, if he will have life by it. The reason is plain, Adam sinning is no more the representative in that covenant, to act for them; so they must take the same way every one for themselves, that he was to have taken for himself and all his posterity. While the pilot manages the ship carefully and skilfully, so as she makes her way towards the port, the passengers have nothing to do for their own safety, all is safe by his management; but if he run the ship on a rock, and split it, and make his escape, every one of the passengers must be pilot for himself, and work for his own life and safety.

But this obedience behoved to be personal in the following respects. It behoved to be performed,

(1.) By man himself, and not another for him, Lev. xviii. 15, fore-cited. The covenant of works knew nothing of a surety or mediator. "In the day thou eatest thou shalt die," plainly imports, that man, the moment he sinned, broke the covenant, and was a dead man in law. If he could have provided a surety who should have obeyed, when he disobeyed, that would not have fulfilled that covenant, or kept it. If a surety was to have place, it behoved to be by a new bargain, wherein a new representation was settled.

(2.) By one person, and not by more; that is, the righteousness of the covenant behoved to be of one piece, and not one part wrought by one, and another part by another. The sinning soul behoved to die; and imperfect righteousness could not be accepted in part, more than it could be in whole, because such righteousness is not righteousness indeed, but sinful want of conformity to the law. Hence it follows,

[1.] That God's accepting of a surety, as well as his providing one for lost sinners in the second covenant, was purely of free grace. For "in him," says the apostle, "we have redemption through his blood, the forgiveness of sins, according to the riches of his grace," Eph. i. 7; he might have held man to the first bargain, and made all mankind utterly miserable without remedy, having once broke the first covenant. But the riches of sovereign free love and grace brought forth a new bargain, wherein a surety was admitted, when that benefit to us might have been refused; yea, and was provided by him too, when we could never have procured one to take that burden on him for us.

[2.] That the purchase of our salvation by the precious blood of Christ, which was a full price for it, is so far from lowering the riches of free grace in it, that it exceedingly heightens the same. When you hear of free pardon and salvation to sinners, through the satisfaction of Christ, beware of imagining, that satisfaction spoils the freedom of it; but remember, that God the Father, Son, and Holy Ghost, might have in justice insisted on our own personal, perfect satisfying of the demands of the covenant of works; and yet such was their love and grace to poor sinners, that the Father parts with his Son to die for us, the Son lays down his life in our stead, and the Holy Spirit freely applies his purchase to sinners. So that all is of free grace to us. If it had been consistent with the nature of God, to have forgiven sin without satisfaction, such remission would have been of free grace; but when there behoved to be a satisfaction made, and God admitted a surety, and provided the same himself, this speaks unspeakable riches of grace; As if a king should give his own son to satisfy the law for a traitor, John iii. 16, " For God so loved the world, that he gave his only begotten Son, that whosoever believeth in him should not perish but have everlasting life."

[3.] That there can be no mixing of our own righteousness, in greater or lesser measure, with the righteousness of Christ, in our justification, by the second covenant, Gal. iii. 12, " For the law is not of faith; but the man that doth them shall live in them." We must betake ourselves wholly to the one or to the other. For the demands of the first covenant must be answered, by that righteousness on which we can be justified; and unless we have of our own a perfect righteousness to produce for that end, nothing we have can be accepted in that point, since there is no admitting of a pieced righteousness. And evident it is, that we cannot pretend to a perfect righteousness of our own, and therefore must go wholly to Christ for one.

The Promise of the Covenant of Works.

Secondly, The promise to be accomplished to man upon his performance of the condition. That was a promise of life, Rom. x. 5, forecited, which was implied in the threatening of death in case of sinning. For understanding the promised life, we must consider the condition to be performed, two ways.

1st, In the course of its performance, while man should have been in the way running the race of his obedience to obtain the crown; while he should have been on his trials for the subsequent reward, holding the way of God's commandments, and walking in the path chalked out to him by the divine law, during the time of his probation, without going off the way in the least. In this case the promise would have held pace with his continuance in the course of obedience. And by virtue of the covenant, he would have enjoyed a concomitant reward of life. " For in keeping of God's commands," says the Psalmist, " there is great reward," Psalm xix. 11. This is evident from the terms of the covenant in the text, which manifestly imply this, namely, While thou dost not eat thereof, thou shalt surely live. Now, this promised life was twofold, natural and spiritual, each of them perfectly prosperous: for, in scripture language, to live is to live prosperously, or in prosperity, 1 Sam. xxv.

6. Aud man's prosperity in the state of integrity, could not be a mixed prosperity, as now in this sinful state, but truly perfect, without mixture of anything that might mar it. And as for the life itself, natural and spiritual, they were both given him in his creation. So then the life promised, and to be accomplished in the course of his performance of the condition of the covenant, was,

A Prosperous Natural Life Promised.

1. A prosperous natural life, perfectly prosperous. The natural life was given to man by God's breathing in him the breath of life, Gen. ii. 7; knitting a rational soul unto his body, and so animating it which was presently discovered by man's breathing at his nostrils. While that union betwixt the soul and body remains, man lives a natural life. And thus man should have lived prosperously, while performing the condition of the covenant. This implied a threefold benefit.

(1.) The continuation of natural life, Rom. vi. 23. Man's body was indeed made of dust; but, by virtue of the covenant-promise, it would have been secured from returning to the dust again. As it was created without any principle of death within it, so the covenant barred all hazard of death from without it, from any other hand, as long as that covenant should be kept. Till the bond of the covenant was treacherously loosed by man himself, there was no loosing of the silver cord that knits soul and body together.

(2.) The vigour of natural life. The keeping of the covenant was a perfect security against all decay and languishing of natural life, which tends unto death. Since man even in that state was to eat, drink, and sleep, no doubt his body was to be supported by these means; but the fruits of the untainted earth were fitted for the preservation of such a life; and while his soul continued pure, he could not but make a regular use of them, according to the appointment of the Creator.

(3.) The comfort of natural life, pure and unmixed with the sorrows of it, which are now felt, but not till sin entered. All men know, that life is one thing and the comfort of life another; but these could not be divided till the wedge of sin was driven to separate them. This lay in these two things:—

[1.] Freedom from all evils and inconveniencies of life, which might embitter it to him. What these are, we all know from experience; a flood of them being let out on the world with the first sin, not to be dried up till the world end, and death and evil be cast into the lake of fire; Gen. iii. 17—19, "And unto Adam he said, Because thou hast hearkened unto the voice of thy wife, and hast eaten of the tree of which I commanded thee, saying, Thou shalt not eat of it; cursed is the ground for thy sake; in sorrow shalt thou eat of it all the days of thy life. Thorns also and thistles shall it bring forth to thee; and thou shalt eat the herb of the field. In the sweat of thy face shalt thou eat bread, till thou return unto the ground; for out of it wast thou taken; for dust thou art, and unto dust shalt thou return." Hence labour was to be without toil, strength without mixture of weakness and uneasiness, health without pain, or sickness, or indisposition of body.

[2.] The comfortable enjoyment of life with the conveniencies of it, Gen. ii. 16, where the Lord God said unto man, " Of every tree of the garden thou mayest freely eat." Life itself sometimes is burdensome now, and the good things of it are beset as with thorns and briers; but innocent Adam could have had none of these things to complain of. He was lord of the inferior creatures, and they were at his disposal. What joy and comfort the creatures could yield to him, he was master of, and could not but have a more exquisite taste of than any man since. He was clothed with the greatest honour, and had it with the profits and refined pleasures of life, together with God's favour.

We know then where to lay the blame of the miseries of this life and death itself. The breaking of that covenant opened the sluice to that flood of them which now overflows the world.

A Prosperous Spiritual Life Promised.

2. A prosperous spiritual life, perfectly prosperous. The soul of man was and is in its own nature immortal, not liable to the dissolution to which the body is subject. But besides, it was endowed with spiritual life, whereby it lived to God in union and communion with him, as bearing the image of God, a lively image of his righteousness and holiness, Gen. i. 7, Eccl. vii. 29. And thus man would have lived prosperously, performing the condition of the covenant. And this implied a fourfold benefit.

(1.) The continuation of the image of God in him, the uprightness of his nature in which he was created. Nothing could have marred that while the covenant was kept. The knowledge of his mind would have remained with him, as would also the righteousness of his will and the holiness of his affections. That glorious likeness to God in which he was created, was a beauty which nothing but sin could mar.

(2.) The continuance of the love and favour of God. He was the friend of God, the favourite of heaven; and as long as he kept the covenant, nothing could dissolve the friendship. Life lies in God' favour, and upon his good behaviour he was surely to enjoy it still

It could never have left him, as long as he kept God's way. For God cannot but love, favour, and delight in his own image, in whomsoever it is preserved entire.

(3.) Ready access to God, and fellowship with him. The covenant was a covenant of friendship; and while sin was kept out there was nothing to mar his intercourse with God. He would still have had immediate communion with God; for there was no need of a mediator where there was no breach, Gal. iii. 20. The means of communion with God, prayers, praises, &c. would at no time have been dry wells of salvation to him; no desertions, nor hidings of God's face, could have place.

(4.) *Lastly*, The daily comfort of his performance. He would still have had the pleasure there is in the very keeping of God's commands, and the comfortable feast of the testimony of a good conscience, upon every piece of obedience performed. And the greater this would have been, the longer he had continued, and the nearer he had come to the end of his race, where was the crown to be received.

Thus we may see God's bounty and man's ingratitude. He had wages in hand allowed him, a present reward of his work, according to that, " Thou shalt not muzzle the mouth of the ox that treadeth out the corn." Yet would he needs better his condition before the time, and so quite marred it.

Eternal Life in Heaven Promised.

2dly, We may consider the condition to be performed, as actually performed, and completely fulfilled. God had appointed to man a time of trial and probation, during which he was carefully to take heed to himself, that he obeyed perfectly and perpetually, as being liable to sin; and so to give proof of himself, of his awful respect to his Creator's will, and his right management of the talents given him by his great Lord to trade with. In this case, viz, upon man's standing in his innocence till that time was expired, eternal life was by the promise secured to him as the reward of his work, Matth. xix. 17. And in it these four benefits were implied.

1. The confirmation of his soul in innocence, righteousness, and holiness, that he should be set beyond hazard of sinning, and that for evermore, as the confirmed angels are. Being justified upon his perfect, personal, and perpetual obedience, this would have followed of course, according to the tenor of the covenant; otherwise he would have been for ever upon trial, which is inconsistent with the nature of the covenant. Mutability is woven into the very nature of the creature, and so Adam was created mutable; but he would have been, upon his obedience, secured from actual liability to

change for evermore. The need of watching would have been over with him in that case, as it is with the saints in heaven.

2. The setting of his body absolutely and for ever out of all hazard of death, even remote hazard. While he was in the state of trial, there was a possibility of death's making an approach to it, viz., on supposition of sin. But had the condition of the covenant once been fully performed, there had been no more any possibility of his dying, Rom. vi. 31, because no more possibility of sinning.

3. The settling of the love and favour of God upon him for ever, without any hazard of his falling out of it. This also necessarily would have followed on his confirmation in righteousness. The sun of favour from God, from that time, should have shone so upon him, as it could never more have gone down. The friendship would have been so confirmed, that there should have been no more a possibility of a breach for ever.

4. *Lastly,* The transporting of him soul and body to heaven, there to enjoy the perfection of blessedness through eternity. He should not always have lived in the earthly paradise, where he was to eat, drink, sleep, &c., but, in God's own time, been carried to the heavenly paradise, to live there as the angels of God. He was happy while he was in the course of obedience, and had communion with God. But there he would have been perfectly happy, and had more near and full communion with God, Psalm xvi. ult.

I am not here to launch forth into the subject of heaven's happiness, which man should have enjoyed by this covenant, had he kept it. Only in a word, for the substance of it, it would have been the same that the saints shall enjoy for ever; for it was the life which Adam lost for himself and his posterity that Christ purchased by his obedience and death for his spiritual seed, Rom. x. 5, compared with Hab. ii. 4, both forecited. And that was eternal life in heaven without controversy. Our Lord Jesus Christ himself proposing the covenant of works to a legalist, holds forth eternal life as the promise of it to be had on the performance of the condition ; Luke x. 25—28, " And behold, a certain lawyer stood up, and tempted him, saying, Master, what shall I do to inherit eternal life ? He said unto him, What is written in the law ? how readest thou ? And he answering, said, Thou shalt love the Lord thy God with all thy heart, and with all thy soul, and with all thy strength, and with all thy mind ; and thy neighbour as thyself. And he said unto him Thou hast answered right ; this do, and thou shalt live." And the weakness of the law to give eternal life now, proceeds only from our inability to fulfil that condition of it, Rom. viii. 3. For which cause, Christ put himself in the room of the elect, to fulfil that obe dience which they were unable to give, Gal. iv. 4, 5, and so consequently gained the life to them which they should otherwise have had if man had not sinned. Besides, it is evident, that by the breach of this covenant man now falls under the sentence of eternal death in hell; therefore, on the grounds of the goodness of God, and the equity of his proceedings, one may conclude that eternal life in heaven was promised.

The difference between Adam's and the saints' heaven.

Yet there would have been considerable difference betwixt innocent Adam's heaven, and the Mediator's heaven, which the saints shall be possessed of; but the advantage lies to the side of the latter. There are four things that would have been wanting (if I may so speak) in innocent Adam's heaven, that will be found in the saints' heaven.

(1.) The additional sweetness of the enjoyment that arises from the experience of want and misery. Two men are set down at a feast; the one never knew what hunger and want meant; the other never got a full meal all his days, but want and hunger were his daily companions. Which of the two would the feast be sweetest to? The case is plain. Sin is the worst of things; there is no good in it; the effects of sin, sorrow, misery, and trouble, are bitter; but God permitted the one, and has brought the other on, in depth of wisdom; for out of these is a sauce drawn that will give an additional sweetness to the supper of the Lamb in the upper house. While the saints walk in their white robes, and remember the filthy, ragged, black garments they went in some time a-day, it will raise their praises a note higher than innocent Adam's, while he should have looked on his, which there was never a spot upon. When after many tossings on the sea of this world, and the numerous floods of difficulties and dangers from sin and Satan which have beset them, the saints happily arrive on the shore of the heavenly Canaan, their relish of the pleasures to be enjoyed there will be the greater and the more delightful.

(2.) The fairest flower in heaven to be seen by bodily eyes, would have been wanting in innocent Adam's heaven, namely, the man Christ. It is a groundless, anti-scriptural notion, that the Son of God would have been incarnate, though man had never sinned, John iii. 16; 1 Tim. i. 15. It was for sinners the Saviour was sent. The ruin of man's nature in the first Adam, was the occasion sovereign love took to raise it up to the highest possible pitch of glory and dignity, in the person of the Son of God. There our nature is personally united to the divine nature, even in the person of the

Son; and the man Christ is in heaven more glorious than a thousand suns. It is true, Adam would have had the sight and enjoyment of God, Father, Son, and Holy Ghost; but he could not have said, as they, Behold God in our nature, our elder brother, &c.

(3.) The charter, written with blood, securing the enjoyment of heaven's happiness. Adam would have had good security indeed for it, by the fulfilled covenant of works; but behold a more glorious charter, the covenant of grace, written with the blood of the Son of God, Heb. xiii. 20. Every draught of the well of the water of life innocent Adam would have had in his heaven, he might have cried out with wonder concerning it, O the gracious reward of my obedience! But the saints shall say of theirs, The glorious purchase of my Redeemer's blood; this is the purchase of the Son of God, Rev. vii. 9, 10, " After this I beheld, and lo, a great multitude which no man could number, of all nations, and kindreds, and people, and tongues, stood before the throne, and before the Lamb, clothed with white robes, and palms in their hands; and cried with a loud voice, saying, Salvation to our God which sitteth upon the throne, and unto the Lamb."

(4.) *Lastly,* The manner of living, as members of the mystical body of Christ. Innocent Adam would have lived for ever in heaven as the friend of God; but the saints shall live there as members of Christ, John vi. 57, and xiv. 19. They shall be more nearly allied to the Son of God than Adam would have been, Eph. v. 30. He will be their husband in an everlasting marriage-covenant, their elder brother, the head, of which they are members, and through whom they will derive their glory, as they do their grace, from the Godhead, as united to Christ, the prime receptacle of grace and glory, Rev. vii. ult., " For the Lamb which is in the midst of the throne, shall feed them, and shall lead them unto living fountains of waters; and God shall wipe away all tears from their eyes." Rev. xxi. 23, " And the city had no need of the sun, neither of the moon to shine in it; for the glory of God did lighten it, and the Lamb is the light thereof."

Thus have I shown you the nature of the promise of the covenant of works, and the life therein made over conditionally to man. If we consider the life Adam could have expected from God, in a course of obedience, though there had been no covenant, we say, Adam performing obedience, according to the natural law written in his heart, would have had a prosperous life and being, while he had a being; this Adam might conclude from the good and bountiful nature of God. But still it would have been consistent with the nature of God, to have withdrawn his supporting hand from man, so as he might have ceased to be any more. And this would have been but taking away freely what he gave freely, being under no obligation to continue it ; for even Adam's innocent works could not have properly merited at God's hand, Rom. xi. 35, " Who hath first given to him, and it shall be recompensed unto him again ?" They could have only merited improperly, by virtue of compact, not by the intrinsic worth of the thing. Here,

[1.] The continuation of life to Adam, even while he continued obedient, was entirely due to the covenant God was pleased to make with him. And here was grace even in the covenant of works, that God was pleased by promise to secure the continuance of man's being, while he continued obedient.

[2.] The right that Adam could have pled to eternal life in heaven, by virtue of his obedience, was entirely founded on the covenant. If God had not revealed to him the promise of it, he could not have known that he should have had it, nor could he have demanded it. The natural law had no such promise. And here was more grace in the covenant of works. And therefore it is no wonder, that though men overturn the gospel-doctrine of free grace, yet they will not take with it. The Pharisees of old, Luke xviii. 11, and the Papists to this day, own free grace in their profession ; and what wonder, since innocent Adam, pleading life upon his works, could not have denied but he was debtor to free grace? But here lies the matter ; they put in their own works, their repentance, holiness, and obedience, (turning faith into a work, that it may go in with the rest), between free grace and them, making themselves but debtors to it at second hand for life and salvation. And if one shall tell sinners, Here you are to do or work nothing for life and salvation, but only receive the free grace gift of life and salvation from Christ by faith, and be debtors at first hand ; though withal we tell them, that repentance, holiness, obedience, and good works, are the inseparable attendants of faith ; they cry out, Error, Antinomianism, Licentious doctrine ! Yet it is the doctrine of the gospel, Tit. iii. 5 ; Eph. ii. 8. And it is not the doctrine of the gospel, nor does the apostle say, " By grace ye are saved, through works ;" for so would Adam have been saved according to the covenant of works, being debtor to free grace at the second hand, which the proud Pharisee was content to be. It is true, Adam's obedience was perfect, ours is not ; but buying is buying still, though one buy ten times below the worth, as well as when he buys at the full value.

The Penalty of the Covenant of Works.

Thirdly, We come now to consider the penalty in case of man's breaking the covenant, not fulfilling the condition. This was death,

death in its full latitude and extent, as opposed unto life and prosperity. This death was twofold. And we may speak of it as a thing that has fallen out.

Legal Death.

First, Legal death, whereby man sinning became dead in law, being a condemned man, laid under the curse, or sentence of the law, binding him over to the wrath of God, and to revenging justice ; " For as many as are of the works of the law, are under the curse. For it is written, Cursed is every one that continueth not in all things which are written in the book of the law to do them," Gal. iii. 10. Thus was man to die the day he should break the covenant ; and thus he died that very moment he sinned, because by his sin he broke the holy, just, and good law of God ; set himself in opposition to the holy nature of God, and cast off the yoke of submission to his Creator. This was an actual liableness to all miseries for satisfying offended justice. Thus the clouds gathered over his head, to shower down upon him ; and thus was he girded with the cords of death, which neither himself nor any other creature could loose.

Real Death.

Secondly, Real death, which is the execution of the sentence, Deut. xxix. 19, 20 ; the threatened evils, and punishments contained in the curse of the law, coming upon him. And of this there are several parts, all which man became liable to, or fell upon him, when he sinned. We take them up in these three ; spiritual, natural, and eternal death.

Spiritual Death.

1. Spiritual death, which is the death of the soul, and spirit of man, Eph. ii. 1, where the apostle mentions a being " dead in trespasses and sins." This results from the separation of the soul from God, by the breaking of the silver cord of this covenant, which knit innocent man to God, causing him to live, and live prosperously, as long as it was unbroken ; but being broken, that union and communion was dissolved, and they parted, Isa. lix. 2. Thus man was separated from the fountain of life, upon which death necessarily ensued. This death may be considered,

1*st,* As immediately seizing him upon the breaking of the covenant. And thus a twofold spiritual death seized him, as the penalty of the covenant ; a moral and a relative death.

(1.) A moral death of the soul, by which it was divested of the image of God, viz. saving knowledge, righteousness, and holiness; and the whole nature was corrupted, Eph. ii. 1; and so left destitute of a principle of vital spiritual actions, that it can no more think, will, or do anything truly good, than a dead man can perform the functions of life, Rom. iii. 10, 11, 12, where a dreadful picture of the corruption of human nature is given; " As it is written, There is none righteous, no not one; There is none that understandeth, there is none that seeketh after God. They are all gone out of the way, they are together become unprofitable, there is none that doth good, no not one." The soul of man was a curious piece of workmanship, made by the finger of God; it was set up, and set a-going for its Master's use, like a watch; but sin broke the chain and spring; so that all the wheels of a sudden stood moveless and could go no more.

(2.) A relative death of the soul, by which the blessed relation man stood in to God was extinguished. He was no more the friend of God, and the favourite of his maker. This was death indeed, Psalm xxx. 5. He enjoyed the friendship, favour, and fellowship of God, upon his good behaviour; he sinned, and so he behoved to lose them. Thus God became his enemy as Rector and judge of the world, and he was set up as a mark for the arrows of wrath.

2dly, As preying upon the soul of man, through the course of his natural life in the world. Sin laid the soul as it were in the grave, the house of death; and there being dead while the man liveth, devouring death works and preys in, and upon it, two ways:—

(1.) In the progress of sin and corruption in the soul, as the body in the grave rots more and more, Psalm xiv. 3. The soul being spiritually dead, the longer it lies in that case, the more loathsome and abominable it becomes. Swarms of reigning lusts breed in it, and are active therein; the remains of the image of God are defaced more and more in it, and the soul still set farther off from God. All actual sins are the workings of this death, the motions of the verminating life of the soul in the grave of sin, Eph. ii. 1, 2. So that they are not only sins in themselves, but punishments of the first sin, which cannot cease to follow on God's departing from the soul; which may persuade us of the absurdity of that principle, That there is no sin in hell.

(2.) In strokes of wrath on the soul. Where the carcase is, there these, like so many eagles, gather together. The sinning soul becomes the centre, wherein all manner of spiritual plagues meet together, as worms do in bodies interred, to feed thereon, Job xx. 26. These are manifold; some of them felt, as sorrows, terrors, anxieties, losses, and troubles, crossing the man's will, and so vexing, fretting, and disquieting him. Those are indeed a death to the soul, having a curse in them, like so many envenomed arrows shot into man; some of them not felt, so as to make the man groan under them, as blindness of mind, hardness of heart, strong delusions, but they are the more dangerous, as wounds that bleed inwardly.

Natural Death.

2. Natural death, which is the death of the body. This results from the separation of the soul from the body. It is twofold; stinged and unstinged death. Unstinged death parts the soul and body indeed, but not by virtue of the curse for sin. This is the lot of the people of God, 1 Cor. xv. 55, and is not the penalty of the covenant of works; for that is death with the sting of the curse, Gal. iii. 10, which death Christ died, which penalty he paid, and so freed believers from it, Gal. iii. 13. So that there is a specifical difference betwixt the death of believers and that death threatened in the covenant of works; they are not of the same kind, no more than they die the death that Christ died.

The natural death, the penalty of the covenant of works, then, is not simply the death of the body, but the stinged death of the body, the separation of soul and body by virtue of the curse; that as they joined in sin against God, they might be separated for the punishment of it for a time; though afterwards to be reunited at the resurrection, with a change of their constitution. For that there will be a change on the bodies of the wicked, as well as on those of the godly, is evident in that they shall continue united to their souls in hell, without food, and under torments; either of which, according to their present constitution, would dissolve their frame, and issue in death. Now, this natural death may be considered two ways, as the penalty of the covenant of works, inwardly and outwardly.

1st, Inwardly, in the body of man. There death got its seat in the day that he sinned; there it spread itself from the soul, where it began that fatal moment of yielding to the tempter. And thus it may be considered three ways; in its beginning, progress, and consummation.

(1.) In the beginning of it. That day that man sinned he became mortal, Gen. iii. 19. The crown of immortality, which he held of his Creator, by virtue of the covenant of works, fell from off his head, and he became a subject of the king of terrors. That day he got his death's wounds, of which he died afterwards. The mutiny then began among the constituent parts of the body, (witness the terror, anxiety, and shame, causing a motion of the blood and spirits, which before their sinning they were unacquainted with); and the end of that was the destruction and dissolution of the whole frame.

(2.) In the progress of it, in maladies and diseases, whereby death carries on its subjects towards the house appointed for all living, Eccl. iii. 20. Every pain, gripe, or stitch, is death's working like a canker in the body of man. Every sickness and disease is a fore-runner of death, coming before to give warning of the approach. The sweat, toil, and weariness that man is liable to, are fore-tokens of the body's falling down at length into the dust, Gen. iii. 19. Man has now his morning, mid-day, and afternoon; and then comes the night. He has his spring, summer, and autumn, and then winter. Like a flower he has his bud, blossom, fading, and then his falling off. But innocent man would have had a lasting mid-day, summer, and blossom. What follows these respectively, is owing to the breach of the covenant.

(3.) In the consummation of it, by the separation of the soul from the body, Heb. ix. 27. The pins of the tabernacle being loosed, it lies along upon the earth at length. The body of man like an old house, falls all down together, while the soul, the inhabitant, makes its escape, and leaves it. They joined in breaking of the covenant, and are punished with separation; the body going to the dust, and the soul to God who gave it, to receive its sentence.

2*dly*, Outwardly, upon the creatures, upon which the body of man has a dependence as to its life and welfare. What dependence we have on the creatures as to this, every one knows by experience. Without the air we cannot breathe; and as the temperature of it is, it is well or ill with our bodies. On the product of the earth we live; the fruits thereof are the support of our natural life, with the beasts that feed on them. The earth depends on the heavens; and according to their influence upon it, so it is serviceable to us. See the chain of dependence among the creatures; Hos. ii. 21, 22, "And it shall come to pass in that day; I will hear, saith the Lord, I will hear the heavens, and they shall hear the earth; and the earth shall hear the corn, and the wine, and the oil; and they shall hear Jezreel." Now man's natural life being so much bound up in these, the life promised him in the covenant could not but comprehend the continuing of these in their original constitution, Gen. i. 31, and fitness for the support of man's natural life and vigour, as means for that end. And so death, the penalty of the covenant, must needs spread itself even to them, and that upon the same score. Thus also it may be considered three ways: in its beginning, progress, and consummation.

(1.) In the beginning of it. And that was the curse laid upon the creature for the sake of the sinner man; Gen. iii. 17, "Cursed

is the ground for thy sake," said the Lord unto Adam. Man became vanity by his sin, and the creatures were made subject to
vanity on his account; so that they could not reach the end of their
primitive constitution, but fainted as it were in the way; "For,"
says the apostle, Rom. viii. 20, "the creature was made subject to
vanity." Nay, such a burden lies on the creation, as makes the
whole to "groan and travail in pain," ver. 22. Where can we turn
our eyes now, but we may see death riding in triumph? The earth's
barrenness often paints death on the faces of the inhabitants thereof, by scarcity and famine; the air is sometimes empoisoned with
pestilential vapours, that kill and sweep away multitudes; the fire
often burns and torments men; the waters swallow them up; beasts
wound, bruise, and kill them; nay, we are not secure from the
very stones of the field. The very sun in the heavens approaching
to them scorches and causes languishing; and removing from us,
causes us shiver with cold; and holding itself under clouds, damps
men's spirits. For death has spread itself over all.

(2.) In the progress of it, Psalm cii. 26. Man's declining in the
several ages, is manifest. Men are of less stature, less bones and
strength, than sometime they were. And why, but because our
mother earth is past her prime, and entered into her old age, and
her breasts afford not such nourishment as in her youth? Hence
man's days are very few now in comparison of what they were before the flood, when the curse had not sunk so deep into the earth,
as it has done from that time, when it had well nigh extinguished
her vigour. And whence is this weakness in the earth, but from
this, that the heavens also faint, are waxed old, and afford no such
influences as before? And whence is that but from the sin of man
in breaking the covenant of friendship with God, pursued by death,
which extends itself to all things that have any hand in preserving
that life, which it has a commission to take away?

(3.) In the consummation of it, in the destruction by fire that is
awaiting the world. For "in the day of the Lord the heavens shall
pass away with a great noise, and the elements shall melt with fervent heat, the earth also, and the works that are therein shall be
burned up," 2 Pet. iii. 10. The visible heavens and the earth are
now like an old worn garment; then shall the old worn garment be
rent in pieces, and cast into the fire. Man's old house, the earth,
that has often been made to shake with earthquakes, shall then fall
all down to ashes together; and the noble furniture of it, God's
works and men's works in it shall be burnt up. The roaring seas
shall be silent at length, and be no more. Yea, the sun, who now
runs his race like a strong man, shall fall as breathless. And the

world, that beautiful fabric of heaven and earth, shall have a dying day. The death threatened in the covenant of works shall pull all down together. And then death itself, with all the appurtenances thereof, shall be pent up in hell for ever, Rev. xx. 14, by the power of the glorious Mediator, Isa. xxv. 8.

Eternal Death.

(3.) Eternal death, which issues from the eternal separation of both soul and body from God in hell, Matth. xxv. 41. This is the full accomplishment of the curse of the covenant of works; and pre-supposes the union of the soul and body, in a dreadful resurrection to damnation; the criminal soul and body being brought forth from their separate prisons and joined together again, that death may exercise its full force upon them for ever and ever. That this was the penalty of the covenant of works, is manifest from the event testified by the holy scriptures, this being the lot of all those who, not embracing the covenant of grace, live and die under the covenant of works. For, says the apostle, 2 Thess. i. 7—9, " The Lord Jesus shall be revealed from heaven with his mighty angels, in flaming fire, taking vengeance on them that know not God, and that obey not the gospel of our Lord Jesus Christ: who shall be punished with everlasting destruction from the presence of the Lord and from the glory of his power." And this death may be considered two ways, as flowing from the sanction of the covenant of works, and from the nature of the creature fallen under that sanction.

1st, As it flows from the sanction of the covenant of works, requiring satisfaction to offended justice, and all the wronged attributes of God. And thus it is a punishment inflicted to satisfy for the offence, and repair the honour of God impaired by man's sin. And that punishment is twofold; the punishment of loss, and the punishment of sense.*

(1.) The punishment of loss; Matth. xxv. 41, " Depart from me, ye cursed." Man having sinned, and this death once seizing him, he is deprived of God's favour, and all comfortable communion with him of any sort is blocked up. The sun sets upon him, and the midnight darkness of God's forsaking of his creature falls on. Justice suffers not one grain of comfort to be put into the sinner's cup. All the least chinks, by which the least beam of the Lord's countenance might shine into the soul are stopt, and the creature is left absolutely comfortless. Thus it is with the damned in hell; and

---

* The reader, if he pleases, may peruse, for a more full account of this awful subject, what our author has said upon it in the Fourfold State. State iv., head 6.

thus Christ, as man's surety, had the sun of his Father's countenance eclipsed, Matth. xxvii. 46, when he cried with a loud voice, " My God, my God, why hast thou forsaken me ?"

(2.) The punishment of sense, in most grievous torments of soul and body; Matth. xxv. 41, " Depart from me, ye cursed, into ever-lasting fire." When death has proceeded thus far with the sin-ner, the waves of God's wrath go quite over his head, arrows of vengeance dipt in the poison of the curse fly at him continually. Who knows the power of them? Psalm xc. 11. The damned are inexpressibly miserable under them for ever and ever. By them was the heart of our glorious Redeemer " melted like wax, in the midst of his bowels," Psalm xxii. 14.

All this is requisite to shew just indignation against sin, and to wipe off the stain left by it on the honour of God.

2dly, As it flows from the nature of the creature fallen under the sanction of the covenant. And thus in this death, these dreadful circumstances do concur.

(1.) An irrecoverable loss of God's friendship, favour and image, Matth. xxv. 41. No more communication for ever can be between God and the creature brought to this dreadful case. All passage of sanctifying influences is stopt; the curse lies on the creature, which bars all emanations of love and favour from heaven, and leaves it under unalterable barrenness. The holy frame of the soul marred by sin, must remain so, never to be mended.

(2.) Perpetual bitter despair, Mark ix. 44. The creature once sunk into this sea of wrath, can never get up its head, nor see the shore; and knows it never shall. Hence absolute despair seizeth them, and all hope is plucked up by the roots. This lies as a talent of lead upon them, and must continually cut them to the heart. When the man Christ was forsaken of his Father, he knew he was able to get through the floods of wrath, and that he would at length joyfully set his foot on the shore; but that was because he was God as well as man. But weak man can never get through.

(3.) Continual sinning. Think and act they must; and how can they but sin, when their corrupt nature remains with them in hell? Submission to just punishment is their duty; but how can they do that in whose hearts is not the least measure of God's grace? Nay, they will gnash their teeth, in rage against God.

(4.) The eternity of the whole. Because they cannot pay out the debt to the full, therefore must they ever lie in the prison. The wrong done by sin to the honour of God is an infinite one, because done against an infinite God; and therefore the satisfaction can never be completed by a finite sufferer. So the yoke of punishment is wreathed about the neck of the sinner for ever and ever, never to be taken off.

This was the penalty of the covenant of works. And thus much of the parts of the covenant.

The Seals of the Covenant of Works.

Thirdly, I shall consider the seals of the covenant of works, whereby it was confirmed to Adam. It has pleased God to append seals to his covenants with men in all ages, for the confirmation of their faith of the respective covenants ; and this covenant seems not to have wanted some seals appended thereto for the same effect. Though innocent Adam was not called to faith in a redeemer, no such object of faith being revealed, or competent in that state ; yet was faith in God always a duty of the first command, and innocent Adam under this covenant was required to have and exercise a faith agreeable to the nature of the covenant he was under. That was, a firm persuasion that he should have life upon his performing of perfect obedience, but should die upon the least disobedience to his Creator. And according as he maintained this faith so was his obedience. Therefore Satan set himself first of all to attack the faith of our first parents, Gen. iii. 4 ; and when he had got it knocked on the head, then he carried his ruining project according to his wish. No wonder then he still sets himself in a peculiar manner against that grace. Now, for confirming this his faith, there were two sacramental seals appended to the covenant.

1. The tree of the knowledge of good and evil, Gen. ii. 17. What sort of a tree it was the scripture doth not determine, nor do the Jews pretend to define. Some gather from Cant. ii. 3, that it was an apple tree. But it is plain from the original text, that these are not the words of Christ, but of the spouse to Christ ; and the book being allegorical, it is too slender a ground at best to build such a fact upon. Whatever it was, it was not so called, as having a power really to make men wise. So the tempter pretended, Gen. iii. 5, but he was a liar from the beginning, John viii. 44. But it was a sign both of good and evil ; sealing to him all good while he should abstain from it, and evil if he should eat of it ; and so confirming his faith in both parts of the persuasion of it. And eventually, by eating of it, he knew good by the loss of it, and evil by the feeling of it. Though it was not to be touched, it might be seen, even as the rainbow, the seal of the covenant with Noah.

2. The tree of life, Gen. ii. 9. The which, though it might be an excellent means of preserving the vigour of natural life, as other trees of paradise also, yet it could not have a virtue in itself of mak-

ing man every way immortal. But it was a notable sacramental sign of life and eternal happiness, according to the nature of that covenant. The which is intimated by the eternal quickening virtue of our Lord Jesus Christ to the perfect happiness of the saints, coming under that name in the New Testament, Rev. xxii. 2; he being that in reality which the tree of life did signify. And thus the eating of it served to confirm Adam's faith, according to that covenant, namely, his persuasion of life upon performing of perfect obedience. The which is clearly intimated, Gen. iii. 22. But man having, by his sin, lost his right to the life signified, could no more be admitted to the partaking of the sacramental sign of it.

The Doctrine of the Covenant of Works applied.

USE. What is said upon this subject, serves for instruction, refutation, and exhortation.

USE I. For instruction. Here as in a glass ye may see several things, concerning God, concerning man in his best estate, concerning Christ, and concerning man in his present fallen state.

1. Concerning God, look into this covenant, and behold,

1st, The wonderful condescension of God, and of his goodness and grace toward his creature man. He stoopt so low as to enter into a covenant with his own creature, a covenant wherein he shewed himself a most bountiful and gracious God towards man. Man was not at his own, but God's disposal. Death was the natural wages of sin, but the life promised could not have been pleaded, but upon the foot of a covenant. Before that covenant man was bound to all obedience; but God was free to have disposed of him, after all, as he should see meet. But he made himself debtor to man for eternal life, upon his performing of perfect obedience; yet in the meantime his strength to obey was all from God, and there was no proportion betwixt man's work and the reward.

2dly, The spotless holiness and exact justice of God against sin. When we look to the condition and the penalty of this covenant, we must needs cry out, "Who is like unto thee, O Lord, glorious in holiness?" Exod. xv. 11, and, "Thou art of purer eyes than to behold evil, and canst not look on iniquity," Hab. i. 13. See here, sinners, how God looks on the least sin. Is it not the abominable thing which he hates with a perfect hatred? Such an evil it is as is enough to ruin a world of creatures among whom it spreads its baleful influence, and to dissolve the whole fabric of heaven and earth.

2. Concerning man in his state of primitive integrity.

1*st*, Man was a holy and happy creature in his first state. He was a spotless creature, meet to transact with God, and to entertain communion with him, immediately by himself without a Mediator. He was able to obey perfectly all the ten commandments. He was happy in God's favour and covenant-friendship. Ah! how is he now fallen like a star from heaven.

2*dly*, Man at his best estate, standing on his own legs, is a fickle creature, liable to change. The penalty set him in the covenant, spake him to be mutable, capable of forgetting his duty to his Maker, and his own interest; and the doleful event confirmed it. Why should men put their trust in men, and make flesh their arm? The most accomplished mere man that ever was on earth, was capable of being unfaithful to his trust, and actually was so. No wonder now that every man be a liar.

3. Concerning Christ the Saviour of sinners, behold here,

1*st*, The absolute necessity of a Surety in the event of a breach of this covenant. The condition was so high, and the penalty so dreadful, in this covenant, that being once broken, it was beyond the power of man to retrieve the matter. He must bear the heavy penalty, and that he could never discharge. He must begin again, and fulfil the condition; and that was beyond his power. Therefore there behoved to be a surety to act and suffer for man, or he was ruined without hope of relief. Hence said our blessed Surety, " Ought not Christ to have suffered these things?" Luke xxiv. 26. No creature was able to have undertaken this important office; it was a burden too heavy for angels. Only he who was God as well as man could perform the arduous task.

2*dly*, The love of Christ to poor sinners in becoming Surety for broken men. " Greater love" (says our Lord, John xv. 13.) " hath no man than this, that a man lay down his life for his friends." " God commendeth his love towards us," (says the apostle, Rom. v. 8.), " in that while we were yet sinners Christ died for us." None less than God man was able to answer the demands of this covenant, when once broken; therefore the Son of God was pitched upon to be the second Adam, to repair the breach made by the first; Psalm lxxxix. 19, " I have laid help upon one that is mighty; I have exalted one chosen out of the people." And when there was no helper, he offered himself to undergo the burden; Psalm xl. 6, 7, " Sacrifice and offering," said this blessed Helper, " thou didst not require; mine ears hast thou opened; burnt-offering and sin-offering hast thou not required. Then said I, Lo, I come." If ever ye would see what Christ has done for sinners, so as to be ravished with admiration of his matchless performance, study the covenant of works which he fulfilled as the second Adam, after it was broken by the first.

4. Concerning man in his fallen state.

1*st*, It is no wonder, that however scarce good works are in the world, yet working to win heaven is so very frequent. Legal principles and practices are natural to men; the covenant of works being that covenant that was made with Adam, and in him with all mankind, and so after a sort engrained in man's nature. And nothing less than the power of grace is able to bring man from off that way, to the salvation by Jesus Christ, 1 Cor. i. 23, 24, " Christ crucified is unto the Jews a stumbling-block, and to the Greeks foolishness; but unto them which are called both Jews and Greeks, he is the power of God, and the wisdom of God." We are like those who being bred merchants, though their stock is gone, must still be trafficking with small wares.

2*dly*, Salvation by works of our own is quite impossible; there is no life nor salvation to be had by the law, Gal. iii. 10, " For as many as are of the works of the law are under the curse." Will ye bring your good meanings and desires, your repentance, your obedience, such as it is, and think to get life, and salvation, and acceptance with God thereby? Remember, if ye will be for doing to live your obedience must be perfect and perpetual; and that if you fail, you are under the curse. That is the tenor of the covenant of works, and it will abate nothing. And therefore ye must quit the way of that covenant, or perish for ever; for ye are absolutely incapable to answer its demands.

USE II. For refutation. With what is said these three things following are inconsistent.

1. That there was no proper covenant of works between God and Adam. The contrary has been already proved from the holy scripture, and the nature of the thing. If we yield that point, the imputation of Adam's sin will have slender grounds to stand on; and if that fail, the doctrine of the imputation of Christ's righteousness will be in hazard.

2. That believers are not wholly and altogether set free from the law as a covenant of works; from the commanding power of it, as well as the condemning power of it. If that be so, believers in Christ are yet in a miserable case; for the commands of the covenant of works are no less than commands of perfect and perpetual obedience, under the pain of the curse; Rom. iii. 19, " Now we know that what things soever the law saith, it saith to them who are under the law; that every mouth may be stopped, and all the world may become guilty before God." Compare Gal iii. 10, " For as

many as are of the works of the law are under the curse." But believers are set beyond the reach of the curse; ver. 13, "Christ has redeemed us from the curse of the law, being made a curse for us." Rom. viii. 1, "There is no condemnation to them that are in Christ Jesus." They are dead to the law as a covenant of works, Rom. vii. 4, "Ye are," says the apostle, "dead to the law by the body of Christ;" and death sets one altogether free. They are under the covenant of grace, and they cannot be under both at once; Rom. vi. 14, "Ye are not," says Paul, "under the law, but under grace."

3. That believers must do good works to answer the demands of the law, as a covenant of works, if they will obtain salvation. Truly our good works will never be able to answer these demands; and if we pretend to do them for that end, as the covenant of works will never accept them, so we cast dishonour on Christ, who has answered all these demands already for believers, by his perfect and perpetual obedience. When God set Adam to seek salvation by his works, he was able for works; it was a thousand times easier to him to give perfect obedience than for us to give sincere obedience. So we may be sure God bringing in a second covenant for the help of lost sinners, would never put them again on seeking salvation by works, after their strength for them was gone.

USE III. For exhortation. Consider seriously of this covenant, with application to the particular state and case of our own souls. Here was a solemn bargain made with our first father, of the utmost importance to him and all his posterity. Will ye not lay to heart your own case with respect to it? Consider,

1. That this covenant was made with Adam in your name, for you in particular, as well as the rest of his posterity. So that you were all once under it, as really as if you had in your own persons consented to the terms of it; and the obedience it required of Adam was equally required of you; and the curse he subjected himself to by the breach of it, lies heavy on you as well as him.

2. Whether ye be delivered from it or not. If ye be, happy are ye; if ye be not, there is a weight lying above your heads that will sink you for ever in the bottomless gulf of perdition, if ye get not loose from that covenant, Gal. iii. 10, forecited.

3. None are delivered from it, but those whom God himself, man's covenant party, has discharged. The breaking of a bargain can never deliver the breaker from it, but lays him under the penalty. Nothing can deliver him but a discharge from the party he bargained with.

4. God discharges none from it, but upon full satisfaction made to all its demands on them. For our Lord has determined the matter thus, "Till heaven and earth pass, one jot or tittle shall in no wise

pass from the law, till all be fulfilled," Matth. v. 18. The sinner shall be obliged to give the law fair count and reckoning, and payment, else he cannot have his discharge. Consider if ye have any experience of this being done in your own case.

5. *Lastly*, The only way to satisfy this covenant, is by faith to lay hold upon Jesus Christ the surety, and to plead his obedience and death. The believer counts up to the law all that Christ has done and suffered, as done for him; so the accounts are cleared, the believer is discharged, the discharge being written with the blood of his Surety. And so he is set free from it for ever.

Thus much of the reality, nature, parts, &c. of the covenant of works·

PART II.

OF THE BREACH OF THE COVENANT OF WORKS.

HOSEA vi. 7,

But they like men have transgressed the covenant.

IN the beginning of this chapter, we have the Jews brought in repenting and turning to the Lord; which looks to that conversion of theirs that is yet to come, and hereby is insured, and that by virtue of the resurrection of Christ. Meanwhile they were to be laid under heavy strokes, and after a sort rejected. They were to be under a long eclipse of God's favour, the valley of vision being turned into a land of darkness. This looks to the Assyrian and Babylonish captivity, and further, to the ruin of the whole nation by the Romans, and their long rejection, which they are under to this day.

The causes of this are specified, to justify God's proceedings against them. (1.) Their inconstancy in that which is good, ver. 4, "Your goodness is as a morning cloud, and as the early dew it goeth away." Sometimes they seemed to promise fair for reformation, but all their fair blossoms quickly fell off. Such was the promising appearance Israel made when Jehu came to the kingdom, and such was that made by Judah in the days of Hezekiah and Josiah. Such too were the hosannas and loud shouts made at Christ's triumphant entrance into Jerusalem, which were soon changed into " Crucify him, crucify him." Therefore did the prophets and apostles testify against them, and denounce the judgments of God against them, and thereby ministerially hew and slay them ; ver. 5, "Therefore have I hewed them by the prophets; I have slain them by the words of my mouth." (2.) Their breach of covenant with God ; quite slighting and perverting, instead of pursuing the ends of the covenant; vers. 6, 7, " For I desired mercy and not sacrifice ; and the knowledge of God more than burnt offering. But they like men have transgressed the covenant ; there they have dealt treacherously against me." (3.) An universal deluge of sin and defection from God, that had spread itself over all ranks. Israel and Judah both were carried away with it, " Israel was defiled," ver. 10, &c.; and Judah was ripe for destruction; ver. 11, " Also, O Judah, he hath set an harvest for thee," &c. Priest and people were quite wrong, vers. 9, 10, magistrates and ministers, church and state ; Ramoth-Gilead, a city of refuge, protecting wilful murderers, or delivering up those they ought to have protected; the priests profane, no better than robbers and murderers, vers. 8, 9. General defection is a cause and presage of a sweeping stroke. It is the second of these that concerns our purpose; "They like men have transgressed the Covenant." Wherein two things may be considered.

1. The crime charged on them, transgressing the covenant, covenant-breaking. This is a crime of a high nature; it strikes at the root of society among men, and therefore is scandalous and punishable though it be but a man's covenant. How much more atrocious is the crime where God is the one party ? God took the Israelites into covenant with himself when he brought them out of Egypt. It was entered into with awful solemnity, Exod. xxiv. The design and ends of it were to lead them to Christ, and so to real holiness in the practise of the duties of the moral law. But, instead of this, they rejected Christ and sat down upon the poor performances of the ceremonial law, ver. 6, without faith and love. So they transgressed the covenant, and broke it, Jer. xxxi. 32; Heb. viii. 9.

2. Whom they resembled in breach of covenant. In this they acted *like men*, as our translators and others turn it; that is vain, light, fickle, and inconstant as man. But the Vulgate, Tigurine, Castalio, Arias Montanus, Rabbi Solomon, Grotius, and the Dutch translation and our own translation in the margin, read, *like Adam*. There is nothing about the Hebrew word to weaken this ; on the contrary, at this rate the word is taken in the proper sense, and this reading is evidently the more forcible of the two; and therefore is the preferable and genuine one, agreeably enough to the context. Besides, as I shewed before, the original word does but twice more occur in the scripture, viz., Job xxxi. 33; Psalm lxxxii. 17; and in both these places is

taken the same way. So the sense is, "They like their father Adam, have transgressed the covenant," for so the word is. He broke covenant with God, and so have they; he the covenant of works, they the covenant of grace, which they externally entered into. God set down Adam in paradise in covenant with him, the end of which was to make him completely happy; but he perverted the end of the covenant, preferred the fruit of a tree to his moral duty to God, so broke the covenant, and was cast out of paradise; and God set Israel down in Canaan, in covenant with him, the end of which was to lead them to Christ, as the end of the law; but they perverted the end of that covenant, and, preferring ceremonial observances to Christ and moral duty, transgressed the covenant, and therefore must be cast out of Canaan. The tree of the knowledge of good and evil was, by God's appointment, a seal of the covenant, fitted to help man to the keeping of it; but he used it the quite contrary way; the ceremonial law was, by God's appointment, for sealing the covenant of grace, and leading the Jews to Christ; but they used it the quite contrary way; and so it was a stumbling-block to them.

The doctrine clearly arising from the text is,

DOCTRINE. Our father Adam broke the Covenant of Works.

In discoursing from this doctrine, I shall,

I. Consider the fatal step by which that covenant was transgressed and broken.

II. How this fatal step was brought about.

III. How the covenant of works was broken by it.

IV. Apply the subject.

The Fatal Step by which the Covenant of Works was broken.

I. I shall consider the fatal step by which that covenant was transgressed and broken. I think I need not stand to prove that this covenant was broken by Adam. The truth of Moses' narration, Gen. iii., puts it beyond controversy; as also doth the doleful experience of his posterity, Rom. v. 12. Our father Adam was once in a flourishing condition, had in his hand a noble portion of holiness and happiness for every one of his children; and he had more in hope for himself and them, which would have made them eternally and completely happy. He had a goodly stock to set up with at first; and a trade with heaven to improve his stock in, which, rightly managed, would have made all his family happy for ever; the which trade was opened to him by this covenant. But, alas! the whole family is ruined, we are all born beggars, we have nothing left us;

nay, we are pursued for our father's debt as well as our own, Rom.
v. 18, " By the offence of one judgment came upon all men to condemnation;" and we are in hazard of dying in prison for evermore.
A plain evidence that our father was broke, his trade mismanaged,
and he run in debt, the communication with heaven stopt; and so
the covenant was broken. Besides the Lord's making a new covenant, a covenant of grace, with Christ, as the second Adam, for
the salvation of lost sinners of Adam's family, is a plain proof that
the covenant of works was broken, and the transgressors thereof
ruined by the first Adam. And what was the fatal step?

It was the eating of the forbidden fruit, Gen. iii. 6, " When the
woman saw that the tree was good, &c. she took of the fruit thereof,
and did eat, and gave also unto her husband with her, and he did
eat." This was that by which the covenant was broken, and man
ruined. No wonder eating and drinking is the destruction of many
to this day; this engine of ruin had too much success in the hand
of the great deceiver, not to ply it still. God gave Adam a dominion over the creatures, to use them soberly for his own comfort and
God's glory. He " put all things under his feet;" he only kept
one tree from him, that he might not eat of the fruit thereof, and
that for the trial of his obedience. He was discharged, under the
pain of death, to meddle with it; to which prohibition he consented;
and yet, over the belly of the solemn covenant, he laid hand on it,
ate of it, and broke the covenant. Here, for the understanding of
this sin aright, consider the progress, the ingredients, and the aggravations of it.

The Progress of the Sin of breaking the Covenant of Works.

First, Consider the progress of this sin. It is not to be imagined,
that Adam and Eve were innocent till they had the forbidden fruit
in their mouths; the coveting of it in their hearts behoved of necessity to be before that; but the eating of it was that whereby sin
and apostasy from God was completed. The beginning of their sin
was unbelief and doubting. At the suggestion of Satan they
doubted the truth of God in the threatening, Gen. iii. 3—6. So, in
this fatal battle, their faith got the first stroke. And it being once
foundered, their heart plied to the temptation, and the lust after the
forbidden fruit arose, and then the sin was completed by actual eating, Gen. iii. 6. The eye of the mind was first blemished; a mist
arose from hell, which they admitted, that by degrees darkened their
understanding, so that they first doubted, and then disbelieved the
threatening of the covenant. Then their will was easily conquered to a compliance with the temptation, and turned away from

the command, the rule of duty. A lust and corrupt affection to the tree seized them, discovering itself at the eye, in a lustful looking at it, Gen. iii. 6. So the hand took it, and the mouth ate it, and the fatal morsel was lodged within the body.

Thus the cool of temptation raised a flame, which quickly spread itself over the whole soul and body. The which is often reached in the case of their sinful posterity, who by these means are frequently cast down from their excellency as it were in a moment, and plunged into a gulf of misery.

There is more ill in doubting and unbelief than men are aware of. It was the devil's master-piece for the ruin of souls under the covenant of works; and so it is still under the covenant of grace; Mark xvi. 16, "He that believeth not shall be damned." Men were first ruined by their doubting and unbelief of the threatening of the first covenant; now men are ruined by their doubting and unbelief of the promise of the second covenant; Isa. liii. 1, "Who hath believed our report?" says the prophet. And what that report is, see 1 John v. 10, 11, "He that believeth on the Son of God, hath the witness in himself; he that believeth not God, hath made him a liar, because he believed not the record that God gave of his Son. And this is the record that God hath given to us eternal life; and this life is in his Son." Though doubting may consist with faith, so that it be not reigning; yet it belongs not but is contrary, to the nature of faith, which in itself is a firm persuasion, more or less firm, according to the strength of it.

The Ingredients of this Sin.

Secondly, Let us consider the ingredients of this sin. If it is opened up, one may see it to be a complication of evils; not a little sin, but a great one, and in some sort the greatest sin.

1. Horrid unbelief was in it. By it the truth and faithfulness of God to his word was questioned, disbelieved, and denied; the lie was given to the God of truth, 1 John v. 11, forecited. And to make the affront the blacker, the devil was believed in his contradiction to God. God said, Yea; Satan said, No; and the decision was in favour of the latter.

2. Pride, ambition, bold presumption, and curiosity, took place in this sin. No less was attempted by it, than to be like God himself; Gen. iii. 5, "Ye shall be as gods," said the old serpent. God had set them in paradise; but they would, in a manner, ascend above the height of the clouds, and set their throne above the stars, as the proud monarch of Babylon did, Isa. xiv. 13, 14. They had full liberty as to the use of all that was in paradise; only God locked up

from them that one tree; and they boldly forced the lock, and ate that which God forbade them to touch; as if nothing was to be hid to them.

3. There was in this sin monstrous ingratitude, and discontent with their condition. They wanted nothing for necessity, convenience, or delight, beseeming their state of trial. A bountiful God had heaped favours on them; they bore God's image, were fit to be companions of angels, were the envy of devils, had the dominion of the lower world, and were God's confederates. But all this was sunk and lost in unthankfulness; and they were so little contented, that they would needs have that in very deed which they had no want of, as is often the case with their children.

4. This sin contained in it contempt of God, rebellion against him, and downright apostasy from him, going over to the devil's side. Thus it was a renouncing of the covenant, and a conspiring with Satan against God. They carry themselves as if they had been decoyed into a foolish bargain; and, forgetting the majesty of God, and their own dependence on him, they break his bands, and cast his cords from them; pretending they would see better to themselves, and so they cast off his yoke at one touch.

5. *Lastly,* In one word, this sin was a breaking of the whole law of God at once. By this one deed, not only was the positive law trampled under foot, but the natural law written in their hearts was broken in all the ten commandments of it at once, as I have shewn elsewhere.*

The Aggravations of this Sin.

Thirdly, Let us view the aggravations of this sin. Consider,

1. The person who did it; righteous Adam; one who was not tainted with original sin, as others now are, but was endued with original righteousness; one in whom Satan had nothing, till he winded it in by his subtilty. There was no blindness of mind, perverseness of will, or unholiness of affections, to graft his temptation on. So having these advantages, the sin was in that respect of all sins the most heinous. And therefore he having found mercy, is a pattern of mercy to all who will believe in Christ.

2. The object by which he was enticed, and for which he broke God's law. It was not a wedge of gold, as in Achan's case; nor thirty pieces of silver, as in that of Judas; but a morsel of fruit. The smaller the thing was, the greater the sin; and the more inexcusable the sinner, whom Satan catched with so sorry a bait. What

* See Fourfold State of Man, state 2. head 1, under the title, "How man's nature was corrupted."

need had he of that, who had enough besides? But when once the mind is bewitched with temptation, it is enough to stir up a longing after fruit, if it be but forbidden; as the wayfaring man in Nathan's parable was entertained by the rich man with his poor neighbour's lamb, though he had a flock of his own.

3. The nature of the thing. Though it was a small thing, yet it was a sacred thing, set apart for a holy use, not to be touched. This sin was theft, and theft of the worst kind, namely, sacrilege. It was a profanation of holy things, and that of the worst kind; profanation of a sacrament, a seal of the covenant. No wonder it brought on a curse.

4. The place where it was committed. In paradise, where every flower was proclaiming the glory of God, where he wanted nothing necessary for him, but was surrounded on every hand with tokens of the Lord's kindness to him. Eden was the pleasantest spot of the virgin earth, and paradise the pleasantest spot of Eden. But there the rebellion was begun against God, who set him in that delightful place. In the presence-chamber, as it were, rebel man, by this act of his, struck at his sovereign Lord. So it was aggravated like the murder of Zacharias, who was slain between the temple and the altar, Matth. xxiii. 35.

5. The time when it was committed. He had not been long in the world, till he lifted up his heel against his Creator. He had stood short while, till, being giddy with pride and ambition, he fell into disgrace. What time Adam fell, is a question. It is the common opinion, that he fell the same day he was created. Some think he stood longer, supposing the events recorded about him, Gen ii. and iii. to require more time than one day. And the deists improve that against the credit of Moses' history, but entirely without ground, I think the common opinion is true. The devil's envy and malice would set him a-work on the first occasion to ruin man; and, for all that appears, whenever he tried it, he carried his point. If our first parents had stood longer, the blessing of marriage would have taken place in a state of innocence. The scripture says, Satan was "a liar, and a murderer from the beginning," John viii. 44. Yet "Adam in honour could not night; he became like as the beasts, they were alike," Psalm xlix. 12. From this text the Hebrew doctors gather, that the glory of the first man did not night with him; and the ancient translators understand it of Adam. The work of redemption is the more illustrious, that man could not stand one day without the Mediator's help.*

* See more on this subject in the author's notes on the " Marrow of Modern Divinity."

6. *Lastly*, The effects and consequents of this sin. These are all evils that came on Adam himself, and on his posterity to this day, and that will come, even to the end of the world. Hereby all mankind were ruined. That sin was the wide gate at which sin and death entered into the world. It spread its malignant influence over the creation, loosed the pins of the fabric of the world, which it will pull down at length altogether, according to the import of the threatening.

How the Fatal step, in the breach of the covenant of works, was brought about.

II. I shall consider how this fatal step was brought about. For clearing of this, three things are to be considered; Satan's tempting to it; God's leaving man to the freedom of his own will in the matter; and man's abusing this freedom of will, and complying with the temptation.

Of Satan's tempting to this Sin.

First, Satan tempted to it. God created all the angels holy spirits, yet mutable, as the event in some of them has proved. Some of them were elected to eternal happiness from eternity, and some of them not elected, 1 Tim. v. 21, where the apostle speaks of elect angels. They were all created the first day, as appears from Gen. i. 1, 2, compared with Job xxxviii. 7. In the former it is said, " In the beginning God created the heaven and the earth." And in the latter place it is said that, when God " laid the foundations of the earth, the morning stars sang together, and all the sons of God shouted for joy ;" by whom are most certainly to be understood the angels. The reprobate angels were not fallen before the sixth day; for it is said, Gen. i. 31, that, on that day, " God saw everything that he had made, and behold it was very good." On the sixth day man was made, and the same day he fell, as has been shewn before. The reprobate angels were fallen before him, and therefore they fell the same day too. And it seems they lost no time, but immediately, with the first occasion, one of them sets to work against man, and gained his point by temptation, John viii. 44, forecited.

Concerning this temptation we may remark,

1. The instrument of the temptation was a serpent, Gen. iii. 1. And,

1st, It was a true and real serpent, as appears from Moses comparing it with the rest of the beasts ; Gen. iii. 1, " Now the serpent was more subtle than any beast of the field." What sort of a serpent it was is not determined. Some think it to have been a beautiful creature of a shining colour; for there are serpents mentioned, Deut. viii. 15, called in the original text *Seraphim*, which is a name given to angels. And so possibly Eve might take the serpent to have been acted by one of the good angels, or Seraphims. Whatever sort it was of, serpents have been of great note in the kingdom of the devil since. The Egyptians worshipped serpents. The genius of a place was painted as a serpent. And in the old Greek mysteries they were wont to carry about a serpent, and cry, *Evah*—a memorial of the extraordinary service it had done the devil.

2dly, It was acted by the devil. For since serpents could not speak, and far less reason, neither of which was wanting in this case, one may surely conclude, that it was the devil who abused the body of the serpent to his wicked purpose, and therefore is called that old serpent the devil and Satan, Rev. xii. 9, and chap. xx. 2.

2. Satan set upon the woman first, the woman the weaker vessel, that having once overcome her, he might by her means the more easily conquer the man. And thus he readily manages his temptations still, observing where the wall is weakest, that there he may make his attack with the more success. And he chose the time when she was alone, not with her husband, from whom she seems to have had the knowledge of the covenant God entered into with him. Had they been together, they might have jointly withstood him who conquered both, one after another.

3. He moveth a doubt concerning the command; Gen. iii. 1, "Yea hath God said ye shall not eat of every tree of the garden?" And thus he does subtilly and ambiguously. He does not at first bring forth the whole venom of the temptation, but pretends, as one in doubt, that he would be informed by the woman. It is hard to tell whether he meant this of God's forbidding to eat of any, or only not of every tree of the garden. It is the design of the tempter to draw us unto a contempt of the commands of God. The woman, however, gives him a round answer, wherein she makes a very ample profession of the truth; vers. 2, 3, "And the woman said unto the serpent, We may eat of the fruit of the trees of the garden, but of the fruit of the tree which is in the midst of the garden, God hath said, ye shall not eat of it, neither shall ye touch it, lest ye die." They may resist at first, who are afterwards overcome.

4. Quitting the attack on the command, which he perceived her to adhere to, Satan falls on the threatening, and contradicts it, Gen. iii. 4, "And the serpent said unto the woman, Ye shall not surely die." He tells her it was not so sure as she imagined, that God

would punish them at that rate. He puts her in hope of escaping punishment. Thus Satan resisted, flies; but where one method fails he will try another, and, through hopes of impunity entertained in one's heart, he often gains his purpose.

5. He proceeds as one that wished well to her and her husband, and pretends to shew how they might both arrive at a high pitch of happiness speedily: even to be as gods, and that in knowledge or intellectual delights; insinuating withal, that, by the very name of the tree, the truth of what he said might appear. For (said the serpent) "God doth know, that in the day ye eat thereof, then your eyes shall be opened; and ye shall be as gods knowing good and evil." Thus the liar and murderer still ruins men, pretending to make them happy, while he carries on their destruction.

6. *Lastly*, She being ensnared, he makes use of her to tempt her husband, and prevails, Gen. iii. 6, "And when the woman saw that the tree was good for food, and that it was pleasant to the eyes, and a tree to be desired to make one wise; she took of the fruit thereof, and did eat, and gave also unto her husband with her, and he did eat." And thus he often conveys his temptations to us, by those whose interest in us and affection to us, we doubt not, and whom therefore we suspect not; and so he rends men with wedges of their own timber, making one a snare to another.

God left Man to the Freedom of his own Will.

Secondly, God left man to the freedom of his own will in this matter. He was not the cause of his fall; he moved him not, nor could he move him to it; James iii. 13, "For God cannot be tempted with evil, neither tempteth he any man." Such is the holiness of his nature. He gave him a power to stand if he would, and he took not away from him any grace given; but, for his trial, left him to his freedom of will, with which he was created. God made him good and righteous, and the natural set of his will was to good only, Eccl. vii. 26. But it was liable to change, yet only to change by himself; he could only be made evil or sinful by his own choice.

If it be asked, why man was not set beyond the possibility of change. It is to be remembered, that absolute immutability is the peculiar prerogative of God himself, and every creature, in as far as it is a creature, is incapable of being so immutable. Yet the creature may be in some sense made immutable, that is, so as it shall not be possible for it actually to fall from its goodness, though there is still a changeableness in its nature. Now, if man had been created without so much as a remote power in himself to change himself, he had not been a free agent; but God might have so established him, as that he could not actually have fallen ; yet that would have been owing to confirming grace. The which why the Lord did not bestow on him, it belongs not to us to define ; only he was no debtor to him for it.

Man abused the Freedom of his Will.

Thirdly, Man abused his own liberty or freedom of will, and complied with the temptation, and so broke the covenant. He only himself was the true and proper cause of his own falling ; not God, for he can never be the author of sin ; not the devil, nor Eve, for they could only tempt and entice, but not force him. It was his own choice, he did it freely without coaction or compulsion ; and he could have stood if he would. And thus was the fatal step made, whereby the covenant was broken.

How the Covenant of Works was Broken.

III. I shall consider how the covenant of works was broken by this fatal step. We may take up this in three things.

1. The command was violated. The covenant required perfect obedience, but it was not given ; perpetual obedience, but man did soon come to a stand in the course of obedience, and went no further. Here he disobeyed, here he shook off the yoke, here he sinned against his God. Thus the condition of the covenant of works was broken.

2. The right and title to the promised benefit by that covenant was undermined. The promised life was lost, man had no more any pretensions to it ; he could no more plead the reward, which was to be given him in hand ; and the prospect of the reward, which before his disobedience he had in hope, was entirely cut off. Thus failing in his performance of the condition of the covenant, he rendered the promise of the covenant null and void, as if it had never been made.

3. He fell under the penalty of the covenant, became liable to death in its utmost extent. As he had no more ado with the promise, the threatening now bound him to bear the wrath threatened for the satisfaction of divine justice. The blessing of the covenant being lost, the curse of it seized him, and he was bound with the cords of death ; the which was let out as a flood, at that breach which was made in the covenant, and overflowed.

(1.) The soul of man, so that it died spiritually, losing the image of God, and losing the favour of God. Man turning from God as his chief end, the image of God in his soul was defaced, Gen v. 1, 3, His saving knowledge was lost ; witness the cover of fig-leaves which our first parents prepared for covering of their nakedness, and their pretending to hide themselves from the presence of God, Gen. iii. 7. The righteousness of his will was lost; witness their aversion to God, hiding themselves from him, their excusing of their sin, transferring of their guilt, the man laying the blame on the woman, the woman on the serpent; nay, Adam not obscurely reflected on God himself. The holiness and regularity of their affections went off; they were filled with disorder, confusion, and shame. They lost God's favour, were seized with horror of conscience, Gen. iii. 8, were driven out of paradise, like a divorced woman out of the house of her husband, declared incapable of communion with God, and debarred from the tree of life, the seal of the covenant.

(2.) The body of man became mortal, death working within it and without it, from that moment the covenant was broken. He was condemned to toil and weariness for life, and then to return to the dust at length, the frame and constitution of man's body having become deadly from the moment of his breaking the covenant. And sorrow and pain in breeding and bringing forth of children, was laid on the female sex, as a particular mark of displeasure with the first sin; and the ground was cursed for man's sake, because of the dependance of the life of man upon it.

(3.) *Lastly*, Soul and body were subjected and bound over to eternal death in hell. For this was comprehended in the threatening of the covenant of works, as has been already shewn.

Thus was the covenant of works broken. Yet man was not, and could not thereby be freed from that covenant; still he was bound to obedience, according to the command of it; and to satisfaction, according to the threatening. Only God was no more obliged to fulfil his promise, since it was conditional, and the condition was broken.

Application of the Doctrine of the Breach of the Covenant of Works.

USE I. Here is a memorial which we have need ever to carry about with us, while we live in this world; A memorial,

1. Of the nothingness of the creature, when left to itself. God left some of the angels to themselves and they turned devils; he left innocent Adam to himself, and he turned apostate. O the need of continual supplies of grace! There was no bent and inclination to evil naturally in them; but in us there is a natural propensity to turn from God. What need have we then to cry, " Lead us not into temptation?" What need of continual dependence upon the Lord?

2. Of the hopelessness of salvation by works. That was the way

which man was first set on, and that is the way which man naturally is set to follow unto this day. But what hope can there be that way? Adam was able to work for life, having sufficient strength laid to his hand, and yet he miscarried in it; how can it prosper in our hands, who are without strength, and whose work-arm is broken; he had less to do than we have now, only perfect obedience was required of him at first; but of us now is required not only perfect obedience, but satisfaction for sin done. We have more work and less strength than Adam had. When he fell a-working for heaven, which work was marred in his hand, it may justly make us to despair of salvation that way. He could not stand, how shall we that are fallen raise up ourselves? How unlikely is it that self-destroyers shall be their own saviours?

USE II. Here is a watchword which we ought never to forget.

1. Watch and pray that ye enter not into temptation. The devil still goes about seeking whom he may devour. No state, while ye are here, can secure you from temptation. Though ye be in a state of friendship with God, he will attack you. No place, though a paradise can protect you. He has malice enough to drive you to the greatest sins; subtilty and long experience to manage the temptation so as it may best take. Do not parley with temptation, listening to the tempter may bring on doubting, doubting will bring on disbelieving, and disbelieving will bring on full compliance. O therefore watch!

2. Take heed of forgetting the covenant of your God. When men lose the sense of the bond of the covenant, they cannot long forbear the breaking of it. We see this in Adam our father, and we may see it daily in men's personal covenants, and the national covenants these lands are under the bonds of. The impression of them is worn off, and so the duties of them are cast behind men's backs. No wonder that this is the sin of the land, and of particular persons, seeing we are all children of the great covenant transgressor, Adam.

USE III. *Lastly*, Here is a demonstration of the absolute necessity of being united to the second Adam, who kept the second covenant, and thereby fulfilled the demands of the first covenant. See your absolute need of him; prize him, and flee to him by faith, behold him with an eye of faith who has repaired the breach. The first Adam broke the first covenant, by eating of the fruit of the forbidden tree; Christ has repaired the breach by hanging on a tree and bearing the curse for his people. Adam's preposterous love to his wife made him sin; Christ's love to his spouse made him suffer and satisfy. In a garden Adam sinned, and therefore in a garden Christ was buried. Eating ruined man, and by eating he is saved again. By eating the forbidden fruit all died; and by eating Christ's flesh and drinking his blood by faith, the soul gets life again, John vi. 57. O then have recourse to Christ; and thus shall you be saved from the ruins of the fall and have an interest in the covenant made with Christ, the condition of which being already fulfilled by him, can never be broken, or they who are once in it ever fall out of it again.

PART III.

OF THE IMPUTATION OF ADAM'S FIRST SIN TO HIS POSTERITY.

ROMANS v. 19,

For as by one man's disobedience many were made sinners, so by the obedience of one shall many be made righteous.

YE have heard of the making of the original contract betwixt God and man, the covenant of works; as also of the breaking of it by our father Adam. This text shews our concern in the breach of that covenant; and it is necessary we be sensible of it, that we be not eternally ruined thereby, but, being convinced of that debt lying on our head, may flee to and make use of the great Surety for removing it from us.

In this chapter, ver. 14, the apostle shews Adam to have been a figure or type of Christ; and from ver. 12, and downwards, he institutes a comparison betwixt these two, the common heads and representatives of mankind, though Christ's representation is not so extensive as Adam's; but each of them represented his seed; Adam his natural seed, and Christ all his spiritual elect seed. Adam by his disobedience broke the first covenant; Christ by his obedience to the death fulfilled the second covenant. The disobedience of the one brings condemnation and death on those that are his; the obedience of the other brings justification and life to all that are his. The reason of both is given in the text; namely, that by the one all his are made sinners, and sinners are justly condemned and die; by the other all his are made righteous, and the righteous must, according to the covenant, be justified and live.

So the text is a comparison made betwixt the effect of Adam's disobedience, and the effect of Christ's obedience. The clauses are quite contrary the one to the other, as light and darkness; and so are the effects redounding from them to those who are respectively affected by them. The former makes men sinners, the latter makes men righteous. It is the former that concerns our present purpose; " By one man's disobedience many were made sinners." Where consider,

1. The malignant cause to which all evil among men is owing; " one man's disobedience." This is the impure fountain of all, the original of all evils. Here two things must be cleared, (1.) Who that one man was. Who but Adam, the first man ; him the apostle had expressly named, ver. 14, as the great transgressor, the head of the rebellion, the fountain of sin, opposed to Christ Jesus as the fountain of righteousness ; and unto him our text in the Greek expressly points, which saith not simply, δι ἑνὸ ; ἀνθρωπον, By one man, &c., but διὰ της παρακοῆς του ἑνος ἀνθρώπου, by that one man's disobedience, that man Adam whom he had mentioned before. (2.) What that disobedience was. No question but Adam was guilty of many acts of disobedience through the whole course of his life after his fall ; but the text speaks of this disobedience emphatically, and as such by way of eminency, that disobedience, plainly referring to the first sin of Adam, that was the sin which first broke into the world, and opened the sluice to death, ver. 12 ; the transgression of Adam, ἡ παραβάσις Αδὰμ, ver. 14 ; that offence or fall, ver. 15. So then this disobedience is Adam's breaking of the covenant of works, by his eating of the forbidden fruit. The transgression of Adam was his transgressing of the covenant, which set him the bounds he was to keep within, on pain of death, Rom. v. 14, compared with Hosea vi. 7. He set off in a course of covenant obedience running for the prize ; but he stumbled and fell in breaking the covenant. Though he was a son by creation, he was God's hired servant by covenant ; but by disobedience to his master he broke the covenant.

2. The answerable effect ; " Many were made sinners." The poisonous fountain being opened, the waters kill wherever they come. Here also two things are to be cleared. (2.) Who these many are. Even the *all* mentioned ver. 12. All Adam's natural seed comprehended with him in the first covenant, as the many made righteous are all Christ's spiritual seed comprehended with him in the second covenant, but the apostle uses the term *many* here, though *all* are meant, not only because *all* are *many*, but because one man, viz., the man Christ, is excepted ; so, in strict propriety of speech, Adam's disobedience did not touch all men simply, but many, there being one man excepted ; and also because the scope of the apostle here is to shew that many shall be made righteous by the obedience of one ; to prove which, proceeding on that principle. That the deed of one

may be imputed to many, he instanceth in Adam's disobedience, who being one man, yet his deed was imputed to many; and he being a type or figure of Christ in that respect, it plainly follows, that as by his disobedience many were made sinners, so by the obedience of Christ shall many be made righteous. (2.) How by Adam's disobedience they were made sinners. There are but three ways how by the sin of another we may be made sinners. [1.] By adopting it through consent and approbation; so Ahab was the murderer of Naboth, though not he, but the magistrates of Jezreel did the deed, 1 Kings xxi. 19. But this is not the way we are made sinners by Adam's disobedience; for infants, and many in the world who never heard of Adam or his sin, and therefore are incapable of adopting it at that rate, are yet made sinners by it. Or, [2.] By imitation, as Pelagians would have it. So indeed one may be made a sinner by imitating sinners. But this cannot be it neither in this case; (1.) Because infants who are not capable of imitation, are involved here as well as others, Rom. v. 14, where death is said to "reign over those who had not sinned after the similitude of Adam's transgression." So also are Pagans included here, who know nothing of the copy that Adam cast us. (2.) Because we are made sinners by Adam's disobedience, as we are made righteous by Christ's obedience. But it is not by imitation, but by imputation of Christ's obedience we are made righteous; therefore it cannot be that we are made sinners by imitation of Adam's sin. (3.) All men of all ages, sexes, conditions, &c., are made sinners. But it is incredible, that, if imitation were the way, there should never have been so much as one mere man to refuse to imitate the ruining example. Therefore, (3.) It necessarily follows that we are thereby made sinners by imputation; even as we are made righteous by Christ's obedience, the same being reckoned our obedience, though not done by us in our own persons. We are not only made liable to punishment by this disobedience, but we are made sinners by it. Not only is the guilt ours, but the fault is ours; we not only die in Adam, 1 Cor. xv. 22, but we sinned in him as our federal head, Rom. v. 12; we broke the covenant in him; that breach in law-reckoning is ours, and is reckoned ours because it is ours by virtue of our being one with him, in his loins, as our natural and federal head.

The text affords the following doctrine, plainly founded upon it.

Adam's Sin in Breaking the Covenant of Works, is the Sin of his Posterity.

DOCTRINE. Adam's breaking of the covenant of works, by his eating of the forbidden fruit, is our sin, our breaking of it, as well as his.

For the illustration of this doctrine, I shall,

I. Consider the extent of this sin which is ours.

II. Shew how Adam's sin of breaking the covenant of works is our sin, our breaking it.

III. Evince the truth of the doctrine, and prove the imputation of Adam's first sin, the sin of breaking the covenant of works, by eating the forbidden fruit, to his posterity.

IV. Shew the ground and reason why this first sin is ours.

V. *Lastly*, Improve the subject.

Of the Extent of the first Sin, which is ours.

I. I shall consider the extent of this sin which is ours. There is a twofold breaking of the covenant of works.

1. There is a private and personal breaking of it by such persons as are still under it. And thus it is to this day broken every day; John vii. 19, "Did not Moses give you the law," said Christ to the Jews, "and yet none of you keepeth the law?" Let none imagine that the covenant of works being broken by Adam, was laid by as an useless thing, which men were no more concerned in. It is true, it is no more useful now as a way to salvation and happiness; but that is not from itself, but from man's weakness, whose weak head, heart, and legs, cannot serve him to walk in so high a way to heaven, from which he fell down headlong before in Adam, and received such a bruise as made him quite incapable for it after. But the covenant itself stands firm still in all the parts of it. The promise of it still stands to perfect obedience, which now takes in suffering as well as doing; as appears from what passed between our Lord and a certain lawyer, Luke x. 27, 28. The lawyer had put the question to him, "Master, what shall I do to inherit eternal life?" Our Lord answered, "What is written in the law? how readest thou?" The lawyer having replied, "Thou shalt love the Lord thy God with all thy heart, and with all thy soul, and with all thy strength, and with all thy mind, and thy neighbour as thyself;" our Lord thereupon said, "Thou has answered right; this do, and thou shalt live." So that if any could answer the demands of this covenant, he should have the promised life. The threatening of it stands firm as mountains of brass, that without satisfying it by one's self or surety, none shall escape; for "without shedding of blood there is no remission," Heb. ix. 22; and "God will by no means clear the guilty," Exod. xxxiv. 7. The commands of the covenant are in as full vigour as ever; for the breaking of a law can never take away the binding force and authority of it; so that it demands perfect obedience of all that are under it, with as much authority still as ever

it did of Adam, Rom iii. 19; For "what things soever the law saith, it saith to them that are under the law." And all men continue under it till they be ingrafted into Christ, be dead to it, and married to Christ, Rom. vi. 14. Wherefore all ye Christless sinners are under it, and are breaking it every day, in every thought, word, and action of yours; and so the curse of it is raining down upon you incessantly; Gal. iii. 10, "Cursed is every one that continueth not in all things which are written in the book of the law to do them." John iii. 36, "He that believeth not—the wrath of God abideth on him."

Some of you stand off from the sacrament of the Lord's supper, and from personal covenanting with God in embracing the covenant of grace, and think ye do wisely to hold your necks out of the yoke of a covenant with God. But, poor soul, thou art hard and fast under covenant to God, the covenant of works, by which thou art bound to perfect obedience, under the pain of God's curse; and every sin of thine is covenant-breaking with God, laying thee under the curse of the covenant. So all this wisdom of yours amounts to a holding fast of the covenant of death, and refusing a covenant of life. But this breaking of the covenant of works, by violating the commands of it now, is not what we aim at.

2. There was a public breaking of it by Adam, the father of all mankind, standing as the representative of his posterity. This breach was made in paradise, where Adam broke the covenant by eating the forbidden fruit. And even this is our sin, and breaking of the covenant; viz. the first breaking of it is ours, and brings us under guilt.

The extent of this breach of the covenant may be considered two ways; in reference to the persons to whom the guilt of it reaches, whose sin it becomes; and in reference to the sin itself.

1st, The extent of this sin may be considered in reference to the persons to whom the guilt of it reaches, whose sin it becomes. And thus we say,

(1.) It extended not to the man Christ. Adam's breaking of the covenant was not his: he sinned not in Adam, as the rest of mankind did. Though he was born of a woman, he was born sinless; hence the angel said unto the virgin Mary, "That holy thing which shall be born of thee, shall be called the Son of God," Luke i. 35. And Heb. vii. 26, he is said to be "holy, harmless, undefiled, and separate from sinners." He came "to destroy the works of the devil," 1 John iii. 8, and "to take away sin," John i. 29, which he could not have been fit for, if he himself had been one of the sinful multitude. If he had needed a sacrifice for himself, he could not have been an atoning sacrifice for us.

He was indeed a son of Adam, as appears from his genealogy brought up to Adam, Luke iii. And it was necessary he should be so, that he might be our near kinsman, to redeem us; that man's sins might be expiated by man's sufferings, and so justice might be satisfied of the same nature that sinned. But Adam was not the man Christ's federal head, nor was he comprehended with him in the covenant of works; forasmuch as he did not come of Adam in virtue of the blessing of fruitfulness given to the man and woman before the fall, but was the seed of the woman only, born by virtue of a spiritual promise made after the breach of the covenant of works. So the breach of that covenant could not be imputed to him, or counted his, by virtue of his relation to Adam.

Nay, he is another public person, as the first Adam was; the federal head in the second covenant, erected to repair the ruins made by the breach of the first; and so he is called the Second Adam, and is represented as the antitype to the first Adam, Rom. v. 14, unto whom the first Adam, having mismanaged his own headship, did as a private person commit himself for salvation, being in a mystical union by faith joined to Jesus Christ, as the quickening Head in the second covenant. But,

(2.) It extended to all mankind besides Christ, without exception of any one from the first son and daughter of Adam, to the last child that shall be born into the world, 1 Cor. xv. 22, " In Adam all die." It is the common portion of all the children of our father's family, from the oldest to the youngest; the common inheritance of the whole tribe of Adam, from the least to the greatest. The man a hundred years old may say, It is my sin; and the child at its first moving in the womb may say, It is mine. The guilt of it is removed indeed from believers upon their union with Christ; but once it lay upon them to condemnation also, as it still lies on all unregenerate persons, Rom. v. 18, " By the offence of one, judgment came upon all men to condemnation." The saints in heaven are singing glory to him who washed them from it in his own blood, and the damned in hell are lying, and will lie for ever under the weight of it.

2dly, The extent of this sin may be considered in reference to the sin itself. There is something in this sin peculiar to Adam's person, in so far as though the whole mass of mankind was concerned in it, yet there was this difference betwixt Adam and his posterity, that he was the representative, they were the party represented; he sinned this sin in his own person, they only in him; and consequently he ruined not himself only, but all the world by it; they ruined themselves only by it. Wherefore, setting aside what was in this sin peculiar to Adam, as the head of the covenant; otherwise,

This sin of breaking the covenant of works is our sin in the whole compass and extent of it. We must look back to the state of innocence, and behold the human nature adorned with the glorious image of God in our father Adam, and us in his loins, taken into covenant with God, a covenant of life upon condition of perfect obedience, which we in him were able to give, and fenced with a threatening of death, which we were not liable to before we sinned. And we must consider, with sorrow of heart, how we broke that covenant in Adam; and, with bitter repentance, shame, and self-loathing, lament over the eating of that forbidden fruit, and all the ingredients of it, our horrid unbelief, pride, ambition, presumption, and bold curiosity, our monstrous ingratitude, &c. The fearful aggravations of it must accent our lamentation, that it was in the state of righteousness of our nature the fact was committed, how small and sorry an object was the covenant broken for, a thing though small yet sacred, the place where, the time when, and the direful effects and consequents of it on ourselves. And we must apply to the Head of the second covenant for our reparation, pardon, and reconciliation with God.

Vain men who have never been deeply convinced of sin by the working of the Spirit on their hearts, but measure their religion more by their corrupt reason than God's word, will be apt to look on these things as idle tales, and to say in their hearts, Would to God we may mourn for our own sins, the sins that we ourselves have been guilty of. Alas, sirs, that sin, with all the ingredients and aggravations of it, as is said, is as really your own sin, as the lies ye have made with your own tongue, the profane oaths ye have sworn, &c., Rom. v. 12, 19, " By one man's sin, death entered into the world, and death by sin, and so death passed upon all men, for that all have sinned." " By one man's disobedience many were made sinners." And if it be not forgiven you, through the atoning blood of Christ, it will sink you into hell; and we know no sins that are forgiven, but they are repented of expressly, if known, and virtually if unknown. We find David mourning over it, Psalm li. 5, " Behold, I was shapen in iniquity, and in sin did my mother conceive me." And so ought all of us to mourn over it every day of our life, and have recourse to the blood of Jesus for pardon of it. And I shall shew,

How Adam's sin, in breaking the Covenant of Works, is the sin of his Posterity.

II. How Adam's sin of breaking the covenant of works is our sin, our breaking it.

1. It is really ours in itself. It is not ours in its effects only, as

a father's sin in riotously spending his estate, reaches his whole family, reducing them to poverty and want. Though the effects of that riotous spending, the poverty, misery, and want, be theirs; yet the riotous spending is the father's only. But so is it not in this case. It is true, the effects of it, the sinful and penal evils following this sin, are ours; we see them, we feel them, and the most stu-;pid groan under them; but the sin itself is ours too. And,

(1.) The guilt of it is ours, Rom. v. 18, "By the offence of one, judgment came upon all men to condemnation;" that is, the guilt of sin, whereby the soul is bound over to God's wrath, by virtue of the sanction of the law. Thus that word is used frequently in the scripture, as appears from John iii. 18, "He that believeth not, is condemned already." Rom. viii. 1, "There is no condemnation to them that are in Christ Jesus;" though it is often mistaken for what we call damnation, by which is understood the full execution of the law's sentence after death. So the guilt of the eating of the forbidden fruit lies on all men naturally as their guilt; though but one man's mouth tasted it, the guilt of the crime seizes all men. Every man is bound over to God's wrath for it, till the Lord Jesus, by an application of his blood to the soul, loose the cords of death.

(2.) The fault of it is ours, Rom. v. 1, "All have sinned," namely, in Adam. The fault lies in its contrariety to the holy commandment; this made it a faulty deed, a criminal action, a sin against God; and as such it is ours. We in Adam transgressed the law, broke through the hedge, and so broke the covenant. If the fault were not ours, a holy God would never punish us for it: but certain it is, that he does punish the children of Adam for it, Rom. v. 14, "Death reigned from Adam to Moses, even over them that had not sinned after the similitude of Adam's transgression." It is true indeed, God may punish one that is not really faulty, for the fault of another, if he do voluntarily substitute himself in the room of the faulty, having a full power so to dispose of himself; and that was the case of Christ the Mediator; but that cannot be pretended to be our case with respect to Adam's sin.

(3.) The stain and blot of it is ours. The whole nature of man was tainted with it, vitiated, and blackened, and, through defilement and loathsomeness thereby, rendered incapable of, and quite unfit for, communion with God, Gen. iii. 24. This sin defiled the whole mass of man's nature, from our father Adam going through all his posterity, like leaven through the whole lump, 1 Cor. xv. 22, "In Adam all die;" their souls die spiritually; his whole race, by this sin, became as dead carcases.

Thus Adam's sin, in itself, is really ours.

2. It is ours in law-reckoning; God imputes it to us, charges it

upon us all once, in our natural state; though whenever a soul believes in Christ, it is disimputed to that soul, Rom. viii. 1, " There is now no condemnation to them that are in Christ Jesus." But, by a sentence passed in the court of heaven, all mankind are decerned sinners, transgressors of the law, guilty of the first sin, and therefore liable to death, the penalty of the covenant, Rom. v. 12, 19, " All have sinned.—By one man's disobedience many were made sinners." And for as much as the judgment of God is according to truth, the matter must stand in itself, as it is found in that law-reckoning; that is to say, because we are really sinners in Adam, therefore we are reckoned in law to be so. So that the imputation of Adam's sin to us, necessarily presupposes its being really ours.

Proof of the Imputation of Adam's First Sin to his Posterity.

III. I shall evince the truth of the doctrine, and prove the imputation of Adam's first sin, the sin of breaking the covenant of works, by eating the forbidden fruit, to his posterity."

1. The scripture plainly teacheth, that all sinned in Adam, and were made sinners by his first sin, which was the breaking of the covenant of works, by eating the fruit of the forbidden tree, Rom. v. 12, 19, both forecited. Where it is to be remarked, (1.) That the apostle speaks of the first sin in both texts; for as in the 19th verse, he calls it " that disobedience;" so in ver. 12, *the* or *that sin,* by way of eminency, as vers. 14, 15, in opposition to *that obedience,* by way of eminency, ver. 19, whereas, speaking of sin in general, ver. 13, he calls it simply *sin.* Besides, he speaks of *that* sin, by which death entered into the world; as by one man that sin entered into the world, and by that sin death; but it is evident, that it was by the first sin that death entered into the world; therefore all sinned in Adam in breaking the covenant of works. This also is clear from the scope of this chapter, which is to account for the justification of sinners by the obedience of Christ, which the apostle does by shewing that Christ died in our room and stead, vers. 7—11, and he sums up the whole matter in this conclusion; ver. 12, " Wherefore, as by one man sin entered into the world, and death by sin; and so death passed upon all men, for that all have sinned ;" and this conclusion he afterwards enlarges upon. The words, it is plain, must have something understood, to make up the sense ; and I conceive it is this ; " Wherefore it is even as by one man that sin entered into the world," &c. *i. e.* The matter of the justification of a sinner before God lies even as the condemnation and death of sinners by that sin of one man, &c. (2.) That the apostle determines all men to have sinned that sin. *For that,* or *in whom** (as

---

* In Greek ἐφ᾿ ᾧ.

Mark ii. 5) all have sinned. But that this is the sense, however, the words be rendered, appears, if it is considered, [1.] That death entered into the world by that sin, and so passed on all men; but, according to the apostle, it could not pass on all men for that sin, but for that all were the sinners; for where death comes, sin must needs be before; by the rule of justice no man can die for a sin he is not guilty of. [2.] If all sinned, infants sinned too; but infants are not capable of having sinned otherwise than in Adam. The apostle teaches very plainly, that infants are comprehended in these all, and that they sinned, ver. 14, " that had not sinned after the similitude of Adam's transgression," which clearly bears them to have sinned another way. (3.) By that sin we were *constituted* or *made sinners*, ver. 19, not by consent and approbation, nor by imitation, but by imputation, as was argued before; and consequently, since the judgment of God is according to truth, we sinned that sin.

2. All are under the guilt of that sin in Adam, till it be removed in justification by faith in Jesus Christ; they are, by virtue of that sin, bound over to death, and the eternal wrath of God. This the scripture teaches evidently, 1 Cor. xv. 22, " In Adam all die." But how can they die in him, if they did not sin in him? Rom. v. 12, " By one man—death passed upon all." Sin then behoved in the first place by him to pass on all; ver. 15, " Through the offence of one many be dead." That offence therefore behoved to be their offence, ver. 18, " By the offence of one, *it was* (viz. the offence) upon all men unto condemnation," *i. e.* the guilt of eternal wrath; but how could they be condemned by a holy and just God for an offence that was not their offence, it being undeniable that they did not substitute themselves, nor were they substituted by another, in the room of the offender? When the apostle tells us, that "there is therefore *now* no condemnation to them that are in Christ Jesus," Rom. viii. 1, does he not plainly teach us, (1.) That all who are not in Christ, are under condemnation, whoever they be, whether guilty of actual sin in their own persons or not, as infants and idiots? (2.) That even such as are *now* in Christ, were under condemnation, all along while they were not in him? Let men take a view of our guilty state in Adam, that wrath which by nature we stand adjudged to, Eph. ii. 3, which the scripture plainly teaches; and then consider the holy, just nature of God; they shall be obliged to own that we sinned in Adam, and that his sin is ours as well as his, and that that wrath on that account is just. But corrupt unsubdued nature firstframes to itself a notion of God's justice, according to its own principles, and then rejects this imputation as inconsistent therewith,

and then puts a sense on clear scripture texts agreeable to its preconceived notions.

3. The universal depravation and corruption of human nature is
a glaring evidence of this. Man is now despoiled of his primitive
glory and integrity, the image of God, the rectitude of his nature,
with which he was created; and instead of it his whole nature is
corrupted, there is in it a bent and propensity to evil. His mind is
darkened, his will perverse, his affections altogether disorderly.
He is born in this case, corruption is woven into his nature from the
time he has a being in the womb; Job xiv. 4, "Who can bring a
clean thing out of an unclean? not one." John iii. 6, "That which
is born of the flesh is flesh." Gen. vi. 5, "Every imagination of the
thoughts of man's heart is only evil continually." Psalm li. 5,
"Behold I was shapen in iniquity, and in sin did my mother conceive me." There is a necessity of regeneration, without a man be
born again he is ruined for ever, John iii. 3. He is naturally dead
in sin, he must be raised from death, he is so marred that he must
be new made, created to good works, else he will lie for ever void of
spiritual life, utterly unable to do anything but sin, Eph. ii. 5, 10.
Such a nature and such a frame of soul is a sin, a fountain of sin.
But without question it is a misery too, and the greatest of miseries
human nature is capable of, as setting men at the greatest distance
from God the chief good. Therefore it must be concluded to be a
punishment of sin too, and of some sin previous to it, which can be
none else but Adam's first sin. And that sin must be our sin, the
sin of all mankind, since it is punished at this fearful rate in us and
all mankind. It is not possible to account for the justice of this
dispensation otherwise. It was inconsistent with the nature of God
to have created man in this case; yet thus we are from the time we
have a being as men. Is this from the Creator otherwise than as a
punishment of sin? Must it not be from ourselves, (Hos. xiii. 9,
"O Israel, thou hast destroyed thyself,") as the authors of our
misery, by sinning against God, namely, sinning this sin, for no
other can have place here? The law of natural generation without
this will not salve the matter; for so justice would have required
either the stopping of generation, or else that even corrupt Adam
should not have generated corrupt children. It is within the compass of omnipotency though not the compass of created power, to
bring a clean thing out of an unclean, as was done in the case of the
man Christ; otherwise the greatest misery and punishment which
might have been averted, is inflicted upon mankind without any
fault of theirs; which is more than absurd.

4. Though men venture to deny sin in infants, who are without

question incapable of actual sinning in their own persons, Rom. v. 14, and ix. 11, yet it is undeniable they are liable to misery, pains, sickness, and die as well as those who are grown person. The groans and tears of parents over the cradles, the moans and distress of poor harmless babes, the graves of the smallest size in the churchyard, are demonstrations of these. Yea, look to the old world, swept away with the flood, and there you will see the infants drowned with the sinners a hundred years old. Look to the overthrow of Sodom, and you will see them burnt in the fire from heaven with the lustful parents that begot them. Look to Jerusalem when it was destroyed, and there you will see them pining to death by famine, with the aged sinners. Then look up to heaven, and behold a holy, just God, who sent these plagues, and consider if it be consistent with his holy nature to treat innocent senseless persons at that rate. And after all look into your Bible, and you will see how God is justified in all these. There you will see the threatening of death annexed to the sin of breaking the covenant of works, Gen. iii. 17, and seeing it executed upon them, ye must needs conclude they are guilty. There you find "death passes on all, for that all have sinned;" Rom. v. 12, "reigns over them that had not sinned after the similitude of Adam's transgression," ver. 14, and thence you must conclude them sinners. There it appears, that "the wages of sin is death," Rom. vi. 23; they receive the wages, they must have then wrought the work of sin; not in their own persons surely, for they were not capable; therefore they sinned in Adam. As for the corruption of their nature, it justifies this procedure indeed; but yet the propagation of it to them is owing to this first sin; and the dispensation of God in that matter must be justified, by their guilt of that sin.

5. *Lastly*, The comparison stated in scripture, betwixt Christ and Adam, plainly evinceth this. The apostle, Rom. v. 14, tells us that Adam was a type or figure of Christ; and 1 Cor. xv. 45, he calls the one the "first Adam," the other the "last Adam." Whence it appears, that as Christ was the federal head in the covenant of grace; so Adam was the federal head in the covenant of works. Whence we may gather,

(1.) That as Christ, in his obedience and death, stood not as a private person, but what he did and suffered, he did and suffered as a public person, to be imputed to all his spiritual seed; 2 Cor. v. 21, "For he hath made him to be sin for us, who knew no sin, that we might be made the righteousness of God in him;" so Adam sinning, and breaking the covenant of works, did what he did not as a private man, whose guilt remains with himself, but as a public person, whose deed was to be imputed to all his posterity, or natural seed; Rom. v. 18, " By the offence of one, judgment came upon all men to condemnation."

(2.) That since Adam was eventually a head of destruction and ruin to all his seed, and Christ a head of reparation and salvation to all that were his seed of the shipwrecked multitude; 1 Cor. xv. 22, " For as in Adam all die, even so in Christ shall all be made alive;" then as God laid on Christ the iniquities of all that are his, making them to meet on him, Isa. liii. 6, so Adam's sin was from him diffused, and came upon all that were his, Rom v. 12; for the one was to repair those whom the other had destroyed; to pay their debts which they had been involved in by the other.

(3.) As believers obeyed and satisfied in Christ their head in the second covenant, so all men sinned in Adam their head in the first covenant. The former is the doctrine of the scripture. " The righteousness of the law was fulfilled in them," Rom. viii. 4. They were " crucified with him," Gal. ii. 20; which further appears, in that they were " raised up, and set in heaven in him," Eph. ii. 6. Hence the latter is established; we broke the law in Adam, and sinned against God in him.

(4.) *Lastly*, As we are made righteous by the obedience of Christ; so we are made sinners by the disobedience of Adam. So says the text. But we are made righteous by the obedience of Christ imputed to us, therefore we are made sinners through the disobedience of Adam imputed to us. Christ's righteousness is really ours, not in its effects only, but in itself, being that very righteousness on which we are acquitted and justified. So Adam's sin is really ours, not in its effects only, but in itself, being that upon which we are all by nature condemned persons, Rom. v. 18. As soon as we have a spiritual being in Christ, and are united to him by his Spirit and by faith, so soon is Christ's righteousness ours; and as soon as we have a natural being as children of Adam, Adam's sin is ours.

So much for the proof of this doctrine, That Adam's first sin, the sin of breaking the covenant of works, by eating the forbidden fruit, is our sin, our breaking of it, or is imputed to his posterity.

The Ground and Reason of the Imputation of Adam's first sin to his Posterity.

IV. I shall show the ground and reason why Adam's first sin, or breaking of the covenant of works, is our sin, our breaking of it. This is the foundation of the imputation of that sin to us, and lies in these two things jointly.

1. He was our natural or seminal head, the natural root of all

mankind, Acts xvii. 26. God set up the human nature in him pure and undefiled, blessed him with fruitfulness, Gen. i. 28, and from him all mankind derive their pedigree. So that as Levi, being in the loins of Abraham, when Melchisedek met him, paid tithes in Abraham, Heb. vii. 9, 10, so we, being in the loins of Adam, when the tempter met him, sinned and broke the covenant in him. But,

2. Which is the main thing, He was our federal head in the covenant of works, our representative in that bargain. There was a proper covenant betwixt God and Adam; and in it Adam was not considered as a private person, but stood as the head of all mankind in it, acting for himself and for his posterity whom he represented; even as the second Adam in the covenant of grace. And thus his sin was ours. Even as Abraham, having the covenant made with him, was the federal as well as natural head of Levi, being the covenant-head of the Jewish nation; and therefore Levi in his loins is reckoned to have paid tithes to Melchisedek.

The sum of the matter lies here; all mankind being originally one in Adam, were made legally one in him and with him, by the covenant of works entered into with Adam, as the head of all mankind, constituted by God himself, the infinitely wise and absolute Lord of all the creatures. By the bond of the covenant superadded to the natural tie betwixt him and us, we were made one with him, to all the purposes of the covenant. And being thus one with him, his sin in breaking of the covenant was ours as well as his. The being of this covenant I have already proved, and have also accounted for the equity and justice of this dispensation.

The Doctrine of the Imputation of Adam's First Sin to his Posterity applied.

Use I. This truth serves to discover, and set before our eyes,

1. The malignant nature of sin. It is an infectious vapour, a plague, a pest to mankind, of a killing nature, wherever it comes. One sinner of mankind infected the whole race; one morsel of that leaven leavened the whole nature of man. It is the spiritual pestilence in the world, that makes more spiritual havoc than fire and sword; an emblem of which God is giving this day in France by a bodily pestilence, with which also he is threatening these nations.* It is Solomon's observation, "That one sinner destroyeth much good," Eccl. ix. 18. This is emphatically represented to us in the case of Adam, and often in the case of many particular sinners

---

* This part of the subject was preached in November, 1721, at which time the plague raged in France. Happily, Great Britain and Ireland escaped that dreadful scourge.

among us, whose sphere of activity is more narrow; but O what destruction do they make within their bounds ! this malignity of it appears,

(1.) In its spreading from the sinner to all that are concerned in him, destroying and breaking down like a flood where it comes. The peace and purity of the whole world was marred by Adam's sin ; and the peace and purity of lesser societies are still marred with the sins of others, Heb. xii. 15. The apostle exhorts Christians to " look diligently, lest any root of bitterness springing up, trouble them, and thereby many be defiled." How many such roots of bitterness are sprung up in our land, wherewith the peace and purity of church and state are both marred together at this day. How many such have sprung up and are still springing up among us, whose pangs of lust mar the quiet of families, leave a blot on them, make the congregation a reproach, and to stink in the nostrils of the sober part of their neighbours.

(2.) In that when the sinner is dead and gone, his sin lives and works after him. It is long since Adam died, but still his sin is working. Jeroboam sinned so in his life, as that he opened such a sluice as ran for several generations after he was silent in the grave. And thus do the sins of many still live and destroy much good after they are gone. And therefore, besides the particular judgment at death, there is a general judgment at the end of the world, where people must answer for the mischief done by the current of their sin in the world after they were gone out of it.

2. The awful and tremendous holy sovereignty of God, whose judgments are always just, but often unsearchable. When one considers how God made the angels independent upon one another as to standing and falling, but comprehended the whole race of mankind under one federal head ; whom also, in the depth of his sovereign wisdom he permitted to fall, when he could have held him up ; so as all mankind are ruined in him ; must we not cry out, " O the depth of the riches both of the wisdom and knowledge of God ! how unsearchable are his judgments and his ways past finding out," Rom. xi. 33. The dispensation was just, he can do us no wrong ; it was becoming the divine perfections, and designed for holy ends in the depth of wisdom. But in the meantime, there is need of a holy, humble spirit to adore the sovereignty of it.

3. The impossibility of our obtaining salvation by the way of this covenant. What hopes can we have of living by doing, when it has misgiven in our head already, when we were fitted for working at another rate than we can pretend to be now ? We have already broken that covenant, fallen under the penalty of it, the which we

must needs discharge before we can have access to begin again on new ground, to look for life by keeping it better. And who of us is able to discharge that debt to the justice of God? "Therefore by the deeds of the law shall no flesh be justified in his sight," Rom. iii. 20.

4. The glory of the contrivance of the second covenant by the ever-blessed Trinity, and of the performance of it by the second Adam in our nature. Look here and behold the necessity of it for our salvation; what could they have done for themselves, who had ruined themselves, and were brought into the world in a state of condemnation? There was a necessity of the obedience and death of Christ in that case; Luke xxiv. 26, "Ought not Christ to have suffered these things?" Behold the suitableness of it; man was ruined by Adam's breaking the first covenant, and the remedy is provided by Christ's keeping the second covenant. Behold the perfection of it. It takes away not only this sin, but all other sins too. How strong is the grace of Christ, that is able to stop the torrent of Adam's sin, increased with innumerable personal sins running with it in one channel? Rom. v. 16.

5. *Lastly*, A notable confirmation of believers' faith as to the imputation of Christ's righteousness and death unto them, upon their embracing the covenant of grace. Is Adam's sin ours by virtue of our union with him as the federal head in the covenant of works? Surely Christ's righteousness, obedience, and death, are no less ours in virtue of our union with Christ, the federal head in the second covenant. That God who imputes the one to all mankind for condemnation, will much more impute the other to believers for justification.

USE II. This doctrine serves to stir up to several duties. And,

1. Be convinced of this sin as your sin. Take it home to yourselves among the rest of the pieces of guilt, chargeable upon you before the Lord. God charges it on all mankind as their sin; all men therefore ought to charge it on themselves, since he is the Amen, faithful and true Witness, and cannot charge any with guilt falsely or by mistake. It is hard to convince men of this; but when the Spirit of the Lord comes to carry the work of conviction through, he will fasten this conviction on the conscience among others; and how can one sue for the pardon of that sin which he will not admit the conviction of?

2. Confess and mourn over this sin before the Lord. Be humbled under the sense of it, and anxiously inquire how ye may be saved from it, and the wrath and curse of God due to you for it. Consider seriously how this debt is on your head by nature, how you are transgressors from the womb, breakers of covenant with God, fallen un-

der the penalty of the covenant of works, by your not fulfilling the condition of it, but transgressing the covenant. Live no more unconcerned about it, but sist your guilty consciences in this point particularly before the Lord; and let that fear and sorrow work in your souls on this head, that ought to be in the case of sins committed by you in your own persons. I shall enforce this with some motives.

MOTIVE 1. Consider that it is really your sin, by which you have offended God, broken his covenant, and made yourselves liable to eternal wrath. And shall it not lie heavy on your spirits, that you have thus sinned? Rom. v. 19. If it be really your sin, your debt ye are involved in by the mismanagement of your first father; can it be safe to be unconcerned about it, while a holy just God is the party ye have to do with?

MOT. 2. It is the fountain of all the sins and miseries that ever have been found with you. Ye are guilty before God of sins of heart, lip and life: these must sometime be a terror to the soul. But whence did all this flow, but from your corrupt nature, averse to all good, and prone to all evil? And whence had you that nature, but from the guilt of this sin lying on you? Ye have been plunged in a gulf of miseries; even from the womb to this day, the clouds have been returning after the rain. Trace them to the spring-head, and you will find they all issue from this sin. And what sin can ye truly mourn over to purpose, if ye do not mourn over the fountain of all? What calls more loudly for repenting and mourning than this leading sin?

MOT. 3. While the guilt of this sin lies upon you ye lose all your labour in striving to get the guilt of other sins removed, or to get your lives reformed. That is but to shut the door while the grand thief is in the house; to labour to dry up the streams, while ye are at no pains to get the poisonous fountain stopt; the which is labour in vain. And it is the overlooking of this that is the cause of the apostacy of many who sometimes have made such a fair appearance; and is also the cause of the prevalence of a legal disposition that is so much at this day among professors.

MOT. 4. *Lastly*, If ye get not the pardon of it, it will ruin you for ever, Rom. v. 18. Hereby ye are condemned; and a pardon only can reverse the sentence. Ye must then sue out the pardon of it; and if you come to God on that errand, be sure your souls will be humbled and broken within you for it.

And if ye would have your hearts duly affected with this sin, (1.) Labour to lay aside your carnal reasonings, and believe God's word as the word of truth and righteousness, which fixes this guilt on all mankind, and particularly on you. These reasonings in this matter are dangerous, and can tend to nothing but hardening the heart, and casting dishonour on God. (2.) How ye naturally trace the steps of Adam in his breaking of the covenant, so bearing fallen Adam's image most lively, as I showed elsewhere.* The consideration of this may serve to prove the fact upon us, while we do so readily fall into the same way again, as far as we have occasion. (3.) Consider the righteousness of Christ, which is to be the same way imputed to all believers, and shall be imputed to you on your believing. There is a gift of righteousness to be imputed, as well as that debt of sin is charged upon you.

Lastly, Let this stir you up to quit your hold of the first Adam and his covenant, and flee for life and salvation to the second Adam in the second covenant, uniting with him by faith. The offer of the gospel is made to you: the Lord has made a grant of his son as a quickening head to poor sinners. Believe it, embrace the offer, accept heaven's gift; otherwise ye will be ruined, not only by the breach of the first covenant, but by despising of the second.

If ye be of those to whom that iniquity is forgiven, ye will highly prize the second Adam; for " unto them that believe he is precious," 1 Pet. ii. 7. Ye will be holy and tender in your walk, the power of sin being broken where the guilt is removed, Rom. viii. 1. Ye will be dead to the law, and denied to your own righteousness, making Christ's fulfilling of the covenant your only plea for life and salvation, Matth. v. 3, Phil. iii. 3.

Thus far of the breach of the covenant of works, and the extent of it.

---

* See " Fourfold State," State ii. Head 1. under the title, " that man's nature is corrupted."

PART IV.

THE CONDITION OF MEN WHEN UNDER THE BROKEN COVENANT OF
WORKS; AND THEIR DREADFUL STATE UNDER THE CURSE.

SECT. I.

THE STATE OF MANY MEN UNDER THE BROKEN COVENANT OF WORKS; WHO THEY
ARE; THE EFFECT OF THAT COVENANT UPON THEM; AND THE REASONS WHY SO
MANY CONTINUE UNDER IT.

GALATIANS iii. 10,

*For as many as are of the works of the law are under the curse; for it
is written, Cursed is every one that continueth not in all things which
are written in the book of the law to do them.*

HAVING discoursed of the breaking of the covenant of works by all
mankind in Adam, we are next to inquire into the state and case of
sinners under that broken covenant. And that the text shews to be
a very lamentable and dangerous one. In a shipwreck, when the
ship is dashed in pieces upon a rock, how heavy is the case of the
crew among the raging waves? The ship can no more carry them
to the harbour, but failing them, leaves them to the mercy of the
waves. If one can get a broken plank to hold by, that is the greatest
safety there; but that doth often but hold in their miserable lives
for a little, till the passengers are swallowed up. Such, and un-
speakably worse, is the case of sinners under the broken covenant
of works, which leaves them under the curse, as we see in the text.
In which we have,

1. The covenant-state of some of mankind, yea, of many of them.
They "are of the works of the law;" it is the same thing as to be
of the law of works; that is, to be under the covenant of works.
So "the works of the law" are opposed to "the hearing of
faith," Gal. iii. 2, that is, the law to the gospel, the covenant of
works to the covenant of grace. But the apostle in our text intimates
their covenant-state by a phrase which, in the first place, designs
their habitual course and practice, viz. to seek life and salvation by
the works of the law; but, in the next place, designs the covenant
they are under, whereof their practice is a plain evidence. They are
opposed to those who are of faith, who, being under the covenant of
grace, by faith look for life and salvation by Christ's works.

The phrase, "As many as are of the works of the law," imports,
that there are others who are not under that covenant. In the

scripture we read of "two covenants," Gal. iv. 24. Each of these have their children; and so the world is divided into two sorts of men; some under the covenant of grace, others still remaining under the covenant of works; which the phrase " under the curse," doth also bear; for since they are under the curse of the law; or covenant of works, they are surely under the law or covenant itself; for whatsoever the law saith, it saith to them who are under the the law," Rom. iii. 19.

2. The state and case of men under that covenant; they " are under the curse." The covenant is broken, and so they are fallen under the penalty; the duty of the covenant is neglected and cast off; and so they are under the curse of the covenant. As the blessing or promise, which they have lost, comprehends all good for time and eternity, soul and body; so the curse comprehends all evil on soul and body, for time and eternity. To be under the curse is to be by the law's sentence separated and destined to evil, according to the threatening, Gen. ii. 17, " In the day that thou eatest thereof, thou shalt surely die."

3. The proof and evidence of this their miserable state and case; " For it is written, Cursed is every one that continueth not in all things which are written in the book of the law to do them." There is an extract of the sentence of the law which is standing against them, Deut. xxvii. 26, " Cursed be he that confirmeth not all the words of this law to do them." That sets the matter in full light, from whence the conscience of every man under that covenant may conclude him under the curse.

The two following doctrines comprehend the full scope of the words, namely,

DOCT. I. There are some, yea, many, of mankind, who are still under the broken Covenant of Works.

DOCT. II. Man in his natural state, being under the broken covenant of works, is under the curse.

DOCT. I. There are some, yea, many, of mankind, who are still under the broken Covenant of Works.

In the prosecution of this subject. I shall,

I. Evince the truth of the doctrine, that there are some, yea many, of mankind, who are still under the broken covenant of works.

II. Describe who they are that are under this broken covenant.

III. Shew what is the effect of the broken covenant of works upon them.

. IV. Shew why so many remain still under this broken covenant.

V. *Lastly*, Apply the subject.

Proof of the doctrine that many persons still continue under the broken covenant of works.

I. I shall evince the truth of this doctrine, that there are some, yea, many of mankind, who are still under the broken covenant of works. This will clearly appear, if ye consider,

1. That there are but "few that shall be saved," Matth. vii. 14. Christ's flock is but a very little flock, Luke xii. 32. But all who are brought from under the covenant of works, are brought into the covenant of grace; Rom. vi. 14, they are not under the law but under grace; and all who are within the bond of the covenant of grace, are of Christ's flock, and shall be saved, Heb. viii. 10. Hence it follows that the most part of mankind are left under the covenant of works. The truth is, all men by nature are under it, and so are born under the curse, Eph. ii. 3. And many live and die under it; and therefore the sentence against the whole wretched herd of the condemned world runs in these terms, "Depart from me, ye cursed, into everlasting fire," &c.

2. The scripture is plain on this head. The apostle tells us that there are some under the law, Rom. iii. 19, to whom the law doth say what it says, for conviction and condemnation; and that is under the law as a covenant of works, for otherwise all are under it as a rule of life. It curseth and condemneth many; Gal. iii. 10, "Cursed is every one," viz., who is under the law; for its curse cannot reach others, there being "no condemnation to them that are in Christ Jesus," Rom. viii. 1. It condemns all unbelievers; John iii. 18, "He that believeth not is condemned already," viz., by the sentence of the law as the covenant of works; for the covenant of grace condemns no man, John v. 45, said our Lord to the Jews, "Do not think that I will accuse you to the Father; there is one that accuseth you, even Moses, in whom ye trust." Chap. xii. 47, "And if any man hear my words and believe not, I judge him not; for I came not to judge the world but to save the world."

3. As all men in Adam were taken into the covenant of works, so no man can be freed from the obligation of it, but they who are discharged from it by God who was man's party in it. This is evident from the general nature of contracts. And none are discharged from it but on a full answering of all it could demand of them, Matth. v. 18. For said our Lord, "Till heaven and earth pass, one jot or one tittle shall in no wise pass from the law, till all be fulfilled." This no man can attain unto but by faith in Jesus Christ, whereby the soul appropriates and applies to itself Christ's obedience and satisfaction offered in the gospel; and so pleading these gets up the discharge; "For being justified by faith, we have peace with God through our Lord Jesus Christ." Rom. v. 1. But certain it is that

all men have not faith, nay, few have it; therefore few are discharged from the covenant of works, but most part are still under it.

4. Freedom from the covenant of works is such a privilege as requires both price and power, each of them infinite, to invest a sinner with it. The sinner is by nature under the covenant of works, bound to perfect obedience to its commands, to complete satisfaction of its sanction. None but Christ was able to purchase the sinner's freedom from that covenant, since none but he could answer its high demands. When the sinner's freedom is purchased, he is so loath to part with that covenant, that none but the Spirit of Christ, in his day of power, can make him willing to come away from under it. So it is the peculiar privilege of the elect, for whom Christ died; yea, of believers, whom the Spirit of Christ has translated from the kindom of darkness into the kingdom of light, Rom. vii. 4; Gal. ii. 19.

5. There are many who still live as they were born; in the same state wherein their father Adam left them, when he broke; who were never to this day in any due concern how to be discharged from the debt he left upon their head, or of the bond of the covenant of works which in him they entered into. How can it be then, but that the debt remains, and the bond is uncancelled as to them? In one of the two Adams all mankind stand to this day; some in the first Adam, bearing the image of the earthly, sin and death; others in the second Adam, bearing the image· of the heavenly, life and salvation. The translation from the first to the second none meet with in a morning-dream; both law and gospel have a part to act in their souls, ere this work can be effected.

6. *Lastly*, There are but two covenants, viz. of works and grace, Gal. iv. 24, as there never were but two ways of life and salvation, by works and by grace; and but two federal heads of mankind, the first and second Adam. Under one of these covenants, and but under one of them, every son and daughter of Adam must be; either under the law or under grace, Rom. vi. 14. The covenant of grace has not been so much as externally revealed or preached to many in the world; and among those to whom it is, how few are there who have really and truly embraced it? how do many stand at a distance from it, as they would do from fetters of iron? Since therefore but few are within the bond of the covenant of grace, it is evident that most men are under the covenant of works.

Hence the case of many, yea, most men, is most miserable, they are under the curse.

Those who are Under the Covenant of Works described.

II. The second thing proposed was, Who they are that are under the broken ovenant of works? This is a weighty enquiry; it is

in effect, who are they that are under the curse? because all that
are under it, now that it is broken, are under the curse. Therefore
take heed to it, and apply what may be offered on this head. I
premise these four things, to make this the more clear.

1. Men may be under the covenant of works, and yet living under
the external dispensation of the covenant of grace. There is a
great difference betwixt one's visible church state, and the state of
their souls before the Lord. The covenant of grace was preached
to Adam in paradise, Gen. iii. 15, yet was he in hazard of running
back to the covenant of works, ver. 22. The Jews had the dispensation of the covenant of grace among them, and the ceremonial
law clearly held out the way of salvation by the Messiah, yet most
of them were under the covenant of works, being sons of the bond-
woman. So, under the gospel dispensation to this day, many to
whom the covenant of grace is offered, continue under the covenant
of works. It is one thing to hear the new covenant proclaimed,
another thing to accept of it by faith.

2. Men may receive the seals of the covenant of grace, and yet be
under the covenant of works. Circumcision was a seal of the covenant of grace, yet many who received it were still sons of the bond-
woman, to be cast out from inheriting with the children, Gal. iv.
24, 25, 30. And so will many who are baptized in the name of
Christ, and have partaken of the Lord's supper, yet be disowned at
the last day, by the Head of the second covenant, as none of his,
Luke xiii. 26, forasmuch as they never truly came into the bond of
that covenant.

3. Men may be convinced in their consciences of the impossibility
of obtaining salvation by Adam's covenant of works, and yet remain
under it still. Where are they who are so very stupid, as to think
that they can obtain salvation by perfect obedience to the law?
The Pharisees of old, and the Papists to this day, will not venture
their salvation on the absolute perfection of their own obedience;
yet the former lived, and the latter do live, under that covenant.
Let no man deceive himself here; such a conviction as hardly any
man can shun, is not sufficient to divorce a man from the law or covenant of works.

4. *Lastly*, Men, upon the offer of the covenant of grace made to
them, may aim at accepting of it, and so enter into a personal covenant with God, and yet remain under the covenant of works. Many
miss their mark in their covenanting with God, and, instead of accepting God's covenant of grace, make a covenant of works with
God, upon other terms than Adam's covenant was, for which there
is no warrant in the word. The Galatians did not cast off Christ's
righteousness altogether, but only mixed their own works with his;

and thus do many still, looking on their faith, repentance, and obedience, such as they are, to be the fulfilling of a law, upon which
they are to be accepted of God.

But more particularly, and directly,

1st, All unregenerate persons are under the covenant of works.
Where is the unconverted man or woman, living in the state of irre-
generacy, strangers to a saving change on their souls? That man
or woman is yet a branch of the old Adam, growing on the old stock,
a stranger to the new covenant, because not in Christ, the head of
the covenant. For "if any man be in Christ, he is a new creature;
old things are passed away; behold, all things are become new," 2
Cor. v. 27. Such an unregenerate person is still under the covenant
of works. This is evident, in that the death contained in the threatening of that covenant has full sway over them, so that they are
dead in trespasses and sins, Eph. iii. 1, 5. They lie yet without spiritual life, as the first Adam left them. They have no communion
with the second Adam, else they had been quickened; for he is a
quickening head, as the other was a killing one.

2dly, All that have not the Spirit of Christ dwelling in them are
under the covenant of works; For "if any man have not the Spirit
of Christ, he is none of his," Rom. viii. 9. And says the same apostle, Gal. v. 8, "But if ye be led by the Spirit, ye are not under the
law." It is one of the first promises of the covenant of grace, the
giving of the Spirit, Ezek. xxxvii. 27, "A new Spirit will I put within you." And the Spirit of Christ once entering into a man never
changes his habitation. For, saith Christ himself, John xiv. 16, "I
will pray the Father, and he shall give you another Comforter: that
he may abide with you for ever." Wo to those, then, that have not
the Spirit of grace, they are under the curse. And such are all
prayerless persons, Zech. xii. 10; ignorant, unconvinced sinners, who
have not yet seen their lost and ruined state, John xvi. 8; refractory
and rebellious ones, who will not be hedged in within the Lord's
way, Ezek. xxxvi. 27; carnal men, who are under the government
of their own lusts and unruly passions, Gal. v. 16.

3. All unbelievers, John iii. 13. Whosoever is destitute of saving faith is under the covenant of works; for it is by faith that one
is brought within the bond of the covenant of grace, is married unto
Christ, being dead to the law. Every soul of man is under one of
the two husbands, Christ or the law. All believers have their
Maker for their husband; and all unbelievers have the law as a covenant of works for theirs, a rigorous husband, a weak one, who can
do nothing for their life and salvation, but for their ruin and destruction. Faith unites the soul to Christ, Eph. iii. 17. The unbeliever,

what though he go about the duties of religion, walk soberly and strictly, he is not joined to Christ, therefore he remains under the covenant of works, under the curse.

4. All unsanctified, unholy persons, Rom. vi. 14. The doctrinal staking sinners down under, and wreathing about their necks the yoke of the law as a covenant of works, is so far from being a proper method to bring them to holiness and good works, that contrariwise they shall never be holy, never do one good work, till such time as they are fairly rid of that yoke, and sit down under the jurisdiction of grace. So that true holiness is an infallible mark of one delivered from the law; and unholiness, of one that is yet hard and fast under it, Gal. v. 18, forecited. Legalism is rank enmity to true holiness, is but a devil transformed into an angel of light, and never prevails so in the church as in a time of apostacy, growing unholiness, untenderness, regardlessness of the commands of God, when all flesh has corrupted their ways. Take for an example, Popery, the grand apostasy. What set of men that call themselves Christians, set up for the law and good works in their doctrine, more than they do? and among whom is there less of these to be found? How can they be but unholy, who are under the covenant of works? for there is no communion with God in the way of that covenant now; so sanctifying influences are stopt, and they must wither and pine away in their iniquity. Whereas when once the soul is brought out from that covenant into the covenant of grace, the course of sanctifying influences is opened, the clean and cleansing water flows into their souls; the head of the covenant is a holy head, conveying holiness to his members; the spirit of the covenant is a sanctifying Spirit; the promises of the covenant are promises of holiness; the blood of the covenant is purifying blood; and, in a word, every thing in the covenant tends to sanctifying and making holy the covenanters.

5. All profane, loose, and licentious men, are under the covenant of works, Rom. vii. 5, and viii. 2. These men of Belial are under that heavy yoke. For under that covenant, being broken, sin and death have the force of a law upon the subjects, as the worms, stench and rottenness, domineer in the grave without control. When one sees so many profane lives, unclean, drunkards, swearers, liars, thieves, cheaters, oppressors, and others, walking after their own lusts; he may conclude all these to be evidences and consequents of the curse of the broken covenant on them; even as when ye go through a field full of briers, thorns, thistles, nettles, &c., ye may sigh and say, These are the product of the curse laid on the earth. These people think they walk at liberty; but what liberty is it?

Even such as that madman enjoyed, Mark v. 4, who had been often bound with fetters and chains, and the chains had been plucked asunder by him, and the fetters broken in pieces; neither could any man tame him. The truth is, they are the arrantest slaves on earth, who are slaves to their own domineering lusts and passions; 2 Pet. ii. 19, "While they promise them liberty, they themselves are the servants of corruption; for of whom a man is overcome, of the same is he brought in bondage." Such kindly slaves are they of the worst of masters, that they have lost all just notion and sense of true liberty, Psalm cxix. 45.

6. All mere moralists, such as satisfy themselves with common honesty and sobriety, living in the meantime strangers to religious exercises, and without a form of godliness. These are under the covenant of works, as seeking justification and acceptance with God by their conformity (such as it is) to the letter of the law, Gal. v. 4. These are they who please themselves, in their wronging no man, doing justly betwixt man and man, and in their pretended keeping of a good heart towards God; while in the meantime, the rottenness of their hearts appears in their ignorance of God and Christ, and the way of salvation by him, their estrangedness from the duty of prayer and other holy exercises. Some of these have that scripture much in their mouths; Micah vi. 8, "What doth the Lord require of thee but to do justly, and to love mercy, and to walk humbly with thy God?" little considering that the last clause thereof writes death on their foreheads. They are under the covenant of works with a witness, having betaken themselves to their shreds of moral honesty, as so many broken boards of that split ship.

7. *Lastly*, All formal hypocrites, or legal professors, these sons and daughters of the bond-woman, Gal. iv. 24, 25. These are they who have been convinced, but never were converted; who have been awakened by the law, but were never laid to rest by the gospel; who are brought to duties but have never been brought out of them to Jesus Christ; who pretend to be married to Christ, but were never yet divorced from nor dead to the law; and so are still joined to the first husband the law as a covenant of works. Though they be strict and zealous professors and therein go beyond many; they are as really enemies to Christ as the profane are; Rom. x. 3, "For they, being ignorant of God's righteousness, and going about to stablish their own righteousness, have not submitted themselves to the righteousness of God." Though they will not let an opportunity of duty slip, but take heed to their ways, and dare not walk at random, as many do; all that they do is under the influence of the covenant of works, and therefore God regards it not, but they remain under the curse.

Of the Commanding, Debarring, Condemning, and Irritating Power
of the Covenant of Works, upon those who are under it.

III. I proceed to show what is the effect of the broken covenant
of works upon those who are under it.

Of the Commanding Power of the Covenant of Works.

First, It has and exercises a commanding power over them, binding them to its obedience, with the strongest bonds and ties of authority. Its commands are contained in the fiery law delivered from
Mount Sinai, out of the midst of the fire, Deut. v. 22. The obedience of them, which it binds unto, is perfect obedience, every way
perfect, Luke x. 27, 28. It has its full commanding power over
them all that are under it. It has become a question whether or
not believers are set free from the commanding power of the covenant of works, as well as from the condemning power of it. We
own the ten commands, which were delivered on Mount Sinai, to be
the eternal rule of righteousness, and that these are given of God in
the hand of Jesus Christ to believers, for a rule of life to them ;
that they require of them perfect obedience, and have all the
binding power over them that the sovereign authority of God
the Creator and Redeemer can give them, which is supreme
and absolute. But that believers are under that law as it
stands in the covenant of works, that these commands are bound on
believers by the tie of the covenant of works, or that the covenant
of works has a commanding power over believers, we must deny.
For believers are dead to the law as a covenant of works, Rom. vii.
4, and therefore as a husband cannot pretend to command his wife
after she is dead and the relation dissolved ; so believers being dead
to the law as a covenant, it cannot have any commanding authority
over them. They are not under it, Rom. vi. 14, how then can it
have any commanding power over them ? They are not under
its jurisdiction, but under that of grace ; so though the commands
be the same as to the matter, yet they are not to take them from
the covenant of works, but from the law as in the hand of Christ.
Our Lord Jesus did, in the name of all his people, put himself under its commanding power, and satisfied all its commands, to deliver
his people that were under it, Gal. iv. 4, 5, " God sent forth his
Son, made of a woman, made under the law, to redeem them that
were under the law." And shall they dishonour him by putting
their necks under it again ? After Christ has got up the bond, having fully paid all the law's demands, shall we pretend to enter in
payment again ?

Let us take a view of the commanding power of the covenant of works, which it has over all that are under it.

1. It commands and binds to perfect obedience, under pain of the curse; Gal. iii. 10, "Cursed is every one that continueth not in all things which are written in the book of the law to do them." Every the least duty is commanded with this certification, and this is the risk they run upon every the least slip. The law in the hand of Christ unto believers commands obedience too, and that under a penalty. But it is a soft one in comparison of that, namely, strokes of fatherly anger; as appears from Psalm lxxxix. 30—33, "If his children forsake my law, and walk not in my judgments; if they break my statutes, and keep not my commandments; then will I visit their transgressions with the rod, and their iniquity with stripes," &c. This penalty is not the curse of a wrathful judge, Gal. iii. 13, "Christ hath redeemed us from the curse of the law, being made a curse for us." But the covenant of works has no less certification, it cannot speak to its subjects in softer terms; so that though the stroke itself be never so small, yet there is a curse in it, if it were but the miscarrying of a basket of bread, Deut. xxviii. 17.

2. It commands without any promise of strength at all to perform. There is no such promise to be found in all the Bible, belonging to that covenant. It shews what is to be done, and with all severity exacts the task; but furnishes not anything whereof it is to be made. So the case of men under that covenant is represented by Israel's case in Egypt, Exod. v. 18, "Go therefore now and work," said Pharaoh to that people; "for there shall no straw be given you, yet shall ye deliver the tale of bricks." Under the covenant of grace, duty is required, but strength is promised too, Ezek. xxxvi. 27, "A new heart also will I give you, and a new spirit will I put within you; and I will take away the stony heart out of your flesh, and I will give you an heart of flesh." And the commands in the hands of the Mediator are turned into promises, as appears from Deut. x. 16, " Circumcise the foreskin of your heart, and be no more stiff-necked." Compare chap. xxx. 6, " And the Lord thy God will circumcise thine heart, and the heart of thy seed, to love the Lord thy God with all thine heart, and with all thy soul, that thou mayest live." Yea, the Mediator's calls and commands to his people bear a promise of help; Prov. x. 29, "The way of the Lord is strength to the upright." But there is no such thing in the covenant of works; the work must be performed in the strength that was given; they must trade with the stock that mankind was set up with at first : but that strength is gone, that stock is wasted ;

howbeit the law can neither make it up again, nor yet abate of its demands.

Of the Debarring Power of the Covenant of Works.

Secondly, The broken covenant of works has a debarring power over them that are under it, in respect of the promise ; it bars them from life and salvation, as long as they are under its dominion, Gal. ii. 16, "For by the works of the law shall no flesh be justified." While Adam kept this covenant, it secured eternal life to him ; but as soon as it was broken, it set it beyond his reach ; and neither he nor any of his descendents had ever seen life, if another covenant had not been provided. The broken covenant of works fixes a great gulf betwixt its territories and life and salvation ; so that no man can pass from the one to the other. If any would be at heaven, they must get out from under the law, and get into the covenant of grace ; so shall they have life and salvation ; but not otherwise. There are two bars which this broken covenant draws betwixt its subjects and life and salvation.

1. There is no life to the sinner without complete satisfaction to justice, for the wrong he has done to the honour of God and his law ; Heb. ix. 22, for "without shedding of blood is no remission." The terms of the covenant were—"In the day that thou eatest thereof, thou shalt surely die," Gen. ii. 17. Now the covenant is broken, the penalty must be paid, in the true sense and meaning of the bond ; the sinner must die, and die infinitely, die till infinite justice be satisfied. Can the sinner get over this bar ? Is he able to satisfy, can he go to that death, a sacrifice for himself, and return again ? Can he pay the penalty of the bond ? No, no. In his blindness and ignorance, he thinks perhaps to get over it by his mourning and afflicting himself for his sin, by bearing as well as he can the afflictions God lays on him ; but all his sufferings in the world are but an earnest of what he must suffer hereafter. For at best they are but the sufferings of a finite being, which cannot compensate the wrong his sin has done to the honour of an infinite God ; and besides, he sins anew in his suffering too ; he cannot bear a cross without some grudge against God, and some impatience, which are new sins. So the sinner in this does but attempt to wash himself in the mire. Wherefore he can never get over this bar. And if he were over it, there is yet a

2. Second bar betwixt him and life and salvation, namely, There is no life and salvation without perfect obedience to its commands for the time to come ; Matth. xix. 17, "If thou wilt enter into life," says Christ unto the young man in the gospel, "keep the command-

ments." This was the condition of the covenant; and it is not enough that a man pay the penalty of a broken covenant, but he must perform the condition of it, ere he can plead the benefit. Perfect obedience to the commands of God is the terms of life in that covenant; no less was proposed to Adam, who broke it; no less to Christ who fulfilled it in the room of his elect, Gal. iv. 4, 5, forecited. As there was a necessity of passive obedience to it, Luke xxiv. 26, " Ought not Christ to have suffered these things ?" so was there of active obedience, Matth. iii. 15, " It becometh us to fulfil all righteousness." And there is no less proposed to all that are under it.

Is the sinner able to get over this bar ? His stock of strength is gone; the fall in Adam has so bruised him, that his arm is broken, he cannot work for life; he is not fit to be God's hired servant now for life; for till he get life of free grace in Christ, he can do nothing, John xv. 5. He must be saved before he can work one good work, saved from sin, the guilt and power of it; saved from the spiritual death he is lying under, as the penalty of the covenant of works; how then can he work for salvation ? The scripture is express on this head, not only that we are not justified by works, but that we are not saved by works: for " By grace are ye saved," says the apostle, " through faith ; and that not of yourselves : it is the gift of God. Not of works, lest any man should boast. For we are his workmanship, created in Christ Jesus unto good works, which God hath before ordained that we should walk in them," Eph. ii. 8—10. " Not by works of righteousness which we have done, but according to his mercy he saved us by the washing of regeneration, and renewing of the Holy Ghost," Tit. iii. 5.

I know the sinner, in his blindness, will think to please God by his doing as well as he can; by his pretended sincerity, though he cannot attain to perfection ; by the will, where he cannot reach the deed. But alas! he considers not that the covenant of works will admit of none of these, all which are rejected by that one sentence of the law, " Cursed is every one that continueth not in all things which are written in the book of the law to do them." Besides that there is not one thing that he does that is well done, while he is not in Christ; there is no sincerity with him, but selfishness ; no will but self-will.

And as there is no getting over either of these bars, so there is no removing them out of the way, that so the sinner may have a passage, without concerning himself with them, Matth. v. 18. Some fancy to themselves a removing of them by mere mercy. God knows that we cannot answer the demands of the covenant of works, so, think they, mercy will pass them for the safety of the sinner. But has not God sufficiently declared the contrary, in the sending of his own Son, who, before he could redeem the elect, behoved to get over them both by perfect obedience and satisfaction in their stead, Rom. viii. 22. If the terms of life and salvation could have been abated, might not God's own Son have expected the abatement in his favour, while he stood in the room of elect sinners? but he got no abatement; how can ye expect it then; See Exod. xxxiv. 7.

Of the Condemning Power of the Covenant of Works.

Thirdly, The broken covenant of works has a cursing and condemning power over them that are under it, in respect of the threatening. " Cursed is every one that continueth not in all things which are written in the book of the law to do them," Gal. iii. 10. Compare Rom. iii. 19, " Now we know that what things soever the law saith, it saith to them who are under the law; that every mouth may be stopped, and all the world may become guilty before God." Every man and woman under it, is in a state of condemnation; they are condemned persons, bound over to the wrath of God in time and eternity, John iii. 18, " He that believeth not is condemned already." So that there have never any come to Christ but with the rope about their necks, as condemned criminals. Christ's kingdom is the jurisdiction of grace, where grace, life, and salvation reign through Jesus Christ. It is peopled by fugitives out of the dominion of the law; and they that flee thither are all such as find there is no living for them at home; they are such as the sentence of death is passed upon, and there is no access for a remission to them under the dominion of the law. And they never think of fleeing into the jurisdiction of grace, till once the sentence of death is intimated unto them, by their own consciences, and they begin to see they are in hazard every moment of being drawn to death; for till then, they will not believe it. Then they bethink themselves of making their escape out of the law's dominion.

This power the law, as a covenant of works, has over them by sin, forasmuch as it was a clause in the covenant, that man sinning should die the death, Gen. ii. 17. It had no such power over man, till once sin entered; but upon the breach of the command, the penalty took place. And since every man is born a sinner, he is also born a cursed and condemned man by the sentence of the law, which abides on him so long as he continues under that covenant. And upon every sin committed, the yoke is wreathed faster and faster about his neck; so that upon every sin committed by persons while in that state, there is a new band by which they are bound over to wrath.

Of the Irritating Power of the Covenant of Works.

Lastly, The broken covenant of works has an irritating influence upon all that are under it, so that instead of making them better, it makes them worse, stirring up their corruptions, like a nest of ants, being troubled by one's touching of them, Rom. vii. 9, 10, 11, "For when we were in the flesh, says the apostle, the motions of sin which were by the law, did work in our members to bring forth fruit unto death.—And the commandment, which was ordained to life, I found to be unto death. For sin taking occasion by the commandment, deceived me, and by it slew me." Men under this covenant, whose corruptions lie dormant after a sort, while the law is not applied to their consciences, when once the law is brought home to their souls, and they are touched with it, their corrupt hearts swell and rage in sin, like the sea troubled with winds. See a notable instance of it, Acts vii. 54, in the case of the Jews after Stephen's speech to them, "When they heard these things, they were cut to the heart, and they gnashed on him with their teeth." And hence is that direction of our Saviour, Matth. vii. 6, "Give not that which is holy unto the dogs, neither cast ye your pearls before swine, lest they trample them under their feet, and turn again and rend you." You may look to another instance, Hos. xi. 2, "As they called them, so they went from them." And thus it is, that by the law sin abounds, and becomes exceedingly sinful.

Now, this is accidental to the law as the covenant of works; for it is holy, and just, and good; and therefore can never bring forth sin as the native fruit of it. But it is owing to the corruption of men's hearts, impatient of restraint, Rom. vii. 12, 13, forecited. While the sun shines warm on a garden, the flowers send forth a pleasant smell; but while it shines so on the dunghill, it smells more abominably than at other times. So it is here. There are two things here to be considered in the case of the law.

1. It lays an awful restraint on the sinner with its commands and threatenings, Gal. iii. 10. The unrenewed man would never make a holy life his choice; might he freely follow his own inclination, he would not regard what is good, but give himself a liberty in sinful courses. But the law is as a bridle to him; it crosses and contradicts his sinful inclinations; it commands him to obey under the pain of the curse, and threatens him with death and damnation, if he shall transgress the bounds it sets him. It is to him as the bridle and spur to the horse; as the master and his whip to the slave. So that the sinner can never cordially like it, but all the obedience it gets from him is mercenary, having no higher springs than hope of reward and fear of punishment.

2. In the meantime it has no power to subdue his corruptions, to remove his rebellious disposition, to reconcile his heart to holiness, or to strengthen him for the performance of duty; "For the law was given by Moses, but grace and truth came by Jesus Christ," John i. 17. As it finds the man without strength, so it leaves him, though it never ceases to exact duty of him. Though no straw is given to the sinner by it, yet the tale of the bricks it will not suffer to be diminished. Hence,

(1.) The very restraint of the law, as the covenant of works, awakens, and puts an edge upon the corruption of the heart, Rom. vii. 11, forecited. It breeds in the corrupt heart a longing after the forbidden fruit, though it have nothing more to commend it than allowed fruit, but that it is forbidden. The sinner perceiving the thorn-hedge of the law betwixt him and sin, conceives a keenness to be over the hedge. And hence it is, that many are never so ready to break out into extravagancies, as after their consciences have been most keenly plied by the word. And thus many never give such a loose to their lusts, as after solemn occasions of communion with God.

(2.) In the encounter betwixt the law and lusts, lusts gather strength by the law's crossing them. They are irritated, provoked, and stirred up the more, that the law goes about to hold them down, Rom. vii. 5. They swell, they rally all their forces, to make head against their enemy, that they may get the victory. The sinner, the more he is plied by the law to hold him back, runs the more fiercely down the steep place into the sea, like the swine possessed by the devil. If the law come into the heart without gospel grace to water the soul, it shall be like one with a besom sweeping a dry floor; the more forcibly one sweeps, the more thick will the dust flee up, and flee about into every corner. The sinner is like the unruly horse, which the more he is checked with the bit, rages the more. And hence the issue often is that which we find in Hos. iv. 17, "Ephraim is joined to idols; let him alone;" and in Psalm lxxxi. 11, 12, "But my people would not hearken to my voice; and Israel would none of me; so I gave them up unto their own heart's lust, and they walked in their own counsels."

(3.) The sinner, finding the case hopeless, hardens himself, and goes on, like treacherous Judah, Jer. ii. 25, "Thou saidst, There is no hope. No; for I have loved strangers, and after them will I go." He looks to the height of the law's commands, and finds himself incapable to reach them; and he looks to the terror of the law's threatenings, and finds them unavoidable. So he gives up with hope, sits down hardened in secret despair, using all means to stop the access of light from the law for his conviction and disquietment. Thus he is like a tired horse, that bears the spur, but will not answer it; or if he be moved by it, turns back to bite the rider, but goes not one foot faster for all it.

(4.) *Lastly*, Hence the heart is filled with the hatred of the holy law, and of the holy God who made it, and holds by it. This is the fearful issue of the matter, Prov. i. 29, " They hated knowledge, and did not choose the fear of the Lord." Rom. i. 30,—"Haters of God." As the condemned criminal hates the judge and the law, so do they. They cannot bring up their hearts to the purity the law requires, and cannot get the law brought down to the impurity of their hearts, but still it reads their doom; hence the heart cannot miss to rise against the law, being girded with the cords of death by it; and against God in secret grudges at his holiness and justice, and secret wishes that he were not such an one as he is.

This is a short account of what is called the irritating power of the law; from which alone one may see, what a fearful case it is to be under the law as it is the covenant of works. It tends to make the heart of man a very hell; and the truth is, in hell it comes to its height; and so they are held like wild bulls in a net.

The Reasons why so many persons still remain under the broken Covenant of Works.

IV. I now proceed to shew, why so many do still remain under the broken covenant of works. As for those who never heard of, nor had the offer of the covenant of grace, we need not inquire much. The case is plain; they know no other way. But men to whom the covenant of grace is proclaimed, yet remain under the covenant of works; they will still hang on about Sinai for all the thunders and lightnings there, and will not come to Zion. The following reasons of this conduct may be given :—

1. It is natural to men, being made with Adam, and us in his loins; it is engrained in the hearts of all men naturally. " Tell me," says the apostle, Gal. ii. 21, " ye that desire to be under the law, do ye not hear the law ?" And there are impressions of it to be found in the hearts of all, among the ruins of the fall. The law as a covenant of works was the first husband that human nature was wedded to; and so it is still natural to men to cleave to it. And we have a clear proof of it,

(1.) In men left to the swing of their own nature; they all go this way in their dealing with God for life and favour. Look abroad into the world, and behold the vast multitudes embracing Paganism, Judaism, Mahometism, and Popery. All these agree in this, that it is by doing man must live, though they hugely differ in the things that are to be done for life. Look into the Protestant churches, and you shall see readily, that the more corrupt any of them is, the more they incline to the way of this covenant. Consider persons among us ignorant of the principles of true religion, who, not having received instruction, speak of the way of life and salvation as nature prompts them, and you shall find them also of the same mind. Finally, consider all unrenewed men whatsoever, having the knowledge and making profession of the expectation of life and salvation in the way of the covenant of grace; yet they in practice stumble at this stumbling-stone, Matt. v. 3.

(2.) In men awakened and convinced, and in moral seriousness seeking to know what course they shall take to be saved, and plying their work for that end. They all take this principle for granted, That it is by doing they must obtain life and salvation, Matth. xix. 16, "What good thing shall I do that I may have eternal life?" Luke x. 25, "What shall I do to inherit eternal life?" And this obtains when they are pricked to the very heart, and the law as the covenant of works has wounded them to the very soul. They never think of a divorce from the law, that they may be married to Christ; but how shall they do to please the old husband, and so be saved from wrath; as is plain in the case of Peter's hearers, Acts ii. 27, when, being pricked in their hearts, they said, "Men and brethren, what shall we do?" and in the case of the Philippian jailor, Acts xvi. 30, who being awakened by a train of very alarming incidents, and trembling through terror, cried out, "What must I do to be saved?"

(3.) In the saints, who are truly married to Jesus Christ, O what hankering after the first husband, how great the remains of a legal spirit, how hard is it for them to forget their father's house? Psalm xlv. 10. Adam having embraced the promise of the Messiah, yet was in hazard of running back to this covenant. There is a disposition to deal with God, in the way of giving so much duty for so much grace and favour with God, in the best, that they have continually to strive with. Self-denial is one of the most difficult duties in Christianity.

2. The way of that covenant is most agreeable to the pride of man's heart. A proud heart will rather serve itself with the less, than stoop to live upon free grace, Rom. x. 3. Man must be broken, bruised, and humbled, and laid very low, before he will embrace the covenant of grace. While a broken board of the first covenant will do men any service, they will hold by it, rather than come to Christ; like men who will rather live in a cottage of their own, than in

another man's castle. To renounce all our own wisdom, works, and righteousness, and to cast away all those garments as filthy rags, which we have been at so much pains to patch up, is quite against the grain with corrupt nature, Rom. vii. 4.

3. It is most agreeable to man's reason, in its corrupt state. If one should have asked the opinion of the philosophers, concerning that religion which taught salvation by a crucified Christ, and through the righteousness of another; they would have said, it was unreasonable and foolish, and that the only way to true happiness was the way of moral virtue. The Jewish Rabbis would have declared it scandalous, 1 Cor. i. 23, where the preaching of Christ crucified is said to be to the Jews a stumbling-block, (in the Greek, *a scandal*); and would have maintained the only way to eternal life to be by the law of Moses. To this day many learned men cannot see the reasonableness of the gospel-method of salvation, in opposition to the way of the covenant of works; and therefore our godly forefathers, who reformed from Popery, and maintained the reformed truth against Popery by their heroic zealous wrestlings even unto blood, while they shewed that acquaintance with practical godliness and real holiness, whereof there is little in our day, are in effect looked upon as a parcel of well-meaning simple men, whose doctrine must be reformed over again, and rendered more agreeable to reason. A rational religion is like to be the plague of this day. But assure ye yourselves, that wherever the gospel comes in power, it will make the reason of the wisest sit down at its feet, and learn, and give over its questions formed by Hows and Whys, 2 Cor. x. 5, It " casts down imaginations, and every high thing that exalteth itself against the knowledge of God, and bringeth into captivity every thought to the obedience of Christ."

Even unlearned and simple men, in whom this appears less, because they do not enter deep into the thought, will be found sick of the same disease, when once they are thoroughly awakened, and take these matters to heart. How will they dispute against the gospel-method of salvation, against the promise, against their believing their welcome to Christ, who are so sinful and unworthy! The matter appears so great, as indeed it is, that they look on the gospel-method as a dream, and they cannot believe it.

4. Ignorance and insensibleness of the true state of that matter, as it now is. There is a thick darkness about Mount Sinai, through the whole dominion of the law; so that they who live under the covenant of works, see little but what they see by the lightnings now and then flashing out. Hence they little know where they are, nor what they are.

(1.) They do not understand the nature of that covenant to purpose, Gal. iv. 21. Any notion they have of it, is lame and weak, without efficacy. They see not how forcibly it binds to perfect obedience and satisfaction, how rigorous it is in its demands, and will abate nothing, though a man should do to the utmost of his power, and with cries and tears of blood seek forgiveness for the rest. They are not acquainted with the spirituality of the law, and the vast compass of the holy commandment, but stick too much in the letter of it. Hence they are alive without the law, Rom. vii. 9. They narrow the demands of it, that so they may be the more likely to fulfil them.

(2.) They are not duly sensible of their own utter inability for that way of salvation; "There is one that accuseth them, even Moses," or the law, "in whom they trust," John v. 45. They know they are off the way, and that they have wandered from God; but they hope they will get back to him again by repentance; while, in the meantime, their heart is a heart of stone, and they cannot change it; and "the Ethiopian shall" be able as soon to "change his skin, the leopard his spots, as they may do good that are accustomed to do evil," Jer. xiii. 23; and there is no coming to God but by Christ, John iv. 6. They know they have sinned, and provoked justice against them; but they hope to be sorry for their sin, to pray to God for forgiveness, and bear any thing patiently that God lays on them; while in the meantime they see not that none of those things will satisfy God's justice, which yet will have full satisfaction for every the least sin of theirs, ere they see heaven. They know they must be holy; but they hope to serve God better than ever they have done; while in the meantime they consider not that their work-arm is broken, and they can work none to purpose till they be saved by grace.

Application of the Doctrine of the Condition of Men under the broken Covenant of Works.

This doctrine may be applied for information and exhortation.

USE I. Of information. Hence learn,

1. That some, yea many of mankind, are under the curse, bound over to wrath. For that is the case of all persons under that covenant. Their necks are under a heavy yoke; they are liable in payment of a penalty, which they will never be able to discharge, and to put off their heads. They may pay more or less of it in this world; but if they get not rid of it another way, it will not be paid out through all the ages of eternity.

2. See here whence it is that true holiness is so rare, and wicked-

ness and ungodliness so frequent in the world. Most men are under that covenant, under which sin and death reign; and there is no holiness, there are no good works under it, Rom. vi. 14. It has, being broken, barred communion betwixt God and sinners under it; and therefore of necessity there must be a pining away in iniquity while one is under it. It is only in the way of the second covenant that sanctifying influences are had.

3. Here ye may see the true spring of legalism in principles as well as in practice. Many are really under that covenant; no wonder then there be many to set up for that way. It is the way that backsliding churches in all ages have gone. It soon began in the primitive apostolical churches; and that mystery of iniquity wrought till it issued in Popery, the grand apostasy under the New Testament.

4. See whence it is that the doctrine of the gospel is so little understood, and in the purity of it is looked at as a strange thing. It is like other things which are not known in the country in which one is bred, and therefore stared at, and often mistaken. Hence it gets ill names in the world. When Christ himself preached it, he was called a friend of publicans and sinners; when Paul preached it, they would not believe but he made void the law by it, and that he opened a door for licentiousness of life, Rom. iii. 8.

Use II. Be exhorted then seriously and impartially to try what covenant ye are under. It is true there is a covenant of grace made, proclaimed and offered unto you, and ye are all under the outward dispensation of the covenant of grace; but yet many are notwithstanding really under the covenant of works still. As ye love your own souls, try impartially, whether ye be under it or not, but under the covenant of grace. For motives, consider

MOTIVE 1. Ye are all born under the covenant of works, being "by nature children of wrath," Eph. ii. 3. It is in the region of the law that we all draw our first breath. And no man will get out from its dominion in a morning dream. We owe it to our second birth, whoever of us are brought into the covenant of grace; but that is not our original state. The law is the first husband to all and every one of Adam's children. I would have you try whether ye be dead to it, and divorced from it or not.

MOTIVE 2. Till once ye see yourselves under the covenant of works, and so lost and ruined with the burden of that broken covenant on you; ye may hear of the covenant of grace, but ye will never take hold of it in good earnest, Gal. ii. 6. Here lies the ruin of the most part who hear the gospel; they were never slain by the law, and therefore never quickened by the gospel; they never find the working of the deadly poison conveyed to them from the first Adam, and therefore they see no beauty in the second Adam for which he is to be desired.

MOTIVE 3. Your salvation or ruin turns on this point. What covenant ye are under. If thou be within the bond of the covenant of grace, thou art in a state of salvation ; " He that believeth shall be saved," Mark xvi. 16. David could say, " God hath made with me an everlasting covenant, ordered in all things and sure ; for this is all my salvation, 2 Sam. xxiii. 5. If thou art under the covenant of works, thou art in a state of death ; for, says the text, " as many as are of the works of the law are under the curse." And is this so light and trivial a matter that thou shouldst be unconcerned which of these covenants thou art under ?

MOTIVE 4. There is no ease for a poor sinner but severity and rigour, under the covenant of works. One may easily see that we are not able to abide that now, when we are become weak and guilty ; for, says the Psalmist, Psalm cxxx. 3, " If thou, Lord, shouldst mark iniquities ; O Lord, who shall stand ?" But while thou remainest under the first covenant, thou canst expect nothing but wrath and fury. There is no pardon under that covenant ; the law-statute being, " In the day thou eatest thereof, thou shalt surely die," Gen. ii. 17. The sinner must die the death. That ever we heard of pardon is owing to the second covenant, which secures pardoning mercy to those who come under the bond of it ; for " by him (Christ) all that believe are justified from all things, from which they could not be justified by the law of Moses," Acts xiii. 39. Though there is no question but the covenant of works requires repentance, a turning to God under pain of the curse ; yet there is no grace for helping the sinner to it under this covenant ; and suppose one could attain to it, it could not help him. There is no accepting the will for the deed under it. It is not good will, but perfectly good works that will satisfy it.

MOTIVE 5. While ye are under that covenant, ye are without Christ, Eph. ii. 12. As a woman cannot, by the law of God, be married to two husbands at once, so one cannot be under the covenant of works and married to Christ at once. The first marriage to the law must be dissolved by death or divorce, ere the soul can be married to Christ, Rom. vii. 4. And being without Christ, ye have no saving interest in his purchase.

Lastly, All attempts you make to get to heaven, while under this covenant, will be vain. The children of that covenant are, by an unalterable statute of the court of heaven, excluded from the heavenly inheritance ; so that, do what you will, while ye abide under it, you may as well fall a-ploughing the rocks, and sowing your seed in the sand of the sea, as think to get to heaven that way ; for what saith the scripture ? " Cast out the bond-woman and her son ; for the son of the bond-woman shall not be heir with the son of the free woman," Gal. iv. 30. The way to heaven by that covenant is blocked up to sinners, the angel with the flaming sword guards the tree of life, so that there is no access to salvation that way, but under a condition impossible for you to perform.

Now, to set this matter in a due light to you, I will,

1. Give some marks and characters of those that are under this covenant.

2. Discover the vanity of some pleas that such have, to prove that it is not to their own works that they trust for salvation, but to Christ.

First, I will give some marks and characters of those that are under this covenant.

1. They have never yet parted with the law, or covenant of works, lawfully, which all the saints have done. There are two ways of parting with that covenant. One is by running away from it; and thus we may apply to this case Nabal's tale concerning David, 1 Sam xxv. 10, " There be many servants now-a-days, that break away every man from his master." They break its bonds, and cast away its cords, value neither its commands nor threats ; for they look on it like an almanack out of date, as a thing that they are not concerned with. This is no lawful parting, and therefore it cannot dissolve the relation betwixt them and it. A servant or a wife that is run away, is a servant or a wife for all that still. And the master can bring back the one, and make him serve or suffer; and the husband the other. And so will this covenant deal with such, and make them sensible they are under it still, in the strictest bonds. It will take them by the throat here or hereafter, saying, Pay what thou owest.

The other is parting with it, after fair count and reckoning with it, and payment instructed ; a parting with it upon a divorce obtained, after a fair hearing given it before the Judge of all the earth. It is brought about in this manner. There is a summons given at the instance of the law, or covenant of works, to the conscience of the secure sinner, to compear before the tribunal of God. Hereby the conscience being awakened, it appears and stands trembling at the bar; in the meantime the King's Son offers himself in a marriage covenant to the guilty soul, with his righteousness, obedience, and satisfaction. The law appears and pleads,

(1.) So much and so much owing by the sinner, for his breaking its commands. Mountains of guilt appear innumerable articles in its accounts ; and the charge must be owned just, for it is just in every particular. Here the sinner, betaking himself to Christ, pleads by faith the satisfaction of Christ for him; and, embracing the gospel offers, he sets betwixt him and the law the death and suf-- ferings of Christ, as full payment of that debt.

(2.) So much to be done before the sinner can be saved, according to the condition of the covenant, perfect obedience due to it by all the children of Adam. The sinner cannot deny the debt; but pleads by faith the Mediator's payment of it, by his obedience even to the death. He counts upon this score unto the law, all that Christ the Son of God did for the space of about thirty-three years on the earth, in the perfect obedience of all its commands.

Thus the sinner, embracing Christ, has wherewith to answer it. And the plea of payment that way is sustained, and the soul is declared free from the law or covenant of works, and so lawfully parted from it. What experience have ye of this? This will, for the substance of it, pass in every soul freed from the covenant of works. But alas! how many are there, [1.] Who were never troubled about that, how to get a discharge of that bargain from the Judge of all the earth, but have lived at ease without it? [2.] Who never saw a necessity of reckoning with the law, in order to their getting clear of it? [3.] Who have still aimed at putting off the demands of the law, with their own obedience and suffering, such as they were?

2. They are of a legal spirit, and have not the spirit of the covenant of grace. Caleb and Joshua had another spirit than the rest of the Jews, so have those who are within the bond of the covenant of grace, Gal. iv. 24. In the saints indeed there are wretched remains of that spirit, but it does not reign in them as in others.

1st, They are of a slavish spirit who are under that covenant; whereas the saints are acted by a son-like spirit. For, says the apostle, Rom. viii. 15; "ye have not received the spirit of bondage again to fear; but ye have received the Spirit of adoption, whereby we cry, Abba, Father." As the slave is moved with fear, not with love; so is it with them. This slavish spirit appears in them thus:

(1.) They are driven from sin, and to their duty, by the fear of hell and wrath, rather than drawn from the one to the other by any hatred of the one, and love of the other, in themselves; like the Israelites of old, of whom it is said; Psalm lxxviii. 34, "When he [God] slew them, then they sought him; and they returned, and enquired early after God." It is the influence of the covenant of works in its terrible sanction, that moves them. Take away that, secure them but from hell and damnation, and they would give themselves the swing in their lusts; they have no other kind of principle to move them to holiness; all is selfish about them.

(2.) They content themselves with the bare performance of duty, and abstaining from any sin, without regarding the true principle, end, and manner of doing; even as the slave who is concerned for no more, but to get his task over, Isa. xxix. 13. It is not their business to get their hearts wrought up to the love of God, concern for his glory, and to the doing of their work in faith; but to get the work done, Luke xviii. 11. It may be they dare not neglect duty, but it is not their concern to find Christ in duty, nor is it their grief if they do not find him.

(3.) Under terror of conscience they do not flee to the blood of Christ, but to their work again, to amend what was done amiss, or make it up by greater diligence, Acts ii. 37. Are not the consciences of men under that covenant affrighted sometimes? But consider how they are pacified again. Not by the sprinkling of Christ's blood on them by faith, Heb. ix. 14, but by resolves to do better in time to come, by prayers, mourning, &c. And hence it is that their corruptions are never weakened for all this, for the law makes nothing perfect; but the believing application of the blood of Christ not only takes away guilt, but strengthens the soul.

2dly, They are of a mercenary spirit; they are acted by the spirit of a hireling, who works that he may win his wages. The covenant of works is so natural to us, that we naturally know no other religion, but to work and win, do good works that we may win heaven by them. Hence the prodigal would be put among the hired servants, when he thought of returning; but when he returned, he insists not on that. This spirit appears in those who are under the covenant of works thus:—

(1.) Their work is for reward, to obtain God's favour and salvation by their works, Rom. x. 3. Whereas the saints look for salvation and the favour of God only through the obedience and death of Jesus Christ, Tit. iii. 5, "Not by works of righteousness which we have done, but according to his mercy he saved us." I own the saints may have an eye to the gratuitous reward promised to them to crown their work and labour of love, as Moses is said to have "had respect unto the recompense of the reward," Heb. xi. 26; and they may be thereby influenced in their duty. But then they look for that reward as coming to them, not for the sake of their work, but for the sake of Christ's work. They are sons, and have a more noble principle of obedience to God, Heb. vi. 10, as God's own children, Rom. viii. 15, who, having the inheritance secured to them another way than by their working, are prompted to obedience by their love to God, and desire to please him. The truth is, those who are under the broken covenant of works, being destitute of saving faith, are void also of true love to God, 1 Tim. i. 5. It is themselves mainly, if not only, that they seek in their duties; and, were it not the hope of gain to themselves by them, they would not regard them. In a word, they serve God, not out of any kindly love to him, but that thereby they may serve themselves.

(2.) The more they do and the better they do, they look on God to be the more in their debt, like Micah, who said, "Now I know that the Lord will do me good, seeing I have a Levite to my priest," Judg. xvii. 13. For it is according to their own doing, not according to their interest in Christ's blood, that they expect favour from the Lord. The publican, Luke xviii. 13, pleads mercy through a propitiation, "Be propitious to me," according to the Greek; but the Pharisee pleads upon what himself had done more than many others, ver. 12, "God, I thank thee," says he, "that I am not as other men are, extortioners, unjust, adulterers, or even as this publican! I fast twice in the week, I give tithes of all that I possess." Hence their hearts rise against God, if they find not their works regarded and rewarded, according to the value themselves put upon them; like the Jews of old, who said, "Wherefore have we fasted, and thou seest not? wherefore have we afflicted our soul, and thou takest no knowledge? Isa. lviii. 3. Hence ariseth a very considerable difference betwixt the children of the two covenants; those of the first covenant, the better they do their duty, their hearts are the more filled with conceit of themselves, their duties, like wind, puff them up, as in the case of the Pharisee, Luke xviii. 11, quoted above. But those of the second covenant, the better they do, they are the more humbled and low in their own eyes; like David, who said, "Who am I, and what is my people, that we should be able to offer so willingly after this sort? 1 Chron. xxix. 14, and like the apostle Paul, "In what am I behind the very chiefest apostles," said he, "though I be nothing? 2 Cor. xii. 11.

(3.) Their duties make them more easy and secure in some one sin or other; like the adulterous woman, Prov. vii. 14, 15, "I have peace offerings with me; this day have I paid my vows. Therefore came I forth to meet thee, diligently to seek thy face, and I have found thee." The Jews, as profane as they were in Isaiah's time, brought a multitude of sacrifices to God's altar, Isa. i. 11. Why did they do so, but because they expected that these would make all odds even betwixt God and them? Just so do many with their duties; they pray to God, and many good things; so they can with the more ease do and say many ill things. By their duties they seem to themselves as it were to pay the old, and they can the more freely take on the new. Thus they "bless God and curse men with the same tongue. Out of the same mouth proceedeth blessing and cursing," James iii. 9, 10. They use their duties for an occasion to the flesh, and turn the grace of God into lasciviousness; than which there cannot be a more speaking evidence of one under the broken covenant of works. Publicans and harlots will enter into the kingdom of heaven, before such persons.

Thus you have some characters of those who are under this covenant, and may perceive that they deal with God in the matter of his favour and salvation in the way of that covenant, and not in the way of the covenant of grace. But it is hard to convince men of this; therefore,

Secondly, I will discover the vanity of some pleas that such have, to prove that it is not to their own works that they trust for salvation, but to Christ.

1. They are so far, say they, from trusting to their own works in this matter, that they really wonder anybody can do it. I answer, that this is rather a sign of the ignorance of the corruption of man's nature, and unacquaintedness with the deceitfulness of your own heart, than of your freedom from that corrupt way of dealing with God. Hazael said so in another case, "Am I a dog to do this thing?" Yet was he such a dog as to do it. Ye know not, it seems, what spirits ye are of. That way of dealing with God is as natural to us, as to fishes to swim in the sea, and birds to fly in the air. The godly themselves are not quite free from it. The disciples needed that lesson, "When ye shall have done all those things which are commanded you, say, We are unprofitable servants; we have done that which was our duty to do," Luke xvii. 10. For they are too apt to think much of any little they do; like Peter, "Behold we have forsaken all," said he, "and followed thee," Matth. xix. 27. The difference then lies here—the godly feel this corrupt way of dealing with God, they wrestle against it, loath themselves for it, and would fain be rid of it; whereas it reigns in others, and has quiet possession.

2. This is rank Popery, and they are true Protestants, believing that we are not saved for our works, but for the sake of Christ. Answer, It is indeed the very life and soul of Popery. But what is Popery, but the product of man's corrupt nature, framing a way of salvation according to the covenant of works? So even Protestants have Popish hearts by nature. A floating principle in the head, received by means of education, or other external teaching, will never be able to change the natural bent of the heart. It is the teaching of the Spirit with power which only can do that. It is an article of the profane Protestant's religion, that there is a hea-

ven and a hell, yet they live as if there were neither of them. That the grace of God teacheth to deny ungodliness and worldly lusts, and to live soberly, righteously, and godly in this present world; yet their life and practice is as far from this principle, as the east is distant from the west. Men do not always live according to their professed principles.; therefore, in this point, the head may look one way, and the heart another.

3. They are persuaded that of themselves, without the grace of God, they can do nothing; that there is no strength in them. Answer, Many have this in their mouths, who never to this day were let into a view of their own utter inability to help themselves. They take up that principle, rather to be a cover to their sloth, and a pretence to shift duty, than out of any conviction of the truth of it in their own souls. Hence none are readier to delay and put off salvation-work from time to time than they; as if they could really do all, and that at any time. But whatever be of that, this is an insignificant plea; the proud Pharisee might have pleaded that as well as you, and yet he stood upon his works with God, Luke xviii. 11, forecited. The matter lies here; they profess they can do nothing without the help of grace; but when by the help of grace they have done their duty, they think God cannot but save them, who so serve him; as if God's grace helped men to purchase their own salvation.

4. They are convinced that they cannot keep the law perfectly, but when they have done all they can, they look to Christ to supply all wherein they come short. Answer. The truth is, that nobody is so far from doing all they can, as such men are who pretend most to it; there are many things they never do, which yet are within the compass of their natural powers. But the Pharisees, who, nobody doubts, dealt with God in this way of works, were convinced as well as you, that they did not keep the law perfectly; but then the ceremonial law afforded them a salve, in their apprehension, for their defects in the duties of the moral law. Just so is the case in this plea, where the deceit lies in that the man lays not the whole stress of his acceptance with God and his salvation on the obedience and death of Christ; but partly on his own works, partly on Christ, thus mixing his own righteousness with Christ's, which the apostle rejects; "The law is not of faith, but the man that doth them shall live in them," Gal. iii. 12. "Christ is become of no effect unto you, whosoever of you are justified by the law," chap. v. 4.

Lastly, They trust in Christ for the acceptance of all their duties, and are persuaded they would never be accepted but for Christ's sake. ANSWER. Men may do this, and yet still keep the way of the covenant of works. Being persuaded that the best of their duties are not without some imperfection, they look to get them accepted as they are for Christ's sake, so as God will thereupon justify and save them, give them his favour, pardon their sin, keep them out of hell, and give them heaven. Thus they make use of Christ for obtaining salvation by their own works; as some Papists teach, that our own works merit by virtue of the merits of Christ, and that they merit not, but as they are dipt in his blood. But the way of the second covenant is to look to Christ alone for the acceptance of our persons, to justification and salvation; and then our persons being accepted, to look to him also for the acceptance of our works, not in point of justification, but of sanctification only. This was Paul's way, Phil. iii. 8, 9, " Yea, doubtless, and I count all things but loss for the excellency of the knowledge of Christ Jesus my Lord; for whom I have suffered the loss of all things, and do count them but dung, that I may win Christ, and be found in him, not having mine own righteousness which is of the law, but that which is through the faith of Christ, the righteousness which is of God by faith."

O deal impartially with yourselves in this matter, and be not too easy in this important point. The heart of man is a depth of deceit, and if you are not exercised to root up this weed of legality, and have felt the difficulty of so doing, it is a shrewd sign ye are yet under the covenant of works; the misery of which condition I am now to open up to you in the second doctrine from the text.

SECT. II.

THE MISERY OF THOSE WHO ARE UNDER THE BROKEN COVENANT OF WORKS.

DOCTRINE II. Man in his natural state being under the broken covenant of works is under the curse.

Here is the case in which Adam left all his children, the case of all by nature. Behold here as in a glass the doleful condition of sinners by the breach of the first covenant,—they are " under the curse." I shall consider this dreadful condition,

I. More generally.

II. Take a more particular view of the dreadful condition of the natural man under the curse of the broken covenant of works.

III. Apply the subject.

A General View of the Curse under which Men in their Natural
State are.

I. I shall consider the dreadful condition in which men in a
natural state are, under the broken covenant of works. And here
let us consider,

1. What curse that is which they are under.

2. What it is to be under the curse.

3. Confirm the doctrine, that man in his natural state, being under
the broken covenant of works, is under the curse.

What the Curse is which Natural Men are under.

First, I shall consider what curse that is which they are under.
It is the sentence of the law as a covenant of works, binding over
and devoting the sinner to destruction. Thus the covenant being
made with the awful sanction of death, Gen. ii. 17, upon the transgressing of it, the curse is pronounced, Gen. iii. And so it is,

1. God's curse, as the sinner's lawgiver and judge; it is his sentence of death against the transgressor, the doom pronounced by him
on the malefactor that has not continued in all things which are
written in the book of the law to do them. It is expressly called
"the curse of the Lord," Prov. iii. 33; and those under it "the people of his curse," Isa. xxxiv. 5. Man's curse is often causeless, so it
miscarries, it comes not, it does no more harm than a bird flying
over one's head, Prov. xxvi. 2. But God's curse is ever on a valid
weighty cause; so his justice requires, and it cannot miss, by reason of his truth, to come, and lie heavy where it does come by reason of his almighty power, John iii. 36.

2. It is the curse of the law, Gal. iii. 13, the curse of the broken
covenant of works, whose penalty is death. So it runs in our text,
"Cursed is every one that continueth not in all things which are
written in the book of the law to do them." The law is armed with
a curse against the disobedient, and therefore when obedience is not
performed it is poured out, Dan. ix. 11. Of old when men entered
into a covenant, they cut a beast in twain, and passed betwixt the
parts, to signify the curse on the breaker, that he should be like
that beast. Hence the Lord threatens covenant-breakers, Jer.
xxxiv. 18, "And I will give the men that have transgressed my covenant,—which they had made before me, when they cut the calf in
twain, and passed between the parts thereof," &c. Compare Matth.
xxiv. 51, "And they shall cut him asunder, and appoint him his
portion with the hypocrites," &c. As for the curse of the gospel,
as the scripture mentions no such thing, it is needless; the law secures the curse and a double curse on those who despise the gospel.

Now, in this curse there are three things to be considered :—

1*st*, The revenging wrath of God is in it, Matth. xxv. 41, " Depart from me, ye cursed, into everlasting fire prepared for the devil and his angels." It is the breathing of fiery indignation by vindictive justice against the sinner. Sin is so opposite to the nature of God, that he cannot endure it; but his wrath (may I say it with reverence) takes fire against the sinner, at the very sight of it, and makes the curse to fly against him. See this awfully represented, Deut. xxix. 20, " The anger of the Lord and his jealousy shall smoke against that man, and all the curses that are written in this book shall lie upon him."

2*dly*, A binding over of the sinner unto punishment, for the satisfaction of offended justice, Gal. iii. 13, " Cursed is every one that hangeth on a tree." As the judge, by his sentence of death, binds over the criminal to death; so God by his curse, binds over the sinner unto death in its whole compass, as in the threatening of the covenant of works. Thus he is bound to suffer till justice is satisfied, which being without the sinner's reach, the punishment comes to be eternal. It is not a punishment for the amendment of the party, as under the covenant of grace; but for reparation of the honour of the Lawgiver and law.

3*dly*, A separating of the sinner unto destruction, though not of his being, yet of his wellbeing; Deut. xxix. 21, " The Lord shall separate him unto evil—according to all the curses of the covenant that are written in this book of the law." Hereby the sinner is exterminated and excommunicated from the society of God's favourites, and set up as a mark for the arrows of wrath. As accursed things were to be destroyed, and not kept for use; so the curse on the sinner is a devoting of him to destruction, as a vessel of wrath, in which justice may be glorified; 2 Thess. i. 9, such " shall be punished with everlasting destruction from the presence of the Lord, and from the glory of his power."

What it is to be Under the Curse.

SECONDLY, Let us consider what it is to be under the curse. Man in his natural state, being under the broken covenant of works, is under the curse, and so,

1. He is under the wrath of God, " a child of wrath by nature," Eph. ii. 3. " The wrath of God abideth on him," John iii. 36. God is displeased with him; he is not, and cannot be pleased with him; as " without faith it is impossible to please God," Heb. xi. 6. God is ever angry with him, Psalm vii. 1, " every day," however he spend the day, better or worse." He cannot endure the sight of him;

" The foolish cannot stand in his sight," Psal. v. 5. That black cloud of the wrath of God is over his head from the moment of his being a living soul, and all along during his continuance in his natural state, under the broken covenant of works. He may be well pleased with himself, and others may be so too, saints as well as sinners ; but God is still wroth with him.

2. He is bound over to revenging justice. It has him by the throat, saying, " Pay what thou owest ;" though perhaps he neither feels the gripe, nor hears the terrible demand, because his conscience is asleep, and all his spiritual senses are fast bound up ; " Now we know," says the apostle, " that what things the law saith, it saith to them who are under the law ; that every mouth may be stopped, and all the world may become guilty before God ;" " guilty" (Gr.) compare Acts xxviii. 4, that is, under revenging justice. The holiness of God gave out the holy commandment in the covenant, justice annexed the threatening of death to the breach of it, truth secures the accomplishment of the threatening, and so lays the sinner under justice, without relief. So that there is no parting of them, till the utmost farthing be paid (2 Thess. i. 9, " punished with," Gr., " suffer justice" or " vengeance, everlasting destruction,") by the sinner himself, or a cautioner.

3. He stands as a mark for the arrows of vengeance ; he is a devoted man in law, tied to the stake, that the law and justice of God may disburden all their arrows into him, and that in him may meet all the plagues flowing from avenging wrath ; " If he turn not," says the Psalmist, " He [God] will whet his sword ; he has bent his bow and made it ready. He hath also prepared for him the instruments of death : he ordaineth his arrows against the persecutors," Psalm vii. 12, 13. Job complains that he was set as a mark for God's arrows, Job. xvi. 12, 13, but natural men have better reason for that complaint. They are in law devoted heads ; on which the law has laid its hand as on the head of a sacrifice, as a signal for cutting off ; Psalm xciv. 23, " He shall cut them off in their own wickedness ; yea, the Lord our God shall cut them off." Psalm xxxvii. 22, " They that be cursed of him shall he cut off."

O ! If men did believe this to be their condition under the broken covenant of works, what rest could they possibly have while in that state ? How would they anxiously inquire, what way they might be discharged from that broken bargain ? But alas ! as the unbelief of the threatening was the cause of the desperate adventure to break the covenant ; so the unbelief of the curse following thereupon, is the cause why they are easy under it. Therefore I shall next confirm the truth of the doctrine.

Confirmation of the truth of this doctrine, That man under the broken covenant of works is under the curse.

THIRDLY, I shall confirm the doctrine, that man in his natural
state, (being under the broken covenant of works,) is under the curse.

1. This is evident from plain scripture testimony. Our text is
express. Therein it is proved from the records of the court of heaven, as to this process; " It is written, Cursed is every one that continueth not in all things which are written in the book of the law
to do them." This sentence is extracted out of Deut. xxvii. 26,
" Cursed be he that confirmeth not all the words of this law
to do them." And the apostle plainly designs the persons against
whom this sentence is passed, namely, those that are under the law,
Rom. iii. 19, compared with chap. vi. 14. Who then can make any
doubt of it ? It is as firm as the truth of God can make it, in his
word, and under his hand and seal.

2. It is evident from the consideration of the justice of God, as a
supreme Rector and Judge of the world ; by which he cannot but
do right, and give sin its due. Two things will clear it.

1st, The breaking of that covenant, whereof all under it are
guilty, deserves the curse. They broke it in Adam, and they are
breaking it every day ; and so they deserve the curse. Now, sin's
deserving of the curse does not arise from the threatening of eternal wrath annexed for a sanction to the commands in the law, as
our new divinity would have it ; that is framed for bringing believers under the curse of the law too. But it arises from sin's contrariety to the command of the holy law ; for it is manifest, that
sin does not therefore deserve a curse, because a curse is threatened
against it ; but because it deserves a curse, therefore a curse is
threatened.

Now look at sin in the glass of the holy commandment, and you
will see it deserves the curse. For the commandment is,

(1.) An image of the sovereign spotless holiness of God ; " The
law is holy," Rom. vii. 12. When God would let out the beams of
his own holiness to man, he gave him the law of the ten commandments, as a transcript of it, and wrote them in his heart ; and
afterwards, the writing being much defaced, he wrote them to him
in his word. So the commandment is holy without spot, as God is.
So that the creature rising up against the commandment, riseth up
against God.

(2.) It is an image of his righteousness and equity, whereby he
does justly to all ; " the commandment is just," Rom. vii. 12. The
commandment is all right in every part, and of perpetual equity ;
" I esteem all thy precepts concerning all things to be right," Psalm

cxix. 128. Look to it as it prescribes our duty to God, to our neighbour, and to ourselves, Tit. ii. 12. It is of spotless and perfect righteousness, as that God is whose righteous nature and will it represents.

(3.) An image of his goodness: "The commandment is good," Rom. vii. 12. It is all lovely, lovely in every part; lovely in itself, and in the eyes of all who are capable to discern truly what is good, and what evil, Psalm cxix. 97, "O how love I thy law!" Conformity to it is the perfection of the creature, and its true happiness, as rendering the creature like unto God, 1 John iii. 2.

Thus the breaking of the covenant, by doing contrary to the holy commandment, is the transgressing of the holy, just, and good will of our sovereign Lord ; a defacing of and doing violence to his image, who is the chief good and infinite good. Therefore sin is the chief or greatest evil, and consequently deserves the curse.

2dly, Since it deserves the curse, the justice of God, which gives everything its due, ensures the curse upon it, Gen. xviii. 25 ; 2 Thes. i. 6. If sin did not lay the sinner under the curse, how would the rectoral justice of God appear ? He will rain a terrible storm on the wicked, not because he delights in the death of the sinner, but because he loves righteousness, Psalm xi. 6, 7, and his righteousness requires it.

3. It appears from the threatening of the covenant; Gen. ii. 17, "In the day that thou eatest thereof thou shalt surely die." That threatening being a threatening of death in its whole extent, ensures the curse on the sinner whenever he transgresseth the command. And the truth of God requires that it take effect, and be not like words spoken to the wind. Here is the case then, man came under the covenant of works, wherein death was threatened in case of transgression ; now the covenant is broken. It behoved then of necessity, that that moment man sinned, he should be bound over to the revenging wrath of God, or fall under the curse. And in that case all natural men lie. And thus the sentence of the law passeth immediately on sinning; Gal. iii. 10, "Cursed is every one that continueth not," &c., in the present tense ; agreeable to the tenor of the threatening, "In the day that thou eatest," &c.

4. If man had once run the course of his obedience, being come to the last point of it, he behoved to have been justified and adjudged to eternal life, according to the tenor of the covenant; Rom. x. 5, "The man which doth those things shall live by them ;" the sentence of the law would immediately have passed in his favour, according to the promise. And therefore man, having once broken the covenant, falls under the curse, and is adjudged to eternal death ; for the

curse bears the same relation to the threatening, that law-justifica-tion bears to the promise. Hence it is that the unbeliever is de-clared to be condemned already, John iii. 18.

Lastly, Christ's being made a curse for sinners is a clear evidence of sinners being naturally under the curse; Gal. iii. 13, " Christ hath redeemed us from the curse of the law, being made a curse for us." He took their place in the broken covenant of works, Gal. iv. 4, 5, that bearing the curse due to them, they might be set free upon their union with him. Hence they who by faith are united to Christ having his satisfaction imputed to them, are delivered from the curse, as borne for them, and away from them, by their Surety, but all others remain under it, as not being reputed to have satisfied it.

Thus far in the general, concerning this dreadful condition. But,

A more Particular View of the dreadful condition of the Natural Man, under the curse of the broken Covenant of Works.

II. We must take a more particular view of the dreadful condi-tion of the natural man under the curse of the broken covenant of works. And here opens the most terrible scene that men are capa-ble of beholding, in time or eternity. Happy they who timely be-hold it, so as to be thereby stirred up to flee to Christ. It compre-hends both the sinfulness and the misery of a natural state, the curse being the chain by which the sinner is bound over to death in its full latitude, as it stands in the threatening of the covenant, Gen. ii. 17, and by which he is staked down under that death. And we shall take a view of this in the natural man's condition, by the breach of the covenant of works, in this life, and after this life.

The Condition of the Natural Man under the Curse, in this Life.

FIRST, The natural man's condition, under the curse of the broken covenant, is very terrible in that part of it which takes place in this life. The execution of the curse is not quite delayed to another world; it is begun in this life, carried further on at death, and full and final execution comes at the last day. As to that part of this condition which takes place in this life, we shall have the more dis-tinct view of it, if we take it up in these following parcels; as to the soul, the body, and the whole man.

The Condition of the Natural Man's Soul under the Curse.

First, Let us view the condition of the natural man's soul under the curse. The natural man's soul is under the curse. It is the most noble part of the man, but the heaviest part of the curse lies upon it. And therefore Christ's soul-sufferings, when he was made a curse for us, were the most terrible of all his sufferings. That is the inward man into which the curse sinks, like water or oil, Psalm cix. 18. In the moment man sinned, his soul fell under the curse. And so,

1. His soul was separated from God, in favour with whom its life lay, Psalm xxxvi. 5; Deut. xxix. 21. The course of saving influences was stopt, the sun went quite down on him, and he lost God, his friend, his life, the soul of his soul. Thus natural men live without God, Eph. ii. 12, separated from him, Isaiah lix. 2. There is no saving intercourse betwixt God and them, more than there is betwixt us and our friends now lying in the grave, Psalm v. 5, Amos iii, 3. They hear his word preached; but, alas! they hear not his own voice, John v. 37. They pray to him, but he hears them not neither; John ix. 31, " God heareth not sinners." They hang on about the posts of his doors, but they never get a sight of the King's face. Be where they will, in the church or in the tavern, in duty or out of it, they are ever at a distance from God. The reason is, they are under the curse, which is as a great gulf fixed betwixt God and them, that there can be no communication between them, none by any means, but what can dry up the gulf, or remove the curse; which the blood of Christ only, applied to the soul, can do.

2. Hence man's soul-beauty was lost; death seizing on him by sin, his beauty went off. As when Christ cursed the fig-tree, it withered away; its blossoms went up as dust, its verdure and greenness were lost ; so the cursed sinner was stript of his original righteousness, the light of his mind, the rectitude of his will, the orderliness of his affections, and the right temper of all the faculties of his soul, Gen. iii. 7, 8. Thus, under the curse, the natural man's soul lies in ruins, "dead in trespasses and sins," Eph. ii. 1, dead to God, dead to righteousness, dead to its primitive constitution and frame, though in a living body.

A dead corpse is an awful sight, where the soul is gone. But thy dead soul, from which God is gone, O natural man! is a more awful one. Couldst thou see thy inward man, as well as thou seest the outward, thou wouldst see a soul within thee of a ghastly countenance, the eyes of its understanding set, its speech laid, all the spiritual senses now locked up, no pulse of kindly affection towards God beating any more; but the soul lying speechless, motionless, cold and stiff like a stone, under the curse.

3. Hence the whole soul is corrupted in all the faculties thereof, Gen, vi. 5, " God saw that the wickedness of man was great in the earth, and that every imagination of the thoughts of his heart was only evil continually," Jer. xvii. 9. " The heart is deceitful above

all things, and desperately wicked: who can know it?" As the soul being gone, the body corrupts; so the soul, being divested of its original righteousness, is wholly corrupted and defiled, having a kind of verminating life in it; Psalm xiv. 3, "They are altogether become filthy." And as when the curse was laid on the earth, the very nature of the soil was altered; so the souls of men under the curse are quite altered from their original holy constitution. This appears in all the faculties thereof.

(1.) Look into the mind, framed at first to be the eye of the soul; there is a lamentable alteration upon it under the curse. "O how is the fine gold become dim!" There is a mist upon it, whereby it is become weak, dull, and stupid in spiritual things, and really incapable of these things; 1 Cor. ii. 14, "The natural man receiveth not the things of the Spirit of God; for they are foolishness unto him: neither can he know them, because they are spiritually discerned." Darkness has sat down on the mind; Eph. v. 8, "Ye were sometimes darkness:" and there spiritual blindness and ignorance reign, not to be removed by man's instruction, or any power less than what can take off the curse. This cursed ground is fruitful of mistakes, misapprehensions, delusions, monstrous and misshapen conceptions in divine things; doubtings, distrust, unbelief of divine revelation, grow there, of their own accord, as the natural product of the cursed soil; while the seed of the word of the kingdom sown there does perish, and faith cannot spring up in it, for such is the soil that they cannot take with it.

(2.) Look into the will, framed to have the command in the soul, and it is in wretched plight. Its uprightness for God is gone, and it is turned away backward from him. It is not only under an inability for good, but having lost all power to turn itself that way; Rom. v. 6, "We were without strength"; Phil. ii. 13, "For it is God which worketh in you to will and to do of his good pleasure;" but it is averse to it, as the untrained bullock is to the yoke; Psal. lxxxi. 11, "My people would not hearken to my voice, and Israel would none of me"; Luke xix. 14, "We will not have this man to reign over us"; John v. 40, "Ye will not come unto me that ye might have life." The will is set in direct opposition and contrariety to the will of God; Rom. viii. 7, "The carnal mind is enmity against God: for it is not subject to the law of God, neither indeed can be." It is a heart of stone, that will break ere it bow to the will of God; and will remain refractory and contumacious against him, till the curse be removed, and the nature of the soul changed, though it should be plied with all the joys of heaven and all the terrors of hell. It is prone to evil, having a fixed bent unto sin; He

xi. 7, " My people are bent unto backsliding from me ;" and this proneness to sin nothing can alter but an omnipotent hand.

(3.) Look into the affections, framed to be the arms and feet of the soul for good, and they are quite wrong. Set spiritual objects before them to be embraced, then they are powerless, they cannot embrace them, nor grip them stedfastly ; they presently grow weary, and let go any hold they have of them ; like the stony-ground hearers, who because they had no root withered away, Matth. xiii. 6. But as for carnal objects, agreeable to their lusts, they fly upon them, they clasp and twine about them ; they hold so fast a grip, that it is with no small difficulty they can be got to let go their hold. Summon them to duty, they are flat, there is no raising of them, they cannot stir ; but on the least signal given them by temptation, they are like Saul's hungry soldiers, flying on the spoil.

(4.) Look into the conscience, framed to be in the soul God's deputy for judgment, his spy, and watchman over his creature ; and it is miserably corrupted ; Tit. i. 15, " Their mind and con-science is defiled." It is quite unfitted for its office. It is fallen under a sleepy distemper, sleeping and loving to slumber. So it is a dumb conscience, often not meddling with the work of directing, informing of the will of God, warning against sin, and exciting to duty ; and thus men are left as when there was no king in Israel, every one doing that which is right in their own eyes. Sometimes being consulted, it gives quite wrong orders, calling darkness light, and light darkness, having lost its right judgment; like those of whom our Lord speaks ; John xvi. 2, " The time cometh, that who-soever killeth you, will think that he doth God service." And ac-cordingly it excuseth where it should accuse ; and accuseth where it should excuse. And if it be once thoroughly awakened, it drives towards despair.

(5.) *Lastly*, Look into the memory, framed to be the storehouse of the soul, and the symptoms of the curse appear there too. Things agreeable to the corruption of nature, and which may strengthen the same, stick fast in the memory, so that often one cannot get them forgotten, though they would fain have their remembrance razed. But spiritual things natively fall out of it, and are soon forgotten ; the memory, like a leaking vessel, letting them slip.

4. Man being in these respects spiritually dead, the which death was the consequent of the first sin, the curse lies on him as a grave-stone, and the penalty binds it upon him, that he cannot recover. So he is in some sort, by the curse, buried out of God's sight. Thus sinners are said to be " concluded in unbelief," Rom. xi. 32 ; shut up, as in a prison, " under the law," viz. with its curse, Gal. iij.

23. So when Christ comes to sinners with his offers of life and salvation, he finds them bound in a prison, Isa. lxi. 1, " He hath sent me—to proclaim—the opening of the prison to them that are bound." They are under chains of darkness, even the chains of the curse on all the faculties of the soul ; which they can no more shake off them, than a dead man can loose and throw off him his dead clothes, hoise up his grave-stone, and come forth to the light. The curse cuts off the communication between God and the sinner, and so closes up all door of hope, while it remains, but by that which can remove the curse.

5. Hence that corruption of the soul grows more and more. As the dead corpse, the longer it lies in the grave, it rots the more, till devouring death has perfected its work in its utter ruin ; so the dead soul under the curse grows worse and worse in all the faculties thereof, till it is brought to the utmost pitch of sin and misery in hell ; 2 Tim. iii. 13, like "evil men and seducers waxing worse and worse." Sin continuing its reign in the soul, must needs gather strength ; and the longer the corruption of nature continues, the stronger it grows. And hence it is, that ordinarily the longer one has lived in an unregenerate state, the pangs of the new birth are the more severe.

6. And hence the corruption of nature shoots forth itself in innumerable particular lusts, according to its growth, Mark vii. 21, 22, 23, " For from within, out of the heart of men, proceed evil thoughts, adulteries, fornications, murders, thefts, covetousness, wickedness, deceit, lasciviousness, an evil eye, blasphemy, pride, foolishness ; all these evil things come from within, and defile the man." These all spring up in the soul under the curse, in such plenty as at length to cover the face of the whole soul, as the cursed earth brings forth thorns and thistles without the pains of the husbandman, and as nettles do the face of the sluggard's vineyard, Prov. xxiv. 30, 31. The man thinks himself very far from such a sin as he has not been tried with ; but when a fit temptation offers, he appears in his own colours? why? but because the soul under the curse was fit to conceive by such a temptation.

7. And these lusts grow stronger and stronger. The man who " first walks in the counsel of the ungodly," proceeds to "stand in the way of sinners," and at length " sits down on the seat of the scornful," Psalm i. 1. The more corrupt one's nature grows, the more nourishment it sends forth to feed and flesh particular lusts. And these lusts, acting according to their nature, gather strength by exercise ; so that custom makes their acting so easy and ready, that they come at length to refuse to be managed, like those of

whom Peter speaks; 2 Epist. ii. 14, "having eyes full of adultery, and that cannot cease from sin." And the man must quit the reins to them, they are quite beyond his control, Jer. xiii. 23.

But this is not all the misery of the soul under the curse; there are additional plagues, which by the curse they are liable to, who are under it. These soul-plagues are of two sorts; silent strokes, and tormenting plagues.

1. Silent strokes, which make their way into the soul with no noise; but the less they are felt, they are the more dangerous; such as,

(1.) Judicial blindness; Eph. iv. 18, "Having the understanding darkened, being alienated from the life of God, through the ignorance that is in them, because of the blindness of their heart." They are naturally blind, and love not to have their eyes opened; John iii. 19, "Men love darkness rather than light, because their deeds are evil." However, some gleams of light get into their minds, while it shines in the word round about them. But they rebel against the light, shut their eyes upon it, and so make themselves more blind; Job xxi. 14, "Therefore they say unto God, Depart from us; for we desire not the knowledge of thy ways." Wherefore God, in his just judgment, causes the light to withdraw, that it shall not enter into their souls, and leaves them to Satan, to be by him blinded more than ever; 2 Cor. iv. 3, 4, "But if our gospel be hid, it is hid to them that are lost; in whom the god of this world hath blinded the minds of them which believe not, lest the light of the glorious gospel of Christ, who is the image of God, should shine unto them."

(2.) Strong delusions. Men living under the gospel-light, having the truth clearly discovered to them, do often keep the truth prisoner; Rom. i. 18, "Who hold the truth in unrighteousness." They receive the true principles into their heads, but they will not allow them to model their lives in conformity to the truth. So they receive not the truth in love. For avenging of which quarrel, they are given up to a spirit of delusion; 2 Thess. ii. 10, 11, "Because they received not the love of the truth, that they might be saved.—For this cause God shall send them strong delusion, that they should believe a lie." This is the curse beginning to work at this day, for the contempt of the glorious gospel; and how the fearful plague of delusion may spread ere it end, God only knows.

(3.) Hardness of heart, Rom. ii. 5. Men's hearts are naturally hard and insensible; but under softening means they harden them more; and God hardens them judicially; Rom. ix. 18, "Whom he will he hardeneth;" withholding his grace from them; Deut. xxix.

4, as Moses said to the Israelites, " The Lord hath not given you a heart to perceive, and eyes to see, and ears to hear ;" blasting all means to them, whether providences or ordinances, whereby others are bettered, so that they do them no good; Hos. iv. 17, " Ephraim is joined to idols ; let him alone ;" exposing them in his holy provi- dence to such objects, as their corruptions make an occasion of sin- ning more, Deut, i. 30 ; giving them over to their lusts, leaving them to the temptations of the world, and to the power of Satan, and suf- fering them to prosper in an evil course. Whereby it comes to pass that they are hardened in sin more than before.

(4.) A reprobate sense, Rom. i. 28, whereby men lose the faculty of discerning betwixt good and evil, as those who are deprived of the sense of tasting know no difference betwixt bitter and sweet. Thus men, who being wedded to their lusts, and can by no means be brought to part with them, but treat that light which discovers the evil of them as an enemy, are sometimes, in the fearful judgment of God, suffered to proceed this length, that they can see no evil even in gross sins, but vile abominations are in their eyes harmless things.

(5.) *Lastly*, Vile affection, Rom. i. 26. Many a time vile affec- tions stir in the soul, and the grace of God in some, and reason and a natural conscience in others, do strive against them, and repress their fury. These are the product of the corruption of nature in all men ; but this soul-plague is more dreadful. In it the soul is given up to these vile affections, so that by them they are commanded, and ruled, and led, like beasts without reason. A fearful case ; reason and conscience are imprisoned, all power and rule over the soul is taken out of their hands ; and the rabble of vile passions and affec- tions manage all, without control. So that the soul is like a ship at sea without a governor, that is tossed hither and thither, being en- tirely under the management of the winds and waves.

2. Tormenting plagues, which make the soul to feel them, to its great pain and uneasiness. Many are the executioners employed against the soul fallen under the curse, who together do pierce, rack, and rend it as it were in pieces. These are tormenting passions, which had never appeared in the soul had it not fallen into sin, and so under the curse. Such tormenting plagues, which the soul under the curse is liable to, are chiefly these following :—

1*st*, Discontent. This haunts the soul like a ghost, ever since men fell from God, sometimes in greater, sometimes in lesser mea- sure. He would not rest contented in God, and from that time he could have no more content within himself. He must have all his will, otherwise he is discontented ; and that he shall never get, till God's will be his will ; and that will never be till he be delivered from under the curse. Hence wretched man is born weeping, lives complaining and discontented, and dies disappointed. What saws, axes, and harrows of iron does this discontent draw through the soul, in fretfulness, impatience, murmuring, grudging, repining, quarrelling with God and men; whereby men become a burden to the Spirit of God, a burden to others, and a burden to themselves? The discontented soul is ruffled and rankled with very small trials, like Ahab, Haman, &c., yea, and often with it knows not what; only there is something wanting, and the mind is uneasy. The mystery lies here, the peace of God is not ruling in the heart, Col. iii. 15; Phil. iv. 7.

2dly, Wrath. This is a fire in the man's bosom, to burn him up; an arrow, a dagger, a sword piercing to the very soul; Job v. 2, " For wrath killeth the foolish man." This fills him with rage and fury, and makes the whole soul like the troubled sea, when it cannot rest, but its " waves toss themselves" and roll up and down, " casting up mire and dirt." The proud heart with temptation swells; and these will no more be wanting to us while here, than the air will be free from midges in the heat of summer, that the man may travel undisturbed. The secret discontent in the soul, following on its loss of God, is the cause of this, as well as of other tormenting passions. Hungry folk are soon angry. The gnawing hunger in the soul after happiness and satisfaction, from which it is barred under the curse, makes them so peevish and wrathful.

3dly, Anxiety, whereby the soul is as it were stretched on tenter hooks, and is drawn asunder by divers thoughts, and put on the rack. Many are the grounds of this torture to the soul. Sometimes it is on the account of carnal things, which come under the name of " the cares of this life," Luke viii. 14, and so as many lusts as a man has to satisfy, so much anxiety how to get them satisfied falls to the share of the wretched soul. Ahab is racked how to get his covetousness satisfied, Haman is racked with his ambition and revenge, &c. Hence the man travaileth with iniquity, Psalm vii. 14, is in pain as a woman with child to bring forth. Sometimes it is on the account of his soul's state before God, how to escape the wrath and curse of God, while the dreadful sound is in the man's ears; Acts ii. 37, " Now when they heard this, they were pricked in their heart, and said,—Men and brethren, what shall we do?" Acts xvi. 30, " Sirs, what must I do to be saved?" This, though it comes to nought in many, yet the Lord makes use of for bringing the elect to Christ.

4thly, Sorrow of heart, which is a weight on the soul pressing it down, the native fruit of sin and the curse. There is a flood of sorrow let out on man under the curse, which divides itself into two great streams. (1.) The sorrow of the world, 2 Cor. vii. 10. Here run over the soul, the floods of sorrow arising from worldly losses, crosses, disappointments, which men meet with in worldly things, in their bodies, estates, reputation, relations, and the like. And this stream never dries up, every day has the evil thereof, Matth. vi. ult. And as if the evils coming on men themselves mediately, or immediately, could not sufficiently cause these waters to swell, such is the disposition of the soul under the curse, that the good which others meet with, often serves to increase them, by means of envy, ill will, and grudge at their prosperity, Job v. 2, " Envy slayeth the silly one." (2.) The sorrows of death, Psalm cxvi. 3, arising from a sight of the guilt of sin lying on the soul before the Lord, which will make the most stout-hearted bow their heads under the weight, Matth. xxvii. 3, 4. These are the most bitter waters caused by sin and the curse; and wo to him with whom they swell to the brim, if Christ be not a lifter up of the head to him.

5thly, Fear and terror, which seizing on the soul puts an end to its ease and quiet. This covereth the soul with blackness, darkness, and tempest; takes away its courage, strikes a damp upon it, and makes it restless. And it is twofold, both effects of the curse on the soul.

(1.) Terror of heart, from the apprehension of danger and misery approaching. Man, having sinned, is by the curse denounced a rebel, yea and adjudged to death; hence he is in God's world like a man under sentence of death, wandering here and there within the King's dominions, ready to be frightened at every accident, and no where secure or in quietness, like Cain, Gen. iv. 14. How can they be fearless among God's creatures, to whom God is an enemy? Guilt is a mother and nurse of fears; and hence it comes to pass, that the sinner sometimes is made to tremble at the shaking of a leaf. In a special manner, any token, presage, or likelihood of the approach of death, the king of terrors, fills the soul with tormenting fear. This is awfully described, Deut. xxviii. 65, 66, 67, " And among these nations shalt thou find no ease, neither shall the sole of thy foot have rest; but the Lord shall give thee there a trembling heart, and failing of eyes, and sorrow of mind. And thy life shall hang in doubt before thee, and thou shalt fear day and night, and shalt have none assurance of thy life. In the morning thou shalt say, Would God it were even; and at even thou shalt say, Would God it were morning, for the fear of thine heart wherewith thou shalt fear, and for the sight of thine eyes which thou shalt see."

(2.) Horror of conscience, arising from the sense of guilt, and apprehension of God's wrath against the soul, Isa. xxxiii. 14, "The sinners in Zion are afraid, fearfulness hath surprised the hypocrites. Who among us shall dwell with everlasting burnings?" This is of all terrors in the world the greatest, and maks a deep wound in the soul, Prov. xviii. 14, "A wounded spirit who can bear?" Cain could not bear it, Gen. iv. 13. Judas could not endure it, Matth. xxviii. 3, 4. Jeremiah prays against it, Jer. xvii. 17, it made Pashur a terror to himself, chap. xx. 4. This is the dreadful workings of the curse in the soul, giving it a foretaste of hell. And we may observe three degrees of it.

(1.) A confused fear as to one's soul's state, making the person uneasy with suspicions and jealousies that matters are all wrong betwixt God and the soul; like that of Herod, Matth xiv. 1, 2, who, hearing of the fame of Jesus, said unto his servants; "This is John the Baptist; he is risen from the dead, and therefore mighty works do shew forth themselves in him." Conscience may sleep long very sound, and yet at length begin to speak, as it were betwixt sleeping and waking, so as it may fill the man with uneasiness with its very may-be's. For under the curse it can never be true to a man's ease, but will one time or other give alarms.

(2.) A sharp pang, though passing like a stitch in one's side, which, while it lasts, fills the soul with horror, and makes the man's heart melt in him like wax, under clear apprehensions that God is his enemy. Such was that of Belshazzar, Dan. v. 6, and Felix, Acts xxiv. 25, "And as Paul reasoned of righteousness, temperance, and judgment to come, Felix trembled, and answered, Go thy way for this time; when I have a convenient season I will call for thee." He felt the fire kindled in his bosom, that it was too strong for him; and therefore immediately orders that there be no more fuel laid to it, lest it should quite burn him up. Such one-day fevers of conscience, no doubt, many natural men do feel under the curse, though by methods of their own, they find means to cause the fit wear off.

(3.) A vehement and abiding horror which they can no more shake off, as in Judas' case, Matth. xxvii. 3, 4. Then the guilt that lay on the conscience like brimstone, is fired, and burns so that they cannot quench the flame. The arrows of wrath, dipt in the poison of the curse, and shot into the soul by an almighty hand, work so as the poison of them drinks up their spirits. The beginnings of hell then are felt. The conscience is, like Mount Sinai, all in fire and smoke. The terrors of God are round about them, as set in battle array against them, and they become a terror to others too. The threatenings of the holy law are no more looked on as scare-crows, by the most obstinate sinner once brought to pass; their lusts then are bitter to them as death; and all the comforts of the world sapless.

Lastly, Despair; Isa. xvii. 11, "In the day shalt thou make thy plant to grow, and in the morning shalt thou make thy seed to flourish; but the harvest shall be a heap in the day of grief and of desperate sorrow." This is the very height of the soul's torment in this world, and puts the copestone on its misery here, and no wonder, for it is the tormenting plague of the damned. A man may be under great horror of conscience, and yet there may be a secret hope of an outgate which supports him; but who can conceive, without experience, the torment of that soul on whom despair hath seized, and hath shut up all doors of hope? What a fearful case must that soul be in, against which the sea of the Lord's wrath so swells and rages, that it is in that case, Acts xxvii. 20, "And when neither sun nor stars in many days appeared, and no small tempest lay on us, all hope that we should be saved was then taken away." This leaves the soul no ease at all, and sometimes hath a most fearful issue, as in Saul and Judas.

The Body is under the Curse.

SECONDLY, The natural man's body is under the curse. The first sin was completed by an action of the body; man ate the forbidden fruit, and with it swallowed down death, by virtue of the curse, which followed sin hard at the heels. God made man a compend of the universe, by his creating power raised a body, a beautiful fabric, out of the dust, and lodged the soul, a spirit, an immortal substance, in it, as in a glorious and convenient habitation, and he blessed the house as well as the inhabitant, Gen. i. 28. But the house he commanded to be kept clean; being defiled by the soul, suddenly he cursed the soul's habitation, and the original blessing was succeeded with a heavy curse; Deut. xxviii. 18, "Cursed shall be the fruit of thy body." And surely the cursing of the fruit implies a curse on the tree it grows on, viz., the defiled body. The condition of the body, thus laid under the curse, we may view in the following particulars :—

1. It is liable to many defects and deformities in the very constitution thereof. Adam and Eve were at their creation not only sound and entire in their souls, but in their bodies, having nothing unsightly about them. But O how often now is there seen a variation from the original pattern, in the very formation of the body! Some are born deaf, dumb, blind, or the like. Some with a want of some necessary organ, some with what is superfluous. Some with such a constitution of body as makes them idiots, the organs of the body being so far out of case, that they are unfit for the actions of

the rational life; and the soul is by them kept in a mist during the union with that body. All this is owing to sin and the curse, without which there had been no such things in the body of man. It is purely owing to mercy that these things are not more frequent; for by the curse all the sons and daughters of Adam are liable to them; and it may be an humbling question, therefore, to the most handsome and beautiful, 1 Cor. iv. 7, " Who maketh thee to differ from another? and what hast thou that thou didst not receive? now if thou didst receive it, why dost thou glory as if thou hadst not received it?" And God makes some such instances, that all may see in them what by the curse they are liable to, John ix. 3.

2. As the temperature of the body was by the first sin altered, so as it disposed to sin, Gen. iii. 7, so by the curse that degenerate constitution of it is penally bound on, by which it comes to pass that it is a snare to the soul continually. The seeds of sin are in it; it is "sinful flesh," Rom. viii. 3, "a vile body," Phil. iii. 21, and these seeds are never removed while the curse lies on it, being a part of that death to which it is bound over by the curse. Thus the case of the man must needs be very miserable, while a sinful soul and sinful flesh remain so closely knit together, in the nearest relation, each a snare to the other; the soul disposing the body to sin, and the body and the soul on the other hand, the corruption of the whole man must make fearful advances under the curse. To this is much owing the crowd of "fleshly lusts which war against the soul," 1 Pet. ii. 11; such as sensuality, gluttony, drunkenness, filthiness, &c. which more and more drown the soul in destruction and perdition. And the sad effects of this distemperature of the body are never wanting, of one kind or another, in all the periods of life; and by means thereof it comes to pass, that the souls of many are in their bodies as sunk in and overwhelmed with a mire of flesh and blood.

3. It is under the curse a vessel of dishonour. By its original make, it was a vessel of honour, appointed to honourable uses, and was so used by the soul before sin entered; and every member had its particular honourable service, serving the soul in subordination to God. But now it is brought down from its honour, and its "members are yielded instruments of unrighteousness unto sin," Rom. vi. 13, and is abused to the vilest purposes; and it is never restored to its honour till, the curse being removed, it becomes the temple of God, by virtue of the purchase of it made by the blood of Christ. But while the curse remains its honour lies in the dust, being bound to such service as it was at first put to, in looking to, taking, and eating the forbidden fruit. See a melancholy

description of this, Rom. iii. 13, and downwards, It is made by the
drunkard like a common sink, by the glutton like a draught, and
often like a weary beast under the load of divers lusts. Every natural man's soul makes it a drudge; in some it must be a slave to
the vanity of the mind, in others to covetousness, in others to wrath
and revenge; in a word, its union with the sinful soul under the
curse is become a yoke of iron.

4. It is liable to many mischiefs from without, tending to render
it uneasy for the time, and at length to dissolve the frame of it.
From the heavens above us, the air about us, the earth underneath
us, and all that therein is, it is liable to hurt. All the creatures are
in a state of enmity to man, while he is an enemy to God; and the
least fly that passeth through the air is able to annoy him now; so
that the natural man is ever in the midst of his armed enemies.
The promise of the covenant was his guard, that while he kept the
commandment, no evil could approach unto him; but now the guard
is removed, and he is laid under the curse, having broken the covenant, whereby not only his covenant defence is departed from him,
but heaven has proclaimed war against him, armed the whole creation
against the men of his curse, and ordered them to be ready to attack
him on a moment's warning. Hence the waters swallow up some, the
fire hurts others, beasts wound and bruise others, and man is
not safe from the stones of the field, yea, every creature's hand is
against him. And not only so, but by the curse men are become
mischievous one to another, fighting, beating, wounding, and killing
one another.

5. There is a seed-plot of much misery within it. It is by the
curse become a weak body, and so liable to much toil and weariness,
fainting and languishing under the weight of the exercise it is put
to, Gen. iii. 19. And not only so, but it hath in it such seeds of
corruption, tending to its dissolution, as spring up in many and
various maladies, which prove so heavy many times, that they make
life itself a burden. By virtue of the curse, death works in the
body, all along from the womb, as a mole under ground, till at
length it lays the whole fabric in the dust, and leaves not, as it
were, one stone on another, in the grave. No part of the body,
without or within, is beyond the reach of diseases and torturing
pains. The greatest care of the body cannot altogether ward them
off. The curse has turned this world into an hospital, where some
are groaning under one distemper, some under another; some at one
time, some at another; and some in that respect are dying daily,
knowing little or nothing of perfect health. The strongest are
liable to be so weakened by diseases, as to be unable to turn them-

selves on a bed; those who enjoy the greatest ease, to tormenting pains; the most beautiful may be a prey to loathsome diseases and sores; and the soundest constitution to infectious plagues.

6. *Lastly,* In all these respects the body is a clog to the soul in point of duty, often hanging like a dead weight upon it, unfitting it for, and hindering it from its most necessary work. The sinful soul is in itself most unfit for its great work, in this state of trial, by reason of the evil qualities of it under the curse. But the wretched body makes it more so. The care of the body doth so take up its thoughts with most men, that, caring for it, the soul is lost. Its strength and vigour is a snare to it, and its weakness and uneasiness often interrupt or quite mar the exercises wherein the soul might profitably be employed. And one may see the forlorn case of the soul of man in this body under the curse, how it is on every hand pulled back from salvation work, in the case of many to whom health and strength is such a powerful snare while it remains, that they will not, and when they are gone, trouble and distress of body do so fill their hand, that they cannot mind their salvation work to purpose.

But it may be objected, That by this account of the condition of those under the curse, the case of natural men and of believers in Christ is alike; since it is evident, that not only these bodily miseries, but many of these soul miseries are common to both. I answer, Though it seem to be alike in the eye of beholders, in regard these miseries are materially the same on natural men and on the children of God; yet really there is a vast difference. On the former they are truly effects of the curse; on the latter they are indeed effects of sin, but not of the curse; "For Christ hath redeemed them from the curse of the law, being made a curse for them," Gal. iii. 13. Sin entering into the world was a fountain of miseries; and till it be dried up, there will be miseries on men's bodies and souls; but the poison of the curse is mixed with these bitter streams to some, but not to others; and that makes as great a difference betwixt the case of the godly and ungodly, as betwixt the case of one man to whom poison, and another to whom medicine is administered. And,

(1.) The stream of miseries on soul or body to a natural man, runs in the channel of the covenant of works; but to a believer, in the channel of the covenant of grace. To the former it comes by virtue of the threatening, Gen. ii. 17, "In the day that thou eatest thereof thou shalt surely die;" To the latter it comes by virtue of that, Psalm lxxxix. 30, 31, 32, "If his children forsake my law, and walk not in my judgments; if they break my statutes, and keep not my commandments, then will I visit their transgression with the rod, and their iniquity with stripes." Running in the channel of the first covenant, they bring the curse along with them ; but in the channel of the second covenant, the curse is not to be found; the waters are healed, however bitter they may be, Isa. liv. 9. When one has a slave, he punishes him for his misdemeanors, by virtue of his masterly authority over him. But if he be freed and adopted for a son, he chastens him, but no more as a slave, but as a son.

(2.) There is revenging wrath in the one, but fatherly anger only in the other, Isa. liv. 9, "For this is as the waters of Noah unto me; for as I have sworn that the waters of Noah should no more go over the earth ; so have I sworn that I would not be wroth with thee, nor rebuke thee." If it was never such a small stroke on the natural man, it is in part of payment of law-debt, for he is under the law, in its commanding, cursing, and condemning power; if it were ever such a heavy stroke on a child of God, it is no part of payment of law-debt, which he is for ever discharged of in his union with Christ. An ungodly man's basket of bread miscarries ; it is no great loss, one would think, he may bear it ; but alas ! there is an impression of wrath upon it, it miscarried by virtue of the curse, Deut. xxviii. 17, "Cursed shall be thy basket ;" and so it is heavier than the sand of the sea, though he, being insensible of his case, feels not the weight of it. Good Eli falls from off his seat, and breaks his neck, 1 Sam. iv 18. O heavy stroke ! we are apt to say ; yea but there was no worse in it than fatherly anger ; the covenant was not broken, though his neck was broken, Psalm lxxxix. 34, " My covenant will I not break." He got a soft fall; as hard as it appeared to spectators, he fell on a pavement of love, Cant. iii. 10.

(3.) The miseries of the ungodly in this life are an earnest of eternal misery in hell; but those of the godly are medicines, to keep back their soul from death ; 1 Cor. xi. 32, " When we are judged, we are chastened of the Lord, that we should not be condemned with the world." Every stroke a man under the curse gets, he may call it " Joseph ;" for " the Lord will add another." The least brook that runs, is making towards the sea, as well as the deepest river; and the least affliction, by virtue of the curse, laid on a man, looks towards hell, as well as the greatest stroke he meets with. Though a piece of money be but small in itself, if it be an earnest-penny of a great sum, it is valued accordingly. And so the least stroke would be frightful to a natural man, if he discerned the nature of it. But in the worst afflictions of God's people, there is a seed of joy

Psalm xcvii. 11, " Light is sown for the righteous ; and gladness for
the upright in heart ;" and the darkest night will have a fair clear
morning.   There was more of heaven in Heman's hell, Psalm
lxxxviii. 15, than there is in the greatest ease, joy, and prosperity
of the wicked.

The Whole Man is under the Curse.

Thirdly, The whole man is under the curse.   The sinner fallen
from God, fell under the curse ; and like a deluge it has gone over
him, and surrounded him on every hand.   Hence our Lord Christ,
being made a curse for us, was beset with sorrows, Matth. xxvi. 38,
" My soul is exceeding sorrowful even unto death," like a man when
the devouring waves are compassing him round about, and from
every hand coming in upon him, ready to swallow him up.   Thus
stands the natural man under the curse ; it is upon him, it is round
about him ; go where he will, there is no shifting of it, all his days
he wades through these waters ; he is in the deep mire, where there
is no firm standing.   He is cursed,

1. In his name and reputation ; " The seed of evil doers shall
never be renowned," Isa. xiv. 20.   Sin laid man's honour in the
grave, and the curse lays the grave-stone upon it ; and it can never
rise again till the curse be removed ; Isa. xliii. 4, " Since thou wast
precious in my sight, thou hast been honourable."   What of it appears before that, is but as it were a ghost, a spectre of honour, that
vanisheth away, which vain men please themselves with a little, as
with illusions of fancy.   The sinner's name may shoot up and flourish
a little ; but it is blasted by the curse, with shame, contempt, reproach, and disgrace.   And no heights of worldly grandeur can secure men against this ; the curse is a worm at the root, which will
work and cause to wither the sinner's name, whatever pains be taken
to hold it green.   A good name is better than precious ointment ;
but where the curse lies, the dead fly will be found there, to cause it
to send forth a stinking savour.   Every man is desirous of a name,
and the raising of it was the snare in which man was first caught,
" Ye shall be as gods ;" but since that time, man has been laid open
to many and deep wounds in it, while by the curse the tongues of
those of his own kind have been as arrows shot from a bent bow
against it, Psalm lvii. 4.

2. In his employment and calling in the world, Gen. iii. 19, " In
the sweat of thy face shalt thou eat bread, till thou return unto the
ground."   Man is put to sore toil, weariness, and distress in his
worldly employment ; and when he has done, O what fruitless pains
and travel he is made to see !   How often do men labour as in the

very fire! and all the issue is, they weary themselves for very vanity. There is sore and hard travel; and after all men must say,
"We have, as it were, brought forth wind." The husbandman toils
in labouring the ground, and the earth by virtue of the curse often
gives him but a poor reward of his labour. The store-master is diligent to know the state of his flocks, and looks well to his herds; but
oftentimes it is seen that that will not effect it, the curse works
against him, and all goes to wreck, Deut. xxviii. 17, "Cursed shall be
thy store." The tradesman is early and late at his work, but often
has much ado to get bread to his mouth and his family. The merchant carefully watches occasions of advancing his interest; but how
often seeking gain does he find loss! and some unforeseen events
discover a secret hand of providence working against him in the management of his affairs. See Hag. i. 6, "Ye have sown much, and
bring in little; ye eat, but ye have not enough; ye drink, but ye
are not filled with drink; ye clothe you, but there is none warm; and
he that earneth wages earneth wages to put it into a bag with holes."
The case of the labour of the mind, is in this respect no better than the
labour of the hands. Solomon tells us, from his experience, the grievous toil of it; Eccl. i. 13, "I gave my heart to seek and search
out by wisdom concerning all things that are done under heaven;
this sore travail hath God given to the sons of men to be exercised
therewith." And he also tells the sorry issue of that toil; ver. 18,
"For in much wisdom is much grief; and he that increaseth knowledge, increaseth sorrow." No set of men have more remarkable
symptoms of the curse on their employment, than those whose labour
is the labour of the mind. The toil is sore, the success small, and
the disappointments innumerable. The physician and the lawyer labour, the one to preserve the body, the other the estate; but after
all their pains, their art fails, they mistake the case, or it is beyond
their power to rectify it. The projects of statesmen, laid in the
depth of their wisdom, how often are they baffled, and by some small
occurrence the whole frame thereof is unhinged! The guides of the
Church, after all their contrivances for a steady management of her
course, how often do they row her into deep waters, from whence
they cannot bring her back, till she is dashed in pieces! Even in
preaching of the gospel, while men shine, they burn and waste; and
when all is done, they must sit down and say, "Who hath believed
our report? I have laboured in vain, and spent my strength for
nought and in vain." Whence is all this, but that man has fallen
under the curse, and it mars whatever he goes about to make?

3. In his worldly substance, Deut. xxviii. 17, "Cursed shall be
thy basket and thy store." Wherever he hath it, he hath the curse

with it; whether it be in the field, Deut. xxviii. 16, or whether it be in the house, Prov. iii. 33. On the meat he eats, on the liquor he drinks, the clothes he wears, and the house where he lodges, there is a curse lying, because they are his. And under the weight of it they groan, as longing to be delivered out of his cursed hands, Rom. viii. 21, 22. And sometimes even providence recovers them out of their hands in this life, as men do goods out of the hands of unjust possessors, Hos. ii. 9, "I will return, and take away my corn in the time thereof, and my wine in the season thereof, and will recover my wool and my flax given to cover her nakedness." Thus under the curse men are liable to melancholy alterations and changes in their outward estate. Riches make themselves wings by virtue of the curse, and fly away, not to be called back again. The man is infatuated in his management, and so is not aware till he has run himself aground. He wants the hedge of the covenant-protection about what is his; and he sustains losses and damages at the hands of those with whom he has to do. Yea, he gathers and heaps up, and diligently watches it; but a fire unblown consumes it, and it melts away like snow before the sun; the curse, like a moth, eats it away, and he is wormed out of that on which he set his heart. Or if it stay with him, it is sometimes locked up from him, so as he has not the comfortable use of it, Eccl. vi. 2, "A man to whom God hath given riches, wealth, and honour, so that he wanteth nothing for his soul of all that he desireth, yet God giveth him not power to eat thereof." And so the man never has a blessed use of it, never has power to use it for the high and honourable ends it is appointed of God unto, when he gives it into their hands as stewards of it for him. The loss he has by it, as it turns to his hurt, is never counterbalanced by the gain. And all this comes on the natural man in virtue of the curse.

4. In his relations. Relations are the joints of society, and sin going through them all, they are all defiled, and the curse goes through them too, Deut. xxviii. 18, "Cursed shall be the fruit of thy body." In them men promise themselves comfort; but there they find sorrow, pain, and smart. There they lean as it were to a wall, and a serpent does bite them. In the state, magistrates often oppress, ensnare, and entangle the conscience, and prove a terror to those that do well. In the church, ministers are unfaithful, unwatchful, unconcerned for the good of souls, or unsuccessful. In neighbourhood, men are unjust, selfish, and snares one to another. In the family, disorder and confusion are found, through every one's unfaithfulness in the duties of their respective relations. How many are there unequally yoked, companions of life, through their jarrings

and discord, a burden and a cross to one another! Husbands such men of Belial that their wives cannot speak to them; wives as rottenness in the bones of their husbands; parents unnatural, and unfaithful to, and careless of their children; children froward, perverse, and stubborn; sons of youth, hoped to be arrows in the hand of their parents, turning to be arrows to pierce them to the heart; daughters, expected to be as corner-stones for their father's family, falling down on the heads of their parents, and crushing their spirits; masters unjust and unfaithful to their servants; and servants perverse, rebellious, and unconscionable in their service. For the curse has gone wide, and in every relation the weight of it is found; though most men that find the weight of it, know it not to be the curse indeed.

5. In his lot, whatever it is, afflicted or prosperous. Afflictions are cursed to the man who is under the curse; he is not bettered by them, though others are. He is not humbled by them, but his spirit is embittered; and, instead of coming to God under them, he runs farther away from him. "Why," says the Lord to Israel, "should ye be stricken any more? ye will revolt more and more," Isa. i. 5. God binds the man with these cords, but he crieth not. He may groan under the weight of his affliction, but he turns not unto the Lord; he saith not, "Where is God my Maker?" Job xxxv. 10. He remains stubborn, incorrigible, and impenitent; Jer. v. 3—"Thou hast stricken them, but they have not grieved; thou hast consumed them, but they have refused to receive correction: they have made their faces harder than a rock; they have refused to return." The man's prosperity in the world is a snare to his soul and ruins him, Prov. i. 32, "The prosperity of fools shall destroy them." If his ground bring forth plentifully, his barns are seen to, but his soul is neglected; as was the case of the rich man in the gospel, Luke xii. 16, &c. If his family prosper, his house be in safety, and his stock thrive, they say unto God, "Depart from us: for we desire not the knowledge of thy ways. What is the Almighty, that we should serve him? and what profit should we have if we pray unto him?" Job xxi. 8—14, 15. "If waters of a full cup be wrung out to them, they set their mouths against the heavens, and their tongue walketh through the earth.—And they say, How doth God know? and is there knowledge in the Most High?" Psalm lxxiii. 8, 9, &c. Youth, health, strength, and wealth together, prove ruining by virtue of the curse. Be the man's lot what it will, there is a curse on it to him, and it tends to his destruction.

6. In his use of the means of grace; Rom. xi. 8, "God hath given them the spirit of slumber, eyes that they should not see, and ears that

they should not hear." The man sits under the dropping of the gospel, but it does him no good. He is as the ground that often drinks in the rain, but brings forth no fruit meet for him by whom it is dressed. He stands cumbering the ground in God's vineyard, for there is a withering curse on him, Good grapes are expected from the pains bestowed on him, but behold, only wild grapes appear. His praying, hearing, communicating, &c., are but like a withered hand that is never stretched out, nor reaches to the throne. His convictions and raised affections quickly settle again, and these fair appearances come to nothing. The gospel, that is a savour of life to some, is a savour of death to him, 2 Cor. ii. 16; and Christ himself, who is set for the raising of many, is eventually for his falling. Thus the curse turns everything against the man, and all is death to him.

7. *Lastly,* In his person. Being a sinful man under the covenant of works, he is a cursed man; For it is written, " Cursed is every one that continueth not in all things which are written in the book of the law to do them." The curse fixeth not only on what is his, but on himself; and it is for his sake that it is laid on other things. The curse, as you have heard, is on his soul, and on his body; for wherever sin is found under this covenant, there the curse also is. And,

(1.) The man is under the power of Satan, Acts xxvi. 18. Into the hand of this enemy man fell, when he broke the covenant of works. Satan having waged war against heaven, set on man, heaven's confederate, and gained the unhappy victory, gained him by temptation to renounce his allegiance to his rightful Lord by breaking the covenant, and so he fell under his power, as his captive taken in war, Isa. xlix. 24, was brought under bondage to this worst of masters, 2 Pet. ii. 19, and is ruled by him at his pleasure, 2 Tim. ii. ult. The curse of the covenant falling on the covenant-breaker, he is thereby laid under condemnation, and adjudged to death according to the threatening; and so he falls under the power of him that has the power of death, that is the devil, Heb. ii. 14. Every natural man is shut up as in a prison, in his natural state; and there he lies in bonds, Isa. lxi. 1. There are God's bands on him, the bands of the curse binding him over to death; and the devil's bands are on him, viz., the bands of strong lusts and corruptions, with which they are laden, as a malefactor in prison is laden with irons. And Satan has the power of gaoler over them. He keeps the keys of the prison, and narrowly watches the prisoners that none of them escape. They are not all kept alike close; but none of them can move beyond the bounds of his jurisdiction, more than the prisoner can get out of the dungeon. Even when the king's word comes to deliver the elect, he will not yield them up; but the prison doors must be broke open, and they forcibly taken out of his hand by a stronger than he.

(3.) The natural man being under the curse is continually in hazard of utter destruction, of having the copestone put on his misery, and being set beyond all possibility of help. If his eyes were opened he would see himself every moment in danger of dropping down into the pit of hell; Psalm vii. 12, " If he turn not, he will whet his sword; he hath bent his bow, and made it ready." The man is constantly standing before God's bent bow, and has nothing to secure him one moment from the drawing of it. The sentence of death is passed against him, John iii. 18, but there is no day intimated for the execution, but every day the dead warrant may be signed against him, and he led forth to death. His name may be " Magor-missabib," a terror round about, Jer. xx. 3. Whither can he look where he will not see his enemies ready to ruin him, on a word of command from that God under whose curse he lies? And what can he do for himself amidst his armed enemies? He is quite naked, Rev. iii. 17, and cannot fight them; he is without strength, Rom. v. 6, and cannot wield armour, though he had it; he is bound hand and foot, Isa. lxi. 1, and cannot flee; and if he could, whither could he flee for safety? Heaven's gates are shut upon him; in the utmost parts of the earth, or the most remote rock in the sea, God's hand would find him out. Justice is pursuing the criminals under the curse, crying for vengeance on the traitors, and their foot shall certainly slide in due time; the law is continually throwing the fire-balls of its curses on them, and will at length set them on fire round about; death is on the pursuit after them, and has gained much ground of them already, and the cloud of wrath hangs over their heads continually in the curse, and the small rain of God's wrath is still falling on them; how soon death may overtake them, they know not; and then the cloud breaks, and the great rain of his strength falls down upon them, and sweeps them away without hope for ever and ever.

The Condition of the Natural Man under the curse, after this life.

SECONDLY, The natural man's condition under the broken covenant of works, is very terrible in that part of it which takes place after this life. Then comes the full execution of the curse, and it is fixed on the sinner without possibility of deliverance. Then will be seen and felt by those who perish under it, what is in the womb of the curse of the broken covenant, whereof all that befals them in this life is but an earnest. The truth is, it cannot be fully represented in words from the tongues of men; but we shall briefly point at it in the following particulars.

Death under the Curse.

First, The natural man under the curse must not only die, but die by virtue of the curse. Death in any shape has a terrible aspect, it is the king of terrors, and can hardly miss to make the creature shrink, being a destruction of nature, and carrying him into another world where he never was before, and putting him into a quite new state, which he has had no prior experience of. But death to the natural man is in a singular manner terrible; it is death of the worst kind. The believer in Christ must die too; but Christ having died for them by virtue of the curse, and that death of his being applied to them by faith, they die not in virtue of the curse; Gal. iii. 13, " Christ hath redeemed us from the curse of the law, being made a curse for us." It is a fatherly chastisement, a medicine to them, yea the most effectual medicine, that cures them of all their maladies, 1 Cor. xi. 30, 32.

But the natural man dies by virtue of the curse of the broken covenant, agreeable to the threatening annexed thereto, Gen. ii. 17. Accordingly, upon man's sinning, the curse seized him; and continuing under that covenant, it is still working in him, till it works his body and soul asunder. Soul and body joined in sin against God, and by sin the man was separated from God; and, as a meet reward of the error, the companions in sin are separated by the curse at length; which would have remained eternally in a happy union, had not sin entered.

Now, that we may have a view of death to a sinner by virtue of the curse, consider,

1. It is the ruining stroke from the hand of an absolute God, proceeding according to the covenant of works against the sinner in full measure; " He shall be driven from light into darkness, and chased out of the world," Job xviii. 18. It is the fatal wound, the wound of an enemy, for the sinner's utter destruction. To a saint, death is a friend's wound, a stroke from the hand of a father, proceeding against his children in the way of the covenant of grace, for their complete happiness. But the ungodly in death fall into the hands of the living God, who then is and ever will be, to them a consuming fire. Having led their life under that covenant, they are then crushed in pieces by the curse for the breaking of it.

2. It is the breaking up of the peace betwixt God and them for ever: it is God setting his seal to the proclamation of an everlasting war with them; after which no message of peace is to go betwixt them any more for ever. It fixeth an impassable gulf, cutting

of all comfortable communication with heaven, for the ages of eternity, Luke xvi. 26. Now the sinner under the curse, living within the visible church, has the privilege of offers of life and salvation; but then there is no more gospel, nor are there any more good tidings of peace, when once death has done its work. The curse which in life might have been got removed by the sinner's embracing Christ, is then fastened for ever on him without remedy. The door is shut, and that for ever.

3. It puts an end to all their comfort of whatsoever nature, Luke xvi. 25. Lazarus is then comforted, but the wicked tormented. It utterly quenches their coal, and puts out all their light, Job xviii. 18, forecited. To the godly, death puts an end to their worldly comforts, but then it lets them into the full enjoyment of their Lord in heaven; but as for the ungodly, at death they leave all their worldly comforts behind them, and they have no comfort before them in the place whither they go. The curse then draws a bar betwixt them and every thing that is pleasant and easy.

4. It is death armed with its sting, and all the strength it has from sin, and a holy just broken law. "The sting of death," whereby it pierces like a stinged serpent, "is sin," 1 Cor. xv. 56, and "the strength of sin is the law." Now, when death comes on the ungodly man, all his sins are unpardoned; the guilt of them all binding him, as with innumerable cords, over to eternal wrath, lies upon him. And these cords of guilt cannot be broken; for the law is their strength, which threatens sin with eternal wrath; and God's truth and faithfulness therein plighted, cannot fail. Thus is death armed against the unbeliever, and herein lies the truly killing nature of it. Where that sting is away, as it is to all in Christ, it can do them no real harm, whatever way they die, whether a lingering or sudden death, a violent or natural one, under a cloud or in the light of comfort, 1 Cor. xv. 55—57.

5. Lastly, It is the fearful passage out of this world into everlasting misery, Luke xvi. 22, 23. It is a dark valley at best; but the Lord is with his people while they go through it, Psalm xxiii. 4. It is a deep water at best; but where the curse is removed, the Lord Jesus will be the lifter up of the head, that the passenger shall not sink. But who can conceive the horror of the passage the sinner under the curse has, upon whom that frightful weight lies? It leads him as an ox to the slaughter; it opens like a trap-door underneath him, by which he falls into the pit, and like a whirlpool swallows him up in a moment, and he is staked down in an unalterable state of unspeakable misery.

Secondly, He is immediately after death haled before the tribunal of that God, under whose curse he lies; Eccl. xii. 7, "The spirit shall return unto God who gave it." Compare Heb. ix. 27, "It is appointed unto men once to die, but after this the judgment." There the soul is judged according to its state, and the deeds done in the body; and there it must receive its particular sentence. And what can it be, but "Depart, ye cursed?" Where can such a soul expect to find its own place, but in the place of torment? Luke xvi. 23. The cause is already judged, the sinner is under the curse, bound over to hell by the sentence of the holy law. And those whom the law has power to curse and does curse while they are in this world, God will never bless in the other world. Consider the sinner under the curse before this tribunal; and,

1. All his sins, of all kinds, in all the periods of his life, from the first to the last breathing on earth are upon him. The curse seals them up as in a bag, that not one of them can be missing; Hos. xiii. 12, "The iniquity of Ephraim is bound up." Where a pardon takes place, the curse is removed, and being once removed, it never returns; so where the curse is, there neither is nor has been a pardon; for these are inconsistent, the one being a binding over of the sinner to wrath, the other a dissolution of that band, so that God will remember their iniquities no more. But where no pardon is, God has sworn he will not forget any of that sinner's works, Amos viii. 7. How fearful, then, must the case be, while the sinner stands before this tribunal with all his sins whatsoever upon him?

2. As the man's sins were multiplied, so the curses of the law were multiplied upon him; for it is the constant voice of the law, upon every transgression of those under the covenant of works, "Cursed is every one that continueth not in all things which are written in the book of the law to do them," Gal. iii. 10. How then can such a one escape, while innumerable cords of death are upon him, before a just Judge, with their united force binding him over to destruction? His misery is hereby insured without all peradventure; and the more of these cords there are upon him, the greater must his punishment be.

3. There is no removing of the curse then, Luke xiii. 25. The time of trial is over, and judgment is to be passed according to what was done in the flesh. When a court is erected within a sinner's own breast in this world, and conscience convicts him as a transgressor of the law, a covenant-breaker, and therefore pronounces him cursed; there is a Surety for the sinner to fly to, an Advocate into whose hands he may commit his cause, a Mediator to trust in and roll his burden on by faith. But before that tribunal there is none for the sinner who comes thither under the curse. As the tree

fell, it must lie; that throne is a throne of pure justice to him, without any mixture of the grace he despised. By the law of works, which he chose to live under, despising the law of grace, he must be judged.

4. *Lastly*, Wherefore he must there inevitably sink under the weight of the curse for ever, Psalm i. 5. He must fall a sacrifice for his own sin, who now slights the only atoning sacrifice, even Christ our passover sacrificed for us. In the course of justice sin must be satisfied for, and without shedding of blood there is no remission. The satisfaction must be proportioned to the injury done to the honour of an infinite God by it. In the gospel, Christ is set before the sinner as the scape-goat before Aaron; he is called to lay his hand on the head thereof, by faith transferring the guilt on the Surety. Since the sinner did not so, but lived and died under the curse, his iniquity must fall and lie for ever on his own head.

Thirdly, The soul is shut up in hell, by virtue of the curse, Luke xvi. 22, 23, " And in hell he lift up his eyes." Thus, by the sentence of the broken covenant, the sinner is cut asunder by the sword of death, and his soul receives its portion, where shall be weeping and gnashing of teeth, being haled from the tribunal into the pit. Then falls the great rain of God's wrath on the men of his curse, the sinner being, to his own conviction, entered in payment of the debt which he can never discharge, and which can never be forgiven. The state of the separate soul under the curse, after its particular judgment, who can sufficiently express the horror of? Consider these things following on that head.

1. Separate souls under the curse, after their particular judgment, are lodged in the place of the damned, called Hell in the scriptures. Then the godly and the wicked change places, who lived together in this world as a mixed company; the soul, which, through faith received the blessing, is carried to heaven; and the soul which parted with the body under the curse, is carried to hell. This is evident from the parable of Dives and Lazarus, Luke xvi. 22, 23. In hell the souls of the wicked are lodged as in a prison, reserved to a further judgment against the great day, 1 Pet. iii. 19. And who can imagine what thoughts of horror must, at its entrance thither, seize the soul, which a little before was in the body in this world, but then goes into an unalterable state of misery, and hath the bars of the pit shut upon it, without hope of relief? O the fearful sudden change it will be to them who lived in wealth and ease, and to them who lived in poverty and distress here! Who can say to which of them it shall be the most frightful change?

2. The dregs of the curse shall there be wrung out to them, and

they made to drink them, in the fearful punishment inflicted upon them for the satisfaction of offended justice, for all their sins, original and actual. Then shall be, more remarkably than ever before, accomplished that passage; Psalm lxxv. 8, "In the hand of the Lord there is a cup, and the wine is red: it is full of mixture, and he poureth out of the same; but the dregs thereof all the wicked of the earth shall wring them out and drink them." The separate soul doth not sleep, nor is void of feeling, nor is it extinguished till the resurrection, as some have dreamed; no, no; it lives, but lives in misery; it feels, but feels nothing but anguish. It is laid under the punishment of loss, being at once deprived of all those things wherein it sought its satisfaction in this world, and of all the happiness of the other world; and it is punished also with the punishment of sense, the wrath of an angry God being poured into it, Luke xvi. 23, 24, which is expressed under the notion of being "tormented in a flame." Then all the joys of the cursed soul are killed, plucked up by the root; and a flood of sorrows surrounds it, having neither brim nor bottom.

3. They are sensible of their lost happiness, Luke xvi. 23. They see it to their unspeakable anguish. Whatever they heard of heaven, and the happiness of those who die in the Lord, while they were on earth, they will get a more affecting discovery of it then, which will cause them to rage against themselves, that ever they should have preferred the pleasures of sin and a vain world to such a blessed state. And how must it pierce the wretched soul, to think that not only all is lost, but lost without possibility of recovery? Luke xvi. 26. O that men would be wise in time, and believe that the state of trial will end with them ere long, and so bend their cares and endeavours, that, amidst the throng of the world's business, cares, vanities, and temptations, they lose not their souls.

4. Their consciences are then awakened, never to fall asleep any more for ever. They will scorch them then like a fire that cannot be quenched, and gnaw them like a worm that never dieth. Without question separate souls are capable of calling things past to remembrance, as is evident in the case of the rich man when in the separate state, Luke xvi. 25, where Abraham bids him remember what a portion he had in this life; the rich man remembers his five brethren, and what a life he and they led, ver. 28. The conscience that was seared till it was past feeling, will then be fully sensible. The evil of sin will then be clearly seen, because felt; the threatenings of the holy law will no more be accounted scarecrows, nor will there be any such fools there as to make a mock of sin. The soul there will be under continual remorse and regret for ever the

ill-spent life, where there is no place for repentance. The soul that would never search and try its ways, while there was occasion to mend what was amiss, will there go through the several steps of life and conversation here; and every new sin that casts up to it as done in the body, will pierce the soul like an envenomed arrow.

5. They will be filled with torturing passions, which will keep the soul ever on the rack Their sinful nature remains with them under the curse, and they will sin against God still, as well as they did in this life; but with this difference, that whereas they had pleasure in their sins here, they shall have none in their sins there; they shall be for ever precluded from acting that wickedness that may give pleasure, and the restraint upon them that way in their prison may contribute to their torment; for, no doubt, the seeds of all sin remain still in them there under the curse; but their sins there shall be their felt misery too. The scripture holds out those torturing passions which they will be filled with, by "weeping, and wailing, and gnashing of teeth;" which intimates to us, that souls there are overwhelmed with sorrow, anguish, and anxiety, with wrath, grudge, murmuring, envy, rage, and despair.

6. *Lastly,* In this state they must continue till the last day, that they be reunited to their respective bodies, and so the whole man get his sentence at the general judgment, adjudging both soul and body to everlasting fire, Matth. xxv. For after they are gone out of this world, their wickedness may be living behind them, and the stream of it may be running when their bodies are consumed in the grave, and their souls have been long in the pit of destruction, like the sin of Jeroboam, who made Israel to sin; all which must be accounted for. And hence it appears, that the expectation of reuniting with their bodies can be no comfortable thought to them but a thought of horror, a fearful expectation.

The Sinner's Body goes to the Dust.

Fourthly, The body goes to the dust in virtue of the curse, Psalm xlix. 14, "Like sheep they are laid in the grave, death shall feed on them." Man's body in the state of innocence was immortal, not subject to death: sin made it mortal, the curse bound it over to death, and to the grave, the dark territory of death, Rom. vi. 23, "The wages of sin is death." Hence our Lord Jesus Christ, becoming a curse for his own, was carried prisoner to the grave, Isa. liii. 9, lay there for a time, bound with the cords of death, Acts ii. 24; but having fully discharged the debt for which he was laid up, disarmed death, and proved the destruction of the grave for all that are his; Hos. xiii. 14, " O death, I will be thy plagues : O grave, I will be thy destruction " But in the meantime death and the grave remain as before to all those who have no saving interest in him ; so that wherever the dead bodies of the wicked are laid up, or however they are disposed of, whether consumed by the fire, eaten up by other creatures, or laid in a grave properly so called; wherever they remain in the state of the dead ; there they are laid up in virtue of the curse. But the bodies of the godly are not so.

The state of the dead body in the grave, under the curse, we may take up in these three things.

It is laid up there as in a prison, like a malefactor in a dungeon, to be kept there till the day of execution. Hence, in the language of the Holy Ghost, Psalm xvi. 10, hell and the grave, or the state of the dead, go under one and the same name ; so that article of the creed, that " Christ descended into hell," is expounded of his continuing in the state of the dead. The bodies of the godly go to the grave too, but it is a place of rest to them, where they rest as in their bed, till the joyful morning of the resurrection, Isa. lvii. 2. For death, armed with the sting, poured out all its venom on Christ, when it had him there, in their room and stead. So it is a hiding-place to them, Job xiv. 13. Whither they are carried from the evil to come, Isa. lvii. 1, and where their eyes are held from beholding grievousness, and an end is put to their toil, Rev. xiv. 13. But in scripture account it is not a place of rest to the ungodly. Remarkable to this purpose is that text, Job iii. 17, 18, " There the wicked cease from troubling; and there the weary be at rest. There the prisoners rest together, they hear not the voice of the oppressor." There are two sorts of men spoke of here, who both go to the grave ; ungodly men, troublers of others, persecutors, oppressors ; godly men, wearied with trouble, imprisonment and oppression. The state of the former in the grave is, they are laid by from doing mischief, causing their terror any longer in the land of the living; the state of the latter is, they are at rest. And as great a difference there is betwixt the two, though one cannot discern it from the posture of their dust, as betwixt a man asleep in his own bed, and a man bound hand and foot in a dungeon, Isa. lvii. 2; 1 Sam. ii. 9 ; Psalm xxxi. 17. And it is their moval or continuance of the curse that makes the difference.

2. Their sin and guilt remains on them there, and that without further possibility of a removal; Job xx. 11, " His bones are full of the sins of his youth, which shall lie down with him in the dust." Sin is a dangerous companion in life ; one had better live in chains of iron, than in chains of guilt ; but happy they with whom sin parts when soul and body part at death. That is the lot of believers in

Christ, who at the Red Sea of death get the last sight of it. There the Lord says to the dying saint, whether he hears it or not, as Exod. xiv. 13, "The Egyptians whom ye have seen to-day ye shall see them again no more for ever." But the man dying under the curse, all his sins take a dead gripe of him never to be let go; and when he lies down in the grave, they lie down with him, and they never part. This is not to be discerned neither in the dust, by bodily eyes, but it is most certain, and as it is represented in the glass of the word, it makes a spectacle of unspeakable horror; Neh. i. 14, "I will make thy grave, for thou art vile;" like a vile, filthy, and loathsome thing, which one cannot endure to look at, and there is no cleansing of; but a hole is dug in the earth, wherein it is covered up with all its filthiness about it. When a saint dies, there is (so to speak) one grave made for him and another for his vileness; and he is to rise again, but his vileness never to rise; but for the ungodly, there is but one, when he lies down and his vileness with him, both to rise together again.

3. All the ruin brought on their bodies there, is done by virtue of the curse; Job xxiv. 19, "The grave consumes those which have sinned." Death makes fearful havoc where it comes; not only doth it separate the soul from the body; but separates the several parts of the body one from another, until it reduce the whole into dust, not to be discerned by the quickest eye from common dust. Thus it fares with the bodies of the godly indeed, as well as the bodies of the wicked; nevertheless great is the difference,—the curse working these effects in the bodies of the latter, but not of the former, stinged death in the one, unstinged death in the other; so all these effects in the one are pieces of revenging wrath for the satisfaction of justice; in the other not so, but like the melting down of the crazy silver vessel, to be cast into a new mould.

The Wicked shall Rise again under the Curse.

Fifthly, They shall rise again out of their graves, at the last day, under the curse; John v. 29, "They that have done evil, shall come forth unto the resurrection of damnation." Compare Matth. xxv. 41, "Depart from me, ye cursed, into everlasting fire, prepared for the devil and his angels." Our Lord Jesus Christ, who became a curse for all his people, was carried from the cross to the grave; but there the debt was fully paid, and the curse was exhausted; the cursing law and justice had no more to exact of him; so he was brought forth out of the prison of the grave, as one free person who had completely discharged the debt which he was laid in prison for. And hence believers in Christ, though they fall down into the grave, as well as others; yet they do not fall down into it under the curse, far less do they rise again, at the last day, under the curse. But the natural man having lived and died under the covenant of works, goes to the grave under the curse; and forasmuch as all that comes on him, in the state of the dead, cannot satisfy completely for his debt, therefore as the curse remains on him all along while he is there, so he rises again under it. And in this doleful event three things may be considered :—

1. They shall rise again out of their graves by virtue of the curse. This is implied in that forecited, John v. 29. When the end of time is come, the last trumpet shall sound, and all that are in the graves shall come forth, godly and ungodly; but the godly shall rise by virtue of their blessed union with Christ, Rom. viii. 11; the ungodly by virtue of the curse of the broken covenant on them. As the malefactor is, in virtue of the sentence of death passed on him, shut up in close prison till the time of execution; and in virtue of the same sentence brought out of prison at the time appointed for his execution; even so the unbeliever is, in virtue of the curse of the law adjudging him to eternal death in hell, laid up in the grave till the last day; and, in virtue of the same curse, brought out of the grave at that day. Hence, by the bye, one may see, that there is no force in that arguing, viz., The separation of the soul and body was not the sanction of the law; else why should the wicked be clothed with their bodies at the resurrection? It is true, that separation was not the whole of the sanction, but it was a remarkable part of it; and there is no inconsistency in the separation and reuniting of soul and body, being both comprehended in the sanction, more than in the laying up of the malefactor for, and bringing him forth to execution, being both comprehended in the sentence of death. The same curse that separated soul and body at death, and separated each part of the body from another in the grave, shall, at the time appointed, have another kind of effect in bringing together the scattered pieces of dust, and joining them together in one body, and joining it again to the soul.

2. All their sin and guilt shall rise again with them; the body that was laid in the grave, a vile body; a foul instrument of the soul in divers lusts; an unclean vessel, stained, polluted and defiled, with divers kinds of filthy impure lusts; shall rise again with all its impurities cleaving to it, Isa. lxvi. 24, "They shall be an abhoring unto all flesh." It is the peculiar privilege of believers to have their " vile bodies changed," Phil. iii. 21. If the bodies of sinners be not cleansed by the washing with that pure water, Heb. x. 22, viz. the blood and Spirit of Jesus Christ; though they be strained in never

so minute parts, through the earth in a grave, they will lose nothing
of their vileness and pollution, it will still cleave to every part of
their dust, and appear again therewith at the resurrection. Then
shall they get a new and horrible sight of the use they made of their
tongues in profane swearing, cursing, mocking at religion, lying, re-
proaching, cruel and unjust threatenings, &c., in undue silence, when
God's honour, their own soul's interest, and their neighbour's good,
required them to speak; of the use they made of their bellies, in
gluttony, and drunkenness, and pampering of the flesh; of their
bodies, in uncleanness, lasciviousness, and wantonness; of their
hands, in pilfering, stealing, unjust beating and abusing their fellow-
creatures, immoderately busying them in the things of this life, to
the neglect of their souls; in a word, of the use they made of their
whole body, and every member thereof; with the qualities and
endowments thereof, its youth, beauty, comeliness, health, and
strength; together with the memorials of dying put into their hands,
as hurts, wounds, weakness, sickness, old age; all of them to have
been improved for God, the good of mankind, and their own eternal
welfare. O, if men could look upon these things now, as then they
will appear, the sweet morsel of sin would be accounted as the poison
of asps.

3. Their appearance will be frightful and horrible beyond expression, when they come forth of their graves under the curse, and set
their feet on the earth again. When, at the sound of the trumpet,
the dead shall all arise out of their graves, and the wicked are cast
forth as abominable branches, what a fearful awakening will they
have out of their long sleep ! When they get another sight of this
earth, upon which they led their ungodly lives; see their godly
neighbours taken out from among them in the same spot of ground
where they all lay, and carried away with joy to meet the Lord in
the air; and when they see the Judge come to the judgment of the
great day, in awful state; and they are going forward to appear before his tribunal; no appearance of malefactors going, under a
guard, to the place of execution; no case of a besieged city taken,
and soldiers burning and slaying, and the inhabitants running and
crying for fear of the sword; can sufficiently represent the frightful
appearance which men risen again at the last day, under the curse,
will make. What ghastly visages will they then have ! How will
the now fairest ungodly faces be black as a coal, through extreme
terror, anguish, and perplexity ! How will they shiver, tremble,
their knees smite one against another, and their hearts be pierced as
with arrows, while they see the doleful day they would not believe !
what roarings and yellings, and hideous noise will then be amongst

the innumerable crowd of the ungodly, driven forward to the tribunal as beasts to the slaughter? What "crying to the rocks and the mountains to fall on them, and hide them from the face of the Lamb," but all in vain! Rev. vi. 16, 17. Then will the weight of the curse be felt to purpose, how lightly soever men now walk under it.

The Wicked appear before Christ's Tribunal under the Curse.

Sixthly, They shall appear before the tribunal of Christ under the curse, like a malefactor in chains before his judge, Matth. xxv. 41. All must appear there, great and small, good and bad; none shall be amissing; Rom. xiv. 10, " We shall all stand before the judgment seat of Christ." But they who now receive the blessing through faith shall be in no hazard of the curse then or there. But it is not possible, that those who lived and died under the curse, should not have it upon them before that tribunal; for after death there is no removing of it. The fearful state of those under the curse before that judgment-seat may be viewed in these particulars.

1. In virtue of the curse they shall be set on the left hand, Matth. xxv. 33. No honour is designed for them, but shame and everlasting contempt; no sentence, but what will fix them in an unalterable state of misery; so no access for them to the right hand amongst the blessed, but they must be ranged together on the left hand as a company of cursed ones.

2. The face of the judge must needs be terrible to them, as being under the curse of him who sits upon the throne, Rev. vi. 16, 17. When they see him, they shall know him to be he, who with his Father and the Holy Spirit gave that law which they transgressed, made that covenant which they broke, whose voice the curse of the law against transgressors was and is; the which must needs take effect in their everlasting ruin, by reason of his justice, holiness, and truth. And he will be in a special manner terrible to such as had the gospel offer made to them, and the more terrible, the more plainly, affectionately, and powerfully it was pressed on them to accept it. O how will it strike them as a dart, when they look towards the throne, thinking with themselves, Lo there he sits to judge me now, and destroy me, who so often made offer of life and salvation to me by his messengers, which I slighted! I might through him have obtained the blessing, but now I stand trembling under the weight of the curse. The despised Lamb of God is turned into a lion against me. Consider this, O sinners, while God is on a throne of grace for you; lest it be taken down, and a tribunal of pure justice be set up for you.

3. To clear the equity of the curse, and the execution thereof upon them, their " works shall be brought into judgment," Eccl. xii. 14.

Their whole life shall be searched into, and laid to the rule of the holy law, and the enormity and sinfulness thereof be discovered. Their corrupt nature, with all the malignity and venom against the rule of righteousness, shall be laid open. Their sins shall be set in the light of God's countenance, in such full tale, that they shall see God is true to his word and oath, that he would not forget any of their works. The mask will then be entirely taken off their faces, and all their pretences to piety solemnly rejected, and declared to have been but hypocrisy. Their secret wickedness, which they re-joiced to have got hid, and which they so artfully managed, that there was no discovering of it while they might have confessed and found mercy, shall then be set in broad day light before God and the world when there is no remedy. Conscience shall then be no more blind nor dumb; but shall witness against them and for God; and shall never be silent any more. The sin and misery brought upon others by their ungodly courses, taking effect when they them-selves were gone out of the world, shall then be pursued in all their breadth and length, laid to their charge, and proved against them; and so the account of their debt to the divine justice shall be fully stated at that day.

4. Their doom shall be pronounced; Matth. xxv. 41, "Depart from me, ye cursed, into everlasting fire prepared for the devil and his angels." Thus shall they receive their final sentence, never to hear more from the mouth of him that sits upon the throne. This determines the full execution of the curse on the whole man, soul and body together. The godly shall get their final sentence too; but, O! the vast difference betwixt "Come ye blessed," and "Depart ye cursed." The unspeakable happiness of the saints in heaven, and the unspeakable misery of the damned in hell, will shew the diffe-rence. But the weight of both lies, you see, in the state of the par-ties, as under the blessing, or under the curse. There is the turning point in respect of one's eternal state.

This World shall be Burnt with Fire.

Seventhly, As they shall be, by virtue of the curse now to be fully executed, driven from the judgment-seat into hell; so, in virtue of the same curse of the broken covenant of works, this world shall go up in flames, and so have an end put to it; 2 Pet. iii. 10, "The heavens shall pass away with a great noise, and the elements shall melt with fervent heat, the earth also and the works that are there-in shall be burnt up." When sin got place in the earth by the breach of the covenant, the curse was laid upon it, and the founda-tions thereof were as it were shaken; by its relation to man, it came within the compass of the curse for his sin, and so was devoted to destruction, which shall then take its full effect. Yea, the whole frame of the creation, having relation to sinful man, was blasted for his sake, being made " subject to vanity," Rom. viii. 20, 21. And so the heaven, which because it is over the head of the covenant breaker, is therefore now sometimes made brass, shall, upon the same account, then pass away with a great noise ; even as the earth, which is sometimes made iron, because it is under him, shall then be burnt up, Deut. xxviii. 23, with 2 Pet. iii. 10, just quoted. So the curse is a train laid in the bowels of the creation, which now and then gives it terrible shocks, but will at last blow all up together. And when once it has done that, and so put an end to this stage of vanity and wickedness; all the effects of it that now lie scattered through the creation, shall be gathered together and cast into the place of the damned (Rev. xx. 14, 15,) with them ; so that though death and misery are everywhere to be found now, it shall be no where then but in that one place ; and all that goes under the name of death shall be in that place. The weight comprehended in the curse lies now on many backs, and so is the more easily borne ; but then it shall all lie on the backs of the men of the Lord' curse, and on theirs only ; and so shall they feel the full weight of it.

The Wicked shall lie for ever under the weight of the Curse in hell.

Eighthly, They shall lie for ever under the weight of the curse in hell, on soul and body together; Matth. xxv. 41, " Depart from me, ye cursed, into everlasting fire." Here is their misery completed, here is the full execution of the curse. The curse was big with wrath, indignation, and fury of a holy, jealous, just God, against sin, and sinners for sin, ever since it first entered, upon the breach of the covenant; and it has since that time still been bringing forth, yet there has likewise still been some allay in it, and the storm of wrath has not yet come to the height. While men, even the men of the Lord's curse, live in this world, much patience is exercised towards them, and partly through the slenderness of the strokes laid on them, partly through their insensibleness, and partly through the mixture of mercy in their cup, they make a shift to live at some ease ; and if their ease be at any time disturbed, yet they ordinarily, though not always, find some means to recover it ; and even while their souls are in hell, during the time betwixt their death and the last judgment, their bodies lie at ease in the grave ; so but the one half of the man is in torment, and a part of him is easy, without any sense or feeling of the least annoyance. But when once the dead are raised again, and the men of the curse have got their last

sentence, and time is absolutely at an end, the mystery of God finish-
ed, and a quite new state of the creation brought in, to wit, the eternal state ; then shall the curse bring forth the threatened death in
its full strength and force on the undischarged covenant-breakers ;
and as Christ, standing surety for the elect, knew by his experience
so shall the men of the curse know by their experience, what was
within the compass of the threatening of the covenant of works ;
Gen. ii. 17, " In the day that thou eatest thereof thou shalt surely
die." Many a commentary has heaven wrote upon it unto men, in
flaming fire, in blood and gore, in sighs, groans, and swooning of the
whole creation ; but never a full one yet, excepting in the sufferings
of the Son of God on the cross. The elect of God get their eyes
opened to read that, and so they make haste and escape out of the
dominion of that covenant to which the curse belongs ; but the rest
are blinded, they cannot read it there. But God will write another
full commentary on it after the last judgment, whence all the men
of the Lord's curse shall, in their horrible experience, learn what
was in it, namely, in the threatening of the covenant of works. The
dregs of the cup of the curse shall then be brought above, and they
shall drink them.

1. In virtue of the curse, the pit, having received them, shall close
its mouth on them. A fearful emblem of this we have, Numb. xvi.
32, 33, in the case of Korah and his company ; " And the earth
opened her mouth, and swallowed them up, and their houses, and all
the men that appertained unto Korah, and all their goods. They,
and all that appertained to them went down alive into the pit, and
the earth closed upon them." Compare that threatening, Psalm xxi.
9, "Thou shalt make them as a fiery oven in the time of thine anger,
the Lord shall swallow them up in his wrath, and the fire shall devour them." They shall be cast into the lake of fire, as death and
hell are, to be shut up there without coming forth again any more,
Rev. xx. 14, 15. By the force of the curse upon them, they shall
be confined in the place allotted for damned men and devils. It
shall so draw the bars of the pit about them, that sooner shall they
remove mountains of brass than remove them. It shall be stronger
than chains of iron to bind them hand and foot that they make no
escape, Matth. xxii. 13, yea and to bind them in bundles for the fire
of God's wrath, that companions in sin may be companions in punishment, Matth. xiii. 30.

2. The curse shall shall then be like a partition wall of adamant,
to separate them quite from God, and any the least comfortable intercourse with him, Matth. xxv. 41. While on the other side of the
wall the light of glory shines, more bright than a thousand suns,

filling the saints with joy unspeakable, and which we cannot com: prehend, and causing the arch of heaven to ring with their songs of praise; on their side is nothing but utter darkness, without the least gleam of light; and there shall be weeping, wailing, and gnashing of teeth. For why, God himself is the only true happiness of the creature, and Christ the only way to the Father; but then there is a total and final separation betwixt God and Christ, and them: The day of the Lamb's wrath is come, all possibility of reconciliation is removed, and patience towards them is quite ended, and the curse hath its full stroke; so God, the fountain of all good, departs quite from them, abandons them, casts them off utterly, and that moment all the streams of goodness towards them dry up, and their candle is quite extinguished. Then shall be known what is in that word, Hos. ix. 12, "Wo to them when I depart from them." And then there is no getting over the wall, no passing of the great gulf for ever, Luke xvi. 26.

3. It shall hence be a final stop to all sanctifying influences towards them. While they are in this world, there is a possibility of removing the curse, and that the worst of men may be made holy; but when there is a total and final separation from God in hell, surely there are no sanctifying influences there. The corrupt nature they carried with them thither, must then abide with them there; and they must needs act there, since their being is continued; and a corrupt nature will ever act corruptly, while it acts at all, Matth. vii. 17. And therefore there will be sin in hell after the last judgment, unless one will suppose that they will be under no law there; which is absurd, seeing a creature, as a creature, owes obedience to God in what state soever it be. Yea, they will sin there at a horrible rate, in blasphemies against God, and other sins akin thereto, as men absolutely void of all goodness, in a desperate state of misery, Rev. xiv. ult.; Matth. xxii. 13. The curse will be a dry wind, not to fan nor to cleanse, but to wither, blast, and kill their souls.

4. It shall be the breath that shall blow the fire continually, and keep it burning, for their exquisite torment in soul and body; Isa. xxx. 33, "For Tophet is ordained of old: yea, for the king it is prepared: he hath made it deep and large; the pile thereof is fire and much wood; the breath of the Lord, like a stream of brimstone, doth kindle it." There the worm which shall gnaw them, shall never die, for the curse will keep it in life; the fire that shall burn them shall never be quenched, for the curse shall nourish it, and be as bellows blowing it, to cause it flame without intermission. The curse shall enter into their souls, and melt them like wax before the fire; it

shall sink into their flesh and bones, like boiling lead, and torment them in every part. It will stake them down there as marks for the arrows of God, which, dipt in the poison of the curse, shall be continually piercing them and burning them up. No pity, no compassion to be shewn any more, but the fire-balls of the curse will be flying against them incessantly; Rev. xiv. 11, "The smoke of their torment ascendeth up for ever and ever : and they have no rest day nor night."

5. *Lastly*, The curse shall lengthen out their misery to all eternity; Matth. xxv. 41, "Depart, ye cursed, into everlasting fire." It binds the sinner to make complete and full satisfaction, for all the wrongs he has done to the honour of an infinite God; it binds him to pay till there be a sufficient compensation made for them all. Now, there being no proportion betwixt finite and infinite, the finite creature can never, by its sufferings, expiate its crimes against an infinite God. Hence, when the sinner has suffered millions of ages in hell, the curse still binds him down to suffer more, because he has not yet fully satisfied; and since he can never fully satisfy, it will bind him down for ever and ever, Rev. xiv. 11, and will bring new floods of wrath over his head; and renew its demands of satisfaction through the ages of eternity, but never, never say, It is enough.

Thus have I endeavoured to open up unto you the nature of the curse of the broken covenant of works, and the dreadful condition of those under it, in this life, and after this life. But after all, who knows the power of God's wrath? No tongue can tell what the frightful experience of those who live and die under it, shall teach them. But thus much may suffice to have shewn you the misery of being under the covenant of works.

Application of the doctrine, That natural men being under the broken Covenant of Works are under the curse.

This doctrine shall be improved in two practical uses; for conviction and for exhortation.

Use I. Of conviction. What has been said on this awful subject may serve to fix convictions in the consciences both of saints and sinners.

First, Saints, who are brought from under this covenant, delivered from it and the curse thereof by Jesus Christ, view this curse in the nature and weight, the length and breadth of it; and say in your hearts before the Lord,

1. Do ye suitably prize and esteem your God, Redeemer and Saviour? Are your hearts suitably affected with the love of God in Christ, that set on foot your deliverance, and brought it about?

Ah! this consideration may afford us a breast full of convictions. What manner of love was this, that the Father did choose you from among the cursed children of Adam to inherit the blessing? that the Son died for you, to redeem you from the curse? that the Holy Ghost applied to you the purchase of Christ's death, to the actual removing of this curse from off you? O where is that love, that warm, glowing love to the Lord, that this requires! The Father's love to you while under the curse, moved him to make his Son to be sin for you, who knew no sin, that you might be made the righteousness of God in him. Christ's love to you made him become a curse for you, and drink the dregs of that cup, which ye should have drank through eternity in hell. The Spirit's love to you made him watch the moment appointed for your deliverance, and bring you out with a strong hand from the dominion of the law, and transport you into the dominion of grace, where there is no more curse. O look back to the dreadful curse which ye were under; look up to the love in delivering of you; keep one eye upon the one, and another eye upon the other, till these cold hearts of yours warm with love.

2. Do ye suitably prize the new covenant, the second covenant? Do ye pry into the mystery of the glorious contrivance, stand and wonder at the device for bringing cursed sinners to inherit the blessing? Would it not become you well to be often looking into it, and saying, "This is all my salvation, and all my desire?" 2 Sam. xxiii. 5. Ah! why have we not higher and more honourable thoughts of the covenant of grace, of the Second Adam, the Head, Surety, and Messenger of the covenant, of the gospel, the proclamation of the covenant, the Bible the book of the covenant, the promises of the covenant, the matchless privileges of the covenant, and even of the public criers of the covenant too? Isa. lii. 7. To help you to this, lay the volume of the two covenants before you; open and read the covenant of works in the first place, where you will find nothing but demands of perfect obedience under the pain of the curse; a promise of life upon conditions impossible to be performed by you, but the curse, wrath, death, hell, and damnation to the sinner. Then turn over to the covenant of grace, and read life and salvation through Jesus Christ by faith; no curse, death, hell, damnation, nor revenging wrath; all these discharged by the Surety. And so raise your esteem of the new covenant in Christ's blood.

3. Do ye walk answerably to the deliverance from this curse? Ah! may not that be applied justly to us; Deut. xxxii. 6, "Do ye thus requite the Lord, O foolish people and unwise? is not he thy Father that hath bought thee? hath he not made thee, and estab-

lished thee?" Obedience to all the ten commands is bound on all under the covenant of works, under the pain of the curse, Gal. iii. 10, " Cursed is every one that continueth not in all things which are written in the book of the law to do them." Obedience to them all is bound on believers too, but by another tie, viz. the tie of their deliverance from the curse, by their God-Redeemer ; Exod. xx. 2, " I am the Lord thy God, which have brought thee out of the land of Egypt," &c. And this, and not the former, is the way in which the law of the ten commands gets any acceptable obedience, 1 Tim. i. 5, from sinful man. O look to the curse of the covenant of works, from which ye are delivered, and be convinced and humbled to the very dust,

(1.) That ye should walk so untenderly, unwatchfully, and uncircumspectly, before the Lord that bought you, and that in the midst of cursed children, a crooked and perverse generation. What can more strike a nail to the heart of a gracious person, than when the Spirit of the Lord whispers into his soul, " Have I been a wilderness unto Israel? a land of darkness? wherefore say my people, We are lords; we will come no more unto thee?" Jer. ii. 31. And, " Is this your kindness to your friend?" Is that your compassion to the world lying in wickedness, to cast a stumbling-block before the blind? You speak, you act untenderly; is that the use of the tongue redeemed from the curse? Is that the use of the eyes, hands, and feet, body and soul, delivered from the curse of the broken covenant? I think, that a believer looking to the cross should say, and abide by it, " To me to live is Christ, and to die is gain," Phil. i. 21.

(2.) That ye should so dote upon this earth, this cursed earth, that the curse of the broken covenant of works has lain upon these five thousand years, and has sucked the sap out of, and so dried up by this time, that it is near to taking fire, and to be burnt to ashes, by virtue of the curse upon it. Let the men of the Lord's curse, who have their portion in it, set their hearts upon it, go upon their belly, and lick the dust, (it is no wonder they cannot get up their back, on whom the heavy curse of the broken covenant lies); but lift ye up your souls unto the Lord, and hearken to his voice; Cant. iv. 8, " Come with me from Lebanon, my spouse, with me from Lebanon; look from the top of Amana, from the top of Shenir and Herman, from the lions' dens, from the mountains of the leopards."

(3.) That ye should perform duties so heartlessly, coldly, and indifferently; with so little faith, love, fervency, humility, zeal, and confidence. O look to the curse of the broken covenant, with the effects of it in earth and hell, that ye may be stirred up to the performance of duty after another manner. I mean not that ye should look upon it as what ye are actually liable to in case of transgression ; for this to a believer, who is never free from sin one moment, may well make his heart die in him like a stone ; it will never kindly quicken him ; it may well drag or drive him to his duty, like a slave ; it will never cause him perform it like a son ; but look upon it as what ye are delivered from, and that will draw, melt, and kindly quicken the heart in love, Eph. ii. 11—13 ; Luke i. 74, 75. Deliverance from wrath is the most powerful motive to obedience.

(4.) That ye should bear your troubles and trials so impatiently, as if your crosses were so many curses. Look to the condition of those under the curse in this world, and you will see your heaviest cross is lighter than their smallest ones, which have the weight of the curse in them, that yours have not, however you cry out under their weight ; yea your adversity is better than their prosperity ; the frowns of providence you meet with, are preferable to the smiles of providence in their lot ; there is no curse in the former, but in the latter there is. Look to the condition of those under the curse in hell ; and that duly considered, ye will kiss the rod, and say, "It is of the Lord's mercies that we are not consumed, because his compassions fail not," Lam. iii. 22. Look how Christ redeemed us from the curse of the law, being made a curse for us, and you will see the poison taken out of the cup, and the pure water of affliction presented to you in your cup to pledge him in ; and why not drink it, and drink it thankfully ? Bear the cross for him, and take blows and buffetings for his sake, and from him for our own good, who has borne away the curse.

4. Have ye due thoughts of the evil of sin ? Is your horror of it suitably raised ? Rom. xii. 9, " Abhor that which is evil," abhor it as hell, so the word may bear. If you duly consider the curse, it may fill you with shame and blushing on this head. There is much blindness in the minds of believers, much hardness in their hearts, and coldness in their affections with respect to spiritual things. The lively sense of the evil of sin is often very small. We dare not own believers to be yet liable to the curse, Christ having, with his precious blood applied to them by faith, freed them from it ; but it is of great and necessary use to them as a looking-glass, wherein they may see the evil of sin, the due demerit of it, what their sins do in themselves deserve, what Christ suffered for these sins of theirs, and what they should have suffered for them, if Christ had not suffered it in their stead. Trace the curse in its effects in this life, and after this life, as they have been represented to you ; so will you see God's

high indignation against sin, the infinite evil that is in the least transgression of the holy law. Behold it in this glass, and you shall conceive a horror of it; and be ashamed that you have entertained so slight thoughts of it.

5. *Lastly*, Are ye duly affected with the case of those who, being strangers to Christ, are yet under the curse? Are ye at due pains for their recovery and deliverance? How natural is it for men, who with difficulty have escaped the greatest danger, to be affected with the case of others who are still in the same danger, in hazard of perishing? But though multitudes are under the curse still, and, it may be, some such as we have a peculiar interest in; yet where is the due care, compassion, and concern for them, that they may be delivered? They are not concerned for themselves, because they have not yet got a broad view of their hazard; but why are not such concerned for them, as have had their eyes opened in their own case. Sure the case of all men by nature is alike, and therefore the past danger of believers gives a clear view of the present danger of unbelievers, unless it be out of mind with them, which it should not be, that once they were " without Christ, being aliens from the commonwealth of Israel, and strangers from the covenants of promise, having no hope, and without God in the world," Eph. ii. 12. The apostle's experience of the terror of the Lord stirred him up to persuade others to flee from the curse, 2 Cor. v. 11; and it well becomes others, who are themselves as brands plucked out of the burning, to act with that concern in the case of others, pulling them out of the fire, Jude ver. 23, and to mourn for the case of those who continue insensible of their danger, as our blessed Redeemer did in the case of Jerusalem, Luke xix. 41, 42.

Secondly, Sinners, ye who are under the broken covenant of works still, not united to Christ by faith, and savingly interested in the covenant of grace, but living yet in your natural unregenerate state, ye may hence be convinced,

1. That ye are under the curse; ye are they who are the people of the Lord's curse, under the sentence of the law, actually binding you over to destruction. Ye are they who by breaking of the original contract have fallen under the penalty, and are decerned in the court of heaven to pay it. Against you, as transgressors of the law, is the sentence passed according to the threatening, Gen. ii. 17, " In the day that thou eatest thereof thou shalt surely die." Against you, and every one of you in particular, is the curse denounced. So the condition of those under the curse, is your condition in particular; and what such are liable to, you are liable to; for your name is in the black roll of the people of the curse, of those

appointed to death, and devoted to destruction, in virtue of the curse of the broken covenant of works.

O Sirs, admit the conviction, and go not about to bless yourselves in your own hearts, putting the thoughts of being under the curse far away from you. There is light enough here to convince your consciences in that point, if ye will not shut your eyes against clear light. All who are under the broken covenant of works are under the curse, but you are under that covenant; therefore you are under the curse. If you be not under that covenant, where is your discharge from it? The believer's discharge may be read; Rom. viii. 1, "There is therefore now no condemnation to them that are in Christ Jesus." Chap. vii. 4, "Ye are become dead to the law by the body of Christ, that ye should be married to another." But where is yours? The unbeliever's discharge is nowhere to be found. It is past dispute that covenant is broken, and that being broken it curseth the breakers; it is undeniable that you are breakers of it, and therefore you must be under the curse.

It is your interest to admit this conviction. What will it avail you to bless yourselves in your own hearts, when God himself in his holy law denounces the curse against you? It is not by the sentence you pass on yourselves that you must stand or fall, but by the sentence God passeth on you in his word. Nay, men's blessing themselves, against whom God denounceth the curse, does but the more expose them to the evils contained in the curse, coming on them speedily and furiously; Deut. xxix. 19, 20, "And it come to pass, when he heareth the words of this curse, that he bless himself in his heart, saying, I shall have peace, though I walk in the imagination of my heart, to add drunkenness to thirst; the Lord will not spare him, but then the anger of the Lord and his jealousy shall smoke against that man, and all the curses that are written in this book shall lie upon him, and the Lord shall blot out his name from under heaven." The admitting of this conviction is among the first steps to a delivery; and there would be good hopes of one's obtaining of the blessing of the gospel at length, if he were once soundly convinced of his being under the curse of the law. And therefore the curse is preached, not that sinners may perish under it, but that they, seeing themselves under it, may stir up themselves to make their escape. The law does its work to prepare sinners for Christ, convincing them of sin, that they are sinners; convincing them of their misery, that they are under the curse; and they that never yet saw themselves under the curse, give a shrewd sign that they were never yet brought from under it. But when once a sinner sees himself concluded under the curse of the law, then he is in a fair way to prize Christ and the blessing of the gospel, and to get himself carefully to inquire what course he should take to be saved. And the believing of the curse of the law with a particular application to one's self, must necessarily go before the so believing the promise of the gospel indeed.

Why should it seem strange in your eyes, who yet are not truly united to Christ by faith, that you should be under the curse of the broken covenant of works? that is the common case of all mankind by nature; and the deliverance from under it befals no man in a morning dream. And sure it is that most men have never been much in pain to get rid of it; and some there are who, striving to get clear of it in a legal way, have but wreathed that yoke faster about their own necks. Do not you know that Christ himself, as the elect's surety, was made a curse? How could that be if they themselves had not been under it, and likewise unable to bear it so as to exhaust it? Now, there is no saving interest in his purchase, till once the soul is brought to Christ by faith, and united to him; which you are not.

It is very consistent with the mercy of God, to lay unbelievers under the curse; for his mercy can never act in prejudice of his exact justice. The covenant being made with Adam for all mankind, the curse behoved to fall on the breakers according to the threatening, by virtue of the truth and justice of God. But mercy indeed has a way made for it towards the miserable under the curse, inasmuch as the prisoners are made prisoners of hope, by having deliverance from the curse proclaimed to them in the gospel; the which may be actually conveyed to them in the way of God's own appointment; namely the cursed sinner's believing on the name of Christ. But what need were there of either purchasing or proclaiming it to you, if you were not under it?

Think not that you cannot be under the curse, because God has done much for you, has given you many blessings, as health, strength, wit, wealth, and prosperity in the world; or because he has wrought many wonderful deliverances for you, has brought you from a low and mean estate to a high one, and mightily increased you in outward comforts and enjoyments. Remember it, and consider well, that all these are but left-hand blessings, which one may have poured in upon him in abundance, and yet be under the curse, and they be cursed to him; Mal. ii. 2, "I will send a curse upon you, and I will curse your blessings; yea, I have cursed them already." Neither think, that because you are poor and mean in the world, have a hard and afflicted lot therein, that therefore you are certainly possessed of God's blessing and not under the curse. Nay, these things are in their own nature effects of the curse, and so they are in very deed to all who are not in Christ, but under the first covenant; and the curse may and doth pursue men in this world, as well as in the world to come; and one may be very miserable in this life and in the other too, by virtue of the curse. Neither deceive yourselves in this matter, with external privileges which you do enjoy in the fellowship of the church. You may be set down at the table of gospel ordinances there, and yet be under the curse, Rom. xi. 9, and by virtue thereof, none of these things doing your souls good.

Wherefore, young sinners and old sinners, yet in your natural unconverted state, be convinced that ye are under the curse which has been described. Lay the matter to heart; what the law saith to them that are under it, it says to you; take it home then to yourselves, and believe you are under the curse.

2. Be convinced that ye are in a very miserable condition, being under the curse; Eph. ii. 3, "By nature the children of wrath." Whatever your outward lot in the world is, your condition is dreadful in this respect. If you had Samson's strength, Absalom's beauty, Solomon's wit and wealth, and Methuselah's long life-time to enjoy them in, your case is miserable beyond expression, being under the curse of the broken covenant of works. The case of a devoted person, loaded with the curses of a city or country, and so put to death, was lamentable; but whosoever thou art who art under this covenant, and so under the curse, thou hast the curse of the Lord of heaven and earth upon thee, binding thee over to eternal destruction, and so art in a thousand times worse case. Your loss is unspeakable, and the whole world cannot compensate it; namely, the loss of God's favour. This burthen is insupportable; for there is that weight in this curse which will sink thee for ever, though now, perhaps, thou feelest it not. The curse binds thee to the payment of a debt to revenging justice, which thou wilt never be able to discharge. You have heard your miserable condition under the curse at large.

To sum it up in a few words; your condition is miserable here, and will be more miserable hereafter, if you die as you now live. In this world, the cloud of wrath hangs over your head, and the small rain of God's indignation is continually falling upon you; in the world to come, the full shower will fall, the floods of wrath will break out and overwhelm you. Your life hangs in doubt every day; and as you live in the most dangerous circumstances, exposed without any covert to the arrows of wrath; so you are not ready to die. On this side death you are in the midst of your armed enemies, and on the other side death you fall into the hands of the living God. O lay to heart your misery ere it be too late.

Refuse not to admit the conviction of the great misery of your condition, because you do not feel yourself so miserable. Remember, that it is not your feeling, but God's word of truth, which can determine you happy or miserable. The judgment of God is always according to truth ; and if you will carry your case to the word, you will see it a most deplorable case ; view it in the glass of the holy broken law which you are under, and you must needs be affected with the horror of it ; " For as many as are of the works of the law are under the curse." You read, you hear the law, with its terrible sentence against the breakers, its fearful curses and denunciations of wrath ; but do you apply them to yourselves ? Nay, you entertain them as if they did not concern you, nor were directed to you ; and if at any time they are like to take hold of you, and grip your consciences, you flee from them, and labour to divert your minds from such thoughts. But remember, " what things soever the law saith, it saith to them who are under the law ;" and consequently it saith them to you, as if your name were expressed in what it saith. And if the law speaks to you indeed, it will have its effect on you, however you may persuade yourself it means not concerning you.

What though you do not feel your misery ? Many think themselves in good case, who in very deed are in a most miserable and wretched condition, as it fared with Laodicea, Rev. iii. 17. They entertain themselves with dreams of happiness, while ruin abides them ; think themselves safe, while they are in the utmost hazard. Nay, there are many who are so far gone under the curse, that they are past feeling, Eph. iv. 19. Neither the sinfulness nor misery of their souls gives them any distress, anxiety, or perplexity of mind. And that is a case miserable to a degree, inasmuch as it is so far a hopeless case.

But why are ye not sensible of your miserable case ? Though ye feel not the weight of it upon you for the present, yea though ye have all ease and prosperity in the world, being neither under trouble of body nor mind, nor any disaster in your affairs ; yet ye ought to remember, that the curse works by silent strokes, as well as by tormenting plagues, as ye have heard ; yea, and that the most terrible workings of the curse are awaiting the people of the curse, on the other side death. Surely then ye have reason to believe, and be convinced, that your state is most miserable, though for the present you feel not the weight of it ; for the curse, working like a moth, insensibly, makes a ruinous condition, in which the breaking will at length come suddenly at an instant ; and they must needs be in a state of unspeakable misery, whom eternal destruction from the presence of the Lord is abiding, ready to seize them at the time appointed.

Wherefore believe the doctrine of the law, concerning the curse, and the misery of sinners under it; believe it with application to yourselves. Believe it upon the testimony of God, who is truth itself; believe it, because God has said it, though perhaps you do not feel it; so shall you come to be duly affected with it, and by that means be stirred up to a concern to be saved from it, which would be a promising step towards a recovery.

3. Be convinced, that your case is desperately sinful while you are under that covenant. While sin remains, the root of misery remains, which will spring up; the fountain abides, which will cast forth waters of bitterness; and it must and will remain in its strength while ye are under that covenant; because, being under that covenant, ye are under the curse. Hence says the apostle, 1 Cor. xv. 56, " The strength of sin is the law." While the law, as the covenant of works, then, hath power over a man, sin will have its strength in him, which he can by no means break. While ye are under that covenant, and so under the curse,

(1.) The guilt of your sin lies on you, the guilt of eternal wrath; and it cannot be removed. The curse stakes you down under that guilt, it binds it upon you as with bands of iron and brass, that it is not possible you should ever get up your head, while the curse is on it; and the curse will be upon it as long as ye are under that covenant, Gal. iii. 10. The covenant in the threatening of it said, If man sin, he shall die; and so sinning he contracted the guilt of death, he came under debt to vindictive justice. The curse of the covenant says, The sinner must die, he must pay his debt to the utmost farthing, he cannot be freed from it without full payment. This you cannot do. The justice and truth of God confirm the curse of the law on the sinner, that it cannot be balked without an imputation of dishonour on them. And since it is not posssible for you to make full satisfaction, and so to exhaust the curse, no, not through the ages of eternity; it is evident, that the curse does inviolably bind the guilt of your sin on you, so that while the former remains on you, the latter is immoveable.

Now consider that ye were born sinners under this covenant, and so born under the curse of it; and that the law is most extensive, both as to parts and degrees of obedience, and so condemns everything you do, because you do nothing in the perfection which it requires. Hence your sins are innumerable, your several pieces of guilt are past reckoning, and you are every day adding to the account; but in the meantime the account never suffers any diminution. The state of a sinner under the curse is an unfathomable gulf, into which the waters are continually running, but not the least drop goes out from it again. New guilt is still added, but nothing of the old or new guilt is removed; the curse lets in more, but it lets none out; all is sealed up under the curse, from your sin in the womb, till your sin of this minute.

Ye will say, God forbid! Surely he is a merciful God. I have been troubled about my sins, and I have repented of them, and begged forgiveness, and I hope he has pardoned me; and I hope to do the same for the time to come, and he will pardon me still. Answer. Not to speak here of what repentance can be found in one lying under the curse of the first covenant, ye should take notice, that you being still under the covenant of works, God deals with you in the way of that covenant, and that covenant admits of no pardon to them who are under it, Acts xiii. 39. For a pardon under that covenant would render the threatening and curse of it vain, and of no effect; and so fasten a blot and stain on the truth and justice of God, and would indeed quite overturn that covenant, and leave it as little regarded by God himself, as it has been by the sinner. Indeed, if you can bear the curse, so as, by your suffering what it binds on you, to exhaust it, and fully satisfy justice; then your crime is expiated, and even in the way of that covenant God and you are friends again; but that is as impossible for you, as to lift the whole fabric of heaven and earth out of its place. The truth is, nothing can procure you the pardon of one sin, but what can remove the curse; while you are under that covenant, you have no saving interest in the blood of Christ, so the curse is not taken off you thereby; and certain it is, that your repentance and begging forgiveness can never remove the curse from off you, for they can never be a full satisfaction to offended justice. And therefore, notwithstanding your pretended repenting and begging pardon, your guilt still remains; there is no pardon in the case; though your guilt is forgotten by you, it is remembered of God still, and is written before him as with a pen of iron, and the point of a diamond.

(2.) Sin has a reigning power over you; and it neither is nor can be broken, you continuing under that covenant, Rom. vi. 14, where the apostle plainly teaches, that they who are under the law are under the dominion of sin. Man, innocent and holy, entered into that covenant; but once turning a sinner under it, he could never turn a saint again under it. It furnished strength to man being clean to keep himself clean, but provided no laver for him once defiled, to wash himself clean again. I know that the men of that covenant do not make, all of them, an alike black appearance in their lives and conversations; some of them bear the devil's mark on their foreheads; others have it in the hollow of their hand, which they can keep from the view of the world. But the whole of them are an unsanctified company, and under the reigning power of sin, which is in them entire and unbroken, Rom. iii. 10—12. So that I say your case is desperately sinful as to the reigning power of sin, while under that covenant; ye neither are nor can be holy under it. And think not this strange. For,

[1.] Since you are sinners under that covenant, you must needs be dead men; for so runs the threatening; Gen. ii. 17, "In the day that thou eatest thereof thou shalt die." Your natural life is yet preserved, therefore your spiritual life then must be gone, Eph. ii. 1. So all the men of that covenant are dead and buried in trespasses and sins. Death preys on their souls, and bears full sway there. Hence it is called "the law of sin and death," Rom. viii. 3, sin and death reigning over all that are under its dominion. And therefore Christ, the head of the second covenant, was made a quickening spirit, death reigning under the first.

What though you perform religious duties under this covenant? They are all but dead works, but the carcases of duties, without life and spirit. They have the matter of duty, but they are not done in a right manner; they are not from a right principle, nor are they directed to the right end; they are all selfish, slavish, and mercenary, and can never be acceptable to God.

[2.] Being under the curse, there is a separation betwixt God and your soul, and so the course of sanctifying influences is blocked up, Isa. lvii. 2. While the curse thus stands as a partition-wall of God's own making, in the course of justice, betwixt God and you, how can there be any saving communion with him? and without that how can ye be made holy? Our Lord Jesus Christ, by his death and sufferings, purchased the Spirit of sanctification for those that are his; plainly importing, that there was no access for the Spirit of sanctification to the unholy creature by the first covenant.

You may possibly find an enlargement of heart in duty under that covenant; but mistake it not for communion with God, there is no communion with him but by Jesus Christ the head of the second covenant, Eph. ii. 18. And for an evidence hereof, you shall observe, that whereas communion with God has a sanctifying and humbling efficacy where it is; these enlargements have no such effect, but on the contrary fill the heart with pride and self-esteem, and so render the soul more unholy, 1 John i. 6.

(3.) That covenant is no channel of sanctification to the unholy creature. To a sinner it is "the ministration of death," 2 Cor. iii. 7, and of "condemnation," ver. 9, a "killing letter," exacting obedience to be performed on the strength given at first, but now quite spent; but promising no new strength for duty, but laying on the curse for non-performance. It is the gospel, or covenant of grace, that is the "ministration of the Spirit," ver. 8. And for this the apostle appeals to the experience of those who have received the Spirit, Gal. iii. 2, "Received ye the Spirit by the works of the law, or by the hearing of faith?"

It is true, that under that covenant you may have been influenced to reformation of life, and prompted to the performing of duty; but all this amounts to no more in that case, but a change of life, and reaches never to a change of one's nature. Fear of punishment and hope of reward, are here the springs of all; not the love of God; and so the result of it is a form of godliness, without the power of it.

[4.] That covenant, instead of having a sanctifying influence on sinners, has an irritating power on their corruptions. The more close it comes upon their consciences, the more their lusts are provoked, as was before explained, Rom. vii. 7. I may herein appeal to sinners' experience. Have ye not sometimes found sleeping corruptions awakened by the law's forbidding of them? and weak lusts gather strength by the very sight of the hedge which the law has set betwixt you and them? And have not your hearts, on some particular occasions, finding how their inclinations were crossed by its commands, awed and frightened by its threatenings and curses, even risen against it secretly, and against the God that made it?—Thus under that covenant your case is desperately sinful.

4. Be convinced, that while ye remain under that covenant, ye remain under the curse; and there is no deliverance from the curse without deliverance from the covenant. "For as many as are of the works of the law are under the curse." It is vain to think one can be under that covenant, being a sinner, and not be under the curse; for the curse will be found to take place in the dominion of the law, wherever sin is found. So as long as ye live under the broken covenant of works, so long ye live under the curse; and if ye die under that covenant, ye die under the curse. When innocent Adam entered into that covenant, it did not curse, nor could it curse him or his, while as yet there was no command of it broken; but when once sin entered, the curse immediately took place, and seized on him and all his posterity; and under it they lie, as long as they remain under that covenant, and are not delivered from that original contract.

This is a weighty consideration, and may pierce the hearts of all who have not got their discharge as to that covenant, who have not got that hand-writing that is so much against them, blotted out with respect to them. Whatever ye do, whatever ye suffer, whatever change be in your conversation, or in the temper and disposition of your spirits, while ye remain under that covenant, the yoke of the curse remains still wreathed about your necks. And, to fasten this conviction the more on you, consider,

(1.) Ye being under that covenant were born under the curse, "by nature the children of wrath," Eph. ii. 3. Adam's sin laid all men under it; and as soon as we are Adam's children we are cursed children, bound over to death by the sentence of the broken law or covenant, Rom. v. 18. Now, there are only two ways how that curse may be supposed to be removed and taken off you, viz., either by your own bearing it for yourselves so as to bear it off, or by another's bearing it for you imputed to you; for that it should be taken off you in a way of mere mercy, without any bearing it to the satisfaction of justice, is inconsistent with God's justice, truth, and covenant, as you heard before. But the former way, it cannot be that ye are or shall be delivered from it; for whatever ye have suffered in your souls, bodies, or any other way, or whatever ye may suffer is still but the sufferings of a finite being, which can never compensate the wrong done to the honour of an infinite God by your sin; and therefore the sufferings of the damned have no end. The breach made by the creature's sin in the honour of an infinite God, is a gulf which swallows up all sufferings of the creature, but can never be thereby filled up. As to the latter, it cannot take place, but in the way of the second covenant, which is inconsistent with your continuing under this covenant. The imputation of Christ's satisfaction, and the delivery from the curse thereby are consequents of the soul's union with Christ, Rom. viii. 1, which is by one's entering into the covenant of grace, whereby they part with the covenant of works which they naturally cleave to, Rom. vii. 4. Therefore it necessarily follows, that while ye remain under the covenant of works, ye remain under the curse, the curse laid on for Adam's sin.

(2.) Suppose that curse were removed, and no curse were lying on you now for the first breach of the covenant; yet ye cannot refuse but that however watchfully you have behaved yourselves, endeavouring to keep the law you have been guilty of some sins in your own persons; you have, sometimes at least, thought evil, spoken evil, and done evil; some duties ye have omitted, some crimes against God and his law ye have committed. Now these lay you under the curse, since you are under the covenant which curseth the sinner; for it is written "Cursed is every one that continueth not in all things which are written in the book of the law to do them." It is not enough to do some things of the law; if all be not done, one is by this covenant staked down under the curse.

(3.) When you have done the best that possibly you can do to keep the commandments, ye still fall under the curse, while ye are under this covenant, because whatever good ye do, ye do it not; for perfection in every point of duty is required under it, Luke x. 27, and not only so, (for that is required under the covenant of grace too, Matth. v. ult.,) but it is required under pain of the curse; for it is written, " Cursed is every one that continueth not in all things," &c. So that if you should omit no duty, external or internal, consistent with one's continuing under that covenant, and should perform them with all the vigour, zeal, and carefulness ye are capable of; yet even for these the covenant would thunder out its curse against you, for that you fail in them in any the least measure or degree.

(4.) Forasmuch as the law requires all perfection in all things, and at all times; and that at no time, in any action, you attain to that perfection, but are still sinning in all your thoughts, words, and actions; therefore the law is still raining down its curse on you, and binding you over with new ties to death, for your new sins, cursing for every thing done amiss. Wherefore since you do nothing but what, one way or other, is done amiss in the eye of the law, it is impossible you should ever get your head lifted up from under the curse while you continue in that covenant.

(5.) *Lastly,* But put the case, though indeed it is impossible that you under this covenant could arrive at perfection, so that you should sin no more, either by omission or commission, either in the matter or in the manner of what you do; but that your obedience should be from this moment perfect in parts and degrees, and that you should obey in as great perfection as the angels do in heaven; I say that, notwithstanding, you remaining under this covenant should still remain under the curse. For it is evident that you are guilty of many sins already, and what is done by you can never be undone; and for that cause you have fallen under the curse already, and your perfect obedience for the present time and the time to come, being a debt you owe for the time wherein it is performed, can never expiate the former guilt or be reputed satisfying for the debt before contracted. Yea, suppose you had never sinned in your own persons, but had perfectly obeyed since you were capable of keeping or breaking God's law; yet being under that covenant you should still be under the curse, as being born under it, on the account of Adam's first sin, which it is plain, on the former grounds, could not be expiated by that your supposed perfect obedience.

Thus it is evident, that while ye remain under this covenant ye remain under the curse.

Say not, that, at this rate, all must be under the curse, since in many things we offend all; for the state of sinners under the two covenants is vastly different. By the first covenant, they that are under it are liable to the curse in case of sinning; but by the second covenant, they that are under it are not liable thereto in any case, but freed from it, Gal. iii. 13. Because Christ's bearing it for them is imputed to them. Sin under the former reigns unto death, but under the latter "grace reigns through righteousness unto eternal life," Rom. v. ult. In justification the obedience and satisfaction of Christ, made for all the sins of all his people, past, present, and to come, are imputed unto believers, and so they are discharged at once of their whole debt to revenging justice, and they can never more fall under the curse, nor be liable to it for their sins, more than a man can be liable in payment of a debt already paid and dis- charged. To pretend that believers may be liable to the curse, and yet not fall under the curse upon their sinning is vain; for if by the law, or threatening, they be liable to the curse in case of trans- gression; the curse must needs seize them when they do actually transgress, in virtue of the truth of God in the threatening; for hath he said it, and shall it not come to pass? Neither is it pro- fitable, in the case of the curse, to distinguish betwixt gross sins, and other sins; for the cursing law makes no such distinction in that point, but where it curseth for one sin, it curses for all, of what kind soever; Gal. iii. 10, "Cursed is every one that continueth not in all things," &c.

So this misery is peculiar to those under the covenant of works.

5. Be convinced, that there is no salvation for you under that co- venant. You must either quit it, and escape out of its dominion, or perish under it. To be saved, and yet be under the curse is in- consistent. But while ye are under that covenant, ye are under the curse; and therefore while ye are under it, ye cannot be saved, but must needs perish. Therefore, I say, if ye abide in that broken ship, ye are ruined, ye will be swallowed up, ye will never see the shore of Immanuel's land. O be convinced of this, that you may despair of ever entering into heaven by that door; that your hopes and expectations by it may die, being plucked up by the roots; and you may look out for another door of hope. Consider,

(1.) That it was the door opened to innocent Adam indeed, but by one wrong step missing it, he could never make his entry by it any more, but was fain to betake himself to another door, even Jesus Christ in the free promise, Gen. iii. 15. How then can ye expect to enter by it? he found that being once a sinner, he was able no longer to live under the dominion of the law, and therefore did be- take himself to the dominion of free grace; his garment of fig-leaves which he made for himself, he parted with as insufficient, and took on the coat of skins (of sacrifices) which the Lord God made unto him. Ye must go and do likewise, or ye perish.

(2.) Sinners being shut up for destruction under this covenant, the door was bolted with the bar of the curse, so that there is no escaping from death by it for them, Gal. iii. 10. When Samson was shut up for death in Gaza, he took the doors of the gate of the city, bar and all, upon his shoulders, and so got out of the city to the mountains, Judg. xv. But this bar of the curse is too heavy for the shoulders of angels, they are not able to bear it, far less are ye able. So there is no access to the hill of God that way for you. That gate is like unto what we read of; Ezek. xliv. 2, 3, "No man shall enter in by it : it is for the prince," the Lord Jesus Christ, the true Samson, who, when all his elect were shut up for death in the prison of the law covenant, barred with the bar of the curse, put himself in their room ; and in his might lifted up the gate, bar and all, and carried them away, and so made a way for them to escape.

Take heed you deceive not yourselves in this matter, with the promises of life you apprehend to be made to your keeping of the commandments of God. It is true, there is a promise of life to obedience in the covenant of works ; but then it is only to perfect obedience. The curse is denounced against the least failure, Luke x. 27, 28, Gal. iii. 10. Now, it is evident you can have no hope by this promise, since you cannot perform the obedience to which it is made. And there is no promise of life in that covenant on any lower condition. Sincere obedience will not entitle you to that promise, though ye could perform it, as ye really cannot; the will cannot be accepted here for the deed ; for the law denounces the curse on every one under it for the least imperfection ; and so staves them off from any benefit by its promise. The promise of life and salvation is in the covenant of grace freely made for the sake of Christ, to be received by faith in him ; and even in it godliness hath the promise of life annexed to it, but is made not to the work, but to the worker being in Christ ; and not for his work's sake, but for Christ's sake. But you being under the covenant of works, have no saving interest in the promises of the covenant of grace, and so have no part nor lot in the life and salvation there promised. And besides, all your obedience is servile and mercenary, unacceptable to God ; so far from having the promise of life, that on the contrary such workers are expressly excluded from it ; Gal. iv. 30, "Cast out the bond-woman and her son : for the son of the bond-woman shall not be heir with the son of the free-woman."

Thus ye see there is no salvation for you under the broken covenant of works.

6. Be convinced, that there is an absolute necessity of being set free from the covenant of works, of being brought into the covenant of grace, and savingly interested in the Lord Jesus, the second Adam. If you be not set free from the first covenant, ye are ruined. For as many as are under the bond of it are under the curse. To put the question to yourselves, Whether you had best quit that covenant, or not? is in effect, Whether you had best remain under the curse, or endeavour to escape? This is a point that in reason can admit no more dispute, than whether a drowning man should be willing to be preserved from perishing? or whether a man should cast burning coals out of his bosom?

If you be not brought into the covenant of grace, interested in Jesus Christ by faith, you can never be freed from the covenant of works. No man shall ever get up that bond, but on his instructing full payment both of the principal sum and of the penalty; that is, both of perfect obedience to the law, and satisfaction to justice for the breach made by sin. This you shall never be able to instruct, do or suffer what you will, unless you embrace and unite with Christ by faith in the second covenant, by means of which his obedience and satisfaction shall be counted up on your score.

Here then is the one thing needful; unless you take this course, ye shall never see life or salvation, but perish for ever.

7. *Lastly*, Be convinced, that your help must come wholly from the Lord Jesus Christ, and that you can contribute nothing by your own working for your own relief; Hos. xiii. 9, " O Israel, thou hast destroyed thyself; but in me is thy help." For being under that covenant, ye are under the curse; and what can one do for himself, acceptable to God, who is under these bonds of death? It is true, sinners will not come to Christ, till they be deeply sensible of their sin and misery; but to require such and such qualifications in sinners before they may come to Christ, is to lay a snare before them, keeping them back from Christ, and teaching them to lay some weight upon their qualifications while they are yet under the curse.

In a special manner to tell sinners that they must truly repent of their sins before they may believe in Christ, or before they may apprehend the remission of sin in the promise, is in effect to say, that they must be holy, and repent in a manner acceptable to God, while they are yet lying under his curse; for the curse is not removed but in justification. The truth is, there is a legal repentance, agreeing to the state of one under the curse, arising from a legal faith, the faith of the curse, that goes before saving faith and remission of sin; and however necessary it is to stir up the soul to prize Christ, it cannot be acceptable to God, since the man is still under his curse.

But no doing no working, no repenting of ours can please God, till once we are from under the curse, through faith in him who justifies the ungodly. And therefore, to effectuate the sinner's passing from the one covenant and its curse, into the other, and the blessing thereof, no doing, no working of ours is required, but only to receive Christ, pardon of sin, deliverance from the curse by faith, they being all offered and exhibited, in the free promise of the gospel, to the sinner under the curse. And so, the curse being removed, the partition-wall betwixt God and the sinner is taken down, and the influences of the Spirit unto sanctification, evangelical repentance, and new obedience, flow into the soul.

Use II. Of Exhortation.

First, Let unbelievers, who are still under this covenant, receive these convictions, and be warned, excited, and exhorted timely to sue to be delivered from under the covenant of works, and for that end to be instated in the covenant of grace, by faith in Jesus Christ. What need is there of further motives than the text gives, in telling us, that all under this covenant are under the curse? which has been explained at large to you. Ah! is it safe to go home and sleep another night under the curse? Is it safe to venture more time under it, when you know not which moment of your time may be the last? As ye have any regard to your own souls, lay this matter to heart, and delay no longer; but haste, escape for your life. Consider, I pray you,

1. The curse is a weight which you will never be able to bear. The weight of God's revenging wrath is in it, and it is a fearful thing to fall into the hands of the living God; on whomsoever this stone falls, it will grind him to powder.

2. It is a growing weight; as your sins grow, the curse grows; Rom. ii. 5, "After thy hardness and impenitent heart, thou treasurest up unto thyself wrath against the day of wrath." The evils thou art bound over to are the greater, and the bonds are the stronger.

3. It is a weight that may be now removed from off you; 2 Cor. vi. 2, "Behold, now is the accepted time; behold, now is the day of salvation." Those whom this weight has sunk down into the pit already, it can never be removed from off them; but ye are yet within the reach of mercy, the Mediator is ready to take the yoke off your jaws.

4. If the weight of the curse be not removed from off you, it will be the heavier that deliverance from it was in your power; Matth. xi. 21, "It shall be more tolerable for Tyre and Sidon at the day of judgment, than for you." The men of that covenant will all

feel the weight of the curse, but it will have a double weight to despisers of the gospel.

5. *Lastly*, It will be an eternal weight, Matth. xxv. 41, " Depart from me, ye cursed, into everlasting fire." There is an eternal weight of glory for the saints in the promise ; and an eternal weight of wrath for sinners in the curse, which they shall for ever lie under, and never get clear of.

Let these motives then excite and induce you to flee from the curse of the broken covenant of works, unto the covenant of grace, where life is only to be found.

Secondly, Believers in Christ, delivered from this covenant, (1.) Be thankful for your deliverance, as a deliverance from the curse. Let the warmest gratitude glow in your breasts for so great a deliverance ; and let your soul, and all that is within you, be stirred up to bless your glorious Deliverer for this unspeakable blessing. (2.) Walk holily and fruitfully in good works, since the bands of death are removed, and your souls are healed. Be holy in all manner of life and conversation ; adorning the doctrine of God your Saviour in all things. Let the whole tenor of your lives testify that you are not under the curse, but that you inherit the blessing of eternal life, by living to the praise and honour of Christ, who hath delivered you from the wrath to come. (3.) Turn not back to the broken covenant of works again, in legal principles, nor in legal practices. The more the temper and frame of your spirit lies that way, the more unholy will ye be ; and the more your duties savour of it, the less savoury will they be unto your God. It is only by being dead to the law, that ye will live unto God.

MEMORIAL

CONCERNING

PERSONAL AND FAMILY FASTING

AND

HUMILIATION.

A MEMORIAL

PERSONAL AND FAMILY FASTING.

ZECHARIAH xii. 12,

" And the land shall mourn, every family apart—their wives apart."

CHAPTER I.

OF PERSONAL AND FAMILY FASTING AND HUMILIATION IN THE GENERAL.

RELIGIOUS fasts, kept in secret, by a particular person apart by himself, and by a particular family apart by themselves, concerning which this Memorial is presented both to saints and sinners, are not indeed the stated and ordinary duties of all times, to be performed daily, or at set times recurring; such as prayer, praise, and reading of the Word are: but they are extraordinary duties of some times, and to be performed occasionally, as depending entirely, in respect of the exercise of them, on the call of providence, which is variable.

They are authorised, and enjoined us, in the Word of God; and therefore, when we shall have performed them, we must say, " we are unprofitable servants, we have done that which was our duty to do;" and must abhor the least thought of meriting thereby.

The particular seasons of them are determined by providence. Wherefore they who would be practisers of them must be religious observers of providence; otherwise God may be calling aloud for weeping and mourning, and girding with sackcloth, while they, not heeding it, are indulging themselves in joy and gladness, Isa. xxii. 12, 13 ; a dangerous adventure ! Ver. 14, " Surely this iniquity shall not be purged from you, till ye die, saith the Lord."

Hence the most serious and tender among knowing Christians, will readily be found the most frequent in these exercises. It is on the pouring out of the Spirit, that the land is to mourn, every family apart and their wives apart, Zech. xii. 10, 12. Paul was a scene wherein corrupt nature shewed her cursed vigour, he being, when he was bad, very bad ; and grace, in its turn, its sacred power, he being, when he was good, very good, and then in fastings often, 2 Cor. xi. 27.

These duties consist of an external and circumstantial part, and an internal and substantial part.

To the external and circumstantial part of them belong time, place, and abstinence.

I. First of all, a proper time must be set apart for these duties. And this is to be regulated by Christian prudence, as best suits the circumstance of the person or family.

We find the saints in scripture ordinarily kept their fasts by DAY. But we have an instance of a personal fast kept by NIGHT, 2 Sam. xii. 16, " David fasted, and went in, and lay all NIGHT upon the earth." This I do the rather notice, to obviate the excuse of those who quite neglect this duty, under the pretence of their not being masters of their own time. If the heart can be brought to it, one will readily find some time or other for it, either by day or else by night. It is recorded to the honour of one of the weaker sex, viz., Anna, that she " served God with fastings and prayers night and day." Luke ii. 36, 37.

As to the QUANTITY of time to be spent in personal or family fasting and humiliation, the duty, I judge, is to regulate it, and not it to regulate the duty. The family fast of Esther with her maidens, observed also by all the Jews in Shushan, lasted three days, Esth. iv. 16. We read of the fasting-day, Jer. xxxvi. 6. Sometimes, it would seem, it was but a part of a day, that was spent in such exercise ; as in Cornelius, his personal fast, which seems to have been over before the ninth hour, that is, before three o'clock in the afternoon ; Acts x. 30, " Four days ago I was fasting until this hour, and at the ninth hour I prayed in my house," before which time of the fourth day, Peter, to whom Cornelius saith this, might be come ; there being but thirty-six miles from Joppa to Cesarea, whither he came on the second day after he set out from Joppa, vers. 23, 24 ; compare vers. 8, 9, 17. Much about that time of the day, Daniel got the answer of his prayers, made in his personal fast, namely, about the time of the evening oblation, or the ninth hour, Dan. ix. 21. And the people being " assembled with fasting, (Neh. ix. 1,) they read in the book of the law of the Lord their God, one-fourth part of the day, and another fourth part they confessed and worshipped the Lord their God," ver. 3. So they continued in the work six hours, from nine o'clock in the morning, as it would seem, till three afternoon ; that is, from the time of the morning sacrifice, to the evening sacrifice, with which the work seems to have been closed, as, it may be presumed, they spent the morning in private preparation for the public duty.

Wherefore I judge, that none are to be solicitous as to what quantity of time, more or less, they spend in these exercises, so that the work of the time be done. Nay, I very much doubt, men lay a snare for themselves in tying themselves to a certain quantity of time in such cases. It is sufficient to resolve, that, according to our ability, we will take as much time as the work shall be found to require.

II. A proper place is also to be chosen, where the person or family may perform the duty without disturbance from others. Time and place are natural circumstances of the action; and all places are alike now, under the gospel; none more holy than another. Men may pray everywhere, whether in the house or in the field, " lifting up holy hands," 1 Tim. ii. 8. Only forasmuch as family fasting is a private duty, it requires a private place; and personal fasting a secret duty, it requires a secret place; according to the caution given us by our Saviour; Matth. vi. 18, " That thou appear not unto men to fast, but unto thy Father which is in secret."

III. Abstinence is included in the nature of the thing; abstinence from meat and drink, and all bodily pleasures whatsoever, as well as ceasing from worldly business. The Jews are taxed for finding pleasure, and exacting their labours in the day of their fast, Isa. lviii. 3. A time of religious fasting, is a time for one's " afflicting his soul," ver. 5, by denying himself even those lawful comforts and delights which he may freely use at other times. Exod. xxxiii. 4, " The people mourned, and no man did put on him his ornaments." Dan. ix. 3, " I set my face unto the Lord God, to seek by prayer, and supplications, with fasting, and sackcloth and ashes." 1 Cor. vii. 5, " Defraud ye not one the other, except it be with consent for a time, that ye may give yourselves to fasting and prayer."

The rule for abstinence from meat and drink, cannot be the same as to all; for fasting, not being a part of worship, but a means to dispose and fit us for extraordinary worshipping, is to be used only as helping thereto; but it is certain, that what measure of it would be helpful to some for that end, would be a great hindrance to others. Wherefore weakly persons, whom total abstinence would disfit and indispose for duty, are not called to fast at that rate; in their case, that saying takes place; Hos. vi. 6, " I desired mercy and not sacrifice." Yet ought they not in that case to indulge them-selves the use of meat and drink, with the same freedom as at other times; but to use a partial abstinence, altering the quantity or quality of them, or both, so as they may thereby be afflicted, as the

Scripture expresseth it, Lev. xxiii. 29. So Daniel in his mourning, Dan. x. 3, " Eat no pleasant bread, neither came flesh nor wine into his mouth."

Meanwhile, all these things are but the outward shell of these duties ; the internal and substantial part of them lies in the following spiritual exercises.

1. Serious meditation, and consideration of our ways, Hag. i. 5. Such times are to be set apart from conversing with the world, that we may the more solemnly commune with our own hearts, as to the state of matters between God and us. In them we are diligently to review our past life. " Search and try our ways."—Lam. iii. 40. And we are to search out our sins, by a sorrowful calling to remembrance the sins of our heart and life, and that as particularly as we can ; and to search into them, by a deep consideration of the evil of them, and of their aggravations, the light, love, mercies, and warnings, we have sinned against ; tracing them up to the sin of our nature, the impoisoned fountain from whence they have all proceeded. And the more fully and freely we converse with ourselves upon them, we will be the more fit to speak unto God anent them, in confession and pleading for pardon.

2. Deep humiliation of soul before the Lord ; the which was signified by the sackcloth and ashes used, under the law, on such occasions. The consideration of our ways is to be pursued, till our soul be humbled within us ; our heart rent, not with remorse for sin only, but with regret and kindly sorrow for it, as an offence to a "gracious and merciful God," Joel ii. 12, 13 ; our face filled with shame and blushing before him, in the view of our spiritual nakedness, pollution, and defilement, Ezra ix. 6 ; and we loathe ourselves as most vile in our own eyes, Ezek. xxxvi. 31 ; Job xl. 4.

3. Free and open confession of sin before God, without reserve. This is a very material part of the duty incumbent on us in religious fasting ; and the due consideration and deep humiliation just now mentioned, do natively issue in it ; producing, of course, extraordinary confession of sin, an exercise most suitable on such an occasion. Hence the Jews spent " one fourth part of the day in confessing and worshipping," Neh. ix. 3 ; and the angel, who brought the answer to Daniel's supplications about the time of the evening oblation, found him still praying and confessing his sin, Dan. ix. 20, 21. For here the sinner duly humbled has much ado, acting against himself the part of an accuser, recounting before the Lord his transgressions of the holy law, so far as he is able to reach them ; the part of an advocate opening up the particulars, in their nature, and aggravating circumstances ; and the part of a judge, justifying God

in all the evil he has brought upon him, and condemning himself as unworthy of the least of all his mercies, and deserving to perish under eternal wrath.

4. The exercise of repentance in turning from sin unto God, both in heart and life, the native result of deep humiliation and sincere confession; Joel ii. 12, "Turn ye even to me—with fasting, with weeping, and with mourning." In vain will we fast, and pretend to be humbled for our sins, and make confession of them, if our love of sin be not turned into hatred; our liking of it into loathing; and our cleaving to it, into a longing to be rid of it; with full purpose to resist the motions of it in our heart, and the outbreakings thereof in our life; and if we turn not unto God as our rightful Lord and Master, and return to our duty again. If we are indeed true penitents, we will turn from sin, not only because it is dangerous and destructive to us; but because it is offensive to God, dishonours his Son, grieves his Spirit, transgresseth his law, and defaceth his image; and we will cast away all our transgressions, not only as one would cast away a live-coal out of his bosom, for that it burns him; but as one would cast away a loathsome and filthy thing, for that it defiles him.

But withal, it is to be remembered, that the true way to deal with a hard heart, to bring it to this temper, is to believe the gospel. As ravenous fowls first fly upward, and then come down on their prey; so must we first soar aloft in believing, and then we shall come down in deep humiliation, sincere and free confession, and true repentance—Zech. xii. 10, "They shall look upon me whom they have pierced, and shall mourn." Therefore the Scripture proposeth the object of faith in the promise of grace as a motive to repentance, that by a believing application thereof the hard heart may be moved and turned; Joel ii. 13, "Turn unto the Lord your God, for he is gracious." One may otherwise toil long with it; but all in vain. "Without faith it is impossible to please God," Heb. xi. 6; and therefore impossible to reach true humiliation, right confession, and sincere repentance, which are very pleasing to him, Jer. xxxi. 18, 19, 20. The unbelieving sinner may be brought to roar under law-horror; but one will never be a kindly mourner, but under gospel influences. When guilt stares one in the face, unbelief locks up the heart, as a keen frost doth the waters; but faith in the Redeemer's blood melts it, to flow in tears of godly sorrow. Hard thoughts of God, which unbelief suggests to a soul stung with guilt, alienate that soul more and more from him; they render it like the worm, which, when one offers to tread upon it, presently contracts itself, and puts itself in the best posture of defence it can; but the believing of the proclaimed pardon touches the heart of the rebel so,

z 2

that he casts down himself at the feet of his Sovereign, willingly yielding himself to return to his duty.

5. Solemn covenanting with God, entering into, or renewing covenant with him in express words. As a fast-day is a day to "loose the bands of wickedness," so it is a day for coming explicitly into the bond of the holy covenant; Jer. l. 4, "Going and weeping, they shall go, and seek the Lord their God." Ver. 5, "Saying, come, and let us join ourselves to the Lord, in a perpetual covenant that shall not be forgotten." Accordingly, this was an eminent part of their fast-day's work, Neh. ix. 38. It follows of course, on due humiliation, confession, and the exercise of repentance, whereby the league with sin is broken. And it lies in a solemn professing before the Lord, that we take hold of his covenant, believing on the name of his Son as the Saviour of the world, and our Saviour, and that in and through him, he will be our God, and we shall be his people; and that we are from the heart content, and consent to take him for our portion, Lord and Master, and resign ourselves to him only, wholly, and for ever. Heb. viii. 10, "This is the covenant, I will be to them a God, and they shall be to me a people." Isa. xlix. 8, "I will give thee for a covenant." Chap. lvi. 6, "Every one that taketh hold of my covenant." John i. 12, "As many as received him, that believe on his name." Psalm xvi. 2, "O my soul, thou hast said unto the Lord, thou art my Lord." Isa. xliv. 5, "One shall say, I am the Lord's."

6. *Lastly*, Extraordinary prayer, in importunate addresses and petitions unto our covenanted God, for that which is the particular occasion of our fast. The confession and the covenanting are, both of them, to be done prayer-wise, as appears from Dan. ix. 4—15; Neh. ix. 6—38. But besides, there must be prayers, supplications, and petitions made for what the person or family hath particularly in view in their fast; Psalm xxxv. 13, "When they were sick, my clothing was sackcloth; I humbled my soul with fasting, and my prayer returned into mine own bosom." And, indeed, the great end and design for which such fasts are to be kept, is, that thereby the parties may be the more stirred up unto, and fitted for wrestling with God in prayer, anent the case which they have particularly at heart. So the Ninevites having their threatened overthrow at heart, it was ordered, that "man and beast" should be "covered with sackcloth, and cry mightily unto God."—Jon. iii. 8; that is, that the men should cry in prayer for pity and sparing; and to the end they might be moved to the greater fervency in these their praying cries, it is provided, that they and their beasts too should be covered with sackcloth; and that their beasts, having fodder and water withheld

from them on that occasion, should be made to cry for hunger and thirst, even to cry unto God, namely, interpretatively, as the "young ravens cry unto him."—Job xxxviii. 41. At which rate, the cries of the beasts, being mixed with the cries of men, would make the solemnity of that extraordinary mourning very great; and the hearts of men being, every now and then during that solemnity, pierced with the cries of the harmless brutes, would be stirred up to a more earnest, fervent, and importunate pleading with God for mercy.

Thus far of *personal*, and *family fasting* and *humiliation* in the general.

CHAPTER II.

OF PERSONAL FASTING AND HUMILIATION IN PARTICULAR.

FROM what is said, it appears, that a PERSONAL fast is a religious exercise, wherein a particular person, having set apart some time from his ordinary business in the world, spends it in some secret place by himself, in acts of devotion tending to his humiliation and reformation, and particularly in prayer, with fasting. Concerning the which we shall consider, 1*st*, The divine warrant for it. 2*d*, The call to it; and, 3*d*, Offer advice how to manage it.

SECTION I.—OF THE DIVINE WARRANT FOR PERSONAL FASTING AND HUMILIATION.

FORASMUCH as will-worship is condemned by the Word, and that can never be obedience to God, whereof his revealed will is not the reason and rule, it concerneth all who would perform this duty in faith, so as to have accepted it of him, to know who hath required it at their hands. And to set that matter in a light sufficient to satisfy and bind it upon the conscience, as a duty owing unto God, let these few things following be duly weighed :—

1. God requires it in his Word, and that both directly and indirectly.

It is directly required; James iv. 9, "Be afflicted and mourn, and weep." It is plain enough from the context, these things are proposed as agreeing to particular persons in their personal capacity. See ver. 8, 10. And what it is that is required of them in these words, could not miss to be as plain to those unto whom they were originally directed; to wit, that it is fasting and humiliation that was intended by them. For this epistle was written to those who were Jews by nation, "the twelve tribes scattered abroad," chap. i. 1. And this is the very language of the Old Testament in that case, the same manner of expression, in which their prophets called them to it. Lev. xxiii. 27.—"On the tenth day of this sventh month, there shall be a day of atonement, and ye shall afflict your souls," to wit, " with fasting." Isa. lviii. 5, " Is it such a fast that I have chosen? a day for a man to afflict his soul?" Or, more agreeable to the original, " Shall a fast I will choose, a day of men's afflicting their soul, be like this?" Joel ii. 12.—" Turn ye even to me,— with fasting, and with weeping, and with mourning." And the *mourning* required in these texts, differs from the *weeping*, as the habit and gestures of mourners differ from their *tears ;* Gen. xxxvii. 34; Eccl. iii. 4, directly pointing unto the duty of fasting and humiliation.

It is also required indirectly in the word, which supposeth it to be a duty the saints will practise, inasmuch as divine directions are given anent it. Now, it is inconsistent with the holiness of God, to give directions for regulating of will-worship, which he doth simply condemn, Matth. xv. 9; Col. ii. 23; Jer. vii. 31. But our Saviour gives directions about personal fasting; Matth. vi. 16, " When ye fast, be not as the hypocrites, of a sad countenance; for they disfigure their faces, that they may appear unto men to fast. Verily I say unto you, they have their reward." Ver. 17, " But thou, when thou fastest, anoint thy head, and wash thy face :" Ver. 18, " That thou appear not unto men to fast, but unto thy Father which is in secret; and thy Father which seeth in secret shall reward thee openly." And it is evident, that these directions do concern secret and personal fasting; for, besides that the text speaks expressly of that which is done in secret, and, therefore, is to be kept secret, contrary to the practice of the hypocritical Pharisees, who made it their business to publish their secret devotions, the outward signs of fasting are commended in the case of public fasts, Exod. xxxiii. 4; Jonah iii. 8; Joel ii. 15—17. In like manner the apostle Paul gives a direction about this duty. 1 Cor. vii. 5, " Defraud ye not one the other, except it be with consent for a time, that ye may give yourselves to fasting and prayer ;" where the consent mentioned as necessary, determines the fasting to be personal; forasmuch as, in the case of public fasts, that matter is predetermined by a superior authority; and in the case of family fasts, it follows of course, on the appointment of such a fast.

2. It is promised that the saints shall perform this duty; Zech. xii. 10, " I will pour upon the house of David, and upon the inhabitants of Jerusalem, the spirit of grace and supplications." Ver. 12, " And the land shall mourn, every family apart,—and their wives apart." Thus, in virtue of the grace of the covenant, this duty is made the matter of a promise, even as other duties of holy obedience are. Accordingly our Lord promised it, in the case of his disciples

in particular, Matth. ix. 15, "The days will come when the Bridegroom shall be taken from them, and then shall they fast;" to wit, personally; for it was not the neglect of the public fast appointed and stated in the law, Lev. xxiii. 27—32, that they were taxed for, but the neglect of personal fasting, used by the disciples of John, upon the occasion of their Master, the friend of the Bridegroom, his being taken from them; and also by the Pharisees, out of their superstitious and vain-glorious disposition, Matth. ix. 14, with Luke xviii. 12.

3. It is recommended unto us by the practice of the saints mentioned in Scripture. It was, as we have already seen, practised by David, a man " according to God's own heart." 2 Sam. xii. 16; Psalm xxxv. 13. By Daniel, a man greatly beloved. Dan. ix. 3. and x. 2, 3; and by the devout centurion, Acts x. 30. It was a frequent exercise of Paul, the laborious apostle of the Gentiles, 2 Cor. xi. 27. These all had the seal of God's good pleasure with their work set upon it, in the communion with God allowed them therein. And it is our duty to go forth by the footsteps of the flock, following their approved example.

4. *Lastly*, That occasional religious fasting and humiliation is a duty required in the word of God, and to be performed by societies in a public capacity, will not, I presume, be questioned. Now, upon that ground, the duty of personal fasting and humiliation may be thus evinced.

1st, There is nothing in the nature of religious fasting and humiliation, that of itself is public, or necessarily requiring a plurality of persons to join therein. The preaching of the word, and celebration of the sacraments, do, in their own nature, require society, and therefore are not to be used by a single person alone in his closet. But it is not so in this case. One may keep a fast alone, as well as he may pray, read the scriptures, and sing psalms, alone. Now, whatever ordinances God hath appointed, and hath not tied to societies or assemblies, nor to any certain set of men, they are the duty of every one in particular, who is capable to perform them.

2dly, The ground upon which the duty of fasting and humiliation is bound on societies, in a public capacity, takes place in the case of particular persons, namely, that extraordinary duties are called for on extraordinary emergents and occasions. If then a church or congregation is called to fasting and humiliation, on such occasions in their case; is not a particular person called to the same, on such occasions in his case? If abounding sin, or judgments threatened or inflicted on a land, require solemn public fasting and humiliation; do not the same things, in the case of a particular person, call for personal fasting and humiliation? Surely every one ought to keep his own vineyard with the same diligence the public vineyard is to be kept; if one does not so, it will be bitterness in the end, Cant. i. 6.

3dly, Extraordinary duties to be performed by a whole nation, church, or congregation, cannot be soon overtaken, because all great bodies are slow in their motions, and sometimes the season may be over, ere they can move thereto in a public capacity; yea, and ofttimes God is calling aloud, by his providence, for national and congregational fasting and humiliation, when the call is not heeded by them, on whom it is incumbent to appoint them. Now, what should particular persons, discerning the call of providence, do in such cases? Must they sit still, and not answer the call as they may, because they cannot answer it as they would? Should they not rather keep personal and family fasts, for those causes for which others either cannot or will not keep public fasts? as in the case of God's pleading with the land of Egypt, "He that feared the word of the Lord amongst the servants of Pharaoh, made his servants and his cattle flee into the houses," Exod. ix. 20. When the Jews are dispersed, some of them in one country, some in another, how shall the land mourn? Must they wait until they be gathered together? No; but the land shall mourn, families apart, and particular persons apart; even as when our neighbour's house is on fire, we do not tarry until the whole town or neighbourhood be gathered; but immediately fall to work ourselves, to do what lies in our power for quenching the flames.

And thus much shall suffice to have spoken of the "divine warrant" for this extraordinary duty.

SECTION II.—OF A PROVIDENTIAL CALL TO PERSONAL FASTING AND HUMILIATION.

THE case of the church, the case of a neighbour, and one's own private case, may each of them separately, and much more all of them conjunctly, found a providential call to personal fasting and humiliation. The prophet Danial kept a personal fast on the church's account, Dan. ix. 2, 3. David on his neighbour's account, Psalm xxxv. 13, and on his own, 2 Sam. xii. 16.

Zion's children should reckon her interest theirs; and as secret personal fasting for public causes, argues a truly public spirit; so it is highly commendable, and being rightly managed, is very acceptable in the sight of God, Dan. ix. 20, 21.

The communion of saints is an article of our creed, and a most beneficial thing in the practice thereof. Considered only in these two parts of it, namely, a communion of burdens, Gal. vi. 2, and a communion of prayers, James v. 16, it is one of the best cordials the

travellers towards Zion have by the way. For one to love his neighbour as himself, whereof secret fasting on his account is a good evidence, is more than all whole burnt-offerings and sacrifices, Mark
xii. 33. And whether it do good to his neighbour or not, it will not
fail, if rightly managed, to return with a plentiful reward into his
own bosom, according to the Psalmist's experience, Psalm xxxv. 13.

Howbeit, it is hardly to be expected that one will be brought to
the practice of this duty on the account of others, till once he has
been engaged therein upon his own account. But surely, if professors of religion were more exercised about their own spiritual
case, this duty of personal fasting and humiliation would not be so
rare as it is. Paul, who had much of this kind of exercise, Acts
xxiv. 16, was "in fastings often," 2 Cor. xi. 27; "kept under his
body, and brought it into subjection," 1 Cor. ix. 27.

Now, any or all of these cases call for this extraordinary duty, in
three kinds of events, other circumstances agreeing, and pointing
thereto in the conduct of providence.

Either, 1, When there is any special evil actually lying upon us,
the church, or our neighbour in whom we have a special concern;
whether it be a sinful or a penal evil. There are some sins that
leave such guilt on the conscience, and such a defilement on the
heart and life, as call aloud for fasting and humiliation, in order to
a recovery from the dismal effects thereof, Jam. iv. 8, " Cleanse your
hands ye sinners, and purify your hearts ye double-minded." Ver.
9, " Be afflicted, and mourn, and weep." Accordingly the Israelites
gathered to Mispeh, being sensible of the abominable idolatries they
had fallen into, " fasted that day, and said, We have sinned against
the Lord," 1 Sam. vii. 6.

In like manner, when the tokens of God's high displeasure are
gone out in afflicting providences, it is time for us to roll ourselves
in the dust; and so to accommodate our spirit and way to the dispensation, humbling ourselves before him with fasting. Thus Nehemiah found himself called to fasting, upon information received of
the continued ruins of Jerusalem, and the affliction that the returned
captives were in, Neh. i. 3, 4; David, and those with him, upon the
news of the defeat of Israel, and the death of Saul and Jonathan, 2
Sam. i. 12; and the people, upon the consideration of the slaughter
which the Benjamites had made among them, Judges xx. 26.

Or, 2, When there is any special stroke threatened and impend-
ing. Thus the inhabitants of Jerusalem, being in imminent danger
from their enemies, were providentially called to weeping and
mourning, though they heeded it not, Isa. xxii. 12, 13. But the
Ninevites took such an alarm, and complied with the call of provi-

dence, Jon. iii. 4—9. So did David, when God struck his child with sickness, 2 Sam. xii. 15, 16. Yea, and so did even Ahaz, when he had heard Elijah's heavy message against him and his house, 1 Kings xxi. 27. When the lion roars, it becomes us to fear ; when God's hand is lifted up, and he appears to be about to strike, it is high time for us to strip ourselves of our ornaments, and to lie in sackcloth and ashes.

Or else, 3, When there is some special mercy and favour to be desired of the Lord ; as was the return of the Babylonish captivity, for which Daniel kept his fast, Dan. ix. 1—3. Christians exercised into godliness, will rarely, if ever, want their particular suits, and special errands unto the throne of grace. The same God, who makes some mercies fall into the lap of others, without their being at much pains about them, will give his own children many an errand unto himself for them, ere they obtain them, because they must have them in the way of the covenant; whereas they come to others only in the way of common providence, in which a blasting curse may come along with the mercy.

To set this matter in yet a clearer light, we shall exemplify these general heads, in one's own private case ; and that in several instances, to be accommodate to the case of the Church, and of our neighbour, by those who are disposed religiously to observe and consider the dispensations of providence. There is a variety of these particular cases, which, with agreeing circumstances to be discerned by each one for himself, call for personal fasting and humiliation. As,

1. When, through a long track of sinning and careless walking, the case of one's soul is left quite in disorder and confusion ; Isa. xxxii. 11, "Tremble ye women that are at ease ; be troubled ye careless ones ; strip ye and make ye bare, and gird sackcloth upon your loins." Certainly the voice of God unto such is, "Thus saith the Lord of Hosts, Consider your ways," Hag. i. 5. Want of consideration ruins many. They deal with their souls, as some foolish men do with their estates, running on without consideration, till they have run themselves aground. But those who adventure so to take a time for sinning, have need to take also a set time for mourning ; for it is not to be expected, that accounts which have been long running on, can be cleared and adjusted with a glance of one's eye. O careless sinner, consider how matters stand betwixt God and you ; are you in any tolerable case for the other world, for death and eternity ? are not matters gone quite to wreck with your soul ? are you not pining away in your iniquity ? is not the state and condition of your soul like that of the sluggard's vineyard, that " was

all grown over with thorns, and nettles had covered the face thereof, and the stone wall thereof was broken down ?" Prov. xxiv. 31. O set about personal fasting and humiliation. Ordinary pains will not serve to recover the long neglected garden ; it must be trenched, digged deep. A little may help the case, that is timely seen to ; but all this will be little enough for thine, which hath lain so long neglected.

2. When one is under convictions, entertaining some thoughts to reform. On such an occasion was that fast kept, Neh. ix. 1, 2, and had very good effects, ver. 38, chap. x. 1, 28, 29. This method is, in such a case, a proper means to bring men to a point in the matter, and to fix their resolutions, otherwise ready to prove abortive. Some have convictions, which, at times, coming and passing away, like a stitch in one's side, set them now and then, to their prayers ; but never prevail to bring them to a settled course of reformation of life ; their disease is too inveterate to be so easily carried off. But were they so wise as to make these convictions a matter of solemn seriousness, setting some time apart on that occasion for personal fasting and humiliation, they might, through the divine blessing, turn to a good account for the interest of their souls.

3. When the conscience is defiled with the guilt of some atrocious sin. Doth national guilt of that kind require national fasting ? and doth not personal guilt of the same kind, require personal fasting ? Yea, sure, God calls men, in that case, to be afflicted, and mourn, and weep, James iv. 8, 9. Strong diseases require strong remedies ; and conscience-wasting guilt, deep humiliation ; as in David's case, Psalm li., and Peter's, Matth. xxvi. 75. This kind of guilt, deeply wounding and stinging the soul, defiling and wasting the conscience, may be without any scandalous enormities of life, appearing to the view of the world. God is witness to secret sins, even to the sins of the heart ; and men of tender consciences will be sick at the heart with such sins as are hid from all the world, and will never move others.

4. When one would fain get over a snare he is often caught in, and have victory over a lust that hath often mastered him. There are not a few who have many good things about them, yet lack ONE thing ; and that one thing is like to part between heaven and them ; marring all their good things, both by way of evidence and of efficacy, Mark x. 21. They know that it is wrong ; they often resolve to amend ; and they would fain get above it ; but whenever a new temptation comes, Satan attacking them on the weak side, down go all their resolutions, like a bowing high wall, whose breaking cometh suddenly in an instant ; and they are hard and fast in the snare

again. O consider, that this kind goeth not out but by prayer and fasting, Matth. xvii. 21. Set therefore some time apart for personal fasting and humiliation, on the account of that very thing, that you may wrestle with God in prayer anent it, and use this method time after time, until you prevail against it ; else that one thing may ruin you ; and you will be condemned for it, not because you could not help it, but because you would not use the means appointed of God for relief in that case.

5. When one is under a dead desertion ; in which case the Lord is departed, the wonted influences from heaven are withheld, but the wound not smarting by reason of spiritual deadness, the party is not much moved therewith. This was the case of the spouse, Cant. iii. 1, " By night on my bed I sought him whom my soul loveth ; I sought him, but I found him not." And for a recovery from it, she made some extraordinary efforts in the way of duty, vers. 2—4. The same appears to be the case of many, with whom some time a-day it was better than now. God hides his face from them; their incomes from-heaven are rare and scanty, in comparison of what they have formerly been ; they are sighing and going backward. Though they go the round of ordinary religious exercises still, yet it is long since they had a token from the Beloved, access to or communion with God in them. O fast and pray for a recovery, as did Israel, when, after they had been long deserted, and very little affected with it, they began at length to lament after the Lord, 1 Sam. vii. 2, 6. It requires much, in the way of' ordinary means, for to go to the ground of such a case, wherein by much slothfulness the building hath decayed, and through idleness of the hands the house droppeth through. Though true grace can never be totally lost, yet it may be brought to such a very low pass, that as some scholars, for retrieving the loss sustained through long absence from the school, must begin anew again ; so some Christians, in order to their recovery, must be carried through the several steps of conversion again, as we may learn from our Saviour's words to Peter, with relation to his fall ; Luke xxii. 32, " I have prayed for thee, that thy faith fail not ; and when thou art converted, strengthen thy brethren."

6. When one is under a felt and smarting desertion ; Isa. xlix. 14, " Zion said, The Lord hath forsaken me, and my Lord hath forgotten me." This is a more hopeful case than the former ; howbeit it goes to the quick ; Prov. xviii. 14, " The spirit of a man will sustain his infirmity ; but a wounded spirit who can bear ?" There are many bitter ingredients in it, which make it a sorrowful case, exquisitely painful to the soul, like that of a woman " forsaken and

grieved in spirit, and a wife of youth—" Isa. liv. 6. To one thus deserted, wrath appears in the face of God, and impressed on every dispensation, Psalm lxxxviii. 7, 8. To his sense and feeling, his " prayer is shut out," Lam. iii. 8 ; and flashes of hell come into his soul," Psalm lxxxviii. 15, 16. Under the pressure hereof, some very grave and solid persons have not been able to contain themselves ; Job xxx. 28, " I went mourning without the sun : I stood up ,and I cried in the congregation." This smarting desertion, in greater or lesser measure, has often been the fearful outgoing from the dead desertion, as it was in the experience of the spouse, Cant. v. 3—7. And it is a loud call to personal fasting and humiliation, Matt. ix. 15, " When the Bridegroom shall be taken from them, then shall they fast."

7. When one is pressed with some outward affliction, whether in his body, relations, name, substance, or otherwise. In such a case, " Job rent his mantle, and shaved his head, and fell down upon the ground, and worshipped," Job i. 20 ; and David's " knees were weak through fasting," Psalm cix. 24. A time of affliction is a special season for fasting and prayer. The Lord often lays affliction on his people on purpose to awaken them to their duty, and as it were to necessitate them to it ; even as Absalom, who having in vain sent once and again for Joab, obliged him at length to come unto him, by causing set his corn field on fire. This is the way to get affliction sanctified, and in due time removed ; Jam. iv. 10, " Humble yourselves in the sight of the Lord, and he shall lift you up." We ought therefore to take heed, that we be not of those who cry not when he bindeth them ; but that in this case we do as Benhadad's servants, who upon a signal defeat of his army, " put sackcloth on their loins, and ropes on their heads, and went out" as humble supplicants " to the king of Israel," who had smote them, 1 Kings xx. 31.

8. When, by the aspect of providence, one is threatened with some such affliction. It is an ungracious hardness, not to be affected when the Lord is lifting up his hand against us. He was a man of an excellent spirit, who said, " My flesh trembleth for fear of thee, and I am afraid of thy judgments," Psalm cxix. 120. Though he was an hero that feared the face of no man, he laid aside that bravery of spirit when he had to do with his God. Wherefore, when the Lord was threatening the removal of a child of his by death, though the continuing of that child in life would have been a lasting memorial of his reproach, yet the impression of the Lord's anger on that threatening dispensation moved him to betake himself to personal fasting and humiliation before the Lord, for the life of that child, 2 Sam. xii. 16, 22.

9. When one would have light and direction in some particular matter of special weight. It is much to be lamented, that men professing the belief of a divine providence in human affairs, should, in confidence of their own wisdom, take the weight of their matters on themselves, without acknowledging God in them; aiming only to please themselves therein, and not their God, as if their fancy, conveniency, or advantage, and not their conscience, were concerned in their determinations and resolves. Hence it is, that wise men are often left to signal blunders in conduct, and feel marks of God's indignation justly impressed on their rash determinations. Thus Joshua and the princes of Israel, in the matter of the league with the Gibeonites, finding no need of the exercise of their faith, but of their wit, vainly imagining they could see well enough with their own eyes, "took of their victuals, and asked not counsel at the mouth of the Lord," and were egregiously overreached by them, as they saw afterward, when it was too late, Josh. ix. 14, 22.

We have a divine command and promise, extending to our temporal, as well as to our spiritual concerns; and very suitable to the necessary dependence we have on God in all things, as creatures on their Creator; Prov. iii. 5, "Lean not unto thine own understanding. Ver. 6, "In all thy ways acknowledge him, and he shall direct thy paths." We ought therefore, in all our matters, to eye him as our director; and steer our whole course, as he directs by his word and providence. Since he hath said, "I will teach thee in the way which thou shalt go : I will guide thee with mine eye," Psalm xxxii. 8, it is unquestionably our duty to "set the Lord always before us," Psalm xvi. 8; to regulate our acting, and ceasing from action, by the divine direction ; even as the Israelites in the wilderness removed and rested, just as the pillar of cloud and fire removed or rested before them, Num. ix. 15—23.

Sometimes, indeed, an affair may be in such a situation, as allows not an opportunity of making an address unto God, for light in it, by solemn prayer ; but we are never so circumstanced, but we have access to lift up our eyes to the holy oracle, in a devout ejaculation ; as Nehemiah did in such a situation, Neh. ii. 4, 5. And there is a promise relative to that case which has been often verified, in the comfortable experience of the saints taking that method to obtain the divine direction; Prov. iv. 12, " When thou runnest thou shalt not stumble." But Christians should accustom themselves to lay their matters before the Lord, in solemn prayer, for light and direction therein, as far as circumstances do permit. So did Abraham's pious servant, with the affair his master had committed to him, Gen. xxiv. 12—14. And accordingly he had a pleasurable experience of the accomplishment of the promise relative to that case, Prov. iv. 12, " When thou goest, thy steps shall not be straitened." And where they are to be determined in a matter of special weight, such as the change of their lot, the choice of an employment, some momentous undertaking, or any the like occurrences in life, whereof serious Christians will find not a few, allowing them time and opportunity to deliberate on them; that is a special occasion for extraordinary prayer with fasting, for light from the Lord, the Father of lights, to discover what is their duty therein, and what he is calling them too in the matter. So the captives returning from Babylon with Ezra, kept a fast at the river Ahava, " to seek of God a right way," Ezra viii. 21.

10. When duty being cleared in a matter of special weight, it comes to the setting to ; in which event, one needs the presence of God with him therein, the divine blessing upon it, and success in it. Thus Esther being to go in unto the king, to make request for her people, there was solemn fasting, on that occasion, used by her and the Jews in Shushan, Esth. iv. 8, 16. And Barnabas and Saul being called of God unto a special work, were not sent away to it, but after fasting and prayer, Acts xiii. 2, 3. We need not only light from the Lord to discover unto us our duty in particular cases, but that being obtained, we need also his presence to go along with us in the thing, that we may be enabled rightly to make our way, which he bids us go. Therefore said Moses, Exod. xxxiii. 15, " If thy presence go not with me, carry us not up hence." Sin hath defiled every thing to us ; and however promising any worldly state, condition, or thing whatsoever, may appear in our eyes, yet if we have not the presence of God in it, and his blessing upon it, to purify it unto us, we will be mired in it, and find a snare and a trap, if not a curse therein to us.

11. When one, having some unordinary difficulty to encounter, is in hazard of being ensnared either into sin or danger. On such an occasion was the fore-mentioned fast at Shushan kept; Esther jeoparding her life, in " going in unto the king in the inner court," not called by him, Esth. iv. 11, 16. The ship has need to be well ballasted, that sails while the wind blows high ; and in a difficult and ensnaring time, there is need of fasting and prayer for Heaven's safe-conduct through it. Men's trusting to themselves in such a case, cannot miss of betraying them into snares.

12. *Lastly,* When one hath in view some special solemn approach unto God ; in which case a special preparation is requisite. Thus Jacob called his family to such preparation, in the exercise of repentance, in order to their appearing before the Lord at Bethel,

Gen. xxxv, 2, 3. The Israelites were called to the same, in order to the awful solemnity of the giving of the law on Mount Sinai, Exod. xix. 10, 11, 15. And it is observable, that, whereas the feast of tabernacles was the most joyful of all the feasts the Jews had throughout the year, a solemn fast was appointed of God to be observed always before it, four free days only intervening, Lev. xxiii. 27, 34. For in the method of grace, none stand so fair for a lifting up, as those who are most deeply humbled, Isa. xl. 4; Luke xviii. 14; Jam iv. 10. Wherefore it is a laudable practice of our church, that congregations keep a congregational fast, before the celebration of the feast of the sacrament of the Lord's supper among them, in order to their preparation for a solemn approach unto God in that holy ordinance. And, for the same reason, secret fasting by particular persons apart, and private fasting by families apart, especially such as have not access to join in the public fast, would be very seasonable on such an occasion. And if those secret and private fasts could more generally obtain, and get place in congregations, some little time before the communion work did begin, it would be a token for good, and might prove like the noise and shaking among the dry bones, that ushered in the breathing on the slain, and the causing them to stand "up upon their feet," Ezek. xxxvii. 7, 10.

These things duly considered, each Christian may be in case to judge for himself, when it is that he is under a providential call to personal fasting and humiliation.

SECTION III.—DIRECTIONS ANENT PERSONAL FASTING AND HUMILIATION.

Having seen the divine warrant for personal fasting and humiliation, and considered the nature of a providential call to that extraordinary duty, it remains to offer some advices or directions for the profitable managing of it in practice.

DIRECTION I. When you find that the Lord is calling you to this duty, prudently make choice of a fit time and place for it aforehand, wherein you may have access to go about it without distraction. And carefully dispose of your ordinary affairs before that time, so as you may have no let nor hindrance from that part which you can prevent. Works of necessity and mercy which are lawfully done on the Lord's day, are much more so in this case, wherein the duty waits not on the time, but the time on the duty. Yea, in case something of worldly business which you could not foresee nor prevent, do fall out in time of your fast, and cannot be deferred or put off without some notable inconveniency, you may, without scruple, dispatch it; for the time is not holy. But in that case, labour that, if possible, your work be not thereby marred; and carefully keep up your frame of spirit for the duty you are engaged in. But Christian prudence to weigh circumstances, for which you are to look up unto the Lord, is necessary to determine herein, according to the general rules of the word, Matth. xii. 3—7.

As for such as are not masters of their time, which is the case of servants, they cannot lawfully dispose of their time at their own hand even for this duty; for our God "hates robbery for burnt offering," Isa. lxi. 8. But then they may endeavour to procure the necessary time at the hand of their masters, to whom, if they be godly and serious, they may modestly hint their design, pitching on a time with so much discretion, as that their good may not be evil spoken of. And if any be so unmindful of their Master which is in heaven, as to refuse such a discreet desire, yet let not the party by any means think, that the sacred nature of the thing he has in view gives him a power to rob his master of so much of his time; for men can offer nothing to God with a good conscience but what is their own, and exercises of devotion are so far from slacking the tie of moral duty to our neighbour that they are nothing but an outward form of devotion, unacceptable to God, so far as they do not influence the party to a careful and religious observance of the duties of morality, such as judgment or justice, mercy, and faith, or faithfulness, Matth. xxiii. 23. Neither yet let him imagine, on the other hand, that he is then no further concerned to look after that extraordinary duty; for no reason can be assigned why one ought not to be willing to be at as much pains or expense for procuring to himself an opportunity of communion with God in that duty, as he will be for an opportunity of attending some worldly business of his own, placing another in his room. But if none of these can effectuate it, then, though the day or time of labouring is the master's, yet the night or time of resting is the servant's; let him give unto God what he has, and it shall be accepted through Christ. But, excepting the case of a providential necessity obliging one to take the night for this exercise, the day is, generally speaking, the most proper time for it, beginning the exercise in the morning.

DIRECTION II. Make some preparation for it the night before, turning your thoughts towards the exercise you have in view, considering of it, and avoiding every thing that hath a tendency to disfit or indispose for it. Shun carnal mirth and sensual delights; sup sparingly; to eat the more, that one is to fast religiously after, is to mock God and cheat one's self. In the intervals of sleep, take heed that your thoughts be not vain, and much more that they be not vile; but that they be such as tend to fit you for the extraordinary duty in view.

DIRECTION III. Rise early in the morning, even sooner than ordinary, unless by reason of bodily weakness that would tend to disfit you for the work; for then you are called, in a special manner, to watch unto prayer, Eph. vi. 18. Sleep is a fleshly comfort, which, howbeit it is necessary, yet one is in this case called to be sparing of. Therefore the priests were bid " lie all night in sackcloth," Joel i. 13; and it is recorded of Ahab, that he in his fast lay so, 1 Kings xxi. 27. A proper means to make one sleep sparingly.

DIRECTION IV. As soon as you awake in the morning, let holy thoughts, with a view to your work, immediately have access into your heart, and beware that carnal or worldly thoughts get not the start of them; for if you allow that, they will be to your soul like water poured upon firewood, that makes it hard to kindle. Surely, if one is at any time to follow the example of the Psalmist David, Psalm cxxxix. 18, " When I awake, I am still with thee," he is to do it at such a time.

DIRECTION V. Let your ordinary duties of prayer and reading of the word, be first of all performed; for extraordinary duties are not to justle out the ordinary, but to be superadded unto them. And in such prayer, beg of God grace to enable you for the work before you, according to his promise. Yea, it may be very expedient, that thereafter you go unto God again by prayer, particularly and purposely for his grace to enable you unto the duty now come to the setting to. And forasmuch as our corrupt hearts are, upon a near view, of a difficult and laborious holy exercise, very apt to wax faint, and our hands to hang down, albeit, the way of the Lord is declared to be " strength to the upright," Prov. x. 29; do you therefore, by all means, study to exercise faith, and labour to believe stedfastly, that his grace shall be sufficient for you, therefore, by all means study to exercise faith, and labour to believe stedfastly, that his grace shall be sufficient for you, to the making of " his yoke easy, and his burden light" unto you, 2 Cor. xii. 9, with Mat. xi. 30. For no man shall ever be able to perform a duty acceptably unto God, without a believing persuasion, in greater or lesser measure, of an allowance made him of grace sufficient for an acceptable performance of it, 2 Cor. iii. 4, 5, Philip. ii. 12, 13. One will otherwise be but a wicked and slothful servant, as our Saviour teacheth, Matth. xxv. 24—26.

DIRECTION VI. After prayer in faith, for the aid of divine grace, as in the preceding direction, begin the work with a solemn review of your sins, in deep meditation, and serious communing with your own heart thereupon; applying yourself to think of them, in such manner as you think of your affairs, when considering how to manage them in cases of difficulty. GOD calls for this at your hand. Hag. i. 5, "Thus saith the Lord of Hosts, consider your ways." Lam. iii. 40, "Let us search and try our ways, and turn again to the Lord." It is recommended to us by the practice of the saints; Psalm lxxvii. 6, "I commune with mine own heart, and my spirit made diligent search;" and cxix. 59, " I thought on my ways, and turned my feet unto thy testimonies." The nature of a religious fast requires it; for how can the deep humiliation therein to be aimed at, be otherwise obtained? or what way else can one be fitted to make a confession suitable to such an occasion? It is observable, that in the fast mentioned, Neh. ix., the "reading of the law" went before the making of the confession, ver. 3. So the first work was to set the looking-glass before their eyes, that therein every one might see his foul face. And the direction given to fallen Israel, in order to a recovery; Hos. xiv. 2, "Take with you words, and say," &c., doth plainly bear, that there should, in that case, be solemn serious thinking before solemn prayer.

Now, to assist you in the practice of this part of your work, the following advices are offered :—

First, Read some pertinent passage of holy scripture, and that with application, as reading your own heart and life therein. Such are those passages, which contain discoveries and confession of sin, as Isa. lix; or lists of sins, or of several sorts of sinners, as Rom. i. 29—32, 2 Cor.; vi. 9, 10, Gal. v. 19—21, 2 Tim. iii. 1—5, Rev. xxi. 8. Particularly, I recommend for this purpose, Ezra ix., Neh. ix., Dan. ix. Of these, or other scriptures of the like nature, you may read such as you shall judge meet.

Secondly, It will be expedient and useful, in this case, to read also the Larger Catechism on the ten commands, in the answers to the questions, "What is required?" and, "What is forbidden?" and especially the latter. For by reading thereof with application to yourself, you will find out your guiltiness in many points, which perhaps would not otherwise come into your mind.

Thirdly, This done, apply yourself to think of your sins, in order to your getting a broad and humbling view of your sinful and wretched case. And for your help herein, I suggest to you these things following :—

1. You may compose yourself, what way you find, by experience, to be best for keeping the mind fixed. It is a piece of Christian prudence in this case, to dispose of every thing so as you may the more readily reach that end, and block up the avenues by which

impertinent thoughts may make their entrance. As, (1.) Because the eyes often betray the heart, through a variety of objects, which present themselves to one's view in the light; if you are in a house you may darken it by stopping the light; if in the fields, you may lie down on your face, and close your eyes. (2.) If you can by no means keep your heart at simple thinking, you may speak to yourself with a low voice, that words may help to fix the mind unto the thing. These are only prudential advices, which they that need may use, they that need not may let alone.

2. It will be very profitable to observe some method and order in thinking of your sins. A confused and indeterminate manner of thinking of our sins, doth, in several respects, fall short of an orderly thought about them. It is true, when the Spirit of the Lord is carrying on a special work of conviction in the heart of a sinner, the man's sins will of course be readily laid to hand, and " set in order before his eyes," Psalm 1. 21. But it is another case, where one is searching out his sins, with an ordinary assistance of the Spirit; herein these do not duly consult their own interest, who refuse the help of method in the search.

And there is a twofold method or order, which may be helpful to you therein; to wit, the order of the time of life, and the order of the ten commandments. Both these are natural, and easy to the meanest capacity.

Thinking on your sins in the order of the time of your life, you will thereby get a general view of your own sinfulness, and that throughout your whole life. And in this method,

1st, You are to consider the sin of your nature. You are to look " unto the rock whence ye are hewn, and to the hole of the pit whence ye are digged," Isa. li. 1. Think what a sinful lump thou wast in thy conception and birth, " shapen in iniquity and conceived in sin," Psalm li. 5; how thou camest into the world, with cords of guilt wreathed about thy neck, binding thee over to wrath under the curse; stripped naked of original righteousness; thy whole nature corrupted, being the very reverse of the holy nature of God; thy soul in all its faculties quite perverted, ready to discover with the first occasion, its wrong set, namely, a propensity to evil, and an aversion to good; and thy body in all its members sinful flesh. In consideration whereof thou mayest well say, with admiration of the divine patience, " O why did the knees prevent me ! Or why the breasts that I should suck !"

2dly, Then turn your thoughts to the sins of your childhood. Soloman in his penitentials tells us, that childhood and youth are vanity, Eccl. xi. 10. Truly, the sins of that early period of our life, are not to be remembered to be laughed at, but mourned over; and so they will be by true penitents; for they are the early sproutings and buds of corrupt nature, that might have been fatal to us, ere we had gone further; behold how in that period thou hast "spoken and done evil things as thou couldst." It is likely that many of these things are forgotten; but yet you may still search out as many of them as may be matter of deep humiliation to you before the Lord. There may be sins of childhood, that will make a bleeding wound, in a gracious heart, on every remembrance thereof, even unto the dying day.

3*dly*, Then take a view of the sins of your youth. Job got a moving view of his, when he was come to a good age; Job xiii. 26, "Thou writest bitter things against me, and makest me to possess the iniquities of my youth." David's heart bleeds at the remembrance of his crying unto God, "remember not the sins of my youth," Psalm xxv. 7. Youth is vain, rash, and inconsiderate; and therefore a dangerous period of life, precipitating some into such steps as make them to halt all their life after, proving fatal to many, and laying up matter of repentance to all. And if the follies of it be not timely repented of, and mourned over, by the sinner, they "shall lie down with him in the dust," Job xx. 11; and present themselves again in full tale, when "for all these God will bring him into judgment," Eccl. xi. 9. Therefore do you take a mournful view of them, and judge yourselves in time.

4*thly*, If you are come to middle age, proceed to the searching out of the sins of that period of your life. In it you cannot miss of matter of deep humiliation; "for man at his best estate is altogether vanity," Psalm xxxix. 5. Every period of life is attended with its proper snares and temptations. And he who, right or wrong, hath made his way through those of youth, doth but enter into a new throng of temptations of another kind, while he enters on the next stage of life; in the which men often, ere they are aware, "pierce themselves through with many sorrows," lose themselves in a cloud of cares and business, and, "troubled about many things," forget the "one thing needful."

Lastly, If you are advanced into old age, go forward and view your sins in that period. Whatever infirmities do attend it, the sins of it must be searched out, and repented of too; for it will not excuse a man, before an holy God, that he is an aged sinner. The corruption of nature, the longer it hath kept its ground, is the more hateful, and will be the more humbling to a gracious soul.

Thus you will have your whole life before you in parcels. And that you may, with the greater distinctness, review any period thereof which you have fully passed, or of which you have passed a great part; you may distinguish the same into lesser periods, according to the more notable events, turns, or changes that were in it, and review them separately; as, for instance, the time before you went to school, by itself; the time of your being at it, by itself; and so in other cases.

But for a more full and particular view of your sins, do you proceed in the order of the ten commandments. The holy law, considered in its spirituality and vast extent, is the proper means for sound conviction; it is the sinner's looking-glass whereby to discern the vast multitude of his spots and defilements, in order to his humiliation. Rom. viii. 7, "I had not known sin, but by the law; for I had not known lust except the law had said, Thou shalt not covet." Wherefore by no means neglect, in this review, to go through the ten commandments; and pause upon every one of them, considering the duties required therein, and wherein you have been guilty by omission of them; and the sins forbidden therein, and wherein you have been guilty by commission of them; guilty in both kinds, in thought, word, and deed. This would be a proper means to shew you the multitude of your transgressions.

But to proceed in both the one and the other order jointly, namely, by reviewing each period of your life separately, in the order of the ten commandments, would, through the divine blessing, be of the most singular use for reaching the most humbling view of your whole life.

Thus far of the second thing suggested for your help to think of your sins, in order to a humbling view of your case. And for your further help therein.

3. Be sure that in a special manner you set before your eyes the signal miscarriages of your life, those sins that have wounded your conscience deepest. I doubt there are but few, if any, of a tender conscience, who see not some such blots in their escutcheon; some remarkable trespasses in heart or life, that are ready to gall them on every remembrance; though perhaps known unto none but God and themselves. Good Eli had such a blot on him pointed out to him under the name of "The iniquity which he knoweth," 1 Sam. iii. 13. And the best of the saints mentioned in Scripture had something of that nature to humble them. Now, as ever you would be duly humbled in your exercise of personal fasting, let these, in your review of your sins, be brought forth by headmark, and set before you in the sight of a holy God; and that, although they be freely pardoned unto you long ago; for the view of these is most likely to affect you; and pardoned sins, inasmuch as they are pardoned, are humbling in

the remembrance of them, Luke vii. 37—47; as Paul's pardoned blasphemy and persecution were to him, 1 Tim. i. 13.

4. In thinking on your sins, take along with you the aggravations of them. Represent to yourself the infinite majesty of God, against whom you have sinned; and as ever you would be duly humbled, entertain high and elevated thoughts of the Lord our lawgiver. This will make you to say with David, Psalm li. 4, "Against thee, thee only have I sinned, aud done this evil in thy sight;" understanding by your own experience what he meant thereby. In your meditation, set God's way of dealing with you, all along from your very birth, over against your way of dealing with him; so shall conviction be brought home on your conscience with a peculiar edge; while considering the mercies he hath heaped on you, the light and warnings he hath afforded you, your guilt will appear of a deepest dye.

5. Having thus seen your extreme sinfulness, consider, in the next place, the just demerit of your sin, even God's wrath and curse, both in this life and that which is to come. "For because of these things cometh the wrath of God upon the children of disobedience," Eph. v. 6. The law is a looking-glass, for sinners, not only in its commands, but also in its threatenings and curse; shewing unto all their cursed state by nature; to unbelievers, what they are actually lying under for their sins, and to believers what theirs do deserve. And, therefore, after you have, as before directed, gone through all the ten commandments, for your conviction and humiliation, do you, for your farther humiliation, set your eyes upon the threatenings and curse of that holy law as a covenant of works; and see therein your just deserving, so as that God may be justified when he speaketh against you, and "clear when he judgeth," Psalm li. 4. And think with thyself, how thou shouldst, without peradventure, eternally perish under his wrath, if he should proceed against thee according to the law and justice; as he hath actually proceeded against many for those very sins wherewith thou art chargeable.

6. In this view of your sins, endeavour all along that your eye may affect your heart. In vain will you rake into that dunghill, if suitable affections or emotions of heart be not thereby excited in you. And these suitable affections are, (1.) Hatred, detestation, and abhorrence of sin, Psalm cxix. 128; Rom. xii. 9. Wherefore, pull the mask from off it, remove the paint and varnish that have been laid over it, that you may see it in its native deformity; and look on it until your stomach turn on the sometimes sweet morsel. (2.) Grief and sorrow of heart for it, Psalm xxxviii. 18. Let your heart be rent, in consideration of the offence thereby given to a gracious

God, its contrariety to his holy nature and will, its dishonouring of his Son, who gave himself a sacrifice for sin, and grieving of his Spirit who sanctifies us. (3.) Holy shame upon the account of it, Jer. xxxi. 19. Behold it as a filthy thing, the very reverse of the beauty of holiness, the holiness of God expressed in his law; and be confounded at the sight. Behold it as a base requital of divine favours, and blush before him. (4.) Self-loathing, Ezek. xxxvi. 31. Pursue the thought of the filthiness of your sin, till you loathe yourself in your own sight, as rendered unclean all over, by abominations of heart and life. (5.) A longing to be rid of sin, the guilt, defilement, prevailing, and indwelling of it. Dwell on the thought of your sinfulness, till your heart, pained and burdened therewith, groan out longing desires of deliverance, as Rom. vii. 24, "O wretched man that I am who shall deliver me from the body of this death!" Who will draw this dagger out of my bowels! this sting out of my conscience! this poison out of my flesh! who will take this load off my back!

All this would be no more than necessary humiliation. For it would be the lot of every sinner either in time or in eternity, to be like the fish that is boiled in the water, which it sometime a day swimmed in. But "blessed are ye that weep now," Luke vi. 21. "Wo unto you that laugh now, for ye shall mourn and weep," ver. 25.

Lastly, It will be very necessary that the whole of this work be mixed with devout ejaculations. For be sure Satan will be at your right hand, to resist you, and to mar your work; your heart will be ready to misgive you in it, to stop, and turn aside; therefore press forward in it, lifting your eyes every now and then to the Lord for help.

With this review of your own sins, let a view of the public sins of the church and land wherein you live, be joined; using the same helps, as in your own particular case, which need not be here repeated.

And in relation to this, I subjoin only three advices.

1. Begin always with your own sins, even though the principle cause of your fast be the state of the church or land. This has been the manner of the saints; Isa. vi. 6, "Then said I, Wo is me! for I am undone, because I am a man of unclean lips, and I dwell in the midst of a people of unclean lips." Dan. ix. 20, "And whilst I was speaking and praying, and confessing my sin, and the sin of my people Israel." The reason hereof is manifest; for one will never be duly humbled for the sins of others, who is not, in the first place, so humbled for his own.

2. Represent public sins to yourself, under such notions as may tend to excite suitable affections and emotions of heart in you. Look on them as they are dishonouring to our gracious God, wounding or ruining to the souls of men, disgraceful to our holy Christian profession, and provoking God to wrath against the land. Hate and loathe them, be ashamed of them, and mourn over them, on these accounts; and long for the day of purging them away.

3. See your own sinful part in them, by all means. Bring them home to your own conscience before the Lord; search out, and see what of the guilt thereof you are, either directly or indirectly chargeable with, in his sight; and be deeply humbled for the same.

Thus far of the review of sin.

DIRECTION VII. After this review of your sins made, go unto God by prayer, and make confession of them. And here, confession is to be the chief part of your prayer; yea, and if the whole of it almost be confession, it will not be amiss. Certainly extraordinary confession of sin is a great part of the work of a religious fast.— Neh. ix. 3; Dan. ix. 20. And the solemn review, in which one's sins are so particularly searched out, natively issues therein.

For the more profitable management of this confession of sin, the following advices are offered :—

1. Take no thought of your voice, farther than to keep it from being unseasonably high. For the voice, in itself, is nothing before the heart-searching God, who regards not the sound of men's throats, but of their heart and affections. "The true worshippers shall worship the Father in spirit and in truth; for the Father seeketh such to worship him," John iv. 23. But sometimes there is a deceit in the voice, to the beguiling of the soul; as it fared with Ezekiel's hearers, "with the mouth shewing much love," Ezek. xxxiii. 31. And one, by an indiscreet management of it, may be fruitlessly weakened; and unfitted for continuing at the work so as need may require. The affections are the best rulers of the voice.

2. Endeavour to bring along into your confession, and carry along, those affections and emotions of heart, of which before; namely, hatred and detestation of sin, godly sorrow, holy shame, self-loathing, and longing to be rid of sin, Psalm xxxviii. 18, "I will declare mine iniquity; I will be sorry for my sin." When the leper was to cry "unclean, unclean," his clothes were to be rent, his head bare, and there was to be a covering upon his upper lip; Lev. xiii. 45. A confessing tongue requires a broken heart, a spirit really weighted with a sense of sin. And the marble, that sweats in foul weather, but yet is never a whit the softer, shall be an emblem of one confessing his sin with a hale heart. Yet let none sensible of the

hardness of their heart, be thereby made to stand aloof from confession, saying, Who will roll away the stone! Let them go forward, and essay it: let them confess their hardness of heart, and unfitness to make confession; for so they may find the stone rolled away to their hand.

3. Be as full as you can in your confession; laying all your spiritual sores before the Lord, so far as you know them. One wound concealed from the physician may prove fatal to the patient; and one sin industriously passed over in confession, may prove fatal to the sinner; "for he that covereth his sins shall not prosper," Prov xxviii. 13. David was aware of this; Psalm xxxii. 5, "I acknowledged my sin unto thee, and mine iniquity have I not hid." It fared ill with Ananias and Sapphira, for that in another case, they lied unto God, and kept back a part, Acts v. And he is no true penitent, that desires to hide any sweet morsel under his tongue, and is not willing to take shame to himself for every known sin.

4. Be very particular in your confession, opening out your spiritual sores before the Lord; Psalm li. 4, "I have done this evil in thy sight;" Joshua vii. 20, "I have sinned; and thus, and thus, have I done." To confess the several kinds of your sin, in general, without descending to particulars, is too superficial work on such an occasion. The particular abominations of *your* heart and life are raised up in meditation, to be laid before the Lord in humble confession. I suppose you to be at this work in a secret place, where you may freely utter before him, what it would not be proper you should say in the hearing of others. No doubt, a great deal of freedom may be used in secret prayer, in narrating of thoughts and actions, with the designation of time, place, and persons, so as may tend to one's deeper humiliation, which would not be to edification in social prayer.

Now, in order to your being the more full and particular in your confession, I would recommend the same method and order to be observed therein, as in the review of your sins. I believe that, so doing, you will find the advantage of it. Go orderly through the several periods of your life, and through all the ten commandments, making your confession; where also you may take in the confession of public sins, always so as may best tend to the further humiliation of yourself. In a special manner, be very particular as to the signal miscarriages of your life, and aggravate your guilt, acknowledging the aggravating circumstances thereof. And unto the confession of your known sins, against all the ten commandments, add a humble acknowledgement of a large void and blank to be left for your unknown sins against every one of them; which you can by no means fill up, but the all-knowing God can: "for who can understand his errors?" Psalm xix. 12. And, considering the commands of the perfect law, as binding you to embrace the Gospel, confess your atrocious guilt in sinning against the remedy of sin, therein revealed, offered, and exhibited unto you.

5. It will be profitable, that, all along through your confession, you approve of the law, as holy, just, and good, Rom. vii. 12. For as black doth best appear when set by white, so sin appears most clearly in its native hue, exceeding sinful, when set over against the pure, holy, just, and good commandment. As, for example, when you are to confess your sins against the first commandment, you may say to this purpose:—"Lord, thou commandest me, saying, 'Thou shalt have no other *gods* before me.' I acknowledge this thy command is most just and reasonable in itself, and most good for me. It was thou alone who made me, thou alone hast preserved me. I never needed another god besides thee, and none but thou couldst ever do the part of a God to me.—Thou didst magnify thy rich grace, in condescending to be, in Christ, a God to me, a most wretched creature. Nevertheless, over the belly of this law of love, my duty, and my interest, I have had many other gods before thee: I have set up my cursed self in thy room and stead—made the vain world my god," &c. And so in other cases.

6. *Lastly*, Let your confession be closed with self-condemning, self-emptying, and a look of faith.

1*st*, Condemn yourself, as did the returning prodigal; Luke xv. 18, "Father, I have sinned against heaven, and before thee." Ver. 19, "And am no more worthy to be called thy son." As you looked to the commandments before, and confessed your sin, so look now to the threatenings and curse of the law, and confess your just deserving. Read there your deserved doom, and pass sentence against yourself. Nothing is more natural than that now you call yourself fool and beast, for that you have followed the wild-fire of your corrupt inclinations, to the miring of yourself thus in sin and guilt; and have broken over the hedge, where now you find the serpent biting you. And here,

(1.) Confess you deserve no good, but all evil, in time. If the cause of your fast be some evil you are at present smarting under, acknowledge God to be just, very just in it. If it is some stroke threatened, and hanging over your head, confess that you well deserve that it should fall on you in its full weight. If it is light that you want, confess you deserve to be left in darkness; or whatever be the mercy you come to make supplication for, acknowledge from the heart that you have forfeited it. Surely, in case your uncircumcised heart be humbled, you will accept of the punishment of your iniquity, Lev. xxvi. 41. And then if your sin has found you out, you will own the procedure against you to be righteous and holy; if your broken bones smart, you will say it is just; if the Lord has turned his former smiles into frowns, mixed your comforts with gall and wormwood, souring them so as to set your teeth on edge, blasted your enjoyments, and squeezed the sap out of them, you will, after confession of sin, say from your very heart, My folly makes it so.

(2.) Confess ye deserve eternally to perish, and that "it is of the Lord's mercies you are not consumed," Lam. iii. 22; that God might in justice wrap you up in the filthy garments of your sin, and cast you out of his sight, into the lake burning with fire and brimstone, as the fittest place for such a sinful lump. Acknowledge yourself to be, in yourself, a wretched creature, justly under the curse and condemnatory sentence of the law, having nothing to say for yourself at the bar of justice, why it may not be fully executed against you, a self-condemned, as well as a law-condemned sinner, Psalm li. 4. Whatever your state be in the sight of God, it is altogether just, that your libel against yourself be not concluded without this.

2dly, Be emptied of yourself, in a humble and hearty acknowledgment of utter inability to help yourself. Having taken a view of the load of sin lying upon you, and laid before the Lord the particulars of your burden, with the sinking weight thereof, acknowledge that it is quite beyond your power to move it from off you. Say from the heart, "Lord, here is a load of guilt lying upon me, which by no doing or suffering of mine can be moved; here is a mighty power of sin I am no more able to grapple with, than a child with a giant; a dead weight I can no more remove, than I can remove a mountain. If thou leave me under it, as justly thou mayest, I perish."

This is true humiliation, where the poor broken sinner lies at the Lord's feet, sensible that he is bound with ten thousand cords of guilt, but unable to loose the weakest of them; that his soul is preyed upon, and like to be devoured by a swarm of living lusts, yet unable to kill or shake off any of them. If we are duly humbled, our humiliation will be carried thus far; for it is the ruin of many, that they see not the absolute need of the blood of Christ for removing of their guilt; and far less the absolute need of his spirit, for breaking of the power of sin in them.

Lastly, Let there be a look of faith out of the low dungeon. Look unto God in Christ, and say, "God be merciful to me a sinner," Luke xviii. 13. And "turn thou me and I shall be turned," Jer. xxxi. 18. Tell him, that, since, according to his holy gospel, there is yet hope in Israel concerning this thing, you must and will take the benefit of the Gospel proclamation of grace and mercy, and lay hold on the horns of the altar; and, therefore, though your weight be heavier than mountains of brass, you do, with humble confidence, at the Father's bidding, lay it wholly over on the blood of his Son the Lord Jesus Christ, trusting thereon allenarly for remission of sin, sanctification, and complete salvation.

Now, as to the two directions last mentioned, I mean not, that what is proposed in either of them must needs be done all at once, without intermission. You may use them, as you are best able to reach them. It is not very likely that those who spent one-fourth of the day in confessing and worshipping, Neh. ix. 3, did make but one confession continued without intermission; so you may make such intermissions in either or both of them as you find necessary. Christian prudence must direct in the matter, to use the means, so as may best conduce to the end.

DIRECTION VIII. After confession of sin, apply yourself to the duty of personal covenanting, explicit entering into, or renewing covenant with God, by taking hold of God's covenant of grace in express words. That this is a necessary part of the work of a personal fast, may be gathered from Jer. l. 4, and Neh. ix. 38, both cited before. And it is clear from the nature of the thing; for to what purpose shall men lay open their wounds before the Physician of souls, if they mind not to put themselves in his hand for cure, in the way of the covenant? or how can they pretend to mourn for sin, if they are not to enter on the way of reformation? A time of personal fasting is a time for the runaway to return to his duty, and to set matters right again, that were put wrong by turning aside from God and his way. And one unwilling to enter into covenant with God, cannot be sincere in his confession of sin, and mourning over it, whatever he may pretend.

For the right managing of this duty of personal covenanting, these three following advices are offered :—

1. See that you understand, and rightly take up the covenant, the covenant of grace, together with the way and manner of a sinner's personal entering into it, and being inflated in it unto salvation; the which are to be learned from the Holy Scripture alone, as being revealed in it only. Mistakes and misapprehensions of these things, may be of very bad consequences in the practice of this duty, for which cause men ought earnestly to pray, that God would, by his own word and Spirit, shew them his covenant, according to the promise, Psalm xxv. 14.

According to the Scripture, the covenant, namely, the covenant of grace for life and salvation, is not left unto you to make, in whole nor in part, by proposing and condescending on terms thereof, as a party contractor; it is made already, completely made and concluded in all the articles thereof, whether conditionary or promissory; and that between God the party contractor on heaven's side, and Christ as Mediator and second Adam, the party contractor on lost man's side. And it is registered in the sacred records, the Holy Scripture. And you are invited into the fellowship of it; Psalm lxxxix. 3, "I have made a covenant with my chosen,—David my servant." 1 Cor. xv. 45, "The last Adam." 1 John i. 3, "That which we have seen and heard, declare we unto you, that ye may also have fellowship with us; and truly our fellowship is with the Father, and with his Son Jesus Christ."

The condition of it is Christ's fulfilling all righteousness in the name of his spiritual seed. Matth. iii. 15, "Thus it becometh us to fulfil all righteousness." This righteousness was stated from the broken covenant of works; and that in three things, namely, perfect holiness of nature, righteousness of life, and satisfaction for sin; all which Christ did fulfil, in his being born perfectly holy, living perfectly righteous, and making complete satisfaction by his death and sufferings. And thus the condition of the covenant, on which is founded the right and claim to the promises of it, is fulfilled already to your hand.

The promise of it, respecting lost sinners, is the promise of eternal life in its full latitude, comprehending all things necessary to make a sinner holy and happy; that God in Christ will be their God, and they shall be his people, Tit. i. 2, "In hope of eternal life, which God, that cannot lie, promised before the world began." Heb, viii. 10, "This is the covenant;—I will be to them a God, and they shall be to me a people." And it is begun to be fulfilled to all who have taken hold of the covenant, and is ready to be fulfilled unto all who shall yet take hold thereof.

This covenant is the plan laid by infinite wisdom for the salvation of lost sinners; upon which they may safely venture themselves, for time and eternity, as upon a bottom infallibly sure, Isa. lv. 3, "I will make an everlasting covenant with you, (Heb.—I will cut to you an everlasting covenant,) even the sure mercies of David; 1 Cor. i. 23, 24, "We preach Christ—Christ the power of God and the wisdom of God." It is heaven's device for repairing the loss we sustained by Adam's fall, whereby we become unholy and miserable, lying in ignorance which we could not cure, under guilt and the curse which we could not remove, and under bondage to sin and Satan, which we could not break;" ver. 30, "But of him are ye in Christ

Jesus, who God is made unto us wisdom, and righteousness, and sanctificatien, and redemption."

The great design of is it to exalt the free grace of God in the salvation of sinners; to shew therein the exceeding riches of his grace to them, in Christ. It is a plan laid for cutting off all ground of boasting from the creature; to make Christ all, and the creature nothing in its own salvation, as being indebted to free grace for the whole thereof. Eph. i. 6, "To the praise of the glory of his grace;" Chap. ii. 7, "That he might show the exceeding riches of his grace, in his kindness towards us, through Christ Jesus;" ver. 9, "Not fo works, lest any man should boast." It is much like unto a contract of marriage, devised and drawn by a wealthy and wise physician, of his own proper motion alone, between himself and a poor woman drowned in debt, weak and witless, and withal overrun with loathsome sores, rendering her incapable to do anything, whether for her own relief, or for his service; and this upon a design to have her wholly indebted to him for her relief, the payment of her debt, the management of her person, and her recovery for action of business.

This covenant is offered and exhibited to you in the gospel, as really as that contract drawn and signed by the physican, would be offered and exhibited to the woman, if he should come and present it to her, for her acceptance; Rom. x. 6, "Say not in thine heart, who shall ascend into heaven? (that is, to bring Christ down from above);" ver. 7, "Or who shall descend into the deep? (that is, to bring up Christ again from the dead,") ver. 8, "But what saith it? the word is nigh thee, even in thy mouth, and in thy heart; that is the word of faith which we preach." So that the righteousness of Christ, to wit, the holiness of nature wherewith he was born, and which he retained unspotted till death, the righteousness of his life, and his satisfaction.made by his sufferings, is in that word freely offered and exhibited to you, as the fulfilled condition of the covenant, being therein revealed unto faith, Rom. i. 17, (Gr.;) as also, the promise of eternal life, as the promise of the covenant to be fulfilled, being therein left you, Heb. iv. 1.

Hence it appears, that the duty of personal covenanting is much mistaken and mismanaged, where the party apprehending that God, in the word, declares himself willing to be his God, upon certain terms, to be by him performed, different from accepting God's full and free covenant of promise, does accordingly make a covenant with God, solemnly taking him for his God upon these terms; promising and vowing, that if God will be his God, pardon his sins, be at peace with him, and save his soul, he will, for his part, be one of his people, and faithfully serve him all the days of his life, watching against all known sin, and performing every known duty. This is just as if the woman, in the case before put, should tell him who offers her the contract, that she is content to take him for her husband, upon certain terms, particularly, that if he will be her husband, and do the duty of a husband to her, she will, for her part, be a faithful wife to him, all the days of her life, doing all that she is able to do for paying off her debt, managing herself and his household to the best of her skill, and taking all pains on her sores, to make her lovely in his eyes; the which being quite contrary to the design and end of that unusual kind of contract, which is to have the wife wholly indebted to the husband for all, doth alter the nature of the proposal, and would quite mar the surprising match, which was in a fair way to be carried on.

But like as in that case nothing remains for the woman to do, to entitle her to the benefit of the contract, but believing it to be a real and serious, not a ludicrous deed, to sign her acceptance; which signing with the hand is necessary, because her belief of the reality of the offered contract, and trusting to it accordingly, being inward acts of the soul, cannot be known among men, but by a proper external sign; even so all that remains for you, to instate you savingly in God's covenant of grace, offered and exhibited to you in the gospel, is to take hold of it, Isa. lvi. 4.

And to the end that, in your aiming to take hold of the covenant, you may not be at a loss, fearing that you may miss any part or parts thereof, lying scattered through the blessed Bible; know that Jesus Christ, the second Adam, head of the covenant, is by his father "given for a covenant" to you, Isa. xlix. 8. So that you have the whole covenant in him; and you take hold of it, by taking hold of him offered and exhibited to you in the free promise of the gospel.

And this is done by faith, or believing on his name, according to John i. 12, "As many as received him, to them gave he power to become the sons of God, even to them that believe on his name." Wherefore, by believing on the name of Christ, we take hold of the covenant, and are instated in it unto salvation. And God hath made believing to be the means of instating sinners personally and savingly in the covenant, in consonancy with the great design and end thereof, declared in the word, and of which before; Rom. iv. 16, "Therefore it is of faith, that it might be by grace." Rom. iii. 27, "Where is boasting then? It is excluded. By what law? of works? Nay; but by the law of faith."

Now to believe on the name of Christ, is to believe or credit the free promise of the gospel, with application to yourself, and accordingly to trust on him as the Saviour of the world and your Saviour, in whom God will be your God, and you shall be one of his people, unto your salvation from sin and from wrath. Mark i. 15, "Believe the gospel." Gal. iii. 2, "The hearing of faith." 1 Thess. i. 5, "Our gospel came not unto you in word only, but also in power, and in the Holy Ghost, and in much assurance." 1 Cor. ii. 4, "In demonstration of the Spirit, and of power;" ver. 5, "That your faith should stand—in the power of God." And Acts xvi. 31, "Believe on the Lord Jesus Christ, and thou shalt be saved." Psalm xxxvii. 40, "He shall save them, because they trust in him." Psalm ii. 12, "Blessed are all they that put their trust in him." Acts xv. 11, "We believe, that through the grace of the Lord Jesus Christ we shall be saved." This believing, or crediting the word, and trusting on the person of Christ, is that which of all things is farthest removed from the nature of a work, according to the scripture use of that word; and, therefore, is the most agreeable means of saving entrance into that covenant, which is of faith, that it might be by grace; not of works, lest any man should boast.

A sinner being by this believing on Christ united to him as the head of the covenant, is thereby personally entered into the covenant; so as, in his right, to have a saving interest in the condition, promise, and privileges thereof, unto his eternal salvation; even as becoming, through natural generation, children of Adam, the head of the covenant of works, we are personally entered into that covenant; so as to be involved in the guilt of the breach of it, and laid under the curse thereof; Rom. v. 19, "For as by one man's disobedience many were made sinners; so by the obedience of one shall many be made righteous." John x. 9, "I am the door; by me if any man enter in, he shall be saved." Eph. iii. 17, "That Christ may dwell in your hearts by faith."

Upon this believing on the name of Christ, crediting and trusting in manner said before, do necessarily follow, an absolute consent to take him for our husband, head, and Lord, and God in him for our God; and unconditional resignation of ourselves unto him, soul and body, to be his only, wholly, and for ever; with an illimited renunciation of all others for him; even as in the case before put, upon the woman's believing the reality of the offer of the contract of marriage between the physician and her, and accordingly, that he will indeed be her husband, follows her consenting to take him for her husband, head, and lord, giving up herself unto him, and renouncing all other for him, absolutely, unconditionally, without limitation or reservation; the which she can never do, till once she believe that. And thus to the word of grace, the covenant offered and

exhibited in the gospel, " I will be to them a God, and they shall be
to me a people," the believing soul answereth, as an echo, " My beloved is mine, and I am his," Cant. ii. 16.

2. Having understood the covenant aright, together with the way
and manner of being personally and savingly entered into it, examine yourselves anent it impartially, as ever you would make sure
work in this weighty matter. Inquire into your sense of your need
of the covenant, your belief of it, and the disposition of your heart
towards it. And upon these heads, pose yourself with these or the
like questions :—

" In the *first* place, O my soul, do I verily believe that I was
lost, ruined, and undone in Adam, by his breaking of the covenant
of works; and that I have ruined myself more and more, by my actual transgressions ? Do I believe, that I am by nature wholly corrupt and sinful, averse to good, prone to evil, and justly laid under
the curse, binding me over to the revenging wrath of God for time
and eternity ? Am I convinced that I am utterly unable to help
myself, in whole or in part, out of this gulf of sin and misery into
which I am plunged ; and that I must needs perish under the guilt,
dominion, and pollution of my sin, without being justified or sanctified, for ever, if I be not relieved by heaven's own hand ?

" *Next*, O my soul, do I believe that there is a covenant of
grace, for the relief of lost sinners, established between God the
Father, and his Son Jesus Christ, as second Adam, wherein, upon
condition of Christ's fulfilling all righteousness, as a public person, is promised eternal life to them, that God in Christ will be
their God, and they shall be his people ? Do I believe, that this is
the plan and device of heaven, for life and salvation to lost sinners, for making them holy, and for making them happy ? Do I
believe, that Jesus Christ hath, by his holy birth, righteous life, sa-
tisfactory death and sufferings, performed that condition of the covenant, and thereby purchased and secured the benefit therein promised for poor sinners ? Then, do I indeed believe, that this covenant already fulfilled in its condition, and certainly to be fulfilled in
its promise, is in Christ crucified, really offered and exhibited to me
in the gospel ; and that I am called to the fellowship of it in him ?
And then, do I verily believe on the name of Christ crucified, offered
and exhibited to me, as the great High Priest, who, by the sacrifice
of himself, hath made the atonement, paid the ransom, and brought
in everlasting righteousness for poor sinners ? That is to say, (1.)
Can I credit his word of grace to me, that he with his righteousness
will be mine, and in him, God will be my God, and I shall be one
of his people ? (2.) And can I, as on a safe bottom, trust on him as

my Saviour, that in him it shall be so unto me, to my eternal life and salvation, to the making of me holy and happy?

"*Finally*, O my soul, how do I like the covenant? Am I pleased with the frame of it, whereby Christ was from eternity appointed, not only the Priest of the covenant, to fulfil the condition of it, but also the Prophet and the King thereof, to administer it? And can I find in my heart to acquiesce in that device for salvation, as all my salvation, and all my desire, for making me holy and happy? Am I content to take Christ the Son of God, for my only Priest, Surety, Intercessor, and Redeemer; and in him, the Father, for my Father, and the Holy Ghost for my Sanctifier; God in Christ for my God? Am I willing wholly to resign myself, soul and body, to him, to be saved by his blood alone, renouncing all confidence in my own righteousness, doings, and sufferings? Am I content to take him for my Head and Husband? Particularly, am I content to take him for my alone Prophet, Oracle, and Guide; to resign and give up myself wholly to him, to be taught, guided, and directed in all things, by his Word and Spirit; renouncing mine own wisdom, and the wisdom of this world? Am I content to take him for my alone King and Lord; to resign myself wholly, soul and body, unto him, to be rescued by his power from sin, death, the devil, and this present evil world, for to serve him for ever, and to be ruled by the will of his command, as to my duty, and the will of his providence, as to my lot? And am I heartily content to part with, and renounce every known sin, and particularly that which most easily besets me, together with my own foolish will, and all other lords besides him, without reservation, and without exception, against his cross? And am I really, as in his sight, willing to have discovered unto me, and upon discovery to part with every sin in me, that I know not!"

Now, howbeit all doubting as to such of these points, as are points of faith, and every the least degree of aversion to the consenting, resignation, and renunciation, is sin before the Lord, and needs to be purged away by the Redeemer's blood; yet they ought not to stop your proceeding, unless they be predominant over your belief and willingness in the matter; Mark ix. 24, "Lord, I believe: help thou mine unbelief;" Gal. v. 17, "The flesh lusteth against the Spirit;—so that ye cannot do the things that ye would," namely, in that perfection that ye fain would do them. But, indeed, if they be predominant, keeping your mind and heart quite unsettled, and wavering like a wave of the sea, that hath nothing to fix it; one cannot advise proceeding in that case; for that would be to lie unto the Lord, with a witness; James i. 6, "For he that wavereth is like a wave of the sea, driven with the wind and tossed." Ver. 7, "For let not that man think that he shall receive anything of the Lord." Howbeit, a sincere belief and willingness in these points, may, indeed waver like a ship at anchor, which is still held fast in the place, notwithstanding of all its wavering therein. And one may take hold of God's covenant of grace unto salvation, even with a trembling hand.

3. *Lastly*, Having, in your self-examination, satisfied your con- science as to these points, go unto God by prayer, and therein so- lemnly and in express words take hold of the covenant. The which may be done in words to this purpose :—

" O LORD, the God and Father of our Lord Jesus Christ, I confess I am by nature a lost sinner, wholly corrupted, and laid under the curse, in Adam, through the breach of the covenant of works; and have ruined myself more and more by my actual transgressions in- numerable. I am convinced, and do acknowledge, that I am ut- terly unable to help myself in whole or in part, out of this gulf of sin and misery into which I am plunged; and that it is beyond the reach of the whole creation to help me out of it; so that I must in- evitably perish for ever, if thine own strong hand do not make help to me.

"But forasmuch as there is a covenant of grace for life and sal- vation to lost sinners, established between THEE and thine own SON, the Lord Jesus Christ, as second Adam, wherein, upon condition of his fulfilling all righteousness, which is now performed in his having been born perfectly holy, lived altogether righteously, and made perfect satisfaction to justice by his death and sufferings, thou hast promised, that thou wilt be their God, and they shall be thy people, to the making of them holy and happy for ever; and that this co- venant is in CHRIST the head thereof, offered and exhibited to me in thy gospel; and thou callest me into the fellowship of it in him. Therefore, upon the warrant of, and in obedience to, thy command and call, I, a poor perishing sinner, do take hold of that covenant for life and salvation to me, believing on the name of Christ cruci- fied, the head thereof, offered and exhibited to me as the Great High Priest, who, by the sacrifice of himself, hath made atonement, paid the ransom, and brought in everlasting righteousness for poor sinners. I credit his word of grace to me, and accordingly trust on him, that he with his righteousness will be mine, and that in and through him, God will be my God, and I shall be one of his people, to the making of me holy and happy for ever.

. "O my God, I do by thy grace acquiesce in that covenant, as all my salvation, and all my desire. With my whole heart and soul, the Son incarnate is my only Priest, my Surety, my Intercessor, and my Redeemer; and, in him, the FATHER, my FATHER, the HOLY GHOST my SANCTIFIER; GOD in CHRIST my GOD. I resign myself soul and body to him, to be saved by his blood alone, renouncing all confidence in mine own righteousness, doings, and sufferings. With my whole heart and soul, he is my HEAD and HUSBAND; and I am his only, wholly, and for ever; to live by him, to him, and for him. I take him for my alone Prophet, Oracle, and Guide; give up myself wholly to him, to be taught, guided, and directed in all things, by his Word and Spirit; and renounce mine own wisdom, and the wisdom of this world. He is, with my heart's consent, my alone King and Lord. And I resign myself wholly, soul and body, unto him, to be rescued by the strength of his mighty hand, from sin, death, the devil, and this present evil world, for to serve him for ever, and to be ruled by the will of his command, as to my duty, and the will of his providence, as to my lot. I am, with my whole heart, content (Lord, thou knowest) to part with, and do renounce every known sin, lust, or idol, and particularly my ———, the sin which most easily besets me; together with my own foolish will, and all other lords besides him, without reservation, and without exception, against his cross;—protesting in thy sight, O Lord, that I am, through grace, willing to have discovered unto me, and upon discovery to part with every sin in me that I know not; and that the doubtings and averseness of heart mixed with this my accepting of thy covenant, are what I allow not; and that notwithstanding thereof, I look to be accepted of thee herein, in the Beloved, thine only Son and my Saviour, purging away these, with all my other sins, by his precious blood.

"Let it be recorded in heaven, O Lord, and let ———, and whatever is here present, bear witness, that I, though most unworthy, have this day here taken hold of, and come into thy covenant of grace, offered and exhibited to me in thy gospel; and that thou art my God in the tenor of that covenant, and I am one of thy people, from henceforth and for ever."

DIRECTION IX. After covenanting with God, set yourself to ply the throne of grace by prayer and supplication, with reference to what is the particular cause or causes of your fast. This is surely the proper order; for then is one in best case to make special requests unto the Lord, when by application of the blood of Christ, in taking hold of the covenant, his conscience is purged; whereas, if one falls to that work before this, he cannot have the confidence towards God necessary in this case, 1 John iii. 20, 21.

And for the right managing hereof, the following advices are offered :—

1st, As it is fit you should, the night before, condescend in your own mind on the causes of your fast; so now again you should review them, partly that the things which you are to lay before the Lord in prayer and supplication may be ready before you; and partly, that you may be duly affected therewith.

2dly, Then go to prayer, and present your petitions anent them to your covenanted God. And pray again and again on these heads, as you shall find your case to require; for the time is set apart for that very end, that you may have opportunity to wrestle with God in prayers and supplications thereanent.

3dly, In these prayers let there be a holy mixture of humility suitable to our unworthiness, of fervency suitable to our pressing needs, and of confidence in God suitable to the access unto him allowed us by the covenant; the which are the special ingredients in prevailing prayer.

1. In all your addresses to the throne of grace, continue an humble supplicant, not forgetting, but maintaining a due sense of your sinfulness, vileness, and unworthiness of the mercies you make suit for. "Lord, I am not worthy that thou shouldest come under my roof, saith the centurion, Matth. viii. 8. "I am not worthy of the least of all the mercies," saith Jacob, Gen. xxxii. 10. Due humility will oblige you to look on yourself as absolutely unworthy of spiritual mercies, though in the meantime you see an absolute need of them; it will keep you from being peremptory in the matter of temporal mercies, and dispose you to a holy submission unto the will of God therein; and it will engage you, in matters of light, to lay yourself fairly open to the divine determination.

If, in this last case, your own inclination do sway you to any one side; yet be sure to have no regard to it before the Lord, but come unto him, as it were in an equipoise, to be cast to what side he will. Such are "the meek will he guide in judgment; the meek will he teach his way," Psalm xxv. 9. Unfair dealing with God in this case is exceeding sinful and dangerous. They who venture on it are therein dissemblers; and will readily throw off their mask, if the answer of God fall not in with the side that their inclination is on; they will repel it; they will not see it, but will take their own way, notwithstanding, to the provoking of the eyes of his glory; whereof we have a remarkable instance in the Jews consulting God as to what they should do, while in the meantime they were aforehand resolved what to do, being bent to go to Egypt, Jer. xli. 17. Chap. xlii. 1—6, 19, 20; chap. xliii. 2—7. Such dealing with God, in the matter of light, sometimes provokes him to give men their will with a vengeance. Thus Balaam got an answer from God, plainly notifying to him that he should not go with Balak's messengers, Numb. xxii. 12. But that answer not suiting his inclinations, which were towards "the wages of unrighteousness," (2 Peter ii. 15,) he went back for another answer more agreeable thereto, and in wrath he got it, vers. 19—22.

2. Be fervent in your addresses, " labouring fervently in prayers," Col. iv. 12. On such occasions the body is afflicted that the spirit may become the more earnest in supplication; the ordinary weight of worldly incumbrances is laid aside, that the soul may the more readily take wing and mount heavenward. "The effectual fervent prayer of a righteous man availeth much," James v. 16.

3. Pray with confidence in God through Jesus Christ; believing not doubtingly and distrustfully; Matth. xxi. 22, "And all things whatsoever ye shall ask in prayer, believing, ye shall receive." Whether your petitions be for temporal or spiritual mercies, present them to the Father in the name of Christ, according to the promises of the covenant relative thereto; believing and being confident on the ground of the merit and intercession of the Mediator, that God will do the best in your case, that your labour shall not be in vain in the Lord, and that what is for his glory and your good shall not be withheld from you, Psalm lxxxv. 12; 1 Cor. xv. 58; Psalm lxxxiv. 11.

4. In the intervals of prayer give yourself to some godly exercise, such as singing of psalms, reading of the word, or meditation. And, particularly, if you be seeking light into a matter, you may enter on thinking about it, in order to your clearing therein; weighing circumstances, with dependance on the Lord, according to the promise; Psalm xxxii. 8, " I will instruct thee, and teach thee in the way which thou shall go; I will guide thee with mine eye." And specially, if you are seeking light into the state of your soul, here is a favourable nick of time for it, the marks and evidences of a gracious state being, upon the back of covenanting with God, in a fair way to be discovered, to the satisfaction of the sincere soul.

5. *Lastly,* Lay no weight on the quantity of your prayers; that is to say, how long or how many they are. These things avail nothing with God, by whom prayers are not measured, but weighed. And what makes the weight in them is the faith, fervency, and humility therein; so that one of those groanings mentioned, Rom. viii. 26, will down-weigh a whole day's prayers, in which these things are wanting. Do you labour to get near God in prayer, and press forward to obtain that.

DIRECTION X. As you have ability and opportunity, let works of charity and mercy be joined with your fast; doing them, whether in the time of it, or before it, or after it. Isa. lviii. 6, " Is not this the fast that I have chosen?" Ver. 7, " To deal thy bread to the hungry, and that thou bring the poor that are cast out, to thy house? when thou seest the naked, that thou cover him, and that thou hide not thyself from thine own flesh." Let the poor be gainers by your fast; for it is the promise of God that "he that watereth, shall be watered also himself." Prov. xi. 25. And one's finding mercy with God, natively issues a merciful disposition towards one's fellow creatures, Matth. xviii. 33 ; Eph. iv. 32.

DIRECTION XI. Before you give over your work, you will do well to consider seriously, that you are now the Lord's, and no more your own ; and forasmuch as your covenanting God supposeth that you are resolved to reform, and to walk more closely with God, lay down resolutions, in the strength of your covenanted God, to watch. And by all means forget not to consider what are those things whereby in a special manner your spiritual condition had formerly been worsted ; and by what means it may be kept right ; and sincerely resolve to eschew the one and pursue the other, that so what gaps have been in your conversation may be filled up, whereby it will appear that by your fast you have been set forward in your Christian course. And withal, review your failures in all the parts of the exercise you have now been employed in.

DIRECTION XII. You may conclude the work with prayer, wherein you may humbly confess your failures in the management of this duty, and apply anew to the blood of sprinkling for purging them away ; avouch your covenant-interest in God, and his in you ; and lay the causes of your fast again before him, and solemnly leave them on him. The laying over a matter on the Lord believingly, in prayer, gives great ease to a burdened heart ; it turns a fast sometimes into a spiritual feast. When Hannah had done so with her case, " she went away and did eat, and her countenance was no more sad," 1 Sam. i. 18. And lay over yourself upon him, for the grace of the covenant, to subdue your corruptions, bear you up against temptations, and carry on your resolutions, that you may go out into the world again, in the faith of his grace sufficient for you in all exigencies.

DIRECTION XIII. When the work is over, take heed to your spirit. And,

1. Beware of spiritual pride. Do not value yourself upon the account of the work done, as they did who said, " Wherefore have we fasted, and thou seest not ?" Isa. lviii. 3. The opinion of the merit of good works, is what the heart of man easily goes off into, by its natural bias ; and there is so much of the old man in the best, that

they are apt to think high of their religious performances and services. Wherefore be on your guard, particularly on that side; and consider the perfection required by the holy law, and keep in view your own mismanagements, so as when you shall have done all those things, you may be obliged to say, " We are unprofitable servants," Luke xvii. 10.

2. Beware of carnal security. Saints sometimes fall asleep quickly after a full meal of spiritual enjoyment; as it fared with the spouse, Cant. v. 1, 2. And Satan, watching the advantage, rallies his scattered forces, and with his wounded men burns the city. So it comes to pass, that, according to Solomon's observe, Prov. xii. 27, " The slothful man roasteth not that which he took in hunting." What was gathered with much pains, is lost through unwatchfulness ere he gets the use of it.

3. *Lastly*, Beware of forgetting the causes of your fast; but in your ordinary addresses to God, remember them, and wait on for an answer; Psalm v. 3, " I will direct my prayer unto thee, and will look up." Prayers may be accepted, and yet not presently answered. In which case, it is necessary that with patience we wait for a return from heaven, meanwhile using the appointed means for obtaining the end. The neglecting hereof may provoke the Lord to continue the symptoms of his anger, or stroke of his hand, which otherwise might sooner be removed; and to leave one perplexed and embarrassed in matters wherein light is needed.

But in your waiting for light, whatever the Sovereign Lord may do, do not you look for impressions, far less for voices, nor extraordinary revelations in any manner of way, to discover your duty in particular cases, 2 Pet. i. 18, 19. But having laid yourself fairly open to the divine determination, and made humble and earnest supplication unto God for light in your particular case, believe that you shall be guided, taught, and directed by him, according to his promise, Psalm xxv. 9; Prov. iii. 6. And then, in dependence on the Lord, weigh the matter and circumstantiate case in the balance of sanctified reason, according to the general directions of the Word, such as Philip. iv. 8, " Whatsoever things are true, whatsoever things are honest, whatsoever things are just, whatsoever things are pure, whatsoever things are lovely, whatsoever things are of good report; if there be any virtue, and if there be any praise, think on these things." And carefully observe the conduct and motions of providence, with reference to it, still comparing them with the Word. And you will find that he will guide you with his eye, according to the promise, Psalm xxxii. 8. And with respect thereto, you may put up that petition unto him in faith, Psalm lxxxvi. 17, " Shew me a token for good."

Thus far of personal fasting and humiliation.

CHAPTER III.

OF FAMILY FASTING AND HUMILIATION IN PARTICULAR.

WHEREIN the substance of this duty, which is the same in all religious fasts whatsoever, doth consist, is already declared. And there being many things common to family fasts, with personal ones of which we have treated at large; it remains only to add here some few things peculiar to family fastings. And,

First, As to the divine warrant for it, one may be satisfied upon these grounds.

1. Forasmuch as every Christian family ought to be a church, Rom. xvi. 5, to receive all ordinances appointed of God, and competent to them in their family capacity; and that religious fasting is an ordinance of divine appointment, in the nature whereof there is nothing to hinder its being performed by a family in their family capacity, it is evident that family fasting and humiliation is a part of family worship; namely, an extraordinary part thereof, to be occasionally performed. Accordingly, it is promised, as an effect of the pouring out of the Spirit; Zech. xii. 12, "The land shall mourn, every family apart." We have also a plain instance of it, in Esther's family, on the occasion of the mischievous decree against the Jews, procured by Haman; Esther iv. 16, "I also and my maidens will fast likewise." And the fasting of the Jews, on the same occasion, in every province whithersoever that decree came, mentioned ver. 3, seems to have been mostly, if not altogether, of the same kind, to wit, family fasting; not only in respect of their circumstances in these provinces, where they were dispersed, chap. iii. 8, but also, that the thanksgiving for their deliverance was appointed to be "kept throughout every family," chap. ix. 28.

2. The ground upon which the duty of fasting and humiliation is bound upon public worshipping societies and upon particular persons, takes place also in the case of families. If national, congregational, and personal sins to be mourned over, judgments to be deprecated, and mercies to be sought, do found a call to a nation, congregation, or person, respectively, to humble themselves with fasting; can there be any reason assigned, why the same should not hold in like manner, in the case of families? Surely, as there are times wherein it goes ill with a land, or with a particular congregation, or person, so there are times wherein it goes evil with one's house, 1 Chron. vii. 23, in respect of special family sins or strokes, and in which there are special family mercies needed. And families

are obliged to the using of the same appointed means for getting rid of the one, and obtaining the other, as other worshipping societies and particular persons are, in their respective cases. And where the concern of members of a family is common, although it be not equal, all of them ought, in reason, to take part of the burden.

3. *Lastly*, The promise made to joint prayers hath weight here, Matth. xviii. 19, "If two of you shall agree on earth, as touching any thing that they shall ask, it shall be done for them of my Father which is in heaven." Ver. 20, "For where two or three are gathered together in my name, there am I in the midst of them." It is certain there is such a thing as extraordinary prayer, which hath a share in the benefit of this promise ; and if the Lord is pleased to lay such a weight on some of his people, their agreeing together to ask a thing of him, or their sounding together, as the word properly signifies ; it is not to be doubted, but extraordinary prayer in families upon some special occasions, is both required by him, and acceptable unto him through Jesus Christ his Son.

Secondly, As for a providential call to family fasting and humiliation : by what is said before, for clearing of one's call to personal fasting, it may be judged of and discerned ; the circumstances of the family being duly considered, and what the conduct of providence towards it appears to point unto. The case of others, in whom the family hath a particular concern, especially the case of the church, may found a call to family fasting, as is clear from the practice of Esther with her maids, Esther iv. 16. And so may the private case of the family itself ; whether in respect of family sins, family strokes, threatened or inflicted, or some special family mercies to be desired. And since the exemplification of these general heads, in one's private case, made in the second section of the foregoing chapter, may, without difficulty, be accommodated to the case of one's family, by persons of the meanest capacity disposed to consider them, it is not necessary here to descend to particulars again.

Lastly, For directions towards family fasting, there are but few that need to be added unto those given before, in the case of personal fasting. It is plain, from the nature of the thing, that the external ordering and management of this matter belongs to the head of the family ; and he or she is discreetly to choose and appoint the time and place wherein the family may perform the duty with least disturbance ; and to see that all be done decently and in order. And,

1. Let the head of the family, some competent time, at least the night before, give notice to them, that such a time is set apart for, and to be spent in, that exercise ; and withal show them the causes of it, and exhort them to stir up themselves to the duties of such a

solemn approach unto God. Common prudence will direct, as well as Christian duty doth oblige, the husband to consult his wife aforehand, as to the fixing of the time to be set apart in the family for that extraordinary piece of devotion.

2. In the morning, let each member of the family go apart by himself into some secret place, and there spend some time in reviewing, confessing, covenanting, praying, and supplicating, as directed in the case of personal fasting, so far as he can overtake them. The more conscientiously this secret work is managed, it will readily fare the better with the family, when met together.

3. Let the head of the family, having taken to himself, and allowed to them a competent time for their extraordinary secret devotions, thereafter call them together. And the family being convened, he may again, if need be, lay before them the causes of their fast, with suitable exhortations and encouragements for exciting them unto the duty. And, after calling on God for the aid of his Holy Spirit, let him sing with them some psalm or part of a psalm, suitable to such an occasion, such as Psalm lxxx. 1, and downwards; Psalm xxxix. 6, to the end; Psalm li. 1, and downwards; read before them some pertinent passage of Scripture, such as those mentioned in the sixth Direction of the preceding chapter, and then pray with them. After prayer made by the head of the family, let the mistress of the family, and such others as he judgeth fit, pray one after another. It is very desirable, that each member of the family, being through grace fit to be employed, do take a part in that work. In the intervals of prayer, there may be singing, reading, or conference, as may be found most expedient.

4. It is fit that, in these prayers, there be extraordinary confession of sin, as particular as may be expedient; together with profession of repentance, and hearty sorrow for sin, and of unfeigned desire to return unto God, and unto the duties of a Christian life; and then, fervent and earnest supplications, upon the matters that are the peculiar causes of the fast.

5. It is proper that the concluding prayer be made by the head of the family; and that therein he resume the confessions, professions, and supplications on the matters of the fast; humbly acknowledge their failures in the management of the work; and profess their looking for pardon and acceptance through the blood of Jesus Christ alone, and also for grace to walk in the ways of new obedience, through the same atoning blood. Then the joint exercise may be closed with singing some part of a psalm, such as Psal. xc. 13, to the end, Psal. lxxxv. 6, to the end, or Psal. lxix. 30, and downward.

6. *Lastly*, The joint exercise of the family being over, let each of

them go apart by himself again, and spend some time in a review
of what they have been employed in, and in secret prayer; the
which is but a suitable conclusion to such solemn work. And family reformation ought to follow hereupon; every member of the
family watching over himself, and all of them watching one over another; that by their holy walking, in peace and unity, and a conscientious performance of their relative duties, it may appear that
they have been sincere and upright before the Lord in their fast.

THE CONCLUSION.

And now, to recommend the practice of these duties to persons
and families, these five things are offered in favour thereof; namely,
that the practice of them is a proper means, 1. To bring strangers
to religion acquainted with it. 2. To recover backsliders. 3. To
prevent relapses. 4. To prepare for a time of trial. And, *lastly*,
To get matters clear for eternity.

First, The practice of personal and family fasting and humiliation, is a proper means to bring strangers to religion acquainted with
it; that those who have not yet dipt into practical religion, may
begin to enter into it. The work of conversion unto God begins at
solemn serious consideration of one's own spiritual state and case;
the which, if sinners could once be brought unto, there would be
some hope of them, as of the prodigal, when " he came to himself,"
Luke xv. 17. And if they would set themselves to the duty of personal fasting, and masters of families would now and then use family
fasts, they might at length be brought to consider of their spiritual
state and case. Wherefore,

1. Ye who are young, and have not yet dipt into the heart of religion, this Memorial is for you. It is presumed ye were baptized
in your infancy, and that now ye are come to the years of discretion;
but have you ever, as yet, taken a solemn deliberate view of your
lost and undone state by nature, under sin, and the curse; and of
the remedy provided for you in Jesus Christ? And have you ever,
as yet, personally entered into covenant with God, by taking hold
of his covenant of grace? You eat, you drink, you sleep, you work,
you play or divert yourselves; and so do young beasts too, the which
when they are dead, are done; but you have an immortal soul that
must eternally live happy in heaven, or miserable in hell. It may
be, you say your prayers too; but have you as yet personally re-
nounced the devil, the vain world, and the flesh? You cannot but
see, that death seizeth some as young and sprightly as you are;
and you know not how soon God may call you off;—have you then
laid your measures for eternity? Alas! you are heedlessly running

about the devil's trap, playing yourselves about the pit's mouth; and should your foot slip now, you are undone for ever. "Thus saith the Lord of Hosts, Consider your ways."

2. Careless sinners, careless about the concerns of the other world, whatever your age or years be, this Memorial is for you. "Ye careless ones, strip ye, and make ye bare, and gird sackcloth upon your loins," Isa. xxxii. 11. What is your religion? Is it not like the foam on the water, no substance in it? What is your life and conversation? See your own picture, Jer. ii. 24, "A wild ass used to the wilderness, that snuffeth up the wind at her pleasure." What condition is your soul in? The emblem of it is the sluggard's vineyard; "All grown over with thorns, nettles covering the face thereof, and the stone wall thereof broken down," Prov. xxiv. 30, 31. Can you really persuade yourselves, that you are "going forth by the footsteps of the flock?" that the saints now in glory took the sinful liberty of thinking, speaking, and acting, that you do? that their soul's state and case cost them as few serious thoughts as yours have cost you? Do you think to stumble on a saving interest in Christ, a pardon, a heaven? No, you will not find it so. Up then, and be doing; set apart some time for considering of, and doing something effectually in your soul's case; that you may go to the ground of the matter, and get it rectified.

Secondly, It is a proper means for the recovery of backsliders, that they may "remember whence they are fallen, and repent, and do the first works," Rev. ii. 5. There are not a few, who sometime a-day blossomed fair, in hopeful beginnings of religion, who are now withered. Their bones are dried, and there is no sap of that kind in them now; and by their sinning against light, they have provoked God to depart from them, so as there is no sap in ordinances, nor in providences, to them, neither; but these are all, as it were, blasted to them, and they are left in the unhappy case of the vineyard, Isa. v. 6, "I will also command the clouds that they rain no rain upon it." And some are not only withered, but are become noisome in their life and conversation; they have not only lost any life of religion they sometimes seemed to have, but their lusts are become rampant in them, as given up to vile affections, defiling the very outward man. "It has happened unto them according to the true proverb, the dog is turned to his own vomit again, and the sow that was washed, to her wallowing in the mire," 2 Peter ii. 22.

O backsliders, your case is a fearful one! Heb. x. 38, "If any man draw back, my soul shall have no pleasure in him." What mind ye to do with it? Will ye continue in it, to your eternal ruin? Oh! no, pity your own souls; there is hope in Israel concerning this thing, bad as it is. Perhaps your hearts tell you, that your case is now gone on too far to be mended; but it is not so; that is but a satanical suggestion. God's Word says otherwise; Jer. iii. 1, "Though thou hast played the harlot with many lovers; yet return again to me, saith the Lord." Isa. liv. 6, "I have called thee as—a wife of youth, when thou wast refused, saith thy God." Wherefore, O backslider, bestir thyself, to answer the Lord's call, and remember that some devils go not out but by prayer and fasting," Matth. xvii. 21. Try this method then for your recovery; try it, as you would not be guilty of wilful dying of your disease. Our heavenly Father kindly meets returning prodigals: the returning backslider will be treated by him as a "dear son, a pleasant child," Jer. xxxi. 20. Return ye then, and "he will restore to you the years that the locust hath eaten," Joel ii. 25. And as yet, "your bones shall flourish like an herb," Isa. lxvi. 14.

Thirdly, It is a proper means to prevent relapses, and to keep one's spiritual case right, when once it is right. Frequent stating of accounts, keeps matters clear which otherwise might come to be perplexed and involved. And the case which, being on the decline, is taken in time, is easily righted, in comparison of that which has long run on; even as when Christ raised to life the young man of Nain, whom they were carrying out to the grave, he only touched the bier, and said, "Young man, I say unto thee, arise," Luke vii. 14. But he wept and groaned once and again at the raising of Lazarus, who had been four days dead, John xi. 33, 35, 38. The unhealthy and sickly disposition of the souls of men, by reason of the remains of corruption that are always in the best, while here, makes the occasional performance of extraordinary duties now and then necessary, over and above the course of their ordinary and stated devotions.

Fourthly, It is a proper means of preparation for a time of trial. It is a piece of Christian prudence to foresee the evil, and hide one's self, while "the simple pass on, and are punished," Prov. xxii. 3. When God is threatening a land with his judgments, it becomes the inhabitants to take the alarm, and prepare to meet their God; and personal and family fasts are proper expedients for that end; since they who in sinning times "sigh and cry for all the abominations done in the midst thereof," stand fair to receive the mark for special favour in suffering times, Ezek. ix. 4. For all the lesser strokes and deliverances these nations have met with of late years, it is, alas! visible to sober men of whatever denomination, that we are not thereby reformed, nor duly convinced of, far less humbled under the

causes of God's flaming controversy with us. And while there is a
God to judge on the earth, we can have no reason to think, that a
generation chargeable with the guilt which we are chargeable with,
is in safety with such a load upon them; but that either God will,
by an unordinary pouring out of his Spirit, awaken, humble, and
make the land to mourn, or else, by some rousing stroke of judgment, will vindicate his own honour, injured to a pitch that our
fathers arrived not at. And the less appearance there is of the
former, there is the greater appearance of the latter. However, we
seem to have no such security against it, as to render it unseasonable to keep personal and family fasts in that view; that we may
mourn over our own sins, and the sins of the nations, and may solemnly commit ourselves and our families to the divine grace, mercy,
and protection, whatever may be the occurrences of Providence in
our day. None know what dark steps may be between them and
the grave; and, therefore, it cannot be an unwise course, timely to
take God in Christ for our guide through the mountains of darkness, for our protector in all dangers, and for our supporter and
helper in the midst of trouble.

Lastly, It is a proper means to get matters clear for eternity, and
so to make us a safe and comfortable passage out of this world. It
was David's unspeakable comfort on his death-bed, that he could
say of the God unto whom his spirit was about to return, " He hath
made with me an everlasting covenant," 2 Sam. xxiii. 5. Jacob,
being an old man, and a dying, comfortably reflected on the place
and time, where and when, in the days of his youth, he had remarkable communion with God, received the blessing, and vowed the
vow, Gen. xlviii. 3, with chap. xxviii. 10—22. Would one be in a
condition to look death in the face, to pass safely and comfortably
to the other world, there is not a more feasible means to reach it
than this. Therefore,

1. Ye who are under doubts and fears, complaining that ye can
never reach clear evidences for heaven, this Memorial is for you.
No wonder they walk in the dark, who will not be at so much pains
to get light into their state. The obtaining of such light, might of
itself be a sufficient ground for such an exercise. Clear evidences
for heaven are such an unspeakable comfort, and so hard to raise
up amidst so much corruption of heart and life, that it is not at all
strange they require something beyond the ordinary course of devotion and application, to obtain the same. And this is a most feasible means for that purpose; for after one has got his soul humbled
by a review of his sins, hath poured out his heart before the Lord in
solemn confession of sin, and personally entered into, or renewed,

covenant with God, by taking hold of God's covenant of grace; if he shall then take the matter in hand, and examine himself as to the evidences of saving grace in him, they will then be as likely to appear clearly as ever.

2. Ye who are, one way or other, getting warnings of approaching death, this Memorial is for you. Do you observe your equals in years, or younger than you, carried off by death? Have you been at any time rescued from imminent danger of your life, arising from some accident or unforeseen occurrence? Are ye now and then visited with sickness? Do you perceive your strength begin to fail, the pins of your tabernacle begin to be loosened? These and the like are loud providential calls to you to prepare for the other world. And preparation for that world, is sufficient to found a call unto such extraordinary devotion; a prospect of approaching death may well be allowed to call one to set some time apart, in order to prepare for it. Preparation for death is work to be done in time of health; and why should it be delayed, since you see that death is approaching? How unreasonable is it for men to leave that work to the sick-bed, where they will have enough ado to die, or may be deprived of their judgment, if they do at all get a sick-bed, and be not suddenly snatched away ere they or their friends are aware! No, Sirs; ye know that death is coming; therefore, while ye are able, set some time apart for that very end, to prepare for it, and to state matters clearly for eternity; otherwise ye are cruel to your own souls, by your negligence, making of death a leap in the dark into the other world.

3. *Lastly*, All without exception, who believe a heaven and a hell, this Memorial is for you. The eternal state is not a matter to venture upon at random. If you do really believe a life to come, ye cannot reasonably think, that this is too much to make a suitable preparation for it. Their hearts are certainly more stout than holy, who, amidst so many instances of mortality as the world is still affording, are not thereby excited to set their own soul's case in order, with an eye to death's coming about to their own door; and thus to set some time apart for that end, is little enough in a case of such vast importance.

AN ALPHABETICAL TABLE,

B.

Backsliders, the cause of, considered, iv., 595.

Baptism, the nature, necessity, and subjects of, ii., 474—479—who have a right to, vi., 125.

Barbarous persecution in Piedmont, ii., 135—whether their sins, while unrepented of, render the liable to eternal punishment, vi., 11.

Believing, what that is by which a sinner is united unto Christ, ix., 581—in order to contentment is, 1. A sure way. 2. A short way. 3. The only way, ii., 344 —in Christ lies in trusting on him as our Saviour, v., 285.

Believers have a true friend in the court of heaven, and cannot finally fall away, i., 475—have in them the old and the new man, vi., 320—in what sense they are said to be dead, iii., 342—the characters of those dead to the world, 344—353— shall have a glorious resurrection, ii., 44—how Christ will acknowledge them after the resurrection, 48—why they should be familiar in the house over which Christ is set, ix., 432—the life of, is a great mystery, and is a strange sight to the world, x., 552—557—this world is a wilderness out of which they come leaning on their Beloved, 559—do enter into rest, v., 291—how they are of God, 303—how they are separated from the world, 304—may know that they are thus separated, 306—why left compassed with infirmities here, xi., 27—50 —though under the law as a rule, yet not under it as a covenant, 197.

Benefits accompanying and flowing from justification, ii., 28—30— flowing to true believers from their union to Christ, viii., 203.

Beware of preaching smooth things, and of closing with a call on account of stipend, v., 37, 38.

Black mark that of a soul who has no more to look for but the world as his portion, ix., 241.

Blessing of the Lord, how to obtain the, iii., 154—159—why men fall short of the, 162.

Blood of Christ, two things in the which wash out the stain of sin, vi., 556—573.

Body, the, is under the curse of the law, xi., 294.

Boston converted by the ministry of the Rev. Henry Erskine, v., 11. See foot note.

Broken heart, what is a, in the gospel sense, ix., 555—how Christ binds up and heals a, 560.

Burdens, the saints lay all their, upon Christ, ix., 511.

Business, the great, of our lives, is to learn to die, v., 453.

C.

Call to come out of the devil's family, i., 644—651—to sinners to awake, iv., 423.

Calling Christ Lord and not obedient to his laws, the folly and sin of, vi., 526.

Case, the, of the thief on the cross no argument for delaying repentance, vi., 469.

Catechism, the Shorter, by whom composed and for what end, i., 9—the Assembly's, a brief explication of, vii., 9— 144.

Causes of the Lord's controversy with us, ii., 667.

Caution to those professing to be married to Christ, v., 533.

Change, the, which sin has brought upon us, how lamentable! i., 184.

Character, the, of those who attend ordinances, but not as becomes them, ii., 442—of many who sit down at the communion table, iii., 13—of the subject in which the mystery of grace is carried on by Jesus Christ, vi., 330—of those who are of God, v., 311—of those personally brought into the covenant of grace, viii., 455.

Charge to depart from iniquity, to whom given, x., 13—in what this departure consists, 14—20—some farther from iniquity at first than ever afterwards, 37.

Children, how to teach to pray, ii., 533.

Christ fulfilled all righteousness as the second Adam, i., 338—is the surety of the covenant of grace, 343—for what he became surety, 344 sinners have abundant security for coming to, 355, 356—the only Redeemer of God's elect, 375—the only physician of souls, iv., 364—is God and man, i., 384—all dying out of must perish, i., 387—is impious to ascribe any part of man's redemption to any other but, 388—the act of assuming human nature was voluntary, 393—calls to his bride to come to his Father's house, iii., 120—in what respects eminently the Beloved One, xi., 150—how we may get into him, 168.

Christ's body not made of any substance sent down from heaven, i., 401—offices in general, 476—484—support of his people under trouble, viii., 223—covenant of grace to whom offered, v., 520— objections to, answered, 520, 521.

Christ a prophet like unto Moses—in what respects, i., 411—458—the sum and hope of the believer's life, iv., 240—as a child born to sinners as his relations, x., 183 —as a prince and counsellor, 204— and the devil contending for sinners, v., 631—longs to show his liberality to sinners, ix., 172—admits of no rival, 380 —is appointed by the Father to heal the broken-hearted, to proclaim liberty to the captives, &c., ix., 550—604—is presented to sinners Wonderful, the great

plained, ii., 393—xiii. 14, explained, iv., 247—x. 22, explained, ix., 399—xi. 16, explained, x., 120—iv. 11, explained, iv., 268.

Heinous, in what respects some sins are more than others, ii., 384—388.

Hell, a part of the other world, v., 404—a close prison, no getting out of, 409.

Help of the Spirit, advices how to get the, xi., 70.

Hinderances to making our evidences for heaven, iii., 51—to repentance, vi., 447.

Holiness, true, what is, ii., 9—11—the absolute necessity of, and motives to come to Christ for it, 13, 14. See vi., 613—615.

Honest servants of Christ must distinguish themselves from others by following the Lord fully, as Caleb, ix., 301—308.

House, what kind of a, the body is to the soul, iii., 23—arguments to provide in time for a better house, 16—house above, what kind of, 32—in Christ's present room, 260.

Hopes of heaven, whatever these be to many, evidences of hell are written on their foreheads, iii., 46.

How to distinguish the joy of the stony ground hearers from that of the true children of God, iv., 50—the Lord helps his people, 53--57--Christ's spouse is to walk, iv., 94—100—we must labour to enter into rest, iii., 288—motives to, 294—heaven is a rest, 303--can a sinner die, or appear before God in judgment without Christ? 386—to hold Christ among us, 434—to become experimental Christians, ii., 653—659—Christ makes men fishers of men, v., 7—can a man love God as his portion when he has empty pantries? v., 73—God hath made over himself to lost sinners of Adam's race as a portion, 77—the soul is humbled and brought down from his heights to Christ, v., 277—Christ calls his people to give up with worldly comforts, v., 379—388—to know whether or not we be travelling to the Zion above, v., 553—those who have part in Christ's service, should serve him, vii., 544—the wicked are driven away in their wickedness, viii., 246—251—Christ the Son of God became the second Adam, 409—it comes to pass that men perform duties, yet not in a right manner, ix., 55—the Lord testifies his displeasure at such, 57—59—may one serve the Lord yet be employed in his worldly business? 471—Christ hath performed the work of preaching good tidings to the meek; ix., 587—they walk who walk by faith, x., 483.

Human nature, the state of, to be lamented, v., 176.

Human nature of Christ, the act of fram-

ing the, in the womb of the Virgn Mary, the effect of the infinite power of God, i., 396.

Humiliation of Christ, i., 490—502—in the humiliation of the soul, this to be considered, v., 400—406.

Humility, our duty, vi., 552—objection to, 553—what it is to humble ourselves under the hand of God, 557—562.

Hypocrites, several things which make fall away, ii., 34, 35—may go far in religion yet fall away, iii., 416. See also ix., 365.

I.

Image of God in which man was created, in what the consists, i., 181.

Images not to be used in the worship of God, ii., 128, 150—bowing to, whether of the whole body or of the knee, is forbidden in the second commandment, 138.

Impediments to self-examination, ii., 507—hindering sinners to come out of the world, v., 365—373—to our making ready to remove to the other world, v., 578—directions to make ready, 579.

Impenitent sinner, the is an unhumbled sinner, vi., 404.

Import of Christ's marking his sighing and groaning people, v., 218.

Important cases respecting the happy prospect of the death of true believers, viii., 262.

Imputation of Adam's first sin to his posterity, proven, xi., 241—246.

In selling all that we may follow Christ, what this consists in, iii., 448—this writes death to several characters, 454.

In what respect a saint's life-time here is night, v., 528.

Incarnation of Christ, i, 391—402.

Inferences from the ten commandments, ii., 373.

Infirmities, believers are accompanied with, what are the, xi., 25.

Influences of the Spirit all humbling, v., 483—all sanctifying, 485.

Inhabitants of heaven, what be, v., 94.

Iniquities, testifying against a man in his addresses to God, iv., 197—199.

Initial sanctification, the Holy Spirit alone acts in, i., 685.

Intercession of Christ, i., 468--474—the soul sees in the, a glorious suitableness to his case, iv., 500—the difference between Christ's and the Spirit's, xi., 60 ---80.

Instating sinners in the covenant of grace, the way of, viii., 577.

Isaiah xxxviii. 19, explained, v., 587—xli. 14, 15, explained, vi., 328—ix. 6, explained, x., 178—liii. 1, explained—x., 268—lix. 2, explained—ix., 17--lv. 4, explained—ix., 128—lxi. 1, explained,

Returning from sin to God, the nature of, vi., 417—428.

Revenge is twofold, public and authoritative, private and personal, v., 172—the sinfulness and dishonour to God in it, 174.

Righteousness, the, of Christ. 1. What. 2. That we are justified by the. 3. How a sinner can be justified by a righteousness not his own. 4. How this way of justifying a sinner consists with the honour of God's justice and law, i., 595. See also, iv., 188—193.

Righteousness, original, man's, viii., 11—was universal and natural, yet mutable, 14.

Righteousness and holiness, the lovely image of God consisted in, i., 185.

Righteousness, believers hunger and thirst after. 1. What this is? 2. What this hungering and thirsting is? 3. The blessedness of those thus hungering and thirsting, iii., 273—279.

Rom. viii. 30 explained, i., 576—iii. 24 explained, i., 581—iv. 11 explained, ii., 465—i. 18 explained, iii., 214—xii. 19 explained, v., 172—vi. 6 explained, vi., 319—viii. 22 explained, ix., 264—ii. 28, 29 explained, ix., 334—viii. 26 explained, xi., 19—v. 19 explained, xi., 233.

Rome, the church of, has half holidays, ii., 204.

Room in Christ's house for sinners of mankind, iii., 260—269.

Rules necessary to be observed for the right understanding of the ten commandments, ii., 69—73.

Rule by which to try doctrines, i., 18.

S.

Sacraments, the, how become effectual means of salvation, ii., 461—464—the use of, vi., 601—of the Lord's supper, when instituted, what meant by the outward elements, ii., 482—487—the believing management of, the best security against the day of wrath, x., 135—143—great, the, sin of profaning the, ii., 470—of the New Testament, only two, the five added by papists are bastard sacraments, ii., 471.

Sacrifice of Christ, what made acceptable to God, and efficacious to men, i., 450.

Sacrilege, the worst theft to profane the Sabbath, ii., 201.

Saints have heaven in right and title, iii., 38—41—many know that heaven shall be their everlasting home, 44, 45—can say of Christ, he is my Lord—iv. 152—a real saint rejoiceth in Christ, iv., 493.

Salvation from hell may prompt to duties without love to God, xi., 137—by works impossible, xi., 218.

1 *Sam.* vii. 12 explained, iv., 52—xii. 21 explained, ix., 500—xv. 22 explained, ii., 51, 52.

Sanctification, the kinds and author of, &c., i., 644—661.

Satan's temptation caused the breach of the covenant of works, xi., 227.

Satisfaction of Christ, the completeness of, grounded on the degrees of his sufferings, i., 453.

Saviour, what kind a sinner has need of, iv., 371.

Schism, the evil and danger of, vii., 595—occasions of, in churches, 600.

Scriptures, the divine authority of the, i., 19—the necessity of the, 24—the only rule to direct us how we may glorify God and enjoy him, and the properties of this rule, i., 37—39—what they teach, 46—48—60, 61.

Searching times, where shall saints be found in? iv., 182—184.

Security in an evil day, the best to be found in Christ, x., 512.

Secret prayer a duty incumbent on all men, ii., 540—545.

Sell what thou hast, the sense which papists put upon, iii., 441—when it is that we are called of God to part with what we have, 442.

Self-denial explained, vi., 309.

Separation, what sins make between God and the soul, ix., 29—34.

Serpent, the, in which the devil appeared to Eve, was a true serpent—was solicited to tempt Eve, by envy, the first native of hell, i., 249.

Several kinds of sins against which the wrath of God is revealed, iii., 242.

Shadow of a great rock, Christ is to his people, ix , 220—sinners have need of Christ as a shadow—what it is to sit under his shadow, iii., 166—172.

Simonides' answer to Hiero, king of Syracuse, who asked him, What is God? i., 77.

Simpson, Professor, the case of, (foot note,) xi., 180.

Sin in general. 1. What law is the transgression of? 2. The nature and evil of. 3. The first sin, and how the eating of the forbidden fruit was the first, &c., i., 256 — 272 — original sin. 1. There is such. 2. In what it consists, 280—292 — is the sickness of the soul, iv., 360—the first, the extent of, xi., 236.

Sin, reigning, perverts the spirit of man, i., 16—the least condemns a man, ii., 391—unto death the nature of the, i., 535—your sin, be sure, will find you out—how sinners try to shift this—how the, makes sin find out the sinner—why sin finds out some in this world and puts off others to the other world—what should one do whose sin finds him out? iii., 181—213.

Sinners to be encouraged to come unto Christ to be united to him by faith, i., 403—may have peace with God, x., 263 in their natural state are far from God and fast asleep, i., 562—cannot come to Christ except they be drawn, 564—living in, are without excuse, vi., 302—earnestly called upon to repent, vi., 429—seriously warned against sin, iii., 612—whom Christ espouses, he espouses for ever, vii., 493 - once interested in Christ shall obtain favour of the Lord, x., 521—527—what they are to do that they may walk with God, x., 595—those out of Christ are engaged in a wearisome labour, ix., 175—how near may they come to Jesus Christ? ix., 408—in order to be saved nothing remains for them but to take hold of God's covenant of grace, already made in eternity, viii., 430—unregenerate, all captives under Satan, ix , 570—life and death set before them, ix., 587—what they come from in coming to God in prayer, xi., 122.

Sinning more terrible than suffering, ii., 638.

Sins, whether all past, present, and to come, are pardoned together and at once, vi., 44.

Sixth commandment explained, ii., 260-275.

Sloth, spiritual, the sources of, iv., 409.

Some take their farewell of Christ with a heavy heart, iii., 490—called Christians, not careful even to appear so before men, ix., 343.

Song iv. 8 explained, iii., 118—ii. 3 explained, iii., 165—viii. 5 explained, x., 550.

Son of God, in man's nature, given to poor sinners as the only remedy of their misery, x., 189—200.

Sorrow, the, of many will turn to no good account, vi., 409.

Soul, as Adam and Eve's, were created immediately of God, so are all the souls of their posterity, i., 180—the, how weaned from the things of time, ix., 48, 50—the, in heaven are blessed and happy in the enjoyment of God, i., 201—gracious, may not a, be very easy even when the Lord seems departed from him? v., 89.

Spirit of God, the, promised to teach the truths of God savingly—the inward illumination of the, necessary for the saving understanding of the Scriptures, i., 35, 36—the, of God, speaking in Scripture, is the Supreme Judge by whom controversies in religion are to be determined, i., 48, 49—Socinians set up reason as the supreme judge, 52—55—the work of, in the washing of a sinner, vi., 575—how the, helps our infirmities in prayer, xi., 21—40.

Strokes, the, which many meet with are pledges of ruin to impenitent sinners, vi., 380.

Success, what that is which the gospel sometimes hath, and that power which sometimes accompanies it, x., 269.

T.

Table of the law, the sum of the second, is love to our neighbour, ii., 79—81.

Take hold of Christ, what it is to, iv., 402—405.

Tale-bearers and slanderers to be discouraged, ii., 316.

Task, a hard, they have to deal with who deal with the world lying in wickedness, v., 346.

Temptation. 1. What meant by it. 2. What meant by leading into it. 3. What the import of this part of the sixth petition in the Lord's prayer. See also a long note on, from the author's manuscript on Gen. ii., 620—635.

Ten commandments, the, were not given to the Israelites as a covenant of works, ii., 89.

Tenth commandment, the, explained, ii., 322.

Terror of God, by the, may a person be driven from iniquity ? x., 32.

Testament, Old and New, what meant by the, i., 20.

Testimony of the gospel, several things imported in the, vi., 295.

Thanksgiving and confession parts of prayer, ii., 536—538.

Thieves and unjust persons, partaking with, is a breach of the eighth commandment, ii., 303—a thief is liable to three tribunals, 305.

Think, if we speak not as we, we do not speak truth—truth must be maintained in both words and deeds, ii., 313—315.

Things to be discerned in our case by sin, iv., 384.

Third commandment, the, explained, ii., 159.

Thirsting sinners, Christ cries to, to come unto him and drink, iv., 459—463.

Those doing what Christ commands, the glorious privileges of, v., 242—who would follow the Lord fully as Caleb, must have another spirit than that of the world, ix., 313—who are the Lord's ought, and will make God's service their chief business, ix., 465—not serving God are serving the devil, ix., 480—finding Christ find life, ix., 499.

Three ways of knowing things, iii., 36—sorts of persons, reproof to, for not holding themselves in readiness for their removal to the other world, v., 573—things which should be considered by those who call Christ Lord, Lord, and do not what he commands, vi., 545—547.

Throne of judgment, God ascending the, also the throne of mercy, iv., 204—of grace, the necessity of the, to poor sinners, vii., 616—628.

with a heap of insignificant ceremonies by the popish and English churches, 155.

Worthy, the, receiving of the Lord's supper, ii., 489.

Wrath or anger, the nature of, in general, v., 151—he that is slow to, is of great understanding, v., 154.

Wrath of God, the, underwent, i., 494 —the state of, viii., 101—objections, 110.

Y.

Years, we can have but a few to come— when these few have sent us off there is no returning; in what respects we can have but a few years to come, iv., 68—70.

Z.

Zechariah xii. 12, explained, iii., 354.

Zion, the citizens of, are no deceivers of themselves, v., 129—are all regenerated, 130—travellers to look for their furniture for the way from Christ, 553.

Zion's mourners, the character of, v., 204 —exhortations to, 212—several sorts of persons blotted out of the number of, v., 210.

Zion's travellers have made Christ their shade and shelter, ix., 244.

THE END.

PRINTED BY
GEORGE & ROBERT KING,
ST. NICHOLAS STREET, ABERDEEN.